The Purpose of Counselling and Psychotherapy

Michael Bennett

palgrave
macmillan

First published 2005 by
PALGRAVE MACMILLAN
Houndmills, Basingstoke, Hampshire RG21 6XS and
175 Fifth Avenue, New York, N.Y. 10010
Companies and representatives throughout the world

PALGRAVE MACMILLAN is the global academic imprint of the Palgrave
Macmillan division of St. Martin's Press, LLC and of Palgrave Macmillan Ltd.
Macmillan® is a registered trademark in the United States, United Kingdom
and other countries. Palgrave is a registered trademark in the European
Union and other countries.

ISBN 1–4039–3596–3 paperback

This book is printed on paper suitable for recycling and made from fully
managed and sustained forest sources.

A catalogue record for this book is available from the British Library.

A catalog record for this book is available from the Library of Congress.

10   9   8   7   6   5   4   3   2   1
14 13 12 11 10 09 08 07 06 05

Printed in China

For Ann

Contents

Acknowledgements   ix

Introduction   1

1 Communicative Rationality   11
     Relativism   12
     Communicative Rationality   15
     Universal Pragmatics   18
     Validity Claims   23
     Systematically Distorted Communication   29
     Argumentation, Discourse Ethics and Postconventional
       Universalism   31

2 Morality, Ethics and Autonomy   37
     Morality and Justice   38
     Ethics and Authenticity   55
     Health   62
     Autonomy   63

3 The Development of Moral Character   69
     Reflexivity   70
     Intersubjective Constitution of Personal
       Identity   71
     Socialization as Evolutionary Stages   80
     Moral Emotions   85
     The Decentred Self   91

4 Communicative Action and Counselling   101
     Communicative Action and Counselling   102
     Non-Judgemental and Value-Free
       Counselling   113

5 Issues in Psychotherapy and Counselling   131
     Transference, Countertransference and Eros   131
     Brief Counselling   139
     Outcomes   147
     Professionalism   153
     Codes of Ethics   157

6 **Abstract Systems and the Colonization of Self**   161
  Legitimation Problems of the State in Late
      Modernity   162
  Abstract Systems   167
  Selfhood in Late Modernity   185

7 **Critique, Resistance and Transformation**   196
  Critique, Resistance and Transformation   199

Notes   212

Bibliography   237

Index   249

Acknowledgements

It is with pleasure that I thank my family, friends and colleagues in Relate Avon for their support during this project.

In particular I am grateful to Donald Godden for his unfailing enthusiasm and help right from the start. Above all I thank my wife Ann and my daughter Samantha.

Introduction

My interest in the subject of the purpose of counselling and psychotherapy has a very practical foundation. I have not undertaken this project within the context of an academic institution, instead it springs from the difficulties that I have faced in working at various levels in a large counselling organization. I think the tone of the argument I present will also reveal that I am not a practitioner in either counselling or psychotherapy. Hence, unlike other considerations of this subject, this is not a work that is concerned with matters of confidentiality and other detailed ethical issues that face the practitioner in their day-to-day work with clients. Important though these issues are there are plenty of other sources of advice. More to the point, however, I shall make the case that practitioners are overly concerned with detailed and small-scale ethical issues such that the broader and deeper concerns with justice, truth and autonomy, which are of genuine interest to them, are often overlooked not just by the practitioners but also by the organizations they work for and the professional bodies who represent them.

I have worked for many years as a manager in a charity providing a counselling service to its local community. For most of this time I was also an elected trustee on the national board of trustees to which my charity was federated. It was in this role of policy-making and resource allocation that I became increasingly aware that decision-making, under very real personnel and financial pressures, had become an almost completely pragmatic matter with little reference to any overarching sense of the purpose of counselling. It gradually dawned on me that, apart from all the very real practical problems that this and most other voluntary organizations face, this state of affairs was compounded by the fact that an articulation of the fundamental purpose of counselling and psychotherapy either did not exist or was well hidden from view. Other than the already mentioned preoccupation with confidentiality and professional codes of ethics, most other statements concerning fundamental purpose turned out to be a loose collection of unconnected values which were in no way based on a rational or philosophical justification. My endeavour in this work is to attempt to address this issue. It is not, however, an abstract philosophical or sociological issue with little relevance to the work of counselling and psychotherapists. Quite the contrary, it is quite clear that without a better understanding of this issue the future direction of these services will almost certainly fail to realize their historic potential not just for the clients they work with but for society as a whole.

It became quickly transparent that a discussion of this purpose was not a psychological question but a philosophical one. Any approach that is purely psychological will expose its proponent to being obliged (often covertly) to import any justifications for the goals chosen from a theoretical framework that is external to psychology and associated disciplines. This leaves counselling and psychotherapy in the dangerous position of being dependent upon an external discourse that is often neither acknowledged nor understood. I have therefore felt it necessary to venture into the realms of philosophy, developmental psychology, sociology and politics, and consider counselling and psychotherapy from these viewpoints. In doing so I freely acknowledge my indebtedness to many theorists in these areas of knowledge. In particular I refer to the work of Jürgen Habermas for providing a profoundly useful platform and overall theoretical framework, and to those works of Anthony Giddens which offer a bridge between sociology and counselling and psychotherapy.

Observed from the outside, counselling and psychotherapy appear to be fragmented. This state of affairs enables the contradictory trends of single schools or traditions claiming a certain level of uniqueness for their methodology, whilst at the same time individual practitioners create their own methodological cocktails from competing traditions. What is absent is a general theoretical framework. I am too circumspect to rise to this particular challenge, but I do believe that I present a reasonable case for proposing that there is a viable framework for considering the purpose of all counselling and psychotherapy. Should this not prove to be the case then hopefully this endeavour will be fruitful if it has in any way stimulated the debate.

The approach that I take is one of critique. By putting many of the received values of counselling and psychotherapy to a radical critical analysis I am not seeking to undermine or destroy these most valuable practices. Rather, I seek to make transparent (much like a therapist) many of the hidden or unconsciously adopted values and presuppositions which have become embedded in them and subject them to a critical investigation from the perspective of an articulated value base that is philosophically grounded and therefore open to rational discourse. In so doing I believe that counselling and psychotherapy will be much more beneficial to their clients and will fulfil their historical and political potential. Many counsellors and psychotherapists are frustrated with the ethical paucity and moral ambivalence that flavours these practices. We are at a cultural crossroads. For Samuels 'the characteristic of late modernity to try to make use of knowledge about itself can be recast as a struggle within our culture to become self-conscious; *our culture struggle to become psychological*' (1993: 8). Once practitioners understand that this struggle is inherently moral, ethical and political, they may well come to see that their work is at the cutting edge of contributing to the beginnings of a new social order.

Throughout I make little distinction between psychotherapy and counselling because in terms of their overall purpose I believe no distinctions are fruitful.

My first concern in this work is with trying to find a rational basis for considering the purpose of counselling and psychotherapy. In a post-traditional world where neither God nor the sheer weight of tradition can provide an objective vantage point from which to define the good, how can we find a philosophical basis from which to judge anything? Under attack from postmodernism the attempt to move out of the position of complete relativism seems hopelessly forlorn. However not to do this leaves us in a significantly worse position. It is at this point that the radical philosophy and social theory of Habermas proves to be extremely useful. In his long-term critique of postmodernism he has developed a theory of rationality that, on the one hand, moves out of the infinite circularity of relativism without, on the other hand, falling back on any metaphysical transcendentalism or religious absolute.

Whilst Habermas is not the easiest of philosophers to understand, the interesting ideas that he generates are well worth the effort. With his concept of *communicative rationality* I follow his investigation of what it means to reach an understanding through communication. Communicative rationality is not a limited form of reason like logic; rather, through a detailed understanding of how communication works, it represents those features of communication that are both *immanent* and *invariable* regardless of individual or cultural context. Through this analysis it becomes clear that to adequately understand our psychic and social worlds the paradigm of the human subject as an isolated, atomized individual consciousness is inadequate and needs to be replaced by a conception of the human subject that is intersubjectively constituted to his or her inner core.

When communicating to reach an understanding we find that there are a small number of features of communication that we cannot dispense with. These are what Habermas calls validity claims. That is, in order to secure sense and understanding, our communications must act in accord with four principles or validity claims. In the first place our utterances must be *comprehensible*, for example, we must as a minimum requirement use a language that all participants can understand. Secondly, what we say must make some claim to be *true*, otherwise we will fail to understand each other. Thirdly, I need to know that what you say is an *authentic* and *sincere* representation of your true interest and identity, otherwise I may have to conclude that your failure to communicate is based on some kind of deception. And finally we have to share some minimal *moral* values. From this seemingly unlikely foundation it is possible to develop the argument that these validity claims are truly universal features of all communication aimed at reaching an understanding, and through their codification into what Habermas calls *discourse ethics* we have arrived at a position that claims to provide a philosophical basis for my investigation into the purpose of counselling and psychotherapy. Just as important is the fact that this process of reasoning is open to disputation.

Because this approach is still quite unusual I felt that it would be useful to spend some time articulating the differences between these validity claims. To make any sense at all morality, which is essentially concerned with justice and equality, must be based on norms that claim to be universal. In the absence of transcendental guarantees, communicative rationality secures this deontologically through processes guaranteed by argumentation and discourse ethics. Morals are concerned with issues that are applicable to everyone, and hold to a symmetry between rights and obligations which distinguishes it from the law which privileges rights. Morality is also a higher value than happiness or well-being. This understanding enables us to take a more reflective and critical perspective on counselling's flirtation with consumer, contractual and human rights. Simultaneously it connects a concern with well-being to the danger of limiting therapeutic interventions to symptom relief and reality adjustment at the expense of the moral and ethical development of the client.

Chapter 2 continues to develop the theme of morality by considering its relationship with solidarity and addressing the problems associated with applying abstract rules to particular cases. But we are still left with the problem of what can motivate us to be moral in a postconventional and secular world. A deontological moral framework gains its credibility precisely because it is 'demotivated', that is, it is not dependent upon extrinsic absolute premises or goods. This kind of morality requires citizens who possess the psychological and emotional competence to act morally. This can be achieved only through adequate socialization processes and it is an important function of psychotherapy and counselling to make up for socialization deficits in our moral development. Following Habermas, ethics and morals can be differentiated because the former does not generate universal norms, instead we find that ethical issues are intrinsically related to questions of self-identity. We judge someone ethically in terms of the degree to which their expressions and actions authentically represent their inner self or identity. A person's competence to be authentic is dependent on their level of self-transparency. To the extent to which they are subject to systematically distorted communication (unconscious processes) their level of authenticity will be compromised as will, by extension, their potential to act ethically. In this context the role of counselling becomes quite clear – by helping the client to reduce the level of unconscious motivation and increase self-transparency the counsellor is making a direct ethical intervention in the client's life. Finally, I introduce two further validity claims – health and autonomy. The concept of autonomy is not new to the therapeutic community but I feel that it has been poorly defined and is often indistinguishable from individualism and consumer choice. Autonomy is, I suggest, the most fundamental value associated with counselling and psychotherapy, and the enabling of autonomy in individuals and society is their ultimate purpose. This sense of autonomy draws on recent debates in sociology which make clear that autonomy cannot be achieved by an individual on his or her own – to achieve autonomy I need everybody else to be autonomous within a social framework that is conducive to autonomous action. In this context the concept of autonomy cannot be encapsulated simply by notions of liberty, instead it involves the deeper notion of freely binding the will to moral obligations.

Traditionally we have been expected to behave morally and ethically by the internalization of external absolute norms which become inner imperatives guiding our action. An instance of this in the Christian tradition would be the Ten Commandments. These are externally and absolutely legitimized by a creator god and operate through the internal, morally driven, motives of the believing individual. This is no longer a successful format and our sense of autonomy is incompatible with such inner compulsion. We have to learn moral character and it is this subject that I consider in the next chapter. The already expressed interest in language and communication enables me to consider those theories of personality development which are dialogical and intersubjective. The development of self through a process of *individuation* is really understandable only when seen as a dialectical or interactive process of mutual recognition whereby my identity becomes real only when others recognize it as such and vice versa. Indeed, much of the therapeutic interaction can be understood in these terms and becomes appropriate when this process fails in real life. The intersubjective theory of personality development enables us to see psychological development as a process that works through evolutionary stages. This process culminates, in the ideal case, with the creation of a decentred and flexible self that is able to act morally and autonomously. In helping people to achieve these goals, counselling is not drawing on a fixed moral code which it bestows on the client; it is more a case of enabling the client to generate a competence to act ethically and morally. One aspect of this competence relates to our ability to respond appropriately to a range of moral emotions extending from guilt to love. They act like antennae supporting us in our relationships with others and we would not be able to act morally or ethically without them. However, we should not see them as somehow raw or natural. They are constituted by our understanding of the world and contain a cognitive content which links them very closely to our sense of self. In this sense they are reflexive and congruent with the validity claims of communicative rationality. Their influence also changes historically with shame becoming more important to us than guilt in recent times.

At the end of the developmental process of individuation we will need a certain kind of self-identity that will enable us to act autonomously. What is the nature of this self? From Copernicus to the postmoderns, mankind has been moved from the centre to the fringes of the universe. This process has gone too far and the decentred type of selfhood that I identify does not lack a core identity albeit that it is flexible and multi-layered. Many postmodern definitions of the self as completely fragmented and centre-less are unhelpful – they also disrespect the real difficulties that people face when their self-identity feels like it is disintegrating. Whilst definitely avoiding fallacies concerning the self as an individual, isolated and self-mastering identity, it is possible to have a plurality of selves that are nevertheless connected and able to maintain a coherent identity over space and time. With the understanding of the decentred self that I develop I suggest it is possible to see how such a person could act with true autonomy. This understanding of personality development and the process of individuation leading to an autonomous decentred subject provides counselling and psychotherapy with the fundamental purpose of enabling people (inside and outside the counselling room) to achieve this objective when other socialization processes have failed them.

In Chapters 4 and 5, I am interested in applying these general observations and considerations to a range of theoretical and practical issues in psychotherapy and counselling. After discussing the theoretical benefits that an understanding of Habermas's theory of communicative rationality would bring I outline how the self-reflective element in therapy is akin to the role of critique in social theory. In both, the role of insight cannot be divorced from enabling a person to understand that many of the psychological difficulties that people experience are the result of domination at both the individual and the social level. Insight and self-awareness are necessarily critical, and counselling provides the individual with her own personal critique. In a society dominated by instrumental or strategic rationality it is easily forgotten that there are different forms of rationality. Moreover when this specific form of rationality is, with some justification, deemed to be 'masculine' we can see how the usage of the concept of rationality in counselling and psychotherapy becomes problematic. This is unfortunate and has the undesirable side-effect of inflating the importance of emotions and feelings. The theory of communicative rationality allows us to redress this imbalance by providing counselling with a framework with which to understand how the ethical and moral actions of clients can be seen to be rational or irrational. It is not the duty of counsellors and psychotherapists to pronounce a 'judgement' on their clients on the basis of this framework, but they must internally hold this moral and ethical frame on behalf of their clients until their clients can hold it for themselves. All these issues, together with an understanding of the increasing extent to which the individual psyche is socially constituted, point to the benefits that accrue from the introduction of a theoretical framework concerning the purpose of counselling and psychotherapy.

Any concern with therapeutic purpose must eventually bring us face-to-face with the issues of value-free and non-judgemental therapeutic interventions. Both these positions are, I submit, untenable. Whilst the obvious point that practitioners should withhold their personal prejudices is true, it is also trivial and serves to mask the deeper argument which claims that the process of communication itself inevitably involves the usage of the validity claims already outlined, which necessarily hold moral and ethical positions. I am similarly sceptical about the adoption of consumerist language and freedom of choice jargon. Some commentators think it possible for practitioners to facilitate the autonomy of their client whilst maintaining their own non-judgementalism. In this scenario the clients are then left to choose their own values as if they were available on a supermarket shelf. If this was simply a matter of the client exercising *taste* in her choice of various cultural artefacts then this position holds some truth, but our understanding of what makes an action authentic, ethical or moral is not a matter of taste and therefore cannot be a matter of choosing from a range values. This limited sense of autonomy as consumption has no substantial place in counselling and psychotherapy.

Whilst practitioners understand that personal prejudices must be excluded from the counselling room, I believe that they often have an insufficient understanding of the social constitution of self and therefore often fail to be aware of the values that operate at an unconscious level. This can result in failing to see that 'individual' problems are heavily influenced by social conflict. There is one value that practitioners should bring into the counselling room, that is, to remain faithful to the client's evolutionary development towards autonomy – *whether or not the client has consciously chosen this.*

Rather than seeing transference and countertransference as negative aspects of therapy I, like some others, believe that these phenomena are essential attributes of the therapeutic relationship – they represent an erotic connection. This movement of love is the same as that involved in the dialectic of mutual recognition already outlined in the process of identity formation. It is the source of energy that provides the motive for people to grow, work through their psychological difficulties and attain autonomous moral action. Psyche needs eros. It is difficult to see how counsellors could achieve the purpose of their work if they did not engage in the erotic process of transference and countertransference.

There are four other issues in counselling and psychotherapy that are cause for concern – brief counselling, outcome measurement, professionalism and professional codes of ethics. Whilst brief counselling may have some merit in specific situations there seems to be a significant and worrying trend whereby case lengths are becoming shorter. The briefer the case the greater the level of counsellor intervention, with the result that the interaction is more likely to be skills- or technique-based and more in the control of the counsellor. This, in turn, tends to result in the reduction of the therapeutic goal to that of symptom reduction which leaves psychotherapy firmly locked into the medical model or metaphor whereby the client is to be returned to some fictional state of equilibrium, health or stasis rather than developed towards a future state of authenticity and autonomy. Instead of a decentred self this approach is more likely to create a 'managed self' that has been fixed by the counsellor-cum-mechanic ready to return to full performance in the same social context that caused the original symptoms. This brief approach is also all too easily able to accommodate the compulsive drive towards the measurement of outcomes. Massive pressure from government agencies, funders (including charitable trusts), insurance companies and corporate clients is forcing counselling and psychotherapy to adopt an increasingly positivistic (as if the well developed critique of positivism did not exist) value system that is extrinsic to what I see as their true purpose. This forces counselling down the road of brief interventions and, for those working in the voluntary sector, it erodes their independence and, by extension, civil society itself.

I am similarly unsure about the benefits that the clients and society gain from the professionalization of psychotherapy and counselling. Clearly the practitioners understandably seek the benefits that professionalization offers – better pay, more status and better conditions as well as the promise of maintaining higher standards for clients. However, counselling and psychotherapy are in danger of becoming a lifestyle option. This aspect of professional aspirations inhibits the more radical and vocational function of counselling being a subversive critic of the dominant culture – a culture which creates so much of the psychological distress that walks into the counselling rooms. Why criticize a society that provides you with your livelihood? Counselling has moved from being a *social movement* to being a form of *service delivery*. As a consequence the discussion of values and ethics has been reduced to a concern with a professional code of ethics that rarely lifts its gaze above issues of confidentiality.

For the remainder of the book I address one of the most neglected aspects of psychotherapy and counselling – their relationship to social and political issues. Given the greater interpenetration between individual and society in late modernity, this neglect is no longer tenable. Counselling has failed to keep pace with the rapid social changes we experience. Globalization, the free movement of capital, ecological crises, changing work patterns and a host of other factors all have an enormous impact on self-identity. In late modernity, governments face the contradiction of having to interfere as little as possible in the economy in order to attract capital, yet they must also limit the social damage caused by capital. Capitalism and democracy are uncomfortable bedfellows, and the state, in order to legitimate itself, attempts to displace the citizen's interest in substantive democracy on to lifestyle and consumer activity. At the same time it proclaims the 'end of ideology and history' which enables the reduction of political issues to technical and managerial processes. Despite these sources of obfuscation, it is always possible for the individual to see through them with, if necessary, the aid of counselling and psychotherapy. However, because of their poor understanding of the connection between the individual and society, these counselling processes may be less than successful in helping the private individual become a public citizen.

Western societies in late modernity are complex. A substantial feature of this complexity is the role of abstract systems in making these societies function. The most obvious of such systems is that of money. Our every-day lives are touched by money in a variety of ways. What is in essence a transaction between a purchaser and a vendor has become so complex that even the experts fail to understand it. The movement of money infiltrates most aspects of our life – from credit cards to pensions; from complex tax systems to international stock exchanges; from the free movement of capital to junk bonds. Other abstract systems include state bureaucracies, international corporations, the Internet, communication systems and so on. What they all have in common is that they seem to be out of our control; hard to understand; not easily held to account; vital for our existence and yet prone to unpredictable failure and collapse. At the other end of the social spectrum are those small-scale social processes in the lifeworld such as the family, friendships, culture activity and socialization processes. The abstract systems create a form of *system integration* that enables complex societies to cohere through our indirect social relations with each other. The social processes of the lifeworld create *social integration* which enables our direct and everyday interactions to function effectively. The problem under consideration is that in late modernity, abstract systems colonize the lifeworld with the result that their social penetration of the individual identity is greatly increased. One only has to think of the impact that the introduction of the TV set has made on domestic arrangements. With a TV set in several rooms in the home we have introduced the processes of marketing and branding not only into hearth and home but into the socialization of our children from the earliest of ages.

This colonization has serious deleterious psychological effects. Our understanding of the world around us becomes fragmented whilst the pervasiveness of money commodifies our relationships. The constant need to monitor ourselves and the limited horizon provided by this instrumental culture instil a depressive loss of meaning. Our reliance on experts to explain the complexities that surround us, coupled with the high risks involved in depending on complex systems, creates a permanent level of anxiety and insecurity. These issues, plus many more, illustrate the extent to which our individual identity is increasingly socially constituted. The extent to which counselling and psychotherapy fail to understand this is the measure of the inadequacy of their ability to fulfil their purpose.

This does not have to be the case. The very processes that have caused this colonization have also generated new forms of selfhood which have the potential to achieve the autonomy that we seek. At the same time these processes have created forms of social interaction that can significantly assist in the generation of autonomous people – namely counselling and psychotherapy. Giddens illustrates how, as a counterpart to abstract systems and globalization, there has been a 'transformation of intimacy'. As intimate relationships have become less defined by traditional roles, a new form of 'pure relationship' based on reflexivity, openness and trust has become a sanctuary for a self seeking meaning. This form of relationship, based on self-reflexive individuals, is only possible to large numbers of people now. They also require the support of a culture that is broadly therapeutic in outlook, and in particular the support of counselling and psychotherapy. Rarely understood by the latter is the fact that by helping their clients they are also sustaining a hugely significant social and cultural transformation. Not only is the self of late modernity redesigning its intimate relationships, but also its successful development towards autonomy is dependent upon other issues of self-identity. For example, by understanding its own social constitution the self can generate a moral outlook. Furthermore, it needs to be reflexive and maintain a narrative structure. And, as previously mentioned, it is a decentred form of identity.

Giddens helps us to understand that not only does a democratic society need the kind of autonomous self that counselling is enabling, but the 'pure' type of relationships that the autonomous self requires (of which counselling is in some ways representative) are themselves open and democratic. The stage upon which counselling and psychotherapy can enact their purpose is therefore truly historic. They have an important role in social and political struggle for control over the tectonic social changes that are erupting out of late modernity. These changes are primarily operating at the *psychological* level. Are counselling and psychotherapy up to this challenge?

CHAPTER 1

Communicative Rationality

If we are to have any level of success in establishing a coherent sense of purpose for counselling, it seems inevitable that we need to investigate what philosophical grounding, if any, can be generated. I want first to attempt to secure as firm a basis as possible for outlining the moral and ethical purpose of counselling before coming to analyze how such roots influence both the values inherent in therapeutic work and the social and political role of counselling.

In a post-traditional world of pluralistic societies, moral obligations can no longer be justified at the social level from a transcendent God's point of view (although it can provide motivation for some individuals). Most religions create an objective vantage point beyond the world from which the world could be created and judged. The move to a secular morality creates the need to reconstruct this perspective within the world itself, whilst attempting to find objective grounds within the world that enable a universal moral perspective. The binding force of religious norms and values came not simply from the naked power of an absolute divinity but from the understanding that divine commands had a rational or true basis. From a non-religious perspective the process of secularization is one in which reason withdraws from the sacred and comes down to earth into the minds of acting subjects, who must set aside moral judgements based on external transcendent guarantees in favour of judgements based on reasons that have a subjective rationality. We obey moral injunctions not from fear of external force but because they carry an authority or truth that 'freely' obligate us. Once the religious foundation has been jettisoned the authority of the moral 'ought' can only be reconstructed on the basis of the reason and the will of living people. The fact that the demise of religious and metaphysical worldviews has not resulted in a whole-scale retreat from morality might reassure us that a secular reconstruction of morality is possible.

How is this to be achieved? Following the theories offered by Habermas and others, I propose that in a world where religion and metaphysics have lost their transcendental guarantees, the only remaining viable source for justifying moral and ethical questions comes from an understanding of the conditions of communicative agreement, that is, communicative

11

rationality. However, before we consider this, it might be useful to consider some of the difficulties thrown up by relativist arguments.

Relativism

In the current climate in contemporary thought the attempt to find some firm ground seems an unlikely venture. The attempt to articulate universal criteria for morality comes under political attack from those concerned with ethnocentrism and postcolonial legacies. Different contexts, different cultural traditions, different worldviews and social practices, it is argued, will necessarily generate different and conflicting conceptions about right and wrong. Western rationalism becomes identified with domination and imperialism. Philosophically, and in everyday life, the notion of a universal reason is becoming less accepted. With postmodernism this process has been accelerated. Postmodernists have not only criticized the modern sense of self, the idea of evolution in history and the validity of high art, but have taken this critique into the heart of reason itself. From this perspective the rationalist claims to differentiate truth and falsehood as well as science and myth are undermined because, given the absence of a sacred guarantor, these distinctions were internal to the traditions of modernity and could not be legitimized outside these traditions.[1] Postmodernism consequently questions philosophy and the possibility of theories of knowledge and justice. Pierce, who is concerned about the impact of postmodernism on feminist thought, summarizes the position well:

> under postmodernism, categories are abolished altogether. Every generalization leaves out something of importance, and our efforts to capture the item left out are endless and lead to a radical particularity. The view is well known: the world as text, subject to endless commentary and particular interpretations, the continual displacement of one text by another... The feminist worry that some stories are marginalized or not told shifts in postmodernism to the view that there are only particular stories, that no rational standards arbitrate between discourses. (1991: 63)

Persuasive as such arguments may seem they contain real problems. At a common-sense level, relativism appears to promote tolerance. A person can both hold the view that, on the one hand, something is right or wrong for her within her own social tradition and yet can, on the other hand, also hold the view that this fact does not enable her to speak for other people in other societies – such a person may *seem* to be tolerant. She appears to be arguing the case that everyone should have the right to make up their own mind. However, the fact that she supports this view does not mean that others are similarly obliged for, without an independent *reason* underpinning this view, it does not mean that others should or would support the same view. Tolerance of opposing views does not ensue from subjectivist or relativist positions. As Williams argues, 'This is seriously confused, since it takes relativism to issue in a non-relativistic morality of universal toleration' (1993: 160).

From a more political and social perspective, relativism seriously undermines the ability to provide a critique of repressive and exploitative social practices. From the position that one ideology is as good as the next and that all are mere fictions, it is the shortest of steps for anyone to create their own ideology in their own image. Such positions, without philosophical justification, can easily take authoritarian forms and lead to cynicism in practical life. To accede to this is to accept the impossibility of providing a moral critique of structural domination inherent in many social conditions. The postmodern ambition to unmask meta-narratives and ideologies makes little sense unless we maintain at least one standard against which such unmasking can take place.

The attempt to find objective knowledge generally takes one of two routes. The first is the objectivist route which postulates an independent 'objective' reality towards which our interpretations converge so that, eventually, they will exactly correspond to this independent reality. The rationality inherent in the interpretations comes to match that found in reality. Some very simple views of science follow this approach such that, given enough time, we will discover the exact true nature of the world out there (as if the concepts we use to understand this world play no part in this process).

On the other hand, the relativist approach adheres to a social constructivist theory of truth. This notion, as we have seen, sees all standards of rationality as particularized to different cultures, traditions and even individuals. The insurmountable difficulty with the objectivist standpoint is that the proponents have to find a neutral (godlike) position outside language in order to demonstrate the nature of objective reality but they can only argue for this from within the limited confines of the language that they use. But the relativist perspective fares no better because, as Habermas (1998c: 135) argues, by conceding to the inevitable contextuality of every linguistically constituted view of the world, they cannot do this without a performative self-contradiction. What is meant by a performative self-contradiction?

Although I shall return to this idea later, it is a simple but compelling criticism of the position of a radical relativist or a sceptic. By using language to articulate his position the relativistic sceptic has at least two problems. First, as he is obliged to use language to make his case that *all* moral positions are relative he has the problem that, by his own admission, the vehicle he is using in order to make a *universalistic* claim about morality is a non-universalistic and context-bound language. Consequently, in terms of successful communications how would the hearer fully understand the point? Secondly, more philosophically, the relativist is in the peculiar position of arguing that his doctrine is somehow above the relativity of judgements he claims to exist in all other aspects of life. So, as Habermas argues in *The Philosophical Discourse of Modernity*, postmodern thinkers like Foucault cannot escape the performative self-contradiction of using the tools of reason to criticize reason – a sentiment which is echoed by Derrida (2003b: 42) in his critique of Foucault.

Where do we go from here? Both the objectivist and relativist approaches are, I suggest, unproductive. We need a different approach. Silverman (1975: 83) begins to shed some light. Truth, he argues, is not so much a series of abstract arguments but the means of establishing truth is linked to the way we *live* together – it is to be found in the public language of a community:

> And this could not be further from the *relativistic* position that, since all assertions are relative to a particular way of knowledge, there is no difference between 'truth' and 'falsity'. As Wittgenstein reminds us, it is through notions of truth and falsity that we live our lives together. So, of course, we *can* assert that there is no difference between the two (language, after all, is not a prison), but, in doing so we would be proposing a non-existent society. For, to see no difference between truth and falsity is for us . . . to be recognisably crazy.[2]

Following Habermas I shall try to make the case that we can extend this argument to not just any linguistic community but to the universal presuppositions of all communication. He argues (1998c: 138–9) that even in the most difficult cases of reaching an understanding, all those involved necessarily appeal to the common reference point of a possible consensus between them. The terrible fear that the terrorist plays on is his total immunity to dialogue and reason. But many of today's leaders were yesterday's terrorists; in the end he has to accept that the change he wants is only possible when both sides attempt to find common ground. Concepts like truth and rationality, although they may be interpreted in various ways and applied using different criteria, play the same grammatical role in every linguistic community. All languages offer the possibility of distinguishing between what is true and what we hold to be true. Rather than projecting a truth 'out there' or, conversely, denying the possibility of any form of truth, this approach looks to our everyday use of communication to see if there are preconditions to communication that are necessary and universal.[3] With the concept of communicative rationality the argument can be developed that, from the possibility of reaching an understanding linguistically, a concept of situated reason can be developed that is both context-dependent and transcendent. It is immanent in that it cannot be found outside the usage of language and transcendent in that as a regulative idea it provides a critique of all activity. In the words of Zizek (2002: 90) the transcendent is not abolished but is rendered *accessible*.

Communicative Rationality

We start from the premise that the primary purpose of communication is to reach an understanding, which may, or may not, result in a social action. Even if this is not always successful the *intention* of participating in a communicative event is that we are trying to reach an understanding. Reaching an understanding is the inherent purpose of human speech. Speech and understanding are not the same thing, but the latter is only possible if sentences are intended to create understanding; reciprocally, sentences have little obvious function if they are not attempting to create understanding.

An agreement on understanding is achieved when the participants in communication, on the basis of reasons, can assent to the content of what is said. As Habermas consistently argues, a communicatively achieved agreement has a rational foundation. This prevents us from accepting as valid any agreement on understanding that is imposed by either party, whether this is a result of a directly coercive intervention in the communicative event or the result of strategic action that indirectly influences the decisions of opponents (for example, bribes or other inducements). It is possible to obtain an objective 'agreement' by force; under the threat of direct or indirect violence people can assent to many things. However, this does not count as a legitimate understanding because, although it may be agreed formally, it cannot count as a subjective agreement if the conditions of communication do not permit a freely motivated assent. The invalidity in law of confessions obtained during torture illustrates the point. Coming to an understanding is a process of mutually convincing one another *and* a process conditional on the fact that this communicative interaction is based on the premise that the parties are motivated to achieve this through reasons. Agreement has to rest on the common convictions of participants able to operate on a rational basis. Consequently, a statement by one person succeeds only if the other accepts the offer (to reach a free and rational agreement) contained in it by taking a position of 'yes' or 'no' on a validity claim that is inherent in any speech act aimed at reaching a mutual understanding. My statement to you – 'It has just started raining' – can only work if you comprehend the vocabulary and grammar (thereby fulfilling the validity claim that our communication must be comprehensible if it is to succeed), and that you freely agree that the validity claim relating to truth (the 'fact' that it is raining) is indeed the case. The uncoerced nature of coming to an understanding is a normative concept – it is a necessary rider; *this norm cannot be discarded on some relativistic whim*. Your agreement to the statement about the rain would lack veracity if it was made under conditions of torture. Therefore, without the norm that understanding must be uncoerced there can be no understanding (even if we have to hold this as a necessary idealization in a world where it can be rarely attained); without the concept that understanding is necessary to the human condition we would, as Silverman says, be 'recognisably crazy'.

In entering into communicative action the speaker and hearer must assume the goal of coming to an understanding to reach an agreement that results in reciprocal understanding, shared knowledge and mutual trust. They commit themselves to recognizing each other symmetrically as responsible subjects capable of orienting their actions to the validity claims inherent in communication. These validity claims, which we shall come to later, are comprehensibility, truth, truthfulness (or authenticity) and justice. In real life there will be many instances where understanding breaks down; in which case the claims to validity must be suspended. In this situation the participants must endeavour, through mutual interpretation, to achieve a new definition of the situation which they can share. If this too fails then communicative action at this level cannot succeed. The remaining options are to reach a compromise, to switch to strategic action (thereby discontinuing the attempt at mutual understanding altogether and agree to interact on an instrumental basis only; for example, the purchase of a newspaper can be achieved without reaching a deep understanding between purchaser and vendor) or to try again to reach understanding by moving to a different level of discourse – the level of argumentation. Since argumentation is merely a reflexive form of communicative action (that is, a form of communication that thinks about and analyzes itself) then the norm of unforced communication also operates at this level. As Habermas suggests '... the presuppositions of communicative action already carry within themselves the germ of morality' (1995c: 132).

Although argumentation draws on the presuppositions of communicative action, they are not identical. Communicative action normally occurs in the everyday language of a world in which we, by and large, share a common normative context and live through received customs and habits and institutionalized patterns of behaviour. Arguments, however, are more abstracted forms of communication, distanced from everyday life by more formal rules of discourse. Indeed, arguments can become highly institutionalized and specialized in the arenas of science, law and art and so on. When my dispute with my neighbour about the fence she is erecting fails to be resolved by common sense, we are obliged to use the more abstract language of the law in an attempt to attain a more specific understanding of our reciprocal obligations. However, the move to abstraction in argumentation should not be confused with the more narrow concept of logical coherence. The latter can be used to demand an internal coherence within the actions and expressions of an individual person but this conception of rationality cannot explain the intersubjective nature of validity claims, nor can it encompass modes of argumentation and the idea of a rational agreement.

Just as communicative reason needs distinguishing from the narrow concept of logic, it also needs to be differentiated from practical reason, that is, it cannot act as a guide to us in practical moral decision-making. Communicative reason is limited to enabling mutual understanding through the process of this understanding being tested by validity claims that are intrinsic to communication itself and also to the production of insights that help us to understand the other person's point of view by means of clarifications gained in argumentation. (If my interlocutor about the rain is dubious about my observation, we can clarify it through argumentation using the specialized language of science.) It is therefore not possible to directly gain practical moral guidelines for action (how we 'should' behave) from communicative rationality. However, moral action and communicative rationality do connect with each other when moral insights need justification because such justification can only be obtained if it fulfils the preconditions of communicative rationality. Even so, communicative rationality provides only a weak motive for moral behaviour, the motive that such behaviour has been rationally justified.

The promising development of the theory of communicative rationality has within it two other developments that need recognizing. First is the demise of the philosophy of the individual subject and its firm replacement by that of intersubjectivity. Second is the move from an interest in language to an interest in communication. With regard to the former, classical philosophy has been overwhelmingly based on the paradigm of self-consciousness, that is, the acting philosophical subject has been that of the relation-to-self of a subject knowing and acting in isolation. The relationship of the classic atomized, individual thinker to the universal is mediated not through intersubjectivity (the sense that the individual is created and sustained by her social relationships) but through the interactions of a self-consciousness – a self-consciousness that will eventually (so the philosopher hoped) link up with absolute knowledge. Habermas and the postmodernists both agree that this paradigm derived from the Enlightenment is exhausted. This consensus is important but beyond it they part company. Some postmodernists argue that in leaving behind the paradigm of the philosophy of consciousness we can also leave behind all other paradigms which inevitably lead us back into the morass of an unendingly regressive circular relativism. Enlightenment rationality definitely does contain real problems; however, unlike postmodern philosophy, we do not have to abandon it all – it is, I suggest, still possible to make real philosophical developments. The paradigm of the philosophy of self-consciousness can be transformed into the paradigm of mutual understanding, that is, of the intersubjective relationship between individuals who are socialized through communication and reciprocally recognize one another. Indeed, as we shall see later on, the thrust of some developmental psychology works from the premise that individual identity is not somehow inherent but is the direct consequence of mutual interaction. The individual can only be such because she is intersubjectively constituted. By this route the critique of Western logocentrism – that is, the domineering thought of subject-centred (some might say patriarchal) reason – results not in the destruction of reason as such[4] but in its reformation into an intersubjectively situated reason. The notion of intersubjectivity is central to my thesis because, once we finally surrender the concept of the isolated, atomistic, primordial, possessive individual,[5] the essential fact that individuals are intersubjectively constituted opens the door to an understanding of common moral and ethical values.

Alongside the demise of the philosophy of consciousness was the development of the interest in studying language rather than 'consciousness'. With the 'linguistic turn' we are no longer trapped in the monological perspective of the philosophy of the subject because language is intrinsically *dialogical* – it is something that operates *between* people. Most linguistic philosophy remained primarily concerned with the analysis of grammar and was therefore highly analytical and abstract. Habermas noticed, however, that Austin's conception of speech acts and Wittgenstein's idea of language-games enabled the evolution of linguistic philosophy into communicative rationality. In the latter, language is placed in the context of the real-life interactions of communication with real people attempting to reach an understanding within the confines of everyday life. This provided the opportunity to study the 'pragmatics' or practical features of the everyday conditions of communication. It also prevented the limiting of communication to speech and embraces other forms of symbolic interaction.

An essential precondition for communication is that the participants, if they intend to reach an understanding, must presuppose a common (or translatable) language, wherein they confer common meanings on the expressions used. Members of a community who share a language must assume that they can understand a grammatical expression in the same way. The expression of symbolically represented thought via signs and grammatical rules carries an ideal status – through language the thought carries its meaning through different contexts. Without this we could have no useful conception of a misunderstanding. Moreover, Habermas notes:

> The presupposition that linguistic expressions are used with identical meanings can often turn out to be false from an observer's perspective, and perhaps this is always the case under the ethnomethodologist's microscope. But even as counterfactual, this presupposition remains necessary for every communicative use of language. (1998b: 19)[6]

Universal Pragmatics

An excursion into the formal pragmatics of language may seem a little distanced from our initial project of trying to establish some non-relativist and rational grounds upon which we may establish the moral and ethical purpose of counselling. This will, I believe, not be a forlorn journey because there is good reason to believe that the presuppositions of communication can fulfil such a purpose, albeit in a somewhat restricted form. In this I echo Habermas's own aspirations:

> I would never have tackled a formal-pragmatic reconstruction of the rational potential of speech if I had not harboured the hope that by means of this approach I would be able to generate a concept of communicative rationality from the normative contents of the universal and ineluctable presuppositions of a *non-circumventable* practice of everyday processes of reaching understanding. It is not a matter of this or that preference, 'our' or 'their' notions of rational life; rather we are concerned here with reconstructing a voice of reason, which we cannot avoid using whether we want to or not in speaking in everyday communicative practice. (1982: 243–4)

This analysis will be brief and runs the risk of satisfying neither the philosopher nor the counsellor but I hope that it may help in illustrating the importance and the unique relevance of the theory of communicative rationality to psychotherapy and counselling.

The already mentioned move within linguistic philosophy towards understanding language in the wider contexts of communication was facilitated by Austin's theory of speech-acts. A speech-act is a *social* event in which the sentences we utter have an *illocutionary force*. When I utter an assertion, a promise or a warning through sentences I am not just uttering the words; rather, I *do* something, I execute an action. These words exist within the context of a real social interaction between the speaker and the hearer so that my intention as the speaker is not just to utter words but to bring about an event in the hearer. Hopefully this corresponding event will be an understanding of my utterance. This understanding is the result of a real psychological process in the hearer – a psychological internal dialogue about the meaning of the speaker's statement and my response, as the hearer, to it. Even if I only achieve a misunderstanding in the hearer, it is still an interactive social event that involves internal psychological work by the participants. To be understood, therefore, every utterance must, at least implicitly, establish an external relation between the parties to the communicative event and an internal relation between each psyche and the meaning to be considered. The illocutionary force of such a speech action is to establish and fix the communicative function of the words uttered such that both parties experience the process of encoding and decoding as one that is active (counsellors are familiar with the term 'active listening') and, if necessary, is also an experience that can involve changing comprehension or perception in both hearer and speaker. This illocutionary force or, in other words, the 'active' element in communicating epitomizes one of the most characteristic features of psychotherapeutic communications – the very fact of communicating presupposes the possibility of mutual psychological transformation.

A speech act can succeed or fail. A speech act between speaker and hearer succeeds if both accept that this communication creates a relationship between them and that this relation is one that the speaker intended. For example, both therapist and client will often go to great lengths to ensure that the intended meanings behind their statements are understood. At the same time the hearer must understand and accept the content uttered by the speaker within the intended relational context between them, that is in this example, within the context of a therapeutic encounter. Behind it is the fact that the speaker and hearer are in an interpersonal relationship. Communication is both an event and a relationship in which the individuals are not isolated atoms but are mutually constituting each other. In 'rational' communication this mutual influencing is free; in distorted or ideological communication (the *perlocutionary effect*) it is subject to domination.[7]

What creates the illocutionary binding or bonding effect that will motivate the hearer to coordinate her subsequent action with the speaker? Why should the client listen to the counsellor? The source of this effect, Habermas argues, is 'the warranty' that the speaker offers to cover the validity claims he raises with his speech act. The value of the warranty is derived from its rational basis; that is, the validity claims inherent in the communication are testable. The universal core found in diverse utterances is based on the fact that language places symbols in a system of validity claims. When a speaker orients herself towards understanding she must raise, and be accountable for, four rationality or validity claims: comprehensibility, truth, norms and truthfulness/authenticity. A rationally motivated agreement or consensus on how to coordinate future action is possible only if the speaker can convince her hearer that her claims are rational:

> I would like, therefore, to defend the following thesis: In the final analysis, the speaker can illocutionarily influence the hearer and vice versa, because speech-act-typical commitments are connected with cognitively testable validity claims – that is, because the reciprocal bonds have a rational basis. (Habermas 1995a: 63)

Thus, speech acts containing such diverse utterances as assertions, descriptions, estimates and predictions and so on have a commonality in that the claim put forward in these different interpersonal relationships is based on their truth content. In our mutual understanding concerning these utterances we are primarily concerned with their relationship to truth – is the estimate accurate or not; will the prediction happen? With reprimands, transgressions and excuses, each being different, nevertheless, the type of interpersonal relationship involved concerns the rightness of the norm applied. If I reprimand someone for their behaviour a key feature of the reprimand being 'heard' will be that the hearer recognizes and accepts the validity of the norm or moral in relation to which she is being reprimanded. If I am censured for my dangerous driving, I am very likely to take heed because I agree with the underlying norm; to be censured for my taste in clothes would make little sense. With utterances concerning personal revelations, promises and intimacies they all express interpersonal relationships whose validity is based on the truthfulness of the participants and their ability to act congruently with their expressions. A client in counselling who is subject to a low level of self-awareness may be subject to communications that failed the third validity test because truthfulness (or sincerity) and congruence would often be compromised. In engaging in counselling, such a client is implicitly (even unconsciously) committing herself to the process whereby she gains the ability to represent herself authentically.

Whichever of the validity claims is involved, speech acts involve commitments to provide rational grounds or to make an undertaking to act in a trustworthy manner. In such communications the hearer can be rationally motivated to accept the speaker's offer of reaching an understanding. The communicative process of reaching an understanding therefore involves the following four validity claims. The speaker must:

1. utter something in a comprehensible expression enabling the speaker and hearer to understand each other;
2. have *something* that she wants to be understood; the speaker must intend to communicate a true proposition in order that the hearer may share this knowledge;
3. express her intentions truthfully or sincerely so that the hearer can believe that the utterance represents the speaker and is not a deception – this creates trust; and
4. must choose an utterance that is right ethically or morally so that the hearer can accept it in the context of a shared normative background.

Communicative action is successful when the participants believe that these reciprocally raised validity claims are justified.

Although genuine communication requires that the illocutionary effects be achieved freely, not all forms of communication proceed in this manner. The illocutionary aim of reaching an understanding through reciprocal influence is a process which happens before the implementation of action to achieve a goal.[8] Such aims, therefore, are achieved only through the (usually implicit) intersubjective recognition of the validity claims. This, in turn, depends on the fact that in reaching an agreement the parties are both autonomous (free from domination) and accountable. Illocutionary aims can only be achieved co-operatively.

When considering the *perlocutionary effect* of an utterance the impact on the hearer is quite different. Here the speaker is intending to produce an effect upon the hearer. In a perlocutionary communication 'the meaning of what is said' is not intended to create mutual understanding, rather the meaning is tied to the interests and intention of the speaker. The speech acts of the speaker are primarily concerned with achieving effects in the hearers which will lead them to action so that the speaker's intentions will be actualized. It follows with this kind of action that the participants no longer need to act co-operatively, nor do they need to respect the validity claims in a manner that is both autonomous and accountable. Obviously such strategic or instrumental actions can be constructive: members of a football team may freely abnegate the expectation that all communications are illocutionary in order to achieve a collective objective just as members of an institution or organization accept that some interactions will be perlocutionary. However, it is not difficult to see that strategic action based on the perlocutionary effect can lead to domination. In such action the initiating agent is only concerned with achieving his intentions. This necessarily creates an attitude towards the hearers such that their free and autonomous existence is no longer relevant as the effect of this type of communication is meant to affect the hearer's subjectivity regardless of their consent and, often, regardless of any rationality. Heteronomy has replaced autonomy. Clients in therapy have typically, prior to therapy, been victims and unwilling participants in strategic interactions subject to perlocutionary effects that deny and prevent both their autonomy and their authenticity. This happens not only within the dynamics of family and interpersonal life, but the predominance of strategic/instrumental values in our culture creates forms of interaction whereby the democratic process of communication through mutual understanding (illocutionary) is overwhelmed by 'communication' characterized by the perlocutionary effect which is often heteronymous. Much of commercial advertising is aimed at creating an effect in the audience that induces them to purchase the relevant products or services, it is not aimed at achieving mutual understanding.

From this it follows that we need to make a clear distinction between two types of social action – communicative and strategic action. The telos inherent in the former is *communicative understanding* and the telos in the latter is *instrumental mastery*. Both forms of action can be rational. A statement is rational when the speaker satisfies the already mentioned conditions required to achieve the illocutionary goal of reaching an understanding with a participant in communication. A strategic or goal-directed action is rational only if the actor satisfies the conditions necessary for realizing his intention to do something in the world. Their rationality is enhanced by the fact that both can fail (an agreement can fail to materialize and the desired instrumental effect can fail to occur) and by the fact that failures can be explained. This distinction between communicative and instrumental action is an important one and not without its critics.[9] Yet, although the philosophical debate on this issue may yet have a little way to run, I shall continue on the basis that communicative action is primary, not just in the sense that it is desirable because it 'ought' to be so, but that the conception of communicative rationality describes an ideal potential already present in every act of communication. The fact that not all linguistic interactions are 'communicative' does not prevent us from defining such events as potentially distorted, nor does it preclude the notion of a conscious historical evolution towards the actualization of a society firmly based on the principle that strategic actions are held secondary to communicative action.

I believe that this distinction also provides a fruitful basis for understanding some of the issues in counselling that we will eventually address. It also helps us distinguish a purpose from a usage. I am seeking to derive the moral and ethical purpose of counselling and psychotherapy from the fact that as a communicative event they are defined by communicative rationality. This does not prevent 'therapeutic' techniques and processes from being 'used' strategically in a whole host of contexts that I would deem contrary to the purpose of therapy; for example, brainwashing, torture, cults, verbal abuse, propaganda and so on. Indeed, it is this attempt to find conceptual clarity that enables us to understand that some of the social exclusion and individual psychopathology[10] experienced in Western society comes from the predominance of strategic action over communicative action. Clients in counselling embody this and maybe counselling agencies should embolden themselves to take a much more radical public stance against it. After all, the counselling interaction ideally represents a pure type of communicative action.

Validity Claims

The rationality of reaching an agreement in communication is dependent on satisfying four validity claims. Presently I shall investigate two of these claims, namely that of normative correctness and that of truthfulness or authenticity, in greater detail. For now I just wish to present a broad outline. The first claim is that of comprehensibility, that is, the sign system used must be grammatically correct and sufficiently shared by the participants to create the technical possibility of understanding. This is not really the subject of this book and truly rests with the study of hermeneutics and linguistics. Henceforth, I shall be referring only to three claims. As my interest lies principally with the issues of morals and ethics, the validity claim to truth will not receive much more attention than the following brief outline.

Truth

Communication involves making statements about facts or proposed facts concerning a state of affairs in the world. We have already rejected the theory that such facts exist independent of our conception of them and simply wait for us to find them. Facts are constituted by members of an interpretation community (this could be the community of scientists, historians and so on) involved in a process of reaching an understanding with one another about things in the world. 'Real', Habermas argues, is what can be represented in true statements, whereas 'true' is explained by one person making a claim, before the interpretive community, asserting a proposition. This truth claim gains validity because it is open to the criticism of the members of the relevant community. A valid or justified truth claim requires its proponent to defend it with reasons against the objections of possible opponents; the intention must be to secure the rationally motivated agreement of the interpretation community as a whole. Moreover, because '... no one has direct access to uninterpreted conditions of validity, "validity" must be understood in epistemic terms as "validity proven for us"' (Habermas 1998b: 14).[11] An example of this could be that of a scientist presenting a new idea in an academic journal which, over time, creates a debate between scientists and leads to further empirical experimentation in order to ascertain whether the idea is 'true' (in whole or part) or not.

The rationality in this aspect of communication is linked to the requirement that such claims should be well-grounded and devoid of errors with regard to facts. Moreover, the person proposing the new idea must be open to reviewing it in the face of contrary observations or facts. If this test is insufficient then the participants must abstract themselves from normal communicative interaction into the more formal mode of communication called 'discourse'. For truth claims the relevant discourse is theoretical. In discourse the participants put to one side the immediate practical issue and orient their communication to the reflexive task of achieving a rational consensus on whether or not the truth claim can be supported by the evidence and argument proposed. Thus discourse acts like an intersubjective court of appeal in which the speaker has the opportunity to defend her claim if challenged.

The truth claim inherent in every speech act implies that the participants intend to achieve an agreement on the difference between that which really is and that which subjectively appears to be the case. This creates and presupposes the essential psychological comprehension of the difference between a public world of intersubjectively acknowledged interpretations and the private world of personal interpretations.[12] The validity claim related to truth is essentially a scientific activity using cognitive and instrumental knowledge in order to ascertain empirical validity about something that is separate from our personal and private feelings and interpretations.

Normative (Moral)

We call people rational if they follow an established norm or moral obligation; for instance, it is generally agreed that causing harm to innocent people is morally wrong. The rationality of this moral is enhanced if the person is able to justify this action by reference to a set of legitimate rules, morals or expectations – thus, the United Nations Declaration of Human Rights justifies the immorality of harming innocent people. The knowledge base in this action refers not to the truth content of states of affairs but to the validity of the norms or morals – terrorism is wrong not because it is 'true' or 'untrue' but because it is immoral. This is moral practical knowledge. In everyday interaction, decisions between contested norms would normally be resolved within the context of established or traditional values – we readily agree that terrorism is wrong. However, if this immediate justification is not successful because say the terrorist describes himself as a freedom fighter, then the communication (if communication is possible at this juncture) takes a reflexive turn and is abstracted up to the level of discourse, that is, a formal level of communication which in this case is concerned with practical–moral issues. At this level the subject of concern is not the initial practical moral conflict (for example, a particular act of terrorism) but the validity claim of the norm underlying the initial normative claim (the issue of the morality of terrorism *per se*). Knowledge gained during moral practical discourse is then handed down ready for application in moral and legal contexts. Moral reasoning is therefore about the normative rightness of an action between people operating at the social level.

Expressive (Ethical)

This type of communication also has a rational basis, although it differs from the other two main validity claims. In an expressive interaction the speaker reveals aspects of his own identity. This can be: making known a desire or intention, making a confession, sharing a feeling or any other form of personal revelation. The main issues are those of transparency and consistency. Transparency is represented by sincerity or truthfulness. Is the speaker faithfully representing himself both at the conscious level (not lying, manipulating or deceiving) and at the unconscious level (that is, is he able to represent all aspects of his personality, even those subject to repression or systematically distorted communication – in other words not self-deceiving)? In the first sense the validity concerns sincerity or truthfulness; in the latter sense the issue is one of authenticity or congruence. A communication is rational and fulfils the validity claim of sincerity if the speaker is, in the ideal case, perfectly transparent and self-transparent. Consistency is related but slightly different. Here we are concerned with the sincerity and authenticity of the person over time. Although individual actions may be either insincere or inauthentic, more important is whether these are isolated instances. If the person consistently fails to follow through stated intentions into successful applications, we would say that he is living an 'inauthentic life' project and, inevitably, he would become existentially judged as an 'inauthentic person'. Validity claims would fail if deliberate lies are exposed or personal revelations can be shown to conflict with other parts of the speaker's psyche, or if stated intentions fail to consistently materialize. The panel of 'critics' in this context will often be informal (intimate partners, family, friends, colleagues and peers) or, in a formal context, may be counsellors, psychotherapists, social workers and psychological professionals. Here the primary orientation to the world is the speaker's relation to his own subjective world.

In the communicative model of action that has been outlined, people have the capacity to use this entire system of validity claims and world relations for coordinating action. This model provides a rich and complex competence on behalf of people enabling them to relate simultaneously to all three worlds – the objective, social and subjective. Moreover, they can relate to them *reflectively*, that is, they have the competence to differentiate the three types of relations and select them appropriately. This psychological competence requires a certain kind of self (the de-centred self) which I shall come to later. We should not be misled, however, into thinking that these validity claims exist in pure and isolated forms. Agreement is not possible if a hearer accepts the truth of an assertion yet doubts its sincerity or normative appropriateness. A counsellor who has experienced a client as insincere, inauthentic and morally ambiguous may well distrust the truth content of many of the client's claims. Similarly, as Ingram (1997: 280) points out, moral arguments aimed at justifying general principles often raise issues of truth concerning the case presented and ethical issues concerning human needs. Nevertheless, Habermas believes that, in principle, reflexive analysis can separate the different validity claims.

In the comments below, Coole makes an excellent summary of Habermas's thoughts on pragmatics. Table 1.1 represents my classification based on Coole's text.

> We thus inhabit three worlds simultaneously, each with its own rationality and validity structure: the objective, the social and the subjective. In orienting themselves to each, rational individuals adopt the appropriate attitude (objectivating, norm conforming, expressive). Each world then contributes its own background certainties (intuitive knowledge, group solidarity/traditional practices, and skills/know-how/body-centred complexes respectively). Language intervenes to reproduce them all: its reproduces cultures, renews social integration and socializes the young, although each has its own potential pathology too: loss of meaning, anomie and psychopathology. Each world is thus lived and, in modernity, reflected upon. Only with the latter are differentiations clear, yielding the three types of validity claims which promised consensus, but also expert cultures (science, jurisprudence, art criticism) whose separation from the lifeworld is an unhealthy dimension of rationalization. Habermas is most insistent that this differentiation of reason should remain and that it is crucial for emancipation, but he would also like to see its three aspects

Table 1.1   Aspects of the Pragmatics of Communicative Rationality

Forms of reason	Science	Morality	Art/expression
Speech person positions	They	You	I
Speech acts	Propositional	Illocutionary	Expressive
Attitude	Objectivating	Norm conforming	Expressive
Validity claims	Empirical validity	Normative rightness	Authenticity, sincerity
Types of knowledge	Cognitive-instrumental	Moral-practical	Aesthetic-expressive
Type of worlds	Objective	Social	Subjective
Background certainties	Skills, know-how	Group solidarity/traditional practices	Intuitive knowledge
Pathology	Loss of meaning	Anomie	Psychopathology
Expert cultures	Science	Jurisprudence	Art criticism and psychotherapy

(somehow) reintegrated in a balanced way within the lifeworld, to yield 'a non-reified, communicative practice of everyday life'. (1997: 229)

It would be unrealistic if this radical programme did not attract critics. Postmodernists, like Lyotard, believe that this approach contains a narrative of emancipation which contradicts the fact that different people and different cultures have worldviews or language-games that are incommensurable. But, as Dews points out:

> Lyotard's arguments depend on a chronic confusion between *language-games* and *validity-claims*. He fails to distinguish between the differentiation of their life-world into three distinct spheres of value, concerned respectively with cognitive, moral and aesthetic questions, and what Habermas terms a 'pluralization of diverging universes of discourse [which] belongs to specifically modern experience'. (1986: 22–3)

Thus while admitting the plurality of language-games, it is possible to argue that validity claims (which are not themselves a specific kind of linguistic activity) cut across this multiplicity.

Luhmann comes from a completely different angle:

> love solves its own attendant communicative problems in a completely unique manner. To put it paradoxically, love is able to enhance communication by largely

doing without any communication. It makes use primarily of indirect communication, relies on anticipation and on having already understood. And love can thus be damaged by explicit communication, by discreet questions and answers, because such openness would indicate that something had not been understood as a matter of course. (1982: 25)

This is to misunderstand the point. It would be perfectly possible for intimate lovers–communicators to omit pedantic linguistic articulations of their subjective states; but not on a long-term basis and not without the competence of the participants to return to the reflexive level of checking the validity of the communication if necessary. If meaning could not be checked how many more intimate moments would be ruined through misunderstanding?

Another group of criticisms clusters around a narrow interpretation of the three aspects of communication and the belief that Habermas favours some language usage as 'normal' and others as derivatives. Norris (1997: 114) points out that Habermas's approach cannot accommodate the notion that the same text contains a host of 'abnormal' features such as metaphors, nuances and accidental connections. White develops this critique noting that linguistic features like humour and irony have the important feature of sensitizing us to the dominating nature of aspects of culture at any historical moment. 'Humour, irony, metaphor, and aesthetic expression in general are what gives us breathing space and weapons in this ongoing struggle to prevent closure in the way we see ourselves, others and the world' (1988: 31). Indeed, the acerbic comedian can cut through a lot of conventions that no longer serve their original purpose. In his commentary on Habermas, White answers his own questions:

A problem with this strategy, which emerges quickly, is that it appears to tie meaning more closely to intentionality than perhaps is warranted. Do speech acts have an ironic meaning only when it is intended by the speaker? ... Perhaps Habermas might have it that he has over-stressed the role of intentionality here, but still defend the key aspect of his scheme by claiming that the quality of irony ... can be recognized only to the extent that *hearers* have mastered the system of validity claims and corresponding distinctions. Moreover, it is precisely here that charges of 'systematic distortion' of communication can begin to be levelled at the speaker. (1988: 31–2)

Indeed, Habermas (1982: 271) makes clear that although features like irony, metaphor and humour are, in his scheme, derivatives, this does not diminish their role in communication. Rather, they rest on intentionally using categorical confusion which we can see through as category mistakes precisely because we have the competence to distinguish the three universal validity claims and the accompanying distinctions between being/illusion, is/ought, essence/appearance.

Systematically Distorted Communication

As I shall develop later in the critique of counselling and psychotherapy, the theory of communicative action that we are considering enables a reflective interaction and control of the communicative process. In other words an understanding of what is intrinsic to communication enables us to gain a degree of awareness and control over our communications. Knowledge of the general structures of communication not only enables access to understanding in a specific context but also provides us with the critical means to reinterpret an understanding from within and transcend it. This, says Habermas (1997b: 130), enables a reflective attitude to the communication. This conception of reflexivity does not make the error of placing the reflecting subject *outside* the communication context (thereby claiming some God's eye or objective point of view), rather it deepens and radicalizes it. In many everyday contexts the move from communicative action up to the critical level of discourse is often blocked by ideology or distortion – for many clients the process of critically reappraising the role that their parents had in the genesis of their current psychological problem which they are bringing to therapy is just too difficult a step because their parents, and the general culture, have placed a taboo on such considerations. Fortunately this can be combated because the radical feature of the concept of communicative rationality is the notion that ingrained in the very structure of action oriented to reaching understanding there exists the critical leverage to break through systematic distortions. It is this leverage that, following Habermas, we shall shortly attempt to develop into rational conceptions of morality and ethics that can inform counselling practice. Just as important, however, it gives us the possibility for a radical critique of the impact of domination socially and at the level of individual psychopathology.

The concept of communicative rationality contains an idealization. By this we do not mean 'false' or 'hopelessly unrealistic', rather that the structures of communication of necessity contain the ideal anticipation of reaching an understanding. When we speak to each other we work on the assumption that we can, eventually, understand each other. In this sense the 'ideal' (reaching an understanding) is rooted in the 'real' (the very process of communicating). So in the conception of communications that have not been subjected to damage can be found a necessary condition (ideal) for individuals to reach an understanding without coercion.[13] Similarly this is true for the identity of an individual coming to an understanding with himself without force. By this move, Habermas notes that we outline *only* formal determinations of the *possible* forms of life and life-histories. It creates the parameters for living an undamaged life but it does not enable us define the concrete shape of an exemplary form of society or the authentic life-history.

In many situations, in oppressive circumstances that prevent rational communication, a person has good reasons to conceal or deliberately mislead others about her 'true' experiences. This can operate at an institutional level where employees may deliberately mislead employers; it can also happen within family situations where one party deceives another. In such cases the person is not raising a claim to truthfulness but is instead masquerading sincerity whilst behaving strategically. Such a manipulator deceives at least one other participant about the strategic (perlocutionary) nature of his communication because he deliberately behaves in a superficially consensual manner. Whilst still holding to the primacy of communicative action over strategic action, it is not possible, in the particular instance, to criticize such strategic expressions on the grounds of their truthfulness or sincerity. Such validity claims pertain only in communications aimed at reaching an understanding. Strategic deceptions are judged in the instrumental sense of whether or not they have achieved the intended perlocutionary effect. Thus, strategic deceptions can be 'rational' in the limited sense of effectiveness in so far as the other person was deceived, but they are not rational in the sense demanded by communicative reason.

If such strategic deception or self-deception has become habitual or impervious to conscious intervention by the person then we can say that the she has become subject to systematically distorted communication. Someone who cannot gain access to her own feeling and moods nor those of others because of an endemic strategic mode of interaction is acting irrationally. Social or interpersonal forms of interaction that have been subject to domination create psychological identities locked into the strategic mode wherein the interests of the manipulator occlude those of the victim. Hence the abusiveness of domestic violence is not limited to physical violence but usually also includes the psychological objectification of the victim, that is, communications in the relationship have not been geared to mutual understanding but are strategic and impersonal in order to meet the sole needs of the dominant partner. Following the validity claim relevant to expression we therefore term 'rational' the behaviour of someone who is both willing and able to free herself from illusions not only with regard to facts, but also with regard to illusions based on self-deceptions about one's own subjective experiences.

> Anyone who systematically deceives himself about himself behaves irrationally. But one who is capable of letting himself be enlightened about his irrationality possesses... *the power to behave reflectively in relation to his subjectivity and to see through the irrational limitations to which his cognitive, moral–practical, and aesthetic–practical expressions are subject.* (Habermas 1997b: 21)

The form of argumentation that clarifies systematic self-deception is 'therapeutic critique'. In this non-strategic communication the psychotherapist and client do not behave like proponent and opponent and their roles are not symmetrical. They are not equal participants in communicative action because the client, in varying degrees, exhibits more self-deception than the counsellor. Therapeutic communication is therefore a special case in which the full rationality of communicative interaction is consciously aimed for but is not currently achievable. The end of therapy signals the equalizing of roles and participation in fully rational communication.

The concept of the three validity claims has, I hope, helped to illustrate how normal communicative interaction aimed at reaching an understanding can only achieve this if it is open to criticism through the usage of these claims to validity. Conflict in everyday life will, however, contest the basis of such a validity claim. In such cases we need to move to another level of discourse from which we can gain reflection upon the contesting claims. This is the level of argumentation which underpins and guarantees everyday communicative validity claims.

Argumentation, Discourse Ethics and Postconventional Universalism

Argumentation (sometimes called discourse) is a more exacting type of communication. It generalizes, abstracts and extends the basic assumptions of specific everyday communication and includes competent participants able to move beyond the limits of their own particular form of life. Discourse ethics (the word 'ethics' in this context should not be confused with its more specific usage later where it is distinguished from the moral) is the attempt by Habermas and others to derive the substance of a universalistic morality from the general presuppositions of argumentation. My intention in taking this path is that it will provide us with good reasons to believe that objective (in the deontological sense – that is, objective 'for all of us' without claiming absolute knowledge) or universal morals can, at a minimal level, be demonstrated. This will then provide us with an entry into the debate about the moral and ethical purpose of counselling which, in the first place, will have actually tried to justify its moral position rather than simply ignoring the issue altogether; and, secondly, it will have already moved us past the sterile position of postmodern relativism which, in everyday counselling, with its limitation to 'particular' truths is easily confused with the futile concept of non-judgementalism.

In argumentation claims to validity have become problematic. In this new form of discourse the participants in argumentation adopt a hypothetical attitude to the disputed validity claims such that it is these claims themselves which are now the object of discussion. Thus, for example, the discussion moves from debating the morality of a particular murder to debating how we might collectively decide, more precisely, what it is about murder in general that makes it immoral. Just as everyday communication necessarily involves the validity claims, argumentation involves universal and necessary presuppositions of communication. Following McCarthy (1973: 145–6) they are:

1. all participants must have an equal chance to employ *communicative* speech acts so that they can at any time initiate and continue a discourse;
2. all participants must have the same chance put forward or call into question statements, interpretations and justifications so that in the long run all opinions are subject to consideration and criticism;
3. all participants must be able to represent themselves sincerely and authentically so that they can make their 'inner nature' transparent to others; and
4. no one should be subjected to domination thereby securing free and equal access to discourse and preventing the privileging of one set of norms.

In summary the presuppositions of argumentation are:

1. no one should be excluded
2. everybody should be given a right to make his or her own claims
3. everyone has the right to criticize others
4. freedom from domination
5. freedom from internal repression
6. the only norms valid are those regulating common interests.

The only force accepted is that of the better argument and thus all motives except that of the co-operative search for truth are excluded. The 'strength' of an argument is measured by the soundness of the reasons – one proof of such cogency is whether or not an argument is able to convince those involved in the discourse and thereby motivate them to accept the validity claim in question. Thus rational arguments require that the participants behave rationally in the sense of exposing themselves to criticism and, if necessary, *subjecting themselves to the psychological process of changing their views (and therefore themselves)* under the force of the better argument. Just as with ordinary communication geared to reaching an understanding, argumentation is an illocutionary communicative event involving the reciprocal subjectivities of the participants. Whilst psychotherapy is not an argument as such, these preconditions and especially the process of mutual psychological influence between therapist and client remind us of the ground rules and experience of psychotherapy and counselling.

This is a significant challenge to the conventional (even patriarchal) conception of argumentation as a purely rational process completely abstracted, via the paradigm of the individual conscience, from embodied feelings and moods and thus somehow operating only in the isolated minds of the participants. If, in Habermas's theory of argumentation, a consensus is reached about the contested validity claim, accepting either the original or a new justification, then this consensus expresses a 'rational will'.[14] This 'rationality' consists in the fact that a common interest was attained without deception. There are three main forms of argumentation:

1. *Theoretical discourse*: which deals with cognitive and instrumental problems by addressing disputed validity claims related to establishing the truth and effectiveness of instrumental actions. Academic debates about counselling theory and practice is such a form of argumentation.
2. *Practical discourse*: dealing with contested validity claims concerning the rightness of norms of action arising out of moral-practical issues.
3. *Therapeutic critique*: concerning problems raised by expressions of self-identity out of which this discourse considers the controversial validity claims relating to truthfulness or authenticity of expressions.

These universal and necessary communicative presuppositions[15] of argumentation entail strong ethical assumptions. Benhabib (1994: 29) deduces two universal principles from this. The *principle of universal moral respect* which recognizes the rights of all to be participants in the moral conversation, and the *principle of egalitarian reciprocity* which guarantees that each has the same symmetrical rights to make his or her claim, criticize other views and reflect upon interpretations and so on. The claim is that the presuppositions of argumentation have a normative content that precedes the moral argument itself. Habermas differs, correctly in my view, from Benhabib when he also stipulates the presupposition that participants must have the competence to act communicatively. This does not just refer to the ability to reason but is also a *psychological* competence – the personal characteristic of authenticity and self-transparency. This is not an abstract principle but something that needs to be practically achieved in the world. Needless to say these presuppositions (sometimes called the 'ideal speech situation') are rarely met in real life and act as ideals against which to measure present conduct. As already mentioned, 'ideal' does not mean 'hopelessly unrealistic', rather that the presuppositions of communication of necessity contain the ideal anticipation of their fulfilment.

Having defined the necessary conditions of discourse or argumentation we have arrived at Habermas's definition of the universal ethic of discourse:

> Only those norms can claim to be valid that meet (or could meet) with the approval of all affected in their capacity as participants in a practical discourse. (1995b: 93)

This ethic, as Benhabib says, '...together with those rules of argument governing discourses, the normative content of which I summarized as the principles of universal moral respect and egalitarian reciprocity, are in my view quite adequate to serve as the only universalisability' (1994: 37). The practical achievement of this is dependent upon the generation of people with the psychological competences (alongside other competences) required by such discourse. Psychotherapy and counselling have no small role in generating such people.

The basic insight behind this approach to universality is that it is procedural, postconventional and deontological. Rather than laying claim to some absolute good, as is found in religions, it claims that the universal principles are a result of procedures which are derived from those presuppositions of communication which are essential if we are to reach an understanding. It is postconventional in that it cannot claim validity simply as a result of inherited traditions, and its deontological nature comes from the refusal to extend the claim to universality beyond the human species into a metaphysical claim about reality as such.

As Pierce notes:

> Universalization in ethics is a purely formal approach to procedures requiring consistency, insisting that people do not make an exception for themselves. As a formal process, universalization in ethics makes statements that do not contain content in the usual narrative sense; that is, universalization in ethics delineates some abstract content such as the notion of equality with some criteria of relevant similarities rather than describing a condition of the external world. Thus the postmodern critique of universalization and generalization in explanatory theories cannot be applied to universalization or generalization in ethics. (1991: 64)

The universalization principle is not a substantive or practical moral in the way that 'do to others what you would have them do to you' is because it is maxims like this that are the very subject matter of moral argumentation as opposed to argumentation *per se*. The universalization principle[16] is a rule of argumentation that expresses the commitment of each and all to be obliged to bind themselves freely (will formation) to the outcome of a genuine argumentative process. This would apply across all the validity claims. In the specific validity claim of normative rightness or morality, discourse ethics does not make pronouncements on right or wrong, rather it establishes a procedure that guarantees the impartiality of the process of judging.

Therapeutic practice can be framed in relation to the principle of universalization and discourse ethics. During the therapeutic process, in one sense, universalization does not apply because, quite simply, the client cannot fulfil the procedural requirements. The most likely scenario is that she is unable to represent herself authentically. This would preclude her from being able to fulfil the condition of will formation, that is, she would not have the competence to bind herself freely to the outcome of a properly constituted argumentative process. The purpose of the therapeutic interaction has the remedial intention of healing the damage that

precludes this competence to thereby enable the client to eventually
re-enter proper communicative action as a person able to act autonomously.
The discourse ethic radically questions traditionally received moral contents
and puts them to the test of a process of rational moral argumentation
with all the presuppositions and procedures involved. This does not make
the counselling a court of law but questions unreflexive moral outlooks
and obliges the participants to be aware that binding morals do exist and
that the dialogue internal to the counselling room is obliged to take into
account communal morals and ethics that are properly and democratically
established. This will, however, be case-dependent. In some cases these
issues have to be suspended in order to facilitate the process of mutual
understanding, otherwise the client may be too defensive. However, by
the end of counselling, if the process has worked, the client will be able to
recognize the validity of certain morals and ethics. The counsellor, in a
sense that I shall outline later, is the custodian of a different set of values –
the morals and ethics inherent in the discourse of therapy. Counselling
can therefore be characterized as an educational process enabling people
to attain full participation in communicative action. At the social level it is
(or could be) a radical force assisting society to shift the balance of social
interactions from the instrumental/strategic to the psychologically and
socially more advanced form of interaction based on communication as
already defined. 'Universality is not the ideal consensus of fictitiously
defined selves, but the concrete process in politics and morals of the
struggle of concrete embodied selves, striving for autonomy.' (Benhabib
1994: 153)

Communicative rationality is not neutral. It privileges a secular, universalist, reflexive way of life in which debates about values as well as conceptions of justice are secured in institutions and everyday practice. But
compared to all other systems of conventional morality it contains a very
significant advantage, which is the fact that it is comprehensively reflexive.
In other words it explicitly knows the presuppositions upon which it is
based and it regularly puts them to open questioning.

> That is to say, only a moral point of view which can radically question all procedures
> of justification, including its own, can create the conditions for a moral conversation
> which is open and rational enough to include other points of view, including those
> which will withdraw from the conversation at some point. In this sense, communi-
> cative ethics 'trumps' the less reflexive 'moral points of view.' It can coexist with
> them and recognize their cognitive limits; communicative ethics is aware not only of
> other moral systems as representing a 'moral point of view' (albeit one which may
> no longer be defensible on rational grounds), but it is also aware of the historical
> conditions which made its own point of view possible. (Benhabib 1994: 43)

It might seem that such an approach might be intolerant of diversity in
culture, religion and personal actions.[17] But the opposite is the case. *Only*

a postconventional universalism can accommodate such plurality and diversity.
Precisely because it can review and subject to debate all its presuppositions,
it alone can provide a public philosophy able to accommodate a tolerant
and pluralist society. To be clear, where the norms of a specific sub-culture
clash with the meta-norms of communicative ethics the former must be
subordinated to the latter. Benhabib's (1994: 45) example is illustrative.
The communicative ethicist would agree that a democratic state should
tolerate the Mormon sect. However, the Mormon practice of polygamy
would not be condoned by the state in so far as it practically precludes the
equal consent of all the participants. Similarly the absolutist claims of
religions can be tolerated in so far as they do not transgress or preclude
the fundamental principles of communicative ethics.

Nevertheless, the usage of a universalization principle carries a special
responsibility – the recognition of otherness. Too often in history the individual has been repressed in the name of a universal principle. Lurking
behind a false universal is the projection of a special vested interest:

> we have to learn from the painful experiences and irreparable suffering of those who
> have been humiliated, insulted, injured, and brutalized that nobody may be excluded
> in the name of moral universalism – neither underprivileged classes nor exploited
> nations, neither domesticated women nor marginalized minorities. Someone who in
> the name of universalism excludes another who has the right to *remain* alien or
> other betrays his own guiding idea. (Habermas 1995c: 15)

CHAPTER 2

Morality, Ethics and Autonomy

In discussing the theory of communicative rationality I believe that we have good reason to propose that we can find a firm basis upon which to construct an argument in favour of the notion that counselling and psychotherapy do have a rational basis for their moral and ethical purpose. I would now like to study in greater detail the validity claims already mentioned and consider the concepts of health and autonomy. This will provide us with six key values that can be founded on communicative rationality:

1. Comprehensibility
2. Truth
3. Justice
4. Authenticity
5. Health
6. Autonomy.

Some or all of these appear in various discussions concerning morality and ethics in counselling but we are rarely given insight into why they are selected and on what grounds their legitimacy rests. This lack of a system and a rational justification leaves the field wide open to all sorts of hunches, intuitions, relativist claims and competing lists of values deemed to be relevant to counselling. Approaching this issue through communicative rationality will, I hope, not only remove the hit-and-miss nature of some of these efforts but, by attempting a rational justification, will also have the benefit of being fallible and open to discussion. In other words, the role of these validity claims will hopefully develop the debate on the purpose of counselling to the deeper level of an argumentative discourse which is connected to other developments in the outside world.

As already mentioned the validity claims of comprehensibility and truth are not the main thrust of this work and will not be developed further. The former is concerned with the technical issue that communication is only possible if facilitated by a cogent grammar and sufficiently shared, or trans-latable, symbols. Although this may hit practical difficulties all communication has sufficient in common that good enough translation is possible. With regard to issues of truth, the truth claim inherent in every act of speech is related to differentiating between what appears to be the case (the sun goes round the earth) and reality (the earth goes round the sun). Reality is constituted in the deontological framework of a reality 'for us'. Again no matter how difficult this is, communication cannot proceed without a recognition of this validity claim even if it can only be anticipated.

Morality and Justice

Apart from any philosophical reasons, moral obligations are socially advantageous. Without the power of morals to provide reasons for our social behaviour, we would only be left with the use of power or manipulation to resolve conflicts. This would be a brutish and cold world.

> Without the emotions roused by moral sentiments like obligation and guilt, reproach and forgiveness, without the liberating effect of moral respect, without the happiness felt through solidarity and without the depressing effect of moral failure, without the 'friendliness' of a civilized way of dealing with conflict and opposition, we would feel, or so we still think today, that the universe inhabited by men would be unbearable. Life in a moral void, in a form of life empty even of cynicism, would not be worth living. This judgment simply expresses the 'impulse' to prefer an existence of human dignity to the coldness of a form of life not informed by moral considerations. (Habermas 2003a: 73)

Morality relates to how people relate to all other people. As counselling is a very real form of social relationship nestling within the wider network of relations we call 'society', it is not unnatural that we should consider the role of morality within the therapeutic relationship itself and its connection with the outside world. Having found a credible conception of universalization in communicative rationality we have, I suggest, found the basis for an understanding of morality. Morality can only rest on issues that are applicable to everyone and moral problems arise when these issues have become a source of conflict. Morality is therefore characterized by a concern with justice and equal treatment and is primarily used against all forms of domination.

The key feature of justice is that it is the only value or good that can and must be *shared by all*. As individuals not only do we have our personal values or preferences, but these are also conditioned by our membership of other social networks (our family, community, religious affiliation, ethnic origin and nation state) such that it is impossible to find one substantial value, good or preference that is common to all *from the outset*. Nobody has yet found a simple given moral value that is acceptable to all. The fact that religions offer competing worldviews would seem to illustrate the failure of the promulgation of one absolute substantive value above all others. In turning to the concept of justice Habermas argues for the priority of the right over the good. The former being those values we follow because they *are agreed by all*, the latter being those values which we follow because *all must agree with them*. Without the priority of the right over the good we cannot have an ethically neutral conception of justice. In pluralistic societies it would be hard to see how equal treatment could be obtained without a conception of justice that was neutral to the competing ethics of different individuals and groups. The attempt to find a universally binding good or value upon which all human beings (including future generations) could agree meets a dilemma. Any value that had real substantive meaning would inevitably be unacceptable to some whilst, on the other hand, a concept that abstracts from all contexts would carry less meaning. For example, the Buddhist concept of Nirvana is an essentially appealing idea (perfect bliss) surrounded by a rich set of images that attract us to the idea, but this salvationist/aesthetic quality makes it unattractive to others. On the other hand, the more abstract notions of justice and duty may be more acceptable to other people but have the problem of being emotionally and aesthetically unappealing.

A concept of justice cannot be generated from competing individual or cultural ethical viewpoints because, from this perspective, it would just be one value amongst others. We would then have the contradiction that moral obligations could be more important for one individual than for another. Of all the possible values of the good life (for example, peace, love, altruism, faithfulness and so on) Habermas's concept of discourse ethics retains only one – justice, which is normative in the strict sense. Issues of justice alone can be settled by rational argument.

Based on the universalization principle which privileges justice (and its counterpart solidarity) this postconventional conception of morality is one of process. That is, as already outlined, contested norms are subjected to communicative rationality as expressed in the process of argumentation. Legitimate norms are those produced by this process and thereby meet an interest that can be applied to all. Moral theory therefore has a limited function. It cannot legitimate a single substantive moral value (God, peace and so on) but it can explain the moral point of view and thereby refute value scepticism. 'Moral philosophy does not have privileged access to particular moral truths' (Habermas 1995b: 211). With the demise of the philosophy of consciousness we no longer ascribe to the philosopher, or anyone else, preferential access to moral truths. Since such truths are inter-subjectively founded they can only be legitimized by a collective, rational process. The philosopher serves the process.

Distinction between Pragmatic, Ethical and Moral Questions

Although moral issues play an important role in the life of all people, there is clearly more to living than being concerned with taking an impartial perspective on the needs of all that may be affected by any action. In addition to moral questions we all face everyday practical problems like repairing the car and making our computers work effectively. Separate from practical issues are ethical questions concerning who I am and who I want to be. We articulate such issues within identity-sustaining networks like the family, friendships and intimate relationships. Most of our time is spent in inter-actions largely untouched by ethical questions except when these ethical questions conflict. In order to understand morals more clearly, I wish to differentiate them from pragmatic and ethical issues. Commentators on counselling often confuse morals and ethics and use the terms inter-changeably. I propose that this confusion is a mistake that works to the detriment of our understanding of both morals and ethics. The concept of ethics will be articulated later.

Pragmatic issues relate to practical problems. If I wish to drive to Bristol and my car breaks down I have a practical or instrumental problem in achieving my goal. In order to solve this problem I make rational choices that will help me to achieve this goal; for example, I may attempt to repair the car or, alternatively, go by train. However, the goal itself may become problematic. The business trip to Bristol conflicted with my need to visit a sick relation elsewhere. Or, in different contexts, should I go to university now or later? Should I take medication for my headache or let nature take its course? When solving such practical issues we make a pragmatic rational choice concerning either a suitable technology or a reliable programme of action. In either case our deliberation concerns alternative possible choices of means or specification of ends. The trip to Bristol is successfully achieved by quick car maintenance, or is supplanted by switching to the different goal of visiting the sick relation. The 'ought' that is working in these cases is a *conditional imperative*, that is, it has a very limited function and is very different from the 'ought' or imperative that is operative in ethical or moral questions. Such conditional imperatives act like a *relative ought* specifying what one 'ought' or 'must' do when faced with a particular problem with regard to realizing certain values on goals.

The rational consideration of important value decisions affecting the whole of one's life is altogether a different matter. Issues taken for granted at the practical level now become problematic. 'Life' decisions involve the clarification of an individual's understanding of herself and level of awareness as well as some conception of what might be a fulfilled or unfulfilled life. This becomes an ethical or existential issue concerning the realization of a personal life project. The choice of a career, one's conduct towards an intimate partner, levels of personal honesty and transparency become a matter of what life I would like to lead and what kind of a person am I now and what would I like to be in the future. Such issues operate at the ethical or existential level and the 'ought' operating here acts as a *strong preference*. The choice between painting my wall with a roller or a brush is a weak or trivial preference, as is the choice of colour and accompanying furnishings. One does not have to provide an ethical or moral justification for such choices which are really based on taste and inclinations. However, decisions about my career, choice of partner and relations to my children involve strong preferences that operate at the level of my character, way of life and, ultimately, my identity. These questions classically belong to the sphere of ethics and are questions concerning the good life, that is, 'Do I lead a good life?' These questions may be asked of myself by others or by myself. Either way, failure is possible. Mistreating my children, ignoring my partner and doing a dishonourable job can leave me with a sense of failure. Not only are such ethical issues of a different order to pragmatic issues but they are issues of great importance to therapeutic practice as, indeed, they are to religious and spiritual practices.

What kind of an 'ought' is involved in ethical questions?

> Ethical questions are generally answered by unconditional imperatives such as the following: 'You must embark on a career that affords you the assurance that you are helping other people.' The meaning of this imperative can be understood as an 'ought' that is not dependent on subjective purposes and preferences and yet is not absolute. What you 'should' or 'must' do has here the sense that it is 'good' for you to act in this way in the long run, all things considered. Aristotle speaks in this connection of paths to the good and happy life. Strong evaluations take their orientation from the goal posited for me, that is, from the highest good of a self-sufficient form of life that has its value in itself. (Habermas 1995c: 5)

The 'ought' here is qualitatively different from issues of taste or practical instrumentality yet does not carry the unconditional or categorical imperative of a moral command that I, *and everybody else*, must follow. The ethical unconditional imperative is something that *I* must follow if *I* am to lead an authentic life – a life that gathers meaning for me through my achievement in fulfilling values that I have set for myself. It is this sense of 'ought' that is, in my view, clearly linked to the inherent values and purpose of counselling and psychotherapy. It is in no sense a command from therapist to client about the content of particular actions, but is a value and purpose held by the therapist for therapist and client until the client, through the therapeutic process, is able to recognize and hold it for herself. The 'ought' of a psychotherapeutic intervention, in this sense, is not an arbitrary subjective value imposed by the counsellor but is necessarily deduced from the rationality inherent in every communication aimed at reaching a mutual understanding. As we have seen, the requirements for such communication involve people who can represent themselves sincerely and transparently and thereby meet the ethical validity claim of authenticity. The psycho-therapeutic intervention is linked to the individual's striving for self-realization in her attempt to live an authentic life. The key purposes and values of this psychotherapeutic or counselling intervention, which, I argue, are universal to all such therapeutic interventions (no matter how distant or unlikely the successful achievement may be), are to create the capacity of the individual to make the existential or ethical decisions that enable her to live an authentic life within the horizon of her own life history and future aspirations concerning the kind of person she would like to be; and to enable her to have the necessary *will* or *resolve* to fulfil this life project. This project of an authentic life is relative to the individual's own life context and particular ambitions, but to be authentic they may not contradict the necessary conditions of authenticity nor may they contravene moral obligations. I cannot achieve authenticity and simultaneously act opaquely by deceiving others or act immorally by dominating others.

> We can imagine how someone like Emma could easily seek to solve her ethical difficulties surrounding her sense of a lack of authenticity by acting in ways which are morally questionable. She was neither abused nor misused as a child. Instead, although her father cared for her, it was in a way he found relevant (providing a good home, clothes and so on); he did not however care for Emma in a way that recognized her as a unique person. Some of this could be attributed to his upbringing and some to his work as a salesman which required him to act in ways that treated other people as 'objects' to be persuaded to his point of view. Other people didn't really exist as genuinely 'other' and this approach had become a habit to her father and was, unthinkingly extended to his treatment of Emma. She was left with feeling unreached, unrecognized and unloved. As such she was never quite sure who she was. What was her authentic voice? Unfortunately her mother's sense of self was even more silent. It was only in therapy that she discovered the layer of anger in her that the distorted communicative patterns of her family and wider culture had repressed and hidden from view. Given time, encouragement and trust by the therapist Emma eventually grew confident in asserting how she truly felt. That is, she was able to act more authentically by making herself more transparent by revealing previously hidden aspects of her personality. However, having achieved some ethical success she began to lose a sense of herself as someone acting in a complex web of interrelationships, that is, someone who has a moral responsibility to others. At work she found herself becoming increasingly angry with colleagues and she was also becoming increasingly irritant with her children. Her ethical need to develop an authentic voice was drowning out the equally authentic needs of others around her. Her therapy then took a moral turn as it worked with her to enable her to limit her anger to more appropriate levels.

From the moral point of view the question of 'What should I do?', when my actions affect others and lead to conflicts that require impartial regulation, involves another category shift. Moral and ethical issues must also be differentiated. From the ethical point of view, other persons and other cultural values are important but only in so far as they connect with my identity and interests within a cultural horizon. In pluralistic societies with competing individual and cultural values, such ethical issues clearly cannot be generalized and we enter into a world of conflicting values – this is the

moral domain. Whether I would *like* to be the kind of person who occa-
sionally breaks motoring speed regulations is not a moral question; for,
from the ethical perspective, it concerns the authenticity of my life. It is
therefore a question of self-respect and possibly how others respect me.
From a moral perspective by breaking a speed limit I am *guilty* of failing
to respect the need of *all* those people who are put at risk by my dangerous
driving.

The moral perspective makes a final move from the individual to the
universal perspective where the 'ought' involved moves from the plane of
the authentically lived life to that of justice applicable to all and involves the
concept of 'duty'.

> A categorical imperative that specifies that a maxim is just only if *all* could will that
> it should be adhered to by everyone in comparable situations first signals a break
> with the egocentric character of the golden rule ('Do not do unto others what you
> would not have them do unto you'). *Everyone* must be able to will that the maxims
> of our action should become a universal law. Only a maxim that can be generalized
> from the perspective of all affected counts as a norm that can command general
> assent and to that extent is worthy of recognition or, in other words, is morally
> binding. The question 'What should I do?' is answered morally with reference to what
> *one* ought to do. Moral commands are categorical or unconditional imperatives that
> express valid norms or make implicit reference to them. The imperative meaning of
> these commands alone can be understood as an 'ought' that is dependent on neither
> subjective goals and preferences nor on what is for me the absolute goal of a good,
> successful, or not-failed life. Rather, what one 'should' or 'must' do has here the
> sense that to act thus is just and therefore a duty. (Habermas 1995c: 8)

Although counselling may often seem more concerned with ethical issues
of authenticity, the moral concern with domination and justice is also of
great importance to counsellors and clients. In relationship counselling,
where both parties are present, issues of justice rarely fail to emanate
because some of the problems presented may result from disparities in power
between both the clients. Unequal distribution of power is a direct (though
not a necessary) cause of injustice. The relationship counsellor will therefore
deal not only with each individual's ethical search for authenticity but also
with the morality of their behaviour towards each other. Domestic violence
in this context is clearly immoral. It is the skill and insight that the counsellor
brings that will determine the therapeutically most effective moment to
address a moral issue. It may take some considerable time to generate
enough trust between client and counsellor before such issues can be
addressed.

As Taylor (1996: 363) argues, following Kant, acting in accordance
with a moral, that is doing a duty, is not onerous but amounts to a freedom.
It is to act in accordance with what we truly are (moral and rational
agents) and is not arbitrarily imposed from outside. Some of our problems

with the concepts of 'duty' and 'guilt' stem from personal memories of duties being externally imposed by arbitrary forces in unequal power situations (parents, teachers and employers). At the cultural level the legacy of a rigid Victorian morality has left us overly suspicious of concepts like duty and our highly individualized conception of 'rights' makes us very resistant to accepting guilt. Morals determined through the process of argumentation are not arbitrarily determined by people who disguise their individual or class interest under the cloak of a special access to some divine or objective source of truth (as, in their days, did the monarchy and the church). As a consequence they do not carry the overtone of being imposed by other people. Their very universality prevents them from marginalizing or excluding the voices of others – be they dissidents or the powerless. Also Habermas's differentiation between morals and ethics creates considerable space for social action that is more individually motivated by the ethics of the authentic life, and minimizes the level of social action that needs to be motivated by duty. From this perspective moral duties can begin to be seen as freedoms as much as they are obligations. One of psychotherapy's roles is to remedy the failed socialization and educational patterns of individuals by enabling them to create within themselves the capacity to act ethically and morally.

Our understanding of the moral point of view becomes clearer with the differentiation between moral and evaluative questions. Moral questions can, in principle, be decided rationally in terms of justice and the process of making interests generalizable (my speeding is bad for everybody because it is unsafe and is a risk to other people). Evaluative questions, however, are about the good life or self-realization (my speeding is good for me because it expresses the free spirit within me) and are 'accessible to rational discussion only *within* the unproblematic horizon of a concrete historical form of life or the conduct of an individual life'. (Habermas 1995b: 108) Indeed, ethics provide an insufficient basis for justice, for, from this point of view, justice is reduced to just one value amongst others. On this construction, moral obligations would vary from person to person and context to context. From the perspective of generalizable interests we must claim the priority of the right over the good.[1]

Some of the key differences between the pragmatic, ethical and moral aspects of practical reason can be expressed as follows:

- moral norms concern decisions about what one ought to do; ethical values inform decisions about what conduct is most desirable;
- legitimate norms place the same obligation on everyone, whereas ethical values express the preferability of things that are held to be good by particular individuals or groups;
- moral norms are things we observe and act in accordance with; ethical values are things we realize or achieve through our action;
- moral questions are held to be either valid or invalid, whilst values are issues of preference with some goods being more attractive than others;

- different norms must not contradict each other when addressing the same issue; ethical values, by contrast, compete for priority; and
- practical reason, therefore, differentiates into issues of: the 'purposive' when relating to pragmatic choices; the 'good' with regard to the resolve of the person seeking to be an authentic or self-realizing subject; the 'just' concerning the free will of individuals capable of moral judgement.

Morality and the Law

Morality and the law are not the same thing. Modern legal systems do not advocate a symmetry between rights and duties; in our individualistic society the law favours rights over duties. The construction of legal individual rights is designed to free 'legal persons' from moral obligations under certain circumstances. Rights are designed to allow individuals the freedom to act according to personal choice on the principle that whatever is not explicitly prohibited is permitted. I have the legal right to enter into a contract with someone even though I know that I will make far more money out of it than they will – something which, from a different frame, may seem immoral. With moral issues, however, there is a symmetry between rights and duties. When acting morally I choose not to act pragmatically in my own interest because the moral 'ought' rationally obliges me to act in accordance with the general interest. Morality protects the integrity of the individual in all aspects. The legal community is quite different. It is always localized in space and time and only protects the integrity of its members in so far as they acquire the artificial status of 'rights bearers'. Consequently, the attempt by counselling to limit the moral and ethical horizon to the rights of clients and third parties is not only mistaken but is symptomatic of the general closing down of the moral universe in counselling in favour of a preoccupation with consumer 'rights', consumer choice and issues of access. A preoccupation with these softer and circumscribed issues enables the world of counselling to ignore its full moral and ethical responsibility to clients whilst similarly ignoring the political dimension of its social role.

The move to universal human rights does not solve the problem of the dichotomy between morals and rights. In the first place, their 'universality' cannot be grounded on some fundamental claim to 'innate' rights as if such claims were radically different to their religious counterparts:

> The texts of historical constitutions appeal to 'innate' rights and often have the solemn form of 'declarations'; both features are supposed to dissuade us from what we would now call a positivist misunderstanding and express the fact that human rights are 'not at the disposal' of the legislator. But this rhetorical proviso cannot preserve human rights from the fate of all positive law; they, too, can be changed or be suspended, for example, following a change of regimes. (Habermas 1999: 190)

The move to 'internationalize' such rights by making declarations of universality through institutions like the United Nations does not solve this problem – they do not become any more 'innate'. Secondly, universal human rights are no more based in morality than their less international antecedents. They are still 'rights' and are heavily coloured by the modern concept of individual liberties and are therefore legal rather than moral in nature. 'What lends them the appearance of moral rights is not the content, and most especially not the structure, but rather their mode of validity, which points beyond the legal orders of nation-states' (Habermas 1999: 190). This is not to deny that the universalization of human rights has benefits; it is just to be clear that such rights are not innate and that they are legally constituted. Therefore, the attempt by some counselling organizations to base their *moral* stance on human rights that are *universal* simply does not solve the problem.

Morality and Happiness or Well-Being

> I do not promise happiness, and I don't know what it is. You New World people are, what is the word, hyped on the idea of happiness, as if it were a constant and measurable thing, and settled and excused everything. If it is anything at all it is a by-product of other conditions of life, and some people whose lives do not appear to be at all enviable, or indeed admirable, are happy. Forget about happiness. (Davies 1983: 475)

Davies' fictional speaker, a psychotherapist, touches a raw nerve in the therapeutic community. Should we, like the American founding founders, be preoccupied with happiness? The argument above obliges us to demure from considering happiness as a 'right', but should it be a principle value or goal in counselling?

Well-being has to do with the avoidance of negative tension and the striving for a physical sense of comfort and relaxation. It requires sufficient nourishment, shelter, absence from anxiety, sexual satisfaction, security, good relationships with family and friends and a sense of belonging to a group. Happiness is directly related to well-being; a person possessing a sense of well-being is happy and satisfied. Governments are concerned with the well-being of their citizens, hence the development of the 'welfare state' – they are not concerned with authenticity or autonomy.

Happiness must be distinguished from the ethical search for self-realization or authenticity, and the preceding Christian concept of salvation. As Guggenbühl-Craig (2001: 27) points out, the path to happiness does not necessarily include suffering. Indeed, for the sake of our well-being we are urged to be happy and not to distress ourselves with questions that have no answers. A person seeking salvation or self-realization wrestles with religious or existential questions concerning life, death and the meaning of existence.

Jungian psychotherapy (and other forms of psychotherapy) distinguishes between happiness and self-realization. To promote well-being by reducing pain and suffering and enabling a more successful adaptation to the world is an important function of counselling and psychotherapy. However, I maintain that this is secondary to the moral and ethical purposes I have outlined. Important as the release of suffering undoubtedly is, all too often counselling and psychotherapy stop at this point. Well-being is more productively conceived as a helpful, though not necessary, condition for acting morally and ethically. In Jungian terms the path beyond well-being is called individuation. Neither happiness nor well-being should be confused with morality or ethics. Emancipation, Habermas argues, '... makes humanity more independent, but not automatically happier' (1994: 107).

Difficulties with the Conception of Morality as Justice

Objections to Kantian moral theories, such as the one proposed by Habermas, come from three main directions:

1. these Kantian theories lean towards a concept of the person that is individualistic, that is, we act as isolated individuals with no necessary affective or communal bonds with other individuals. From this perspective it is difficult to generate ideas such as compassion, love and connectedness;
2. Kantian moral theories are criticized for being too abstract. In order to gain sufficient generality they become so abstracted from concrete, particular issues that the application of such abstract norms is dogged with difficulty; and
3. giving priority to the 'right' over the 'good' inevitably leads to problems with regard to the issue of why people should conform to a moral duty. Without the power of ethical symbols (such as 'salvation', 'redemption', 'self-realization' and so on) it is difficult to comprehend why people would feel obliged to act morally.

These three issues can be defined as relating to problems with solidarity, application and motivation.

Solidarity: The Morality of Care

The most famous critic of Habermas's moral theory from this perspective is Gilligan *et al.* (1988). She was concerned that a definition of morality as justice inevitably emphasized a sense of personal and emotional detachment. Justice requires impartiality and objectivity; the personal qualities of distance and detachment become the mark of mature moral judgement. The model of personality required to work with such morality is typified by 'masculine' qualities of disconnected, rational detachment. Gilligan subjected this to a feminist critique by the suggestion (later withdrawn) that there are in fact two types of morality such that the morality of justice should be complemented by a morality of care. Rather than emphasizing distance between people, the morality of care was concerned with connection. Rather than abstract rules of justice, care is concerned with particular people in particular contexts by promoting attachment, closeness and affective bonds as means of maintaining relationships, fostering the welfare of others, preventing their harm or relieving their pain and suffering. In this context detachment becomes a source of moral danger because it represents a loss of connection with others. The caring personality must be flexible and, through imagination, able to understand and experience the feelings of others. Many counsellors will fall into one or other of these categories which they would tend to define in terms of the 'masculine' and the 'feminine'. This duality and subsequent splitting is not helpful as it tends to camouflage the complexity of moral issues and act as a defensive posture relieving the counsellor of moral tension.

This creation of an 'extra' morality of care doesn't work. First, the separation between justice as dealing with the universal and care as dealing with the particular is confusing. The issue of applying universal rules to particular cases is always a perennial problem with issues of justice, but it could not be otherwise. A successful legal system is attempting to do this every day of the week. The problem is overcome by improving our competence in the interpretive understanding and insight into the specific nature of individual cases and the sensitive application of universal rules to them. In other words, this is a problem of application (which we will address shortly) rather than a problem with the fact that moral norms must have a justification couched in universal terms. This obviates the necessity of creating a separate realm of morality dealing with the particular which is framed in the language of care.

Secondly, rather than being separate, the morality of care is an integral part of justice, and communicative ethics as a whole:

> This can be seen if we look at a key element of what being context-sensitive requires within the communicative model. Emotions such as caring and compassion, which are integral to the second voice, are also integral to communicative ethics, because they stand in an 'internal relation' to the sort of cognitive achievements expected of discourse participants. That is, there are necessary 'emotional conditions' for the post-conventional, cognitive operations of seriously engaging others in moral dialogue, as well as of imagining the harm which alternative norms may actually entail for the needs and interests of others. In other words, a communicative ethics is crippled if it proceeds in an emotional vacuum. (White 1988: 85)

Although Habermas himself does not go overboard using the language of emotions and attachment, the framework he provides can easily accommodate this perspective and, as White indicates, requires it. Indeed, using a slightly different language, Habermas opens up the concept of justice by revealing its necessary link to the notion of solidarity. By this concept he makes it clear that a necessary concomitant of morality as justice is the fact that moral consciousness itself depends on people recognizing that they are members of a moral community and thereby have welfare connections (compassion, caring and affective bonds) with fellow members. 'If we interpret justice as what is equally good for all, then the "good" that has been extended step by step to the "right" forms a bridge between justice and solidarity' (Habermas 1999: 29).[2] Universal justice also requires that each of us should take responsibility for another. Within the concept of 'right' remains that aspect of the 'good' which reminds us that moral consciousness depends on a particular and crucial self-understanding of moral persons who recognize that they *belong* to the moral community. All individuals who have been socialized into any communicative form of life at all belong to this community.

Since moralities grow in response to the needs of fragile human beings who individuate through socialization, they must always face two ways. The individual is secured by the stance of equal respect for the dignity of each individual, whilst moralities must also protect the network of social relationships fostering mutual recognition that is essential for any individual to survive as a member of a community. To these two aspects correspond the moral principles of justice and solidarity, such principles being two aspects of the same thing. Justice requires equal rights and equal respect for individual whereas its reverse side, solidarity, concerns the welfare of members of a community who share a form of life and who therefore need to maintain the integrity of this form of life itself.[3] Respect for the individual necessarily requires concern for one's neighbour. The root of all this is a process unique to the human species, that is, the individual can only individuate through association with others. This makes the individual vulnerable to, and dependent on, other members of her community. Morality therefore cannot protect the individual without protecting the community.[4] By an overwhelming preoccupation with the former, psycho- therapy neglects the latter and, consequently, necessarily fails to promote individuation because it ignores the social transformations necessary to effect and sustain individual development. This leads to my growing concern that psychotherapy remains primarily a force that adjusts people to an unquestioned social background. This process is accelerated by the continual erosion of the provision of counselling and psychotherapy in the voluntary or independent sector, accompanied by the increase in counselling in the health and commercial sector where needs are more likely to be 'medical- ized'. At the same time, the provision of counselling and psychotherapy is increasingly privatized. Individual private practitioners, who have no obligation to provide a service to those that cannot afford it (although some do), are, it could be argued, more likely to pursue personal interests of career development and professional status at the expense of solidarity and welfare. The failure to understand the moral purpose of counselling and psychotherapy seems to uncannily suit the needs of 'professionals' who become preoccupied with the imported ideologies of 'consumer choice' and managerial control. Perhaps counselling and psychotherapy might be better seen as a vocation rather than as a profession.

Application

The need to base morality on universal principles inevitably results in a process of rational abstraction from the particular case. The problem with universalism is that it would require the intellect of a genius. How do I work out the moral basis of how I should act towards my stepson when I don't even like him?! It is rarely clear how we could answer the basic moral question 'What ought I to do?' by the singular translation of universal rules into concrete, context-dependent situations. (There is no absolute code anywhere, as far as I know, giving us golden rules of behaviour towards stepchildren.) Fortunately, we have no need of such an intellectual capacity because this idea misconceives the role of universalization. The role of universalization is one of justifying the norms that underlie everyday interaction and not of immediate application.

> Discourse ethics . . . makes a careful distinction between the validity – or justice – of norms and the correctness of singular judgements that prescribe some particular action on the basis of a valid norm. Analytically, 'the right thing to do in the given circumstances' cannot be decided by a *single* act of justification – or within the boundaries of a single kind of argumentation – but calls for a two-stage process of argument consisting of justification followed by application of norms. (Habermas 1995c: 35–6)

A deontologically grounded morality cannot avoid the troublesome process of abstraction from concrete circumstances. Without this process, competing and conflicting norms could not be resolved through rational processes that would gain the approval and legitimation of all those concerned. This process is reversed by the impartial application of rationally grounded and agreed rules to individual cases. A developed legal system represents this process in action, but is, as already mentioned, restricted to the domain of legal rights and relates to us only in our identity as 'legal persons'. The issue of the application of general norms to concrete specific cases can only arise after problems of justification have been resolved. As already mentioned the rapid pace of technological development is creating new problems of applying valid norms with regard to genetic engineering.

Just as discourse ethics can defend itself against criticisms concerning the morality of care, I believe it can also remain viable in the face of concerns over abstraction and forms of application. However, this is not quite sufficient. A reflexive, postconventional morality requires that the participants operate at a similar level of moral consciousness. Without citizens able to operate at this psychological level it would be difficult to achieve prudent applications of universal morals and hard to support the individual in his personal motivation to translate his moral insights into moral action. 'Only those forms of life', suggests Habermas, 'that meet universalist moralities halfway in this sense fulfil the conditions necessary to reverse the abstractive achievements of decontextualization and demotivation' (1995b: 109). It is a real and practical task to develop citizens and the social structures that sustain them to enable individuals to operate a post-conventional moral consciousness. In this context, counselling has the social role of being consciously aware that its wider purpose is to help people develop themselves into the postconventional moral and ethical consciousness required by both a society and other individuals who want justice and personal autonomy. In order to achieve this it must take the further step of doing all it can at the organizational level to influence the political agenda in favour of this set of values. Please remember that this does not deny that the everyday process of therapeutic interaction is also concerned with the relief of pain and suffering. But I am attempting to place this within a broader framework of moral and ethical purpose. Many clients may not experience symptom relief and may not develop very far towards autonomy. This does not necessarily mean that the therapy was a failure; it may mean that the damage was too ingrained. Nevertheless, I suggest that the intention of counselling and psychotherapy must be, no matter how far in the future, to help the client achieve the ability to perform ethically and morally.

Motivation

The problem is simple. Postconventional morality has to operate in a 'demotivated' fashion if it is to achieve impartial and universal norms. 'Demotivated' means that the participant, when acting morally, must have no ulterior motive other than freely consenting to the norm in question. Helping you to unload your supermarket trolley is hardly moral if I steal your purse at the bottom of the trolley!

But how, in practice, do we have the motive to act without personal motive? Having disconnected morals from religion and traditional ethical sources we are left, in the social arena, with just conventions and customs[5] which have only a low power of motivation. By excluding sacred sources of hope for personal salvation and redemption we suffer an enormous loss in the power of motives for obeying moral commands. Discourse ethics deliberately separates moral judgement from immediate action and locates it in rational discourse. Clearly, moral judgements tell us what we should do, and the fact that moral judgements are rationally based will affect our will. By 'will' I mean our volition or conscious intention to act. Thus the rational basis of morality gives us a disposition to conform to the moral imperative. This is illustrated by the guilt or bad conscience we feel when we fail to conform to our better judgement. To this extent guilt is a constructive moral emotion for both the individual and society. However, the problem of weakness of will or indisposition to act morally even when the subject 'knows' that this is irrational or 'immoral' reveals that rational moral insight is a weak moral motive when contrasted with pragmatic motives for action. 'When we know what is morally right for us to do', observes Habermas, 'then we know that there are no good (epistemic) reasons to act otherwise. But that does not mean that other motives will not prevail' (1999: 35). Duties point the will in a certain direction but do not have the power to compel in the way that impulses do.

Why be moral? The power of rational insight is important but insufficient. Philosophers, as philosophers, can no longer provide any guidance about the meaning of life that is generally binding. Philosophical theories are important because they can correct poorly argued theories that undermine the moral intuition. They can demonstrate the moral point of view and defend its universalism against a relativism that deprives moral commands of their meaning and force. Thus, moral theories can effectively clarify the moral point of view but they cannot provide a strong motivation to be moral.

The next step is a little surprising but only because we are still hankering for some religious or metaphysical absolute grounding. The impossibility of this creates the possibility for counselling and psychotherapy to understand the importance of their moral and ethical role for individuals and society. A postconventional morality remains unfulfilled until it is brought into real life by motivated people. They must, in some way, be disposed to act according to conscience and obligation. This morality therefore depends on socialization processes that prepare people by engendering agencies of conscience, that is, through the internalization of moral principles in the personality system. In a postmodern world Habermas takes a bold step:

> I will defend the thesis that does not sit well with the spirit of the times: that anyone who has grown up in a reasonably functional family, who has formed his identity in relations of mutual recognition, who maintains himself in the network of reciprocal expectations and perspectives built into the pragmatic of the speech situation and communicative action, cannot fail to have acquired moral intuitions... (1995c: 114)

It is at this point that the critical power of this approach becomes evident because this virtuous moral socialization process becomes undermined by distorted communication. It is distorted *specifically* within 'dysfunctional' family arrangements and it is distorted *systematically* by the social, political and economic structures of 'advanced' capitalist societies. Later, I shall consider the issues of: moral personality development and socialization; moral and ethical emotions which foster moral sensitivities and inclinations; and the social context of systematically distorted communication. The point I wish to make here, however, is that moral action does require socialization processes to engender citizens who possess the psychological and emotional competence and will to act morally and ethically. Such people must meet the universal principles of postconventional morality halfway because they cannot rely on religious or metaphysical guarantors to do the work for them. The role of counselling in this context is to help people make up for educational and socialization deficits; to undo, deconstruct or rewrite the distorted communications or texts of their own life and thereby help them gain the competence to act morally and ethically. And, to reinforce the dialectical point, in order for any particular individual to achieve this it is necessarily the case, because we are socially constituted, that we need to work to create the conditions conducive to enable *all* people to achieve this moral identity. The counselling and psychotherapeutic voice, if it is to achieve individual psychological transformations, must make itself heard in a radical manner at the social and political levels. In Buddhist thought the Bodhisattva represents a similar principle; although attaining personal self-enlightenment, the Bodhisattva refuses entry into Nirvana until all other creatures have developed themselves to the point of self-enlightenment. This is not so much an ethic of sacrifice as the acceptance that the authenticity of my life is dialectically contingent on the authenticity of yours.

Moral consciousness and personal identity have an internal link which creates a connection between ethics and morals within the individual psyche. A consciousness able to operate at the postconventional level of morality needs to be supplemented by an ethical self-awareness that the integrity of my core identity is dependent on the fact that I can only respect myself as an authentic person if, as a general rule, I undertake the actions I take to be morally right. This, in turn, requires that I am open to moral emotions such as guilt and shame; that my moral sense is connected to feelings of solidarity and care; and that I possess hermeneutic empathy when applying universal norms to particular contexts. In other words, moral consciousness requires maturity and autonomy. This seems obvious. With conventional moralities in the naive attitude moral maturity is indeed an achievement, but it is distinctly aided by beliefs in religious or metaphysical certainties. At the postconventional level such certainties no longer exist so moral maturity and autonomy reflect psychological achievements within the context of effective socialization patterns.

The problem of motivation does not undermine a postconventional morality, rather the latter helps us by being clear about the fact that motivation is provided by factors other than moral theories themselves. Although I shall return to some of these themes later, we are disposed to act morally for the following reasons. First, because postconventional morals are universal and rationally justified this cognitive element helps us to identify with them – I feel more secure in my moral actions if I can rationally justify them. Secondly, successful socialization patterns create personal identities that, in order to achieve congruence and authenticity, must follow moral imperatives. Successful parenting will not enable children to feel personally fulfilled if their actions harm others, that is, I cannot feel ethically authentic and morally guilty simultaneously. A third reason is that moral and ethical emotions like guilt and shame operate very powerfully on us and provide strong incentives not to transgress normative codes. We know that these reasons are insufficient. The fourth factor, therefore, is the fact that moral consciousness is awakened by the compelling power of rhetoric and art. People do not fight *for* vague abstractions, they fight *with* engaging and compelling images (flags, metaphors, barnstorming speeches and so on). This is the power of art. Art is world-disclosing, that is, it induces us to see things in a radically different light. It also uses richly textured images whose aesthetic quality enables us to identify with them.[6] However, it is important to note that postconventional morality and consciousness require that we have a reflexive relationship to such compelling images. That is, their attraction and ability to create identification does not operate in a naive or direct fashion but is mediated through a consciousness which has the ability to choose such identifications rather than be chosen by them.

Finally, perhaps the most powerful, and also the most dangerous, source of moral and ethical motivation is love, eros or desire. Nothing can be so inspiring as love and yet nothing can create such moral torment. Whilst the aesthetic experience connects me to an image or a text, erotic desire connects me to another moral being. Granted, such desire can be blocked or fixated on the other person as an object, but these rigid objectifications are distorted or unfulfilled forms of attraction. People with adequate identity formations feel the motivating power of love as a mutual process. Luhmann, who has developed a systems theory of love, articulates this mutual process of self and other transformation:

> Love orients itself towards the world of another system; in other words, in its consum-
> mation it changes what it observes. Love cannot distance itself, but makes itself part of its
> 'object'. Its object does not stay put, for it absorbs the operation and as a consequence
> changes. The being experienced by the other becomes a component of operative repro-
> duction. Self-reproduction and external reproduction remain divided according to
> systemic context, and yet are nevertheless consummated *uno acto*. (1982: 175)

When set in a moral and ethical context, love has an inordinate power to motivate people to act in accordance with moral and ethical obligations.

It is my belief that counselling and psychotherapy have a strong connec-
tion to four of these five reasons. It is not the function of counselling to design moral theories. I have already alluded to their role as making up for socialization deficits. Understanding and working with moral emotions is a mainstream endeavour in therapy. Whilst one does not expect therapists

to be artists they do have a responsibility to morally inspire the clients through the use of inspirational imagery. Jungian psychotherapy, for one, clearly acknowledges this. Finally, we need to clearly understand that the therapeutic relationship between therapist and client is at heart an erotic relationship. Failure to integrate these understandings into counselling practice runs the risk of leaving clients who, outside the counselling room as citizens, are morally and ethically confused.

Ethics and Authenticity

When discussing the validity claim of morality I was inevitably drawn into making comparisons with ethics. It is now my intention to consider the validity claim of ethics in greater detail so that, among other things, we can see that, as a form of communicative action, it has a rational core. In terms of communicative reason ethical action is an expressive interaction in which the speaker reveals aspects of her own identity which are thereby made accessible for assessment (and enjoyment) by others. These expressions can be the sharing of an emotion, revealing a desire or intention, confessing an action and various other forms of personal revelation. The main issues concerning validity are those of transparency and consistency.

Transparency is represented by sincerity or truthfulness and authenticity. Sincerity or truthfulness is operative when the speaker faithfully represents herself at the conscious level (not lying or deceiving) and authenticity is in place when she represents herself at the unconscious level (not hiding aspects of her personality, or self-deceiving). In the ideal case, the communication is rational when the validity claim of transparency is fulfilled. In practice we are interested in the validity of the speaker's intentions (and, therefore, in the personal identity behind the expression) not just in individual utterances, but in their communicative action over time. In this sense we assess their sincerity and authenticity by the consistency of their actions over an extended period. Are the occasional insincerities minor blemishes or indicative of a flawed character? If I consistently failed to enact my stated intentions, I and my family and friends would know that the project of my life had failed and that I was living inauthentically. The sincerity of an expression or the authenticity of a life cannot be proved or disproved through argument (as can truth or rightness claims); it can only be *shown* by the level of consistency between expressed intentions and past or future actions. Unlike morals which compare my actions to universal standards, ethical values relate to the trajectory of my life or that of an identifiable group or community.

> Imagine Max a forty-seven year old computer analyst. When his fourth marriage began going the way of the others he knew not only that something was wrong and that 'something' was in him, but also that his recurring depression was linked to his

sense of shame that he could not successfully maintain a significant relationship. The project of his life was failing as he failed to represent his intentions in consistent action. Fortunately, his therapist was able to persuade him that his recent flirtation with soft drugs was not the answer. Through his work in therapy he came to realize that when the women in his marriages failed to maintain a high level of intimacy this would remind him of his unresponsive mother whose lack of intimacy encouraged him to be emotionally distant. In his increasingly desperate attempt to reverse this process in his marriages his invasive intensity would mean that when his wife retreated from him Max would feel abandoned. This feeling was so intense that his patterned reaction was to run, psychologically and physically. Which is what he did three times. This not only left him emotionally and financially drained it left him alienated from the authentic person he knew he could be. Only when this pattern became transparent through therapy could he begin to value himself as an authentic person able to maintain a coherent identity over time.[7]

Ethical questions have a self-referentiality. What is good for me or for us in this situation? When considering whether or not to divorce my spouse, the ethical questions concern what would be best for me, for my spouse and for the children. To approach divorce in this fashion is only possible in a society where divorce and separation are no longer morally objectionable. In this latter case I would be concerned with the rightness of leaving my spouse rather than with issues of rerouting my life on to a more authentic path whilst minimising the damage in the process. (That is, would I be breaking a norm that applied to all people in this situation? For example, a Christian may be more concerned with the failure to uphold a sacred promise and feel divorce as a moral failure.) This 'egocentricity' at the individual level is paralleled by an 'ethnocentricity' at the political level when a tribe, community or nation represents or protects its own way of life or cultural values. At either level, self-reference represents an internal relation between an ethical question (Should I leave my spouse?) and how I should understand myself (Do I feel shameful in leaving my spouse?). Thus the question 'What is the best thing for me?' has to be answered in relation to the question 'Who am I, and who do I want to be?' The ethical outlook addresses the individual's (or group's) striving for self-realization and the resolve to fulfil an authentic life so that his concern over who he is and what he would like to become operates through his life history. Throughout, the crucial issue is that my identity is at stake, and because it is *my* identity and self-understanding that is at issue explains why ethical questions do not generate answers that are valid for everyone.

Ethical insights influence how we orient our lives. They bind our will or volition by forming a conscious plan of our life within which our free will operates. This life-plan permeates all parts of our life:

> everyone is in some sense aware of the reflexive constitution of modern social activity and the implications it has for her or his life. Self-identity for us forms a *trajectory*

across the different institutional settings of modernity over the *duree* of what used
to be called the 'life cycle'...Each of us not only ' has', but *lives* a biography reflexively
organized in terms of flows of social and psychological information about possible
ways of life. Modernity is a post-traditional order, in which the question, 'How shall
I live?' has to be answered in day-to-day decisions about how to behave, what to
wear and what to eat – and many other things – as well as interpreted within the
temporal unfolding of self-identity. (Giddens 1991: 14)

The authentic life is like a narrative. And only if we write this story ourselves,
or own our life history,[8] can we see in it the realization of our selfhood.
'Responsibly to take over one's own biography', argues Habermas, 'means
to get clear about *who one wants to be*, and from this horizon to view the
traces of one's own interactions as *if* they were deposited by the actions of
a responsible author, of a subject that acted on the basis of a reflective
relation to self' (1998a: 98–9).

If we have defined ethics in terms of the authenticity of an individual or
group, have we not opened the door to the complete relativism that we
have been trying to combat? If the self is defined by its ethical choices, and
these choices are arbitrary, then each individual or group forms its own
ethical universe closed to any kind of rational assessment. Whilst ethics do
not create universal obligations in the fashion of morals, they are open to
some rational criticism. They are measured by the authenticity of the self-
understanding of the individual or group. An individual who consistently
acts insincerely and has an opaque relation to aspects of her identity will be
unable to act authentically and may well be so judged by peers and, in
extreme cases, by relevant professionals (social workers, mental health
workers and so on). This kind of critique of an ethical life is not based on
a judgemental comparison between the ethical choice of this person as
opposed to that of an other person, rather it operates internally to this
specific person, or form of life, by considering the level of authenticity of
the process, that is, how authentically is the chosen ethical life being lived.
Addicts (alcohol, drugs and so on), in their desperate attempt to overcome
their addiction, exemplify the critical importance to a sense of selfhood of
being able to be seen to authentically live a life of which they are consistently
the author.

Moreover, the preferences and goals by which I steer my life are not
simply given but are themselves open to rational reflection. Since my chosen
values depend on my self-understanding, and since this self-understanding
can undergo reasoned change (as represented by the therapeutic process),
the values themselves are open to critique by myself *and by others who share
the social world within which I constitute myself.* Indeed, apart from issues
of authenticity and inauthenticity, our social actions are also open to
assessment by the other validity claims inherent in communicative action.
In order to reach a mutual understanding we must also: communicate
comprehensibly, make statements that are true rather than false, follow

moral obligations, act autonomously and maintain a healthy balance between these validity claims. Whilst our ethical life is indeed our own individual life project it must nevertheless be compatible with the other validity claims.

Authenticity and Counselling

The ethical life is a striving for the conscious realization of an authentic life. By its very nature this is a difficult struggle and is only achievable when the individual attains a reflective distance from her own life history. But this is not achievable by the individual alone. Her life project exists within a social frame of other individuals pursuing their own life projects within a context of social institutions and processes. Consequently, when her life becomes inauthentic and subject to unconscious determinations which cause her anxiety or depression, her friends and family are potential participants who can act as constructive critics in her process of gaining a self-clarification of why her life is going awry. This intervention acts as a catalyst in her process of searching to understanding herself in order to bring about future personality change. In societies which generate this type of personality formation this cathartic role is often occupied by psychotherapists and counsellors. Therapy is an important process whereby I can recover the trajectory of my life project.

But this recovery could also be defined as a 'critical reconstruction'. Entry into a therapeutic relationship, from the ethical viewpoint, only makes sense on the basis of the client's intention of consciously enacting an authentic life. The therapist offers the possibility of the client reconstructing her life in the sense of reorienting it, and this process is critical because it questions the ethical tenets of the life lived hitherto. A life based on a personality susceptible to insincerity and self-deceptions, which may show themselves in symptoms of projection, splitting, depression and similar phenomena, is offered to the therapist to generate a critique of the client's behaviour using the idea of a conscious and coherent mode of life as a yardstick. This critique, which is subject to lengthy amendments in the continuing relationship between therapist and client, gains its therapeutic effect when it is eventually accepted and internalized by the client as an accurate account of the inauthentic aspect of the client's biography to date so that this reconstruction enables the possibility of a future life that is free of self-deceptions. In so doing, counselling and therapy work with the six validity claims inherent in communicative action.[9]

> If illusions are playing a role, this hermeneutic self-understanding can be raised to the level of a form of reflection that dissolves self-deception. Bringing one's life history and its normative context to awareness in a critical manner does not lead to a value-neutral self-understanding; rather, the hermeneutically generated self-description is

logically contingent upon a critical relation to self. A more profound self-understanding alters the attitudes that sustain, or at least imply, a life project with normative substance.[10] In this way, strong evaluations can be justified through hermeneutic self-clarification. (Habermas 1995c: 5)

Transparency, Authenticity, Pure Relationships and Eros

James Hillman, a truly perceptive Jungian theorist, caught the spirit of the times in the early 1970s at about the same time that Habermas was developing his theoretical perspective, when he noticed that the psychological identity of modern man was being increasingly characterized by the issue of transparency.

> Now our image of the goal changes: not Enlightened Man, who sees, the seer, but Transparent Man, who is seen and seen through, foolish, who has nothing left to hide, who has become transparent through self-acceptance; his soul is loved, wholly revealed, wholly existential; he is just what he is, freed from paranoid concealment, from the knowledge of his secrets and his secret knowledge; his transparency serves as a prism for the world and the not-world. For it is impossible reflectively to know thyself; only the last reflection of an obituary may tell the truth, and only God knows our real names. (Hillman 1972: 92)

As we have seen, transparency is a key feature of authenticity. Revealing our true selves to others in a mutual interplay is the only way that we can both be truly known by others and also truly know others. Only by transparency can we be held by ourselves and others to account on the authenticity of our life. By the same process it is only through transparency that mutual trust can be engendered. A person who attempts to live authentically over a period of time is someone in whom I can place my trust because his actions contain a certain rationality and predictability in relation to the core identity that is being authentically enacted. This is made possible by the transparency of the person which enables me to monitor the authenticity of his actions in relation to his core self and stated ideals of goals. Arendt (1998: 244) indicates how this phenomenon is linked to the importance of making a promise. The price of freedom as a citizen in a democratic society is that we are subject to the unpredictability of our own psychological nature and to the same nature in others. The function of promising is to create a level of certainty and predictability in a very uncertain world. The only alternative would be to subject oneself and others to the mastery of a sovereign ruler, that is, tyranny. Promises are only possible to the extent that people are authentic and autonomous.

In an open society we can no longer assess a person's character through their place and status in a rigidly hierarchical structure. In the fast pace of highly mobile interactions the mark of the authentic woman is no longer her office, status, badge or uniform; it is the authenticity of her identity made accessible to assessment through transparency. Authenticity is rendered accessible by transparency which, in turn, facilitates trust. As Kop (1985: 18) illustrates, '...if I am transparent enough to myself, then I can become less afraid of those hidden selves that my transparency may reveal to others...But who can love me, if no one knows me? I must risk it, or live alone. It is enough that I must die alone'.

It was not always so. In fact, according to Hochschild (1982), this is a relatively recent phenomenon. During the sixteenth century in England and France, opportunities for social upward mobility increased. Guile and the careful management of self in presentation to others became an important tool for class advancement. Acting a part, playing a role and not displaying one's true self became a useful tool for taking advantage of new opportunities. Guile, cunning, deceit and a manipulative role-playing became tools for self-advancement. Sincerity came to be judged as the polar opposite of its current positive image. It was seen as an inhibition to act before a multiplicity of audiences or, as Hochschild indicates, an absence of the psychic detachment necessary for acting. Thus in the literature of the time the 'honest soul' was portrayed as being simple, unsophisticated or simply naive. In the modern period, interest has moved away from the issue of sincerity into a move inward, that is, we are preoccupied with how we fool ourselves. In a world where our psyche is seduced by brand images, regimented by employment discipline, rendered almost obsolete by a technicized corporate science it is little wonder, argues Hochschild, that we are concerned and worried about our authentic self.

At this point I wish to develop the connection of ethics and authenticity with eros, love and desire because Habermas does not take it far enough. His prime interest is with regard to an individual's, or a group's, relation to itself. That is, am I representing myself authentically and am I acting congruently? Although this clearly involves others, their role is largely one of assessing me for my benefit, or securing trust in me for their benefit. What he doesn't clearly elucidate is the role this plays in the close, mutual interaction of people in an intimate relationship – people who can act at the level of 'we'. Granted, Habermas is insightful about the dialectic between counsellor and client in the therapeutic relationship and this, as we shall see, is not short of erotic connection; but the therapeutic relationship is temporary and is primarily focused on the needs of one of the participants. What specific role does self-revelation, transparency and authenticity have in intimate, loving relationships?

For many, the road on which I travel towards my ethical, 'good' or authentic life is that of love as expressed in marriage or other forms of committed, intimate relationships. On this 'royal road' the ethical imperative for authenticity is essential not just for my own destiny but also for my attachment to my loved ones. Sincerity and authenticity also underpin the validity and genuineness of my love, emotional attachment and erotic desire for another. Transparency engenders trust which, in turn, enables faith and confidence in loving relationships. It enables my 'I' to meet your 'I'; it connects my inner self to your inner self. The more aware I am of my own self the more I can reveal to you and, as our path of individuation requires mutual recognition, greater transparency necessarily results in an erotic attraction to others similarly developed. With individuation the erotic connection becomes deeper and more differentiated and requires the trusting security generated by greater authenticity. Just as morality, defined in terms of justice, has solidarity as its necessary flip side, the ethical concern with personal identity and authenticity is necessarily linked with the need to connect with other identities for mutual recognition through the connecting power of eros and love. The extension of this phenomenon to significant portions of the population is peculiarly modern and is a natural extension of the process of interactive individuation rather than just being a contemporary search for intimacy in an impersonal social world. Giddens, in an attempt to capture what's new about these arrangements, calls them 'pure relationships'.

> Intimacy has its own reflexivity and its own forms of internally referential order. Of key importance here is the emergence of the 'pure relationship' as prototypical of the new spheres of personal life. A pure relationship is one in which external criteria have become dissolved: the relationship exists solely for whatever rewards that relationship as such can deliver. In the context of the pure relationship, trust can be mobilized only by reflexive process of mutual disclosure. Like self-identity, with which it is closely intertwined, the pure relationship has to be reflexively controlled over the long term, against the backdrop of external transitions and transformations.
>
> Pure relationships presuppose 'commitment', which is a particular species of trust. Commitment in turn has to be understood as a phenomenon of the internally referential system: it is a commitment to the relationship as such, as well as to the other person or persons involved. The demand for intimacies is integral to the pure relationship, as a result of the mechanisms of trust which it presumes. (1991: 7)[11]

This pure kind of relationship brings into being a new form of eros, which Giddens calls 'confluent love'. Romantic love is superseded because it is often unequal in terms of power with women historically coming worse off, and also because romantic love does not operate at the reflective level – we are subject to it rather than vice versa. Confluent love presumes an equality in emotional give-and-take and the ethical ability to act authentically by revealing one's needs and vulnerabilities to each other. This applies not just to the initiation of such a relationship, but to a reflexivity that is present throughout its life and, where relevant, its dissolution. As we shall see in greater detail later, this is also part of a greater process of democratization. For Giddens, the possibility of intimacy creates a promise of democracy in relationships which is not limited to those that are sexual. He envisages the development of an ethical framework for a 'democratic personal order, in which sexual relationships and other personal domains conform to a model of confluent love.... The changes that have helped transform personal environments of action are already well advanced, and they tend towards the realization of democratic qualities' (1992: 188–9).

Health

Having articulated four validity claims so far, we are still left with a problem. Individuals, groups and whole cultures have an unhealthy record of failing to keep all of them in balance. Communicative reason, which outlines the conditions required in communications to effect a mutual understanding, works on the principle that all the claims to validity must be present. Clearly, in different contexts, the differing claims will assume varying levels of relative importance or appropriateness. For example, issues of comprehensibility will be of more significance between two people of different languages and cultures than it will be between two people who share the same language and culture. The pragmatic question of which means of transport I should choose to reach my destination can carry more or less weight when put in the context of whether or not this journey has significance for the fulfilment of my life project. But when considering the actions of an individual, group or a whole society, I agree with Habermas that all the validity claims must be present and held in a reasonable balance. Serious imbalances can be dangerous. The environmental problems facing the planet have a direct relationship to the predominance of the scientific worldview, applied through technology, found in advanced industrial societies unable to critically reflect on the ideology of economic growth. In other contexts the predominance of a heavy moralizing outlook can create fundamentalist movements in all faiths, often leading to extreme human rights violations. Similarly, narcissistic counter-cultures can be consumed by a passion for the 'authentic path' at the expense of moral obligations and pragmatic effectiveness.

   Although a significant aspect of Habermas's achievement with the concept of communicative rationality has been the decentring of an instrumental conception of rationality into the different validity claims – he is also keen to maintain the organic links between these claims as being parts of the same whole that is practical reason. Ignoring the connections will only undermine the emancipatory interest in the whole theory. The overly rationalized everyday life of an individual or group cannot be rescued from its false limitations and impoverishment by the imposition of another cultural domain, say religious fundamentalism, without replacing one tyranny by another. 'In the communicative praxis of everyday life', observes Habermas, 'cognitive interpretations, moral expectations, expressions and evaluations must interpenetrate one another. The process of reaching understanding which transpires in the lifeworld requires the resources of an inherited culture *in its entire range*' (1997a: 49).[12]

Thus the validity claim of health or equilibrium acts like a criterion monitoring all the other validity claims to keep them all interrelated in a balanced (though contextually sensitive) way. Health is often used as a systems-monitoring concept in relation to holding balances between various parts of a system. However, when used clinically in a therapeutic environment, we are never sure about what it means because the 'system' is not defined. The concept of communicative rationality provides a framework or system within which this notion of health can derive meaning.

Autonomy

That autonomy is an important concept for counselling and psychotherapy is not a new idea. What I am trying to do here is to explain why it is important and how it connects to the other values already articulated. Without having taken this route we could not be clear whether autonomy is really a form of ethics or an expression of morality. Moreover, as we shall see in the next chapter, if our concept of the autonomous person is not firmly placed in a dialectical relationship with other people or the community, then most usages of the concept are likely to over-identify autonomy with a privatized individuality. Autonomy is our sixth and final value, with which the other five constitute the core values that give counselling and psychotherapy their purpose. However, unlike the others it does not operate like a validity claim securing communicative interactions or, rather, it does so in a different way. In the ideal model of interactions which are in accordance with the preconditions of communicative reason the most successful communicative agreements are only achieved by fully autonomous people. Such people, in turn, will achieve autonomy only when they have fully internalized the ability and motivation to act in accordance with the other validity claims. These other claims guarantee specific aspects of communication and their organic equilibrium, whereas autonomy is both dependent upon these claims and also their fulfilment. Through successful socialization processes that provide us with personal identities (that are also sustained by supportive social systems) enabled to act in accordance with the other validity claims, we thereby produce autonomous people who, in turn, are able to act in accordance with the necessary conditions of communicative action. Thus autonomy, like the other values or validity claims, is not arbitrarily selected but is deduced from communicative rationality; it has a necessary character and is rationally linked to the other values. This does not mean that other values cannot operate in therapeutic interactions. It does mean, however, that they may be shown to be derived from the six values outlined; if not, they would be obliged to prove their validity. The advantage of being clear and open about using communicative rationality as the basis for selecting these values is that we show *why* we think they are necessary and therefore make them accessible to rational debate. A loose assortment of counselling values that can vary between the different therapeutic schools and are unable to give cogent reasons for their validity is less than useful and provides an inadequate protection against the invasive power of ideological values from the dominant, external culture.

I want to be a little more specific about our understanding of the concept of autonomy from the perspective of communicative reason. As Holmes and Lindley (1989: 228) point out, it can be used to endorse a range of conflicting ideas from a conservative defence against state intervention on the grounds that it interferes with personal autonomy, to an extreme libertarian personal selfishness. Holmes and Lindley derive their concept of autonomy from within the liberal democratic tradition of John Stuart Mill combined with psychotherapeutic insights into the nature of emotional disturbance. They are clear, and I agree with them, that it does not mean selfishness or an isolated independence from other people. They place themselves in that school of psychotherapy based on the works of John Bowlby which is critical of other psychotherapeutic schools that overvalue independence, seeing dependency '...as an undesirable relic of childishness which the mature individual can, with therapeutic help, outgrow' (1989: 228–9). Rather, autonomy is the flip side of mutuality and interdependence. I would also agree with them that psychotherapy has developed the concept of autonomy by showing how '...self-knowledge and the internalization of good relationships...may provide an important route to overcoming heteronomy' (1989: 229).

This leads them to the conclusion that autonomy is at the centre of psychotherapy because: it is a fundamental value; it has long been recognized in western thought; and it is a unifying assumption shared by most psychotherapists. Whilst sympathizing with their broad outlook it does not tell us *why*, in a philosophical or rational sense, autonomy should have such a primary role in counselling and psychotherapy. Placing the concept in a historical tradition has little effect when that tradition is quite correctly heavily criticized by both postmodernists and critical theorists like Habermas. It is because of the existence of these critical attacks that autonomy, and all other values associated with counselling and psychotherapy, cannot be assumed to be true. Without a true conviction based on accessible, yet defendable, rational arguments, notions about the concept of autonomy and other values have little power or influence.

Giddens develops the concept of autonomy more successfully:

> The principle of autonomy provides the guiding thread and the most important substantive component of these processes. In the arena of personal life, autonomy means the successful realization of the reflexive project of self – the condition of relating to others in an egalitarian way. The reflexive project of self must be

developed in such a fashion as to permit autonomy in relation to the past, this in turn facilitating a colonising of the future. Thus conceived, self-autonomy permits that respect for others' capabilities which is intrinsic to a democratic order. The autonomous individual is able to treat others as such and to recognize that the development of their separate potentialities is not a threat. Autonomy also helps to provide the personal boundaries needed for the successful management of relationships. (1992: 189)

Here the link between autonomy and self-reflexivity is clear, as is the sense that this is a life project over time. Both of these notions clearly link autonomy to our concept of authenticity, that is, the leading of a genuine life over the trajectory of a life span. Although not stated here, like Habermas, Giddens understands that this ethical autonomy, or the autonomous leading of an authentic life, is dependent on the trust enabled by the evidential proof of authenticity facilitated by transparency of self to oneself and to others. Mutuality is also expressed by the need to relate to others in an egalitarian and democratic fashion. However, this approach, still does not give the idea of autonomy a philosophical or sound rational basis. Because this has not been achieved, unlike Habermas, Giddens cannot give the concept any sense of why it is 'necessary', as opposed to arbitrarily selected, and, consequently, he cannot link autonomy successfully to the other values of truth, comprehensibility, morality and health. It is the embeddedness of autonomy in communicative rationality and practice that gives the concept its powerful and necessary relation to psychotherapy and counselling.

Without this theoretical structure it is possible for commentators like Holmes and Lindley to confuse the concepts of ethics and morality:

> Psychotherapeutic autonomy is pluralistic in that it aims to help people to find and follow their *own* various goals and desires, without imposing any particular view of what is right upon them. Part of the process of therapy is helping people to recognize whether a particular decision for course of action feels right for *them*. (1989: 229)

I have difficulty with this for the following reasons. In the first place, it ignores the difference between ethics and morals whereby we may well be concerned, in ethical terms, with what is good for 'me', but I feel that we have shown that our moral interactions with others cannot be a matter of choice in this sense, nor can they be issues limited to my own perspective. Secondly, our understanding of ethical issues is that, in almost all cases, they cannot contradict moral imperatives. My third concern is that even with the issue most closely connected with counselling and psychotherapy, that is the notion of authenticity, authentic actions and life projects involve ground rules that are not open to individual choices and values. The concept of autonomy must include the concept of ethical authenticity, in which case we must live in conformity with the relevant validity claims of transparency (to oneself and others) and the resolve to be transparent and authentic over our life span. Inevitably this must place significant restrictions on our choice of actions. In the fourth case, autonomy bears a similar relationship to truth. Notwithstanding our acceptance of the appropriate methodological acceptance of an untruth during therapy, this is not acceptable at the end of the therapeutic process. Thus, truth is also a limitation on client choice.

Moreover, a therapist would be failing in her duty if she condones, either by silence or by affirmation, a client's personal identity formation if the relationship between the various forms of actions as expressed in the validity claims is excessively out of balance. This concept of health does not need to be rigid and can tolerate profiles that show greater interest in some areas above others, but all need to be present and accessible. A further concern is that this concept of autonomy completely ignores the idea that certain autonomous decisions must bear no relation to personal motivations and must be completely demotivated. Finally, this *laissez-faire* sense of autonomy does not have the possibility of being developed into the better conception of autonomy as that stage of personal identity required in order to achieve successful communicative agreements as well as being a precondition for behaviour in a fully developed democracy. As a consequence the understanding of autonomy proposed by Holmes *et al.* inflates and misconceives the notion of personal choice of values and goals that are available to the client. It is also far too soft on the counsellors' responsibilities.

Habermas takes the concept of autonomy further. Although his language is very Kantian and somewhat abstract, I believe that the sense of it is relatively clear and relates to stages of personal development not unknown to transpersonal, existential and humanistic psychotherapies. Our interest is in the concept of volition and the freely chosen binding of our will. That is, once freely accepting a moral obligation we have 'no choice' but to act in accordance with its imperative. When we act pragmatically by using technical skills to solve a problem, the binding of our will to the technical rule is chosen purely in relation to a successful practical outcome. If I wish to attach a screw to the wall I need to use a screwdriver and not my mobile phone. I limit my personal choice to that which will achieve a successful practical outcome. It has no ethical or moral significance. In ethical actions the binding of our will to imperatives concerning authenticity is still relative to our personal preferences and life goals. The fact that it is essential to me to express myself by playing the guitar does not have any implications for others. Moral obligations (I must not harm others), however, acquire an unconditional or categorical validity that is not found in pragmatic or ethical action; but this is only the case if the individual's will, or volition, is freed from all personal, or other, influences and determinations (my desire to play the guitar should not persuade me to steal it from somebody else). In other words, my personal wishes are subordinated to the imperatives of practical reason. From this platform, Habermas notes that '...the contingent goals, preferences, and value-orientations that otherwise determine the will from without can then be subjected to critical evaluation in light of norms that are justified from the moral point of view' (1999: 32). In this sense of autonomy, freedom is not conceived in terms of the act of an ego choosing from a shopping list of wishes in line with its personal desires and preferences, or even its authentic life project. Rather, when such issues are no longer resonant, our autonomy expresses our freedom to choose to bind itself to moral duties that not only apply to me, but apply to everyone. In so doing my interests are the same as everyone's interests because they conform to practical reason.[13]

> An autonomous will is one that is guided by practical reason. Freedom in general consists in the capacity to choose in accordance with maxims; but autonomy is the self-binding of the will by maxims we adopt on the basis of *insight*.[14] Because it is mediated by reason, autonomy is not just one value alongside others. This explains why *this* normative content does not impair the neutrality of a procedure. A procedure that operationalizes the moral point of view of impartial judgement is neutral with respect to arbitrary constellations of values but not with respect to practical reason itself. (Habermas 1999: 99–100)

At this higher level only the will that is guided by moral insight can be called autonomous.

> The categorical 'ought' of moral injunctions, finally, is directed to the *free will*, emphatically construed, of a person who acts in accordance with self-given laws; this will alone is autonomous in the sense that it is completely open to determination by moral insights.[15] In the sphere of validity of the moral law, neither contingent dispositions nor life histories and personal identities set limits to the determination of the will by practical reason. Only a will that is guided by moral insight, and hence is completely rational, can be called autonomous. All heteronymous elements of mere choice or of commitment to an idiosyncratic way of life, however authentic it may be, have been expunged from such a will...the autonomous will is efficacious only to the extent that it can ensure that the motivational force of good reasons outweighs the power of other motives. (Habermas 1995c: 9–10)

The language may be grand but I believe that it does express something quite tangible and real. Many people are able to achieve this autonomy in aspects of their lives. Most parents will often be self-sacrificing with regard to their children; many people can achieve this sense of autonomous action when caring for vulnerable friends or relations; and many of our everyday actions can proceed in this way. Naturally, our autonomy is really tested only when a moral duty is in conflict with an important personal need. Nevertheless, many people can achieve this and some are probably able to act all the time in accordance with this sense of autonomy. Even if we cannot reach such sublime levels, this definition of autonomy is a useful ideal against which we can measure our actions. It is a much richer definition than that offered by other theorists. Whilst autonomy can be achieved without counselling and therapy, the ultimate goal of therapeutic work is to enable people to act autonomously.

CHAPTER 3

The Development of Moral Character

In my articulation of the validity claims connected to morality and ethics I noted that Habermas's theory of discourse ethics does not entirely resolve the motivational issue of why we should act morally. We can generate arguments showing that there is a rationality inherent in moral and ethical actions, but arguments and rational insights have a limited motivational effect in concrete life situations. The question I wish to address here concerns some aspects of how we socialize people to act morally; how do we anchor the inclination to act morally in personal identity? There has to be some congruence between discourse ethics and the development of social institutions and individual subjectivity.

> For unless discourse ethics is undergirded by the thrust of motives and by socially accepted institutions, the moral insights it offers remain ineffective in practice. Insights . . . should be transformable into the concrete duties of everyday life. This much is true: any universalistic morality is dependent upon a form of life that *meets it halfway*. There has to be a modicum of congruence between morality and the practice of socialization and education. The latter must promote the requisite internalization of superego controls and the abstractness of ego identities. In addition, there must be a modicum of fit between morality and socio-political institutions . . . Moral universalism is a *historical result*. (Habermas 1995b: 207–8)

This is a new and different way of understanding moral action. Conventionally our understanding of why we should be moral has been based on epistemological arguments. Because religions and traditional moralities have claimed direct access to 'truth' or the 'good life', moral action has been a process of gaining or internalising this truth, from which point we act in accordance with the appropriate dogma. Since discourse ethics bars the possibility of communicating any such absolute knowledge, this approach is not open to us. Acting morally is not something that the cognitive part of our consciousness 'knows' and then enforces. The internal command 'I must be good' doesn't necessarily result in moral outcomes. Rather, acting morally involves a complete process of psychological development involving our feelings, thoughts and desire, and it requires a different concept of the self.

69

The conventional way in which norms are internalized and self-monitored was connected to societies whose norms and values were grounded in traditional or religious forms of legitimation which were accepted in an unreflective fashion and internally reinforced by guilt mechanisms. Having already rejected these forms of legitimation we need to articulate different means by which morality can be embedded in real personal identities. Classical conceptions of the 'superego' and other forms of internal censoring, no longer adequately describe the process of identity formation. With the availability of models of ideal communication and democratic discussion, we have a different basis for legitimizing norms and values and therefore have, in some way or other, to develop different models which explain how people do internalize norms. This alone is a huge project so I will concentrate on a brief consideration of some of the key elements that this project would involve: reflexivity, intersubjectivity, evolutionary stages of psychological development, moral emotions and decentred conceptions of character and identity. Hopefully, this will begin to provide an alternative conception of the development of a moral self. This morally and ethically constituted self will therefore require a moral and ethical response when its soul becomes troubled and enters the domain of therapy.

Reflexivity

'There is no route back from reflectiveness' (Williams 1993: 163). In this succinct statement, Williams catches some of the essential nature of reflexivity or self-awareness. Having achieved a reflective consciousness there is no way that we can consciously take ourselves back from it. Williams continues '...in the individual case, though we can consciously embark on a course to reduce reflection, we cannot consciously assume that course, and if we are successful, we will have to forget it' (1993: 164). Reflexivity is an essential feature of evolutionary psychological development; it guarantees its irreversibility, and a postconventional moral self would be impossible without it.

Nevertheless, the fact that we cannot consciously step back from reflexivity does not prevent unconscious processes from repressing reflective consciousness. Someone who is generally competent at a particular stage of development will develop the corresponding moral consciousness. However, sufficient external pressure and/or unconscious pressure may exert conflict on a person such that she falls back in her moral performance and judgement to a level lower than her general competence. Thus, although reflexiveness does not enable a conscious regression, it does not always prevent an unconscious regression. Habermas indicates that, indirectly, this observation can act as a useful guide to the individual's general stability in her current developmental stage: 'Because it places the acting subject under an imperative for *consciously* working out conflicts, moral consciousness is an indicator of the degree of stability of general interactive competence' (1995a: 92). Later on, when discussing the decentred self, I will consider in greater detail how reflexivity influences the kind of self required by the communicative understanding of morality.

Intersubjective Constitution of Personal Identity

> Whether one calls it a growth tendency, a drive toward self-actualization, or a forward-moving directional tendency, it is the main spring of life, and is, in the last analysis, the tendency upon which all psychotherapy depends. It is the urge which is evident in all organic and human life – to expand, extend, become autonomous, develop, mature – the tendency to express and activate all the capacities of the organism, to the extent that such activation enhances the organism or the self. (Rogers 1993: 35)

It is this kind of approach, with its unclear links with individualism, drive theory and organic urges, that has had an enormous influence on psycho-therapy and counselling. It desperately needs updating with intersubjective accounts of personal development. The 'linguistic turn' in thinking enables us to break out of this monological perspective. Communicative action is, by its very nature, *dialogical*. Communication towards reaching a mutual understanding is a reciprocal process between speaker and hearer. The process of personal development is equally reciprocal.

It is not possible to deduce a normative concept of autonomy, which we have argued is the highest form of ethical and moral development, from the intentional action of isolated individuals. Only the theory of communicative action can establish an intrinsic moral norm – the idea of 'unforced intersubjectivity'. In communicative action oriented to reaching understanding, speaker and hearer enter into an interpersonal relation in which they commit themselves to recognize each other symmetrically as responsible subjects who are able to submit their actions to the authority of the validity claims inherent in communication. Simultaneously, participants in communication are also connected to the normative context of the world around them. 'In this way', Habermas argues, 'the necessary presuppositions of communicative action constitute an infrastructure of possible communication constructed around a moral core – the idea called unforced intersubjectivity' (1995c: 131). Since all socialization processes must operate through the medium of communicative action, they are subject to the necessary presuppositions of such action which already contain within themselves this moral element.

Our journey through the terrain of discourse ethics arrives at a moral theory that sets aside conceptions of personhood that ignore the social construction of identity. Only in relations of reciprocal recognition can we create and maintain identity. Intersubjectivity is constitutive of our identity – it is something we cannot step out of. All aspects of our identity are connected to others who share a community of communicative relations. I can only be myself through the recognition of others who reciprocally need my recognition to be themselves. Our socialization from infancy is a long process which makes the self vulnerable to the vagaries of the social interactions through which it is generated. There is no guarantee that the self's need to depend on others will be forthcoming – not all parents naturally provide the level of care that the child needs. Morality therefore serves the purpose of protecting this fragile identity from an undue lack of reciprocal recognition or care. Reproduction of the species requires socialization processes that create mature adults able to be autonomous in moral and ethical actions and also morally competent to reproduce these qualities in their offspring. Counselling and psychotherapy can be seen as agents of socialization that need to be available for those individuals and groups for whom the regular processes of socialization provided by the family and the education system and so on, have failed.

Unlike Rogers, I do not see the process of self-actualization as one that is carried out by an independent subject working in isolation and freedom, but as a process of socialization embedded in communicative action that simultaneously connects me with others whilst creating my biography or life-history that is self-reflexive. As others attribute agency, intentionality and accountability to me, I gradually internalize these qualities through the recognition bestowed by others. The ego which appears to be peculiarly mine and validated as such by self-consciousness cannot be maintained solely by me on the basis of my power alone. It does not 'belong' to me as such, but retains an intersubjective core.

The socialization process required for the creation of a postconventional moral outlook presupposes a non-conventional kind of ego identity. Self-identity needs to be seen not as a monolithic ego structure that controls all, but as a reflexive self able to sustain and reconcile multiple and sometimes conflicting identities. These reconciliations are achieved not by the impositions of a masterful ego but through an identity which can reflexively live with and accept difference and complexity. This capacity is based on a cognitive and emotional acceptance of intersubjectivity and autonomy. 'The very concept of a self, of an I, of a me, is something which is constructed only through intersubjective interactions, which take place always in contexts of shared meanings.[1] Similarly, my identity as this specific individual is constructed through my participation in communities, institutions and systems of meaning...' (Weir 1995: 264).

Habermas's critics[2] clearly acknowledge that the intersubjective theory of identity construction is both powerful and uniquely his own. However, whilst he recognizes the importance of the emotional side of relationships to this process of mutual recognition, he does not develop it. To gain a better understanding of how identity is generated in the affective bonds of early life it might be useful to turn to the work of Benjamin (1988).

The key idea that Benjamin constantly brings to our attention is that, from the intersubjective perspective, the subjectivity of the individual grows in and through the relationship to other *subjects*. Thus the development of my identity is critically dependent on the fact that I recognize that the self that I meet in interactions is also a self or subject in his or her own right. We recognize that the other is different yet also alike; separate yet capable of sharing similar mental experiences. Indeed, successful communication requires two subjects that are able to experience similar mental states. The idea that the infant has the capacity, need and desire from birth to relate to others has significant consequences. Following Benjamin we can see that Freud's original view (which object relations has already seriously criticized) of the subject as a discreet, individualized energy system needs revising in favour of intersubjective theory. I am similarly doubtful about the school of ego psychology which developed in the USA in the late 1960s which portrays the newly born child as existing in a symbiotic union with the mother. The problem with this approach is the idea that we separate *out* of oneness rather than growing and becoming more of a self *within* relationships. The intersubjective view holds that the infant is never completely undifferentiated from the mother, but, from the beginning, relates to others. Once this is accepted the important issue is not only one of separation but also how we connect and recognize others; rather than freedom from others it is active engagement with others which enables us to know ourselves through mutual recognition with others.

Using another frame of reference we might call this dynamic of mutual recognition the dialectic of erotic identification; the movement of recognition is also the movement of love. The development of this erotic interaction into adult confluent love becomes a key target for the socialization of the infant into a fully competent moral and ethical adult. This, as we have seen, is necessarily connected to the ethical quality and validity claim of authenticity. Because the dynamic of mutual recognition requires us to recognize the 'other' as a subject in her own right, at higher developmental stages this recognition will no longer be naively given but will be dependent upon the other proving that she is an authentic person by making her subjectivity transparent and open to verification such that her 'subject-status' can be shown to be genuine. This condition applies to all participants in the process of mutual recognition or erotic identification.

It is not my view that intersubjective theory should replace intrapsychic theory, rather the latter should yield its dominance to enable a complementary relationship between these two psychological theories. The intrapsychic perspective conceives of the person as being a discreet entity with a complex internal psychological structure; this approach is particularly interested in the unconscious. Intersubjective theory requires that such an approach be placed within the dynamic context of the construction of self through interactions with other selves.[3] Later on we shall also consider how intersubjectivity can resolve some of the limitations found in object relations theory.

The dialectics of mutual recognition are paradoxical and intriguing:

> The need of the self for the other is paradoxical, because the self is trying to establish himself as an absolute, an independent entity, yet he must recognize the other as like himself in order to *be* recognized by him. He must be able to find himself in the other. (Benjamin 1988: 32)

> The need for recognition entails this fundamental paradox: at the very moment of realising our own independence, we are dependent upon another to recognize it. At the very moment we come to understand the meaning of 'I, myself,' we are forced to see the limitations of that self. At the moment when we understand that separate minds can share the same state, we also realize that these minds can disagree. (Benjamin 1988: 33)

A person comes to feel their own agency and authorship by being with another person who recognizes her feelings, her intentions, her existence and independence. My ability to assert myself is dependent on the recognition provided by others. This recognition is reflexive in so far as it includes not only the act of the other confirming my identity but also my response to that confirmation.

The difficult problem, however, is recognizing the other. Establishing myself is dependent upon gaining the recognition of the other which, in turn, requires me to acknowledge that the other exists for herself and not just for me. As the person matures she will become less dependent on the physical presence of others to provide recognition – this is possible only to the extent that the other has been *internalized* within the psyche of the individual. But in early childhood the child's confirmation of internal and external reality is based on the child's confidence in early figures of care, usually the mother and the father. 'As developed through the loving attentions of early caretakers', notes Giddens 'basic trust links self-identity in a fateful way to the appraisals of others' (1991: 38). For Giddens the 'other' is also not an unknowable, unconnected external entity, rather self and other are inherently connected. Trust in others is essential for the experience of a stable external world and an integrated sense of self-identity. Trust is established through intimate affective bonds which must also conform to the validity claims of communicative action so that the authenticity of such bonds is guaranteed by their morality, truth, comprehensibility and transparency. Without mutual transparency neither self nor other can exist as real identities. 'It is "faith" in the reliability and integrity of others which is at stake here . . . Trust, interpersonal relations and a conviction of the "reality" of things go hand in hand in the social settings of adult life' (Giddens 1991: 51–2).

Once we place ideas of mutual recognition in the context of the early family life experienced by most children in Western societies other issues become apparent. I am well aware that there are many family structures currently available, but in most of them it is the mother that still does the bulk of primary care-giving to children. Whilst some of what follows can also apply to fathers who occupy the same primary care-giving role, the unique features of the role of women in a patriarchal society gives them extra difficulties in the role of motherhood when placed within the process of mutual recognition. This process requires not only that we recognize the other as someone distinct from ourselves, but that, critically, the other must be recognized as an independent *subject* and not simply as an object in the external world or an adjunct of the child's ego. The child needs a mother who acts as a real person with real needs that are reflected back to the child, rather than a de-selfed maternal figure who represses her own identity in order to create space for the invasive tendencies of the child's imperial ego. The cultural stereotyping of selfless mothering (which, although in decline, is still powerful) and the mutual recognition needs of the child for a real concrete subjectivity in his mother create powerful and dangerous contradictions in our conventional conceptions of child-rearing.

> The recognition a child seeks is something the mother is able to give only by virtue of her independent identity. Thus self psychology is misleading when it understands the mother's recognition of the child's feelings and accomplishments as maternal mirroring. The mother cannot (and should not) be a mirror, she must embody something of the not-me; she must be an independent other who responds in her different way. (Benjamin 1988: 24)

If the process of mutual recognition breaks down and one party denies the other, destroys her identity and wishes to control her, then he has negated himself because there is no longer an other to recognize him; there is no longer an other for him to desire. Thus if the mother gives the child no boundaries and sets no limits to his imperial ego, if she denies her own interests and identity needs and effectively removes her 'self' (by always putting the child's needs first), then she is no longer able to be a credible other for him. As Benjamin says, she is effectively destroyed, and not just in fantasy. Unfortunately, the same movement reversed simply locates the problem in the child. If the mother tries to break the child's will and refuses any compromise then it is her ego that is imperial in its invasion of the child's psyche. In these circumstances, the child must now obliterate his ego. There can be no winners in a process where mother and child alternately deny themselves and then seek retaliatory vengeance. Only mutual recognition between real subjects will enable both of them to develop into ethical and moral subjects equipped with the motivation and ability to operate successfully with the interactive communicative requirements demanded by a postconventional world. The values of autonomy, morality and authenticity which are derived from communicative reason are only possible between people who are able and willing to treat other people as subjects like themselves. Intimacy and confluent love is only possible between such people. The difficulties often experienced in the relations between mothers and sons are illustrative of how this process can fail.

Since women are almost universally the primary care-takers of small children, then the process of differentiation and mutual recognition for both boys and girls is heavily geared to only one parental gender. This can create special difficulties for boys; for, whilst all children identify with their first loved one, boys, in their need to define themselves as a different sex, must dissolve this identification. Boys achieve their masculinity by denying the original identification with their mothers. With this hiatus the boy risks losing his capacity for mutual recognition. There is a danger that the feelings of emotional attunement, harmony and empathic understanding of mother's needs and feelings become associated with the femininity that gets abandoned in his dis-identification with his mother. He is still able to cognitively accept that the other is separate; but as emotional attunement is now experienced as dangerously close to losing one's newly found masculine identity, his capacity to recognize the other as a real subject is seriously diminished, and in some cases eliminated. As a consequence, the other, and especially the female other, becomes related to as an object. In this process of objectification, rationality (that is, the limited instrumental and strategic form of rationality), rather than feelings and emotions,[4] becomes the mode of exchange in relationships. This form of objectifying rationality suppresses the other's subjectivity, and Benjamin defines it as a 'false differentiation'. Once initiated the process of false differentiation carries high costs for the boy that becomes a man, for the women in his life and for the ecological environment of a society dominated by objectifying instrumental reason. His ability to interact in mutual erotic love is diminished with the result that erotic love becomes psychological and physical domination. The woman ceases to become an independent subject but is projected as an object, as nature, less than human. With the breakdown of mutual recognition, male identity resides on only one side of the equation of reciprocity: difference, separation and self-sufficiency triumph over sharing, connection and dependency. Such socialization processes can only fail to create adults equipped with the competences to act ethically and morally.

This identification of the lack of maternal subjectivity is not meant to be an attack on mothers, rather it offers a critique of the distorted social processes that inhibit such subjectivity. In the meantime, it seems to me that counselling and psychotherapy cannot be 'value-free' on such issues. They have a clear moral and ethical commitment, as defined by communicative rationality, not just to offer help to the victims (both women and men) of this distorted socialization process, but also to understand that such help is not simply the reduction of stress and symptoms but also involves the creation of an opportunity for such people to rewrite the narrative of their distorted past in the light of an autonomous and authentic future identity.[5]

If mutuality is deformed by objectification, the opposite of this process is not absolute 'oneness'. Benjamin is clear that sameness and difference exist simultaneously in mutual recognition. Mutual fusion is not the goal. Feelings and experiences of similarity and sharing must leave enough room for difference if they are to feel real. Indeed, it is the very fact that self and other are not merged that gives feelings of extreme closeness and intimacy their depth and soulful yearning. It is only the externality of the other that gives intimacy its richness. Mutuality is the ability to share feelings and intentions without desiring or demanding control, to experience similar states whilst acknowledging difference. This finds its most notable expression in adults' erotic union:

> The capacity to enter into states in which distinctness and union are reconciled underlies the most intense experience of adult erotic life. In erotic union we can experience that form of mutual recognition in which both partners lose themselves in each other without loss of self; they lose self-consciousness without loss of awareness. Thus early experiences of mutual recognition already prefigure the dynamics of erotic life. (Benjamin 1988: 29)

The intersubjective viewpoint is to be distinguished from that of self psychology (as represented by Kohut 1977) and much of psychoanalytic theory. These theories tend to disparage dependency and inflate the importance of independence as the goal of maturity. They have difficulty in distinguishing other people, as subjects in their own right, from their role as an 'object' for the active subject. From this perspective development occurs through separation and individuation, by taking something from the object and internalizing it – the independent and isolated subject is seen as taking something from the other who acts as an object. From this viewpoint, socialization acts like a strategic and instrumental process and is clearly at odds with the mutuality required by communicative rationality.

Object relations theory offered a development on psychoanalytic theory and self psychology. In object relations theory the need for relationships is understood. Sometimes relationships are with whole persons, other times they are with parts of persons. These 'objects' can be both external and internal to the self. With the phenomena of projection internally experienced objects are felt to be outside, and with introjection external objects are felt to be internally experienced. Benjamin argues that these concepts do not sufficiently articulate the active, reciprocal and mutual nature of exchanges between infants and adults. Object relations theory misses the importance of the paradoxical balance between the recognition of the other and assertion of the self. I would argue further that because object relations theory is not grounded in a more comprehensive intersubjective tradition like that provided by communicative rationality, it cannot generate the latter's ethical and moral positions. Moreover, this strictly limits the ability of object relations to develop critiques of the social and political environment within which it rests. Samuels offers us a useful insight:

> Object relations dealers focus on intrapsychic and interpersonal explanations for personality development and dysfunction. They tend to rule out sociopolitical or other collective aspects of psychological suffering. The version of personality that object relations theory presents, with its accent on the decisive part played by early experiences, maternal containment, and the move toward the depressive position or stage of concern, is, in many senses, little more than a reproduction of the kind of personality that the culture which surrounds object relations theory already valorizes. If we want to apprehend personality, we have to consider the historical context in which personality exists. For us in the West, this implies that the personality-ideal (to coin a phrase) will reward personality theories that are congruent with our humanistic–romantic–individualistic traditions. Hence…object relations theory cannot avoid supporting the present-day arrangements over political power and social structures…Object relations theories may have attained their popularity, not because they mount a challenge to the existing order, but because of this secret alignment with the existing order. (Samuels 1993: 275–6)

Whilst Samuels acknowledges that projective identification is a useful therapeutic tool, it is limited '…because the concept of projective identification just does not get hold of the collectivity of persons, of where they are already joined together on a psychosocial level, of where things are shared. Hence, projective identification is a relatively weak tool of political analysis' (1993: 277). Intersubjective socialization theories developed from communicative rationality do not have this problem because, from the beginning, the individual and society are inextricably linked. From the necessary presuppositions of communicative action we can generate not only intersubjective conceptions of socialization but also moral theories. This not only enables us to understand the path of an individual life in terms of its authenticity, but also provides a critical analysis of the structures of a society which oppress and otherwise distort the individual's ability to lead a moral and ethical life. Later on I shall spend some time considering how communicative rationality provides us with a radical critique of contemporary society and the role of counselling in this context. For the moment I wish to express my agreement with Samuels when he says:

> The unavoidable way in which innate and environmental realms are first positioned with regard to a single person, so that the object relations consensus can perform its soldering function, makes it difficult to go beyond the individual perspective to a more collective analysis…The assumption that a good-enough environment is all that innate potential of an individual requires to flower, and that this is determined within the nuclear family and in the first months of life, is hopelessly passive in the face of problematic social and political structures…wellbeing may not be achievable in a society characterized by alienation. The time-honoured values of humanistic

ethics are not free of political bias and complicity in the construction of an oppressive and conformist society. (1993: 271)

The power of Benjamin's account is that it enables the radical critique that Samuels (1993) and Cushman (1995) find wanting in other developmental psychologies. The theory of intersubjectivity can easily articulate the origins of domination and the dialectics of control. In order to exist for myself, I have also to exist for an other. There is no way out of this dependency and interdependency. Following Benjamin, we can see that if I destroy the other then there is no one to recognize me – I would be connected to a dead or empty subjectivity, which is no connection at all, with the result that I cannot see myself because the other does not recognize me. Counsellors will have experienced domineering men and women who have so oppressed their partner that the 'satisfaction' obtained in this expression of power is soon undermined by the lack of recognition gained from this empty other. 'If the other denies the recognition, my acts have no meaning; if he is so far above me that nothing I do can alter his attitude toward me, I can only submit. My desire and agency can find no outlet, except in the form of obedience' (Benjamin 1988: 53). Benjamin calls this the dialectic of control:

> If I completely control the other, then the other ceases to exist, and if the other completely controls me, then I cease to exist. A condition of our independent existence is recognising the other. True independence means sustaining the essential tension of these contradictory impulses; that is, both asserting the self and recognising the other. Domination is the consequence of refusing this condition. (1988: 53)

In mutual recognition we accept that others are separate but nonetheless are able to share like feelings and intentions. The loss of complete sovereignty and imperial control is compensated by the pleasure and love of sharing communion or solidarity with another conscious subject. Extreme self-sufficiency and independence leads to the detachment from the other, whilst the opposite condition of extreme dependency obliterates the separate reality of the other. The consequence of both these positions is either domination or submission.[6] Omnipotence and servitude reflect the absence of intersubjectivity, the breakdown of connection and differentiation. A relationship characterized by domination is one in which mutuality has been replaced by complementarity. Whereas mutuality is the connection between subjects, in complementarity the self is subject and the other is object so that my subjective needs are fed by the other who acts as passive object.

> In the radical separation of subject and object we perceive again the inability to grasp the aliveness of the other; we hear the echo of the unmovable, unmoving character of the master. Yet again the denial of recognition leaves the omnipotent

self imprisoned in his mind, reflecting on the world from behind a wall of glass. (Benjamin 1988: 190)

Socialization as Evolutionary Stages

There have been many theories of psychological development using the concept of evolutionary stages; for example, those of Piaget, Kohlberg, Maslow, Wilber, Erikson, Habermas and Kegan. My purpose here is not to provide an in-depth summary of this position, rather to indicate how such a perspective can be generated from the intersubjective model and how it links to moral development.

From the range of theorists in this area I am primarily interested in Kegan because his work is the most successful in explaining the continual process of development in terms of the intersubjective processes of mutual recognition. Like Benjamin he distances himself from the dominant tradition, which extends from Freud to Rogers, with its conception of growth that emphasizes autonomy, separation and distinctness over dependency and connectedness. Kegan is committed to a psychology that respects both poles and the relationship between them. Similarly he distances himself from Kohlberg and Piaget who concentrate on an abstract notion of personal construction. Whilst this approach is important, it ignores the equally important mechanisms of the construction of self through affective relationships of mutual recognition, what Kegan calls 'making meaning':

> this constructive-developmental perspective [Kohlberg and Piaget – MB] has taken no interest whatever in the equally important, but quite different, side of the same activity – the way that activity is experienced by a dynamically maintained 'self,' the rhythms and labours of the struggle to make meaning, to have meaning, to protect meaning, to enhance meaning, to lose meaning, and to lose the 'self' along the way. The Piagetian approach, viewing meaning-making from the outside, descriptively, has powerfully advanced a conception of that activity as naturally epistemological; it is about the balancing and re-balancing of subject and object, for self and other. But what remains ignored from this approach is a consideration of the same activity from the inside...the 'participative.' From the point of view of the 'self,' then, what is at stake in preserving any given balance is the ultimate question of whether the 'self' shall continue to *be*, a naturally *onto*logical matter. (1981: 12)

'Meaning' in this context bears a strong resemblance to our notion of communicative action geared towards reaching an understanding. For Kegan, meaning-making is the primary human activity and is irreducible. It depends on someone who recognizes you. As he says, we may be fit and healthy but we can still perish without meaning.

The proposition is that human development is an evolutionary activity that is both cognitive and affective – we *are* this activity. The emergence of our feelings and our cognitions is directly related to the continual attempt by the person to create a sense of a 'centre' or a self out of the push and pull of the interaction between myself and others. 'I am suggesting that the source of our emotions is the phenomenological experience of evolving – of defending, surrendering, and reconstructing a centre' (Kegan 1981: 81–2). Maintaining, losing and reintegrating this balance at higher stages is a constant feature of evolutionary growth. At each stage the other gains a little more recognition of its own subjectivity and integrity.

At lower stages of personal growth you are an instrument which I use to satisfy my needs and express my will, but, as I develop, this aspect of you becomes internalized such that I may now fulfil my own instrumental needs. Later on the recognition of the other develops further so that the other is recognized as being separate from me but not really different. A teenager in a gang of friends needs the others to recognize and affirm his identity, but the other friends are not really understood to be separate subjects. Eventually the other becomes an individual and so do I. However, at this stage the developing self is so concerned with its own sense of separateness that it becomes closely identified with the task of psychologically managing itself and its formal relationship to the world through duties, performances, roles and careers. This can lead to a highly individualized and atomized sense of self. Nevertheless, at this stage I develop the capacity to observe my performance so that my self is less at risk from the grave humiliations associated with performance failure. With this growing confidence in performance a new self emerges whose community stretches beyond itself, indeed: 'The community is for the first time a "universal" one in that all persons, by virtue of their being persons, are eligible for membership. The group which this self knows as "its own" is not a pseudo-species, but the species' (Kegan 1981: 104).

It is at this level that the postconventional moral and ethical subject emerges; the evolutionary process of mutual recognition reaches the stage where both parties in communicative action are able to recognize each other as true subjects. Intimacy is more acceptable. Through the dynamic of mutual recognition the self surrenders independence for interdependence. A self able to interact with internal psychological subsystems is also more able to share itself with real external psyches; the individual itself is able to give itself up to an other and share experiences whilst respecting mutual distinctness.

Kegan defines the two orientations of connection and separation as the two greatest yearnings in human experience.[7] Whilst describing these as 'yearnings' gives us a sense of how we feel them, I believe that Habermas's theory of communicative reason has given us a means of analyzing and understanding them. However, what is of interest to both Kegan and Habermas, is not just these yearnings but the *relation* between them. This lifelong tension creates the dynamic and motion to evolve to higher states of balance between these two poles. Each balance or equilibrium resolves the tension in a different way.

What Habermas, Benjamin and Kegan have in common is the notion that the transition to the postconventional results from, and creates, the problematization of our hitherto customary and naive acceptance of the givenness of our understanding of self and the external world. The legitimacy of existing norms is no longer taken for granted and they are now subject to rational justification. Young adults expect their parents to be able to explain why something like visiting their grandparents (which often feels boring) should be enacted. Respect for the law is not sufficient, rules must be shown to be rational and valid. At this level the essential feature of moral action is that the resolution of conflict is based on justified reasoning alone.

> As we have seen, this syndrome disintegrates when a hypothetical attitude is introduced. Before the reflective gaze of a participant in discourse the social world dissolves into so many conventions in need of justification. The empirical store of traditional norms is split into social facts and norms. The latter have lost their backing in the certainties of the lifeworld and must now be justified in the light of principles. Thus the *orientation to principles of justice* and ultimately to the *procedure of norm-justifying discourse* is the outcome of the inevitable moralization of a social world become problematic. Such are the ideas of justice that, at the postconventional stage, take the place of conformity to roles and norms. (Habermas 1995b: 165)

Once the postconventional level has been reached, further psychological development cannot be described in terms of natural stages. Once a subject reaches this reflective level of moral consciousness, neither the psychologist nor any other expert can identify further stages as if they followed each other in the same naturally evolutionary way that they do at lower levels. The asymmetry between the psychological expert and the subject disappears as both now inhabit the same postconventional level. The same is true for the relationship between client and psychotherapist once the client has developed to the postconventional stage. From this point onwards the psychotherapist, scientist, psychologist and philosopher do not occupy a ground superior in moral development than anybody else. Any of these who are involved in making moral judgements at the postconventional level are participants in a joint venture in which the sole arbiter of competing claims is the better argument.

That the fulfilment of the psychological evolutionary process ends in a postconventional consciousness which is anchored in self-reflexiveness does not come without a price. For some the price is too high, but this is, I believe, a misunderstanding. White reminds us that Foucault and his sympathizers are ambivalent about the rational, self-reflective subject of the humanist tradition because it '...becomes all too easily an accomplice in those modern networks of power which subjugate and provide authoritative scripts for our "bodies and pleasures" ' (1988: 145). Thus the theories I have outlined become, in the view of this tradition, state-endorsed processes that create conformity through *self*-discipline and *self*-policing.

> From the Foucauldian point of view, the self-reflective, responsible, Habermasian subject shares this danger. Not only is its developmental genesis one of distancing itself from 'inner nature,' but it is also easily drawn into networks of 'normalising' 'bio-power.' In both these ways, the Habermasian subject apparently shows itself to be inhospitable to its own pre-rational, embodies otherness. (White 1988: 145–6)

We are already familiar with this viewpoint in our comments on the work of Rose (1999). Although such Foucauldian criticisms dutifully keep us aware of some congruence between state processes and identity formation they are hopelessly totalizing and gloomy. To my mind, Weir captures much more accurately the paradox and, in the balance, the advantages of a reflexive postconventional identity.

> The capacity, and the responsibility, to problematize and define one's own meaning (one's own identity) is both the burden and the privilege of modern subjects. As a subject who is no longer defined by a fixed position in a social system, I am (relatively) free (or, at the least, I aspire to a normative ideal of freedom) to determine, through my practises, who I am and who I am going to be. The flip side of this freedom is the burden of self-defining; every action, every position is open to question. This freedom and this responsibility are absolutely inescapable in our daily lives. At the same time, along with the increasing need for self-definition goes an increasing production and differentiation of identity-attributes: of possible roles, attachments and affiliations, values, beliefs and commitments, needs and desires, styles and modes of expression. We are exposed to more and more frameworks for reflection on and demystification of the constitutive influences which shape our identities (such as family and relationship dynamics, unconscious processes, collective identities...) (Weir 1995: 264)

From this very brief analysis I believe that we have outlined some indications of how socialization creates a self that is competent to act morally, ethically and lovingly. At the same time we can see how this process takes the form of evolutionary developmental stages which involve the whole personality rather than just the rational-cognitive faculties, and Benjamin has revealed to us how distorted socialization can lead to domination.

Kegan helps us to understand that this evolutionary path is not just any road but is a universal psychological highway. As we develop we become more in tune with the limited range of possibilities made available to us by the necessary preconditions of communicative action. The counsellor helps us to find this path when we lose our way.

The heart of the constructive-developmental framework – and the source of its own potential for growth – does not lie so much in its account of stages or sequences of meaning organizations, but in its capacity to illuminate a universal ongoing process (call it 'meaning-making,' 'adaptation,' equilibration,' or 'evolution') which may very well be the fundamental context of personality development. Accordingly, it is to this process and its experience, rather than to stages, that I would direct the invested attention of the constructive-developmental counsellor. (Kegan 1981: 264)

The constructive-developmental clinician locates himself or herself in the processes of growth. She regards the client's disorder not as his sickness, nor his undoing, but as the throes of his own becoming...That development she seeks to facilitate is itself the growth of the truth. (Kegan 1981: 294–5)[8]

Finally, Wilber provide us with a group of concepts that may improve our understanding of this process of evolutionary development. There are two types of movement – *translation* and *transformation*. The former represents a change in the surface structure and the latter a change in the deep structure of consciousness. He invites us to comprehend the difference between these concepts through the analogy of a multi-storey building. If we move the furniture around on the fourth floor, that is translation; if we move them to the fifth floor, that is transformation. Once on the fifth floor we may then engage in new acts of furniture moving or translating. Psychological development requires both. Transformation to a higher level will not be possible until we have done sufficient translation at our current level; however, endless translation will not achieve transformation. Wilber continues: 'Any psychosocial institution that validates or facilitates translation we call *legitimate*; any that validates or facilitates transformation we call *authentic*' (1990: 266).

Legitimacy acts on the horizontal axis and measures the degree of integration, coherence and stability of a given level of psychological development. One of the greatest needs of individuals is to find legitimacy for the present level of development. Legitimacy therefore is an intersubjective process providing mutual recognition and confirmation that one's identity is appropriate to the evolutionary stage attained. Legitimacy is linked to levels of translation achieved within a specific level. We also need a measure of the degree of vertical transformation – the concept of authenticity provides this. Thus we may well act legitimately at one level by having a high degree of integration and stability at that level; however, when compared to social expectations we may well be 'stuck' at a lower level than is appropriate and therefore be acting, in Wilber's terms, inauthentically. Consequently, any social practice related to the production of psychological development (for example, the family, the education system or any religious systems) should be judged on the basis of its success in creating legitimate and authentic identities. To merely confirm and validate a person at his or her present stage of adaptation would be a failure to work on the authentic axis of achieving development to higher psychological levels.

Counselling and psychotherapy can be so judged. Whilst providing security and safety for people experiencing distress at their current level of development, including relief from symptoms, is a legitimate therapeutic task, if the counselling process does not also provide the opportunity for authentic development, it is failing. It may well be that the authenticity axis of going into deeper self-understanding may have to wait until the clients are sufficiently well held (by which time some clients may have left counselling). It may also be the case that developmental issues may need to be addressed by a different therapist. In any and every case it should be the ideal therapeutic intent to offer the client the real possibility of psychological development over and above symptom relief, and to provide suitable encouragement to the client to make use of the opportunity at a pace that suits them. Whilst providing choice for the client is important, the current consumerist tone of such recommendations seems more suited to the marketing model of a shopper selecting goods from a supermarket shelf than to the idea of a person making existential choices. 'Choosing' to transform to a higher level is a difficult concept because we are unconsciously tied to the obviousness of the present (troubled) level. Current counselling practice is becoming increasingly conservative and conformist as freedom of choice becomes limited to acts of translation (rearranging the furniture) at the current level, and less concerned with transformation. It is also politically conservative because it leaves clients ill-equipped to challenge the social–political construction of their identity (and its malaise) as developmental work becomes increasingly marginalized under the impact of brief counselling, behavioural therapy and counselling provided by non-independent institutions.

Moral Emotions

I have spent some considerable time discussing various aspects of morals and ethics, and it now seems appropriate that we should draw our attention to the role of moral emotions and feelings. It would not be possible to develop our moral character if we do not learn a sensibility towards moral feelings. During our brief survey of moral emotions it is worth remembering that, although they have an important role in sensitizing us to moral phenomena, they cannot provide a sound basis for moral judgement. Moreover, in the culture of therapy, feelings tend to be over-rated. This is partially (and to some extent understandably) a reaction to the highly rationalized and patriarchal dominant culture; on the other hand it is simply a conceptual and phenomenal mistake.[9] There is a danger that we perceive feelings as being primal, raw and natural. Rather, we should see them as being structured, constituted, possessors of a history and having cognitive content. Like most other things, they are also constructed by social interaction:

> Suppose that the world either was impervious to our emotions, or instantly and utterly capitulated before them. Suppose, for instance, that, whenever we loved someone, our love was never returned, not out of indifference or because love had been pledged elsewhere, but because the thought of such reciprocity never occurred to the person. Or suppose that, whenever we were angry, the object of our anger dropped down dead. Our emotions either totally determined the lives of others, or made no impact on them whatsoever. Furthermore suppose that this was, not only how the world was, but how, in our fantasies, we represented it. Our emotions would, I suspect, die of the lack of interaction, of the lack of narrative. (Wollheim 1999: 224)

Emotions cannot simply be feelings like a racing heart, butterflies in the stomach or a yearning for fusion. Although these experiences may accompany certain feelings, there is also a cognitive content to feelings. For example, my feeling of anger is linked to a belief that some unjust harm has being done, and my feeling of intimate love for another is connected to a belief concerning the good character of the loved one. Indeed, emotions would be of little interest to us if they were simply things that 'happened to us'.

Before looking at the particular nature of specific moral feelings like guilt and shame it might be helpful to consider some of the more general functions associated with moral emotions. For example, we would not be able to experience certain conflicts of action as morally relevant unless we felt that the integrity of a person was under threat or in danger of being violated. It is the intuitive feeling of worry or anxiety that stimulates us to understand the moral danger our daughter is in when she exhibits behaviour that is self-abusive. Feelings enable us to *perceive* something as moral. They give a texture or a timbre to an event such that a person who cannot interpret moral phenomena will be blind to moral feelings and vice versa. Our moral sensibility enables us to feel sympathy or compassion for a vulnerable person. Also our moral feelings orient us in making moral judgements, although they do not provide a rational basis for such judgements they do provide us with an experiential basis for our initial intuitive judgements.

The cognitive content of emotions is shown by the fact that we do not regard feelings of guilt, shame, loyalty and so on as simply being expressions of sentiment and preference. The guilt I feel in perpetually being late for appointments will be interpreted by others not as a quirk of my character but as the expected emotional response to a failure of character. Finally, if we recall Habermas's concept of solidarity we may recall that the flip side of justice is solidarity – concern for the fate of all others is important when justice depends on a process of people participating in discourse. We need to care about others before we judge them.

Certain moral emotions also express something in addition to a cognitive content. They relate to a person's sense of self – the sense that the person has of herself. Emotions like pride, guilt, humiliation and shame are experienced as deviations from some norm. The self is the object of these emotions which provide an assessment of that self. Moral emotions therefore provide an attitude that is reflexive. They are also directly linked to the person's sense of authenticity – the validity claim that we have discussed previously becomes the person's judgement on her own validity as an authentic person. These moral emotions are therefore congruent with the validity claims inherent in communicative action. Coming from a very different tradition, Wollheim develops a conception of the authentic very similar to our own:

> I claim that what is more directly involved is that awareness which the person, any person, has of himself, and which allows him to think of himself as an ongoing person: influenced by his past, living in the present, and concerned for his future. The moral emotions . . . are triggered by something that the person experiences as a disturbance of, or as a threat to, this sense of himself. There is a fall in his sense of security, and this gives rise to anxiety. (1999: 151)

The norm against which moral emotions of self-assessment like guilt and shame judge us is that of the authentic person or the person with integrity. As Taylor (1985: 108–9) indicates, the person capable of experiencing the emotions of self-assessment sees herself as a moral agent, as someone who thinks about herself and her life evaluatively. If her identity and self-perception is to successfully see herself as a moral agent, then she must be seen by self and others to act in accordance with her moral precepts. In other words, she has to act with a moral consistency which brings us back to the validity claim of authenticity.

Guilt and shame are not the only moral emotions. However, I am especially interested in them because they are emotions of self-assessment, and because, in the late twentieth century and early twenty-first century, the relationship between these two emotions is changing. With guilt we feel self-recrimination because our actions have transgressed a legitimate norm. Usually this also involves, either intentionally or unintentionally, causing harm to others, though the fact that I can feel guilty about wasting my time watching a stupid TV programme when I am harming nobody but myself suggests that the crucial element in guilt is not harming others but doing something that is forbidden. The experience of feeling guilt is usually that of feeling criticized, exposed and subject to the critical comments of others (be they real or internalized) which often stimulate feelings of fear and anxiety. We usually feel guilty with regard to a specific action that we have done rather than with our whole identity, and the usual, though not necessarily, response is to repair the damage done to others. By failing to make the crucial phone call that my manager asked me to do, a client had a wasted journey. My feeling is one of guilt and I may well seek to make amends to both the client and the manager. With everyday guilt the self is not totally damaged, rather we feel that we have brought some temporary and localized damage to a self that otherwise remains the same. On the positive side, guilt has the obvious social function of maintaining social order, and, as mentioned earlier, guilt provides the individual with useful antennae helping him to maintain a good balance between self and other in social relationships.

Whilst I am collecting all these emotions under the umbrella conception of moral emotions, it might help to recollect my earlier distinction between morals and ethics. In this context guilt is usually understood as a moral emotion in the narrower sense of relating to universal moral codes, whereas shame is more of an ethical emotion linked to the self's sense of authenticity. Taylor would agree:

> There is no reason to deny that shame in all its occurrences is a moral emotion, provided that morality is not thought of just in terms of adhering to or breaking certain moral rules, but is taken to include personal morality, a person's own view of how he ought to live and what he ought to be. The final self-directed adverse judgement in shame is always the same: that he is a lesser person than he should be ... (1985: 76–7)

Shame is therefore only possible if a person has a pre-existing sense of self-worth, self-respect, integrity or authenticity. Such a person has to believe in certain ethical values concerning her life project and what constitutes an authentic representation of fulfilment of this project over time. There has to be a self to respect, and that self must already be committed to a significant set of values that gain credibility only through their enactment and fulfilment. Shame cannot be the result of trivial failures. The sense of crushing failure and humiliation that represents the feeling of shame comes from significant failures of the self to enact or embody the personal, ethical values it has designated as being an authentic representation of its own identity. This is why the act of being unfaithful to an intimate partner can cause such terrible anguish for our deceit and lack of loyalty are shocking illustrations of our lack of integrity. When acting with integrity we maintain our sense of selfhood through the feeling of self-respect that is achieved when our actions are congruent with our own ethical system. The sheer negativity involved in feeling shame therefore provides a massive incentive to us to act with authenticity. The opposite of shame is pride or self-esteem – confidence in the integrity of the narrative of our self-identity.

When feeling shame all aspects of self feel under attack. The feeling of degradation associated with shame comes not just from the witnesses to the shameful deed, but our own self is degraded in our own eyes and absolutely so. The sense of exposure involved reveals to the subject that he is inferior to what he believed or hoped himself to be. The revelation that his identity is inferior generates feelings of helplessness and hopelessness such that there seems to be nothing he can do about it. But this isn't quite the case. A person that felt no shame would have abandoned completely any values that he lived by; he would have jettisoned the person he once was. Paradoxically, because shame only exists in relation to a valued sense of self, he still has some hold on the person he once was so that there is still the possibility that he can regain his old identity. He may do this by constructively rejecting the standards by which others judged him, or he may change the standards.

Guilt and shame relate to integrity in different ways. Taylor (1985: 134–5) argues that when she feels guilty the agent interprets herself as having done something that she regards as alien to herself with the result that she is in danger of splitting and disowning the guilty act. A further anxiety connected to guilt is that, if this splitting takes place, the aspect of her personality which did the forbidden deed might assume control; consequently, it is important to the person feeling guilt to purge herself of this alien aspect and thereby regain a measure of control. Guilt is therefore different from shame in that it involves the recognition of the emergence of a worse self, rather than a recognition of the failure of a worthy self. These differences explain other contrasting features:

> They explain why guilt but not shame is rightly connected with fear and anxiety; an alien self whose doings conflicts with the agent's evaluations is indeed something to fear and feel anxious about. In shame the agent himself is diminished, and a diminished self need not be feared; it is to something to be despised ... For this reason there is in cases of shame a loss of competence in either his values or in his capacity to live up to them which is not to be found in cases of guilt. (Taylor 1985: 135–6)

Drawing from Wollheim (1999: 155–6) and Giddens (1991: 68) we can outline other differences between shame and guilt (see Table 3.1). Kohut (1977) and Giddens (1991) draw interesting parallels between the development of modern civilization and a move in general consciousness from the prevalence of guilt to the new prevalence of shame. As we have seen, guilt carries the connotations of moral transgression: it is derived from a failure in personal content to comply with a moral imperative.

> It is a form of anxiety which is most prominent in types of society where a behaviour is governed according to established moral precepts, including those laid down and sanctioned by tradition. Shame is more directly and pervasively related to basic trust than is guilt, because guilt concerns specific forms of behaviour or cognition rather than threatening the integrity of the self as such. Unlike guilt, shame directly corrodes a sense of security in both self and surrounding social milieu. The more self-identity becomes internally referential, the more shame comes to play a fundamental role in the adult personality. The individual no longer lives primarily by extrinsic moral precepts but by means of the reflexive organization of the self. This

Table 3.1   Comparison of Guilt and Shame

Guilt	Shame
Related to discreet acts that violate something that is forbidden	Related to issues of self-identity – the whole person
Asks others to forgive what we have done	Asks others to forget what we have become
Autonomy is achieved by surmounting repressions	Autonomy is achieved by insight into the nature of the narrative of self-identity
Exposes transgressions	Exposes aspects of self
Feeling of wrongdoing towards an other	Feeling of inadequacy towards an other
Trust is based on an absence of betrayal	Trust is based on transparency – knowing and being known by the other
Improvement is represented by the desire to make reparation	Improvement is represented by the desire to change the self

> is an important point, since it follows that modern civilization is not founded, as Freud thought, on the renunciation of desire. (Giddens 1991: 153)

If Giddens's hunch about the growing empirical prevalence of shame is correct then it provides indirect support for our thesis. A postconventional moral consciousness has abandoned the naive acceptance of given moral codes in relation to which guilt acts as the emotional warden. A postconventional morality requires evolutionary socialization processes that create self-reflexive mature adults able to act authentically and autonomously. Such people must have a highly developed sense of self which is able to maintain itself in multiple roles and in a manner that guarantees its authenticity by displaying a transparency to others and to one's own self. It is through this medium of transparency that the moral emotion of shame operates in support of the authentic self. 'Shame requires a sophisticated type of self-consciousness...It is plainly the state of self-consciousness which centrally relies on the concept of another, for the fault of being seen as one might be seen by another is the catalyst for the emotion' (Taylor 1985: 67).

Whilst having concentrated on guilt and shame, it is important to acknowledge those moral emotions which are not connected with self-assessment, for sorrow and love are emotions that are linked to connection with others. Our intersubjective theory of personality development clearly underlines the importance of the dialectic between self and other. With guilt and shame the emphasis is on the critical judgement of the self by others. Love and sorrow pick up the theme of affective bonds created in the process of mutual recognition and are moral emotions concerned with our making and breaking of connections with others. Love and sorrow act as moral emotions supporting our ability to care for oneself and for others by informing our understanding of how one should act in a caring capacity – they enable us to see experiences of our attachment and detachment as relevant to our moral development. All these moral emotions can therefore not be interpreted as being either value-free or simply just 'feelings'. The therapist needs to be aware that they express a moral or ethical inner core and signify that the process of therapeutic interaction with such emotions is necessarily a moral act.

The Decentred Self

> Since Copernicus, we have known that the earth is not the 'centre' of the universe. Since Marx, we have known that the human subject, the economic, political or philosophical ego is not the 'centre' of history – and even, in opposition to the Philosophers of the Enlightenment and to Hegel, that history has no 'centre' but possesses a structure which has no necessary 'centre' except an ideological misrecognition. In turn, Freud has discovered for us that the real subject, the individual in his unique essence, has not the form of an ego, centred on the 'ego', on 'consciousness' or on 'existence' – whether this is the existence of the for-itself, or the body-proper or of 'behaviour' – that the human subject is de-centred, constituted by a structure which has no 'centre' either, except in the imaginary misrecognition of the 'ego', i.e. in the ideological formations in which it 'recognizes' itself. (Althusser 1971: 201)

When considering the definition of a decentred self that is appropriate to our project we must bear in mind the debt that this conception owes to the poststructuralist and postmodern traditions and then distance ourselves from this interpretation. We have already noted the importance of the Copernican revolution in terms of the postmodern critique of the hegemony of the philosophy of the subject. The rejection of man as the measure of all things has opened up the possibility of the many insights that Althusser enumerates. However, this process and the ensuing relativism have gone too far. Consequently, we have used Habermas's theory of communicative reason to provide, what I hope is, an effective rebuttal. Similarly, the postmodern dismembering of the self into the decentred self needs substantial revision so that we may create a notion of the decentred self that not only has an intuitively better sense of fit with lived experience, but is also consonant with the precepts of communicative rationality and evolutionary developmental psychology.

Giddens, using an argument that can be traced back to Wittgenstein (1953), reminds us about the extremity of the postmodern attack on essentialism. Nothing has an essence, so this argument goes, and everything is constituted in the ever-flexible and mobile interplay of signifiers. If meaning is a linguistic and conceptual process which operates through defining a thing by what it is not, then such concepts as 'self-identity' falsely indicate an 'essentialist unity'. I agree with Giddens and Wittgenstein that this attack is misplaced. Of course difference plays a role in defining meaning, but this is not an infinite process nor is it a never-ending circle. Meaning is anchored in everyday, pragmatic concepts of use or, in Habermas's terms, the pragmatics of speech embedded in communicative action. There is therefore no philosophical reason why an acceptance that language is context-dependent prevents us from legitimately understanding that a concept like self-identity represents a human characteristic that can maintain itself over different contexts of space and time and is by that fact a meaningful concept. Whilst postmodernism does provide us with some useful conceptions that will help us create a useful notion of a decentred self, we are not obliged to follow this mode of thought to the point where self and self-identity have no meaning. Labouvie-Vief indicates how this once fertile tradition has ended up with a very fixed outlook: '... they have tended to erect a new form of dogmatism, according to which integration, holism, and universality are 'out' and to be avoided at all cost' (1994: 262).[10]

Feeling that the concept of self-identity does contain real meaning I shall outline a number of characteristics of self-identity that are compatible and constitutive of our conception of the decentred self. Following these 'unifying' aspects of our definition I shall consider how the decentred self can also be constructively theorized in terms of a plurality of selves. The decentred self has the following aspects of self-identity. This list owes much to Giddens (1991), Taylor (1996) and MacIntyre (1982).

Self as a Reflexive Project

> This is what distinguishes the classical writers from followers of Descartes, Locke, Kant, or just about anyone in the modern world. The turn to oneself is now also and inescapably a turn to oneself in the first-person perspective – a turn to the self as a self. This is what I mean by radical reflexivity. Because we are so deeply embedded in it, we cannot but reach for reflexive language. (Taylor 1996: 176)

In a post-traditional world our identity is no longer a phenomenon that we can naively accept nor is it something that our social role will completely define for us. Rather, it is a *self*-identity which we must constantly and consciously maintain and present to others. The reflexive project of the self consists in sustaining a coherent biographical narrative which is also open to revision and transformation. It takes place in social scenarios where we are constantly making multiple choices. Our lives are subject to constant planning decisions both in the short-term (meeting people involves complicated diary scheduling) and in the long-term sense of consciously making a life-plan.

In pre-modern times, transitions in people's lives have always involved the reconstruction of their identity. This was often ritualized into rites of passage; for example, the transition from adolescence to adulthood. In relatively stable cultures the change in identity was clearly defined. In modernity, such ritual processes barely exist so the process of psychological transformation has to be undertaken by the self in a reflexive operation on the self. Self-identity is not simply a set of characteristics of the self maintained across time and space; instead *it is such continuity* as interpreted reflexively by the person. This is confirmed by the ability to use 'I' in different contexts.

The Self as a Project Spanning the Past and the Future

The conscious sense of one's own lifespan becomes the characteristic metaphor and sense of destiny of the self. One's own history is interpreted and often rewritten in the light of an anticipated and projected future. Our sense of self derives a coherence and integrity from a conscious ordered awareness of the phases of our life from cradle to grave.

Reflexivity is Continuous and Pervasive

The self is not simply a discreet part of our identity that has certain moments to call its own. It becomes a pervasive feature of conscious life through which the individual constantly questions herself about her actions.

Self-identity Presumes a Narrative

Some theorists who question the existence of self-identity will argue that the different stages in a person's life represent different people rather than different aspects of the same person. The flaw in this argument is that personal identity is reduced to the sole factor of self-consciousness. Much more convincing is the argument that in order to have a sense of who we are, we need to have an understanding of our history and an anticipated future. As Taylor says, '... I can only know myself through the history of my maturations and regressions, overcomings and defeats. My self-understanding necessarily has temporal depths and incorporates narratives' (1996: 50). In order to communicatively interact with others in everyday life, the individual must have a biography that is recognizable to others and it must have a degree of authenticity in order for the actor to be taken as a real person. Such a person must integrate internal and external events and construct them into an ongoing narrative or story about the self.

I am what I may justifiably be taken by others to be in the course of living out a story that runs from my birth to my death; I am the *subject* of a history that is my own and no one else's, that has its own peculiar meaning. When someone complains – as do some of those who attempt or commit suicide – that his or her life is meaningless, he or she is often and perhaps characteristically complaining that the narrative of the life has become unintelligible to them, that it lacks any point, any movement towards a climax or a *telos*. Hence the point of doing any one thing rather than another at crucial junctures in their lives seems to such a person to have been lost. (MacIntyre 1982: 202)

Reflexivity Extends to the Body

Reflexive management of the self is extended to management of the body. To a greater degree than before the self finds expression and identity through the body. Negative aspects of this are represented by such conditions as anorexia, bulimia, obesity, fashion fetishism, working-out and so on. Lasch (1985) would interpret this as expressing a latent narcissism that is characteristic of late capitalist societies.

Evolutionary Development Maintains a Dynamic Relation between Opportunity and Risk

Giddens gets hold of this idea for us:

Letting go of the past, through the various techniques of becoming free from oppressive emotional habits, generates a multiplicity of opportunities for self-development. The world becomes full of potential ways of being and acting, in terms of experimental involvements which the individual is now able to initiate. It would not be true to say that the psychologically liberated person faces risks while the more traditional self does not; rather, what is at stake is the *secular consciousness of risk*, as inherent in calculative strategies to be adopted in relation to the future. (1991: 78)

The Need for Authenticity

To be the subject of a narrative of one's life is to be accountable for the actions that compromise this narrative. That is, the story of my life is open to be held accountable in terms of its authenticity. Similarly, my story is part of somebody else's narrative so that I may hold them to account. The theme of authenticity, of being true to oneself, runs through the narrative of my life. To act authentically involves more than using our self-knowledge. It means discovering or, more accurately, constructing our 'true' self by working through the emotional blocks that prevent us from understanding ourselves as we really are. If we ignore the emotional obstacles we will, as Freud says, be condemned to repeat them.

The Life Course is Seen as a Series of Transitions

Transitions like puberty, leaving home, marriage, parenting and divorce become reflexively understood as constituent factors in our self-development.

Modern self-identity is a complex phenomenon characterized by its reflexive nature. I have attempted to show that there is a lot more involved than mere 'self-awareness'. These concepts of self-identity bring a thematic unity to our understanding of the development of self and the nature of modern character.[11] I now want to illustrate how these notions of self-identity are compatible with a more pluralistic understanding of the self.

Postmodernism and poststructuralism are not the only traditions to have a concern with a plurality of selves. Jungian psychology has a similar outlook ranging from the more simplistic opposites of masculine and feminine to Hillman's much more radical conception of psychological polytheism:

> An archetypal psychology that would give proper due to many dominants, that would recognize the interpenetrating psychological reality of many Gods – and not merely the highest: Yahweh, Zeus, ego, or self – and the psychological legitimacy of each cosmos, is forced to question, even abandon, psychological monotheism and its emphasis, for instance, upon the ego-self axis, which is, after all, only the usual Judeo–Protestant monotheism in psychological language. This language usually presents the ego in a direct line of confrontation and covenant with a single self, represented by images of unity (mandalas, crystals, balls, wise men, and other patterns of order). But according to Jung the self has many archetypal instances. The puzzling relation between self and the archetypes reduces the ancient enigma of the many-in-the-one and the one-in-the-many. In order to give full value to the differentiated manyness of both the archetypal world of divine figures, *daimons*, and mythic creatures, as well as to the phenomenal world of our experiences, where psychological actually is vastly complicated and manifold, we shall focus intensively upon the *plurality* of the self, upon the many Gods and the many existential modes of the effects. We shall leave to one side theological fantasies of wholeness, oneness, and other abstract images of a goal called self. (1972: 265)

Hillman, Lacan and others may well have provided us with a valuable service with their critique of those ideological conceptions which equated the person solely with the ego or with a sentimental ideology of the supremacy of the individual. However, I agree with Samuels (1993) in that this critique goes too far. It simply replaces one extreme with another; the completely unified self simply is replaced by the completely plural or fragmented self. The human subject is not dead. The perspective of a coherent self-identity can coexist with its manifestation in a plurality of forms such that 'the many contains the unity of the one without losing the possibilities of the many'. Samuels (1989: 12) goes on to propose that the psyche can be seen as containing relatively autonomous spheres of activity each of which can, over time and according to context, have its dominance. Rather than having a rigid hierarchy with an organising ego always at the top, at any one time several self-images and personal myths may be operating within us. Consequently, the contemporary person '. . . has *always been* a decentered subject, an actor playing many roles in many scripts, characterized by lack, somewhat faded as well as jaded, jerky, marginalized, alienated, split, guilty, empty, Imaginary. The Person has *always been* a Trickster in his or her attitude to Psychological growth, Machiavellian in his or her understanding of Politics' (Samuels 1993: 203). Finally, Samuels argues that this model would '. . . give equal weight to the multiplicity *and* to the unity of the personality. This would redress the tendency to give greater weight to unity and integration, which is found in both linear and spiral models. There would be no need to insist that every feature of development has a *telos* or goal . . .' (1989: 22–3).

I am not discomforted by the observation that our psyche can, at various times, be somewhat ramshackle with competing self-images and personal myths, as well as having various tricksterish and mercurial characteristics. Similarly, our theory of psychological development does not have to be totalizing in its demand that every aspect of the psyche comply with the need to grow in a particular direction towards moral consciousness. But there is a limit. The relatively autonomous spheres of psychic activity that Samuels discusses can dominate our attention over time and differing contexts, *but for an autonomous person acting with postconventional moral consciousness* these quasi-random experiences or personal attributes can contradict neither any relevant moral imperatives nor the authenticity of one's self-identity. It is possible to accommodate a range of psychic sub-personalities, archetypal figures and personal images. The purpose of evolutionary psychological development is not to rigidly and uniformly control such phenomena, but, through psychic labour, to translate and transform them into members of an inner psychic cabinet who are democratically and reflexively aware that their individual existence is only possible through a coexistence with each other and through a coexistence with other real people in the external world. Successful interactions between social subjects require a self-identity able to autonomously follow moral imperatives and present an authentic representation of itself in processes of mutual recognition. These external and interactive conditions are constitutive of the nature of an authentic self-identity in accordance with which the internal psychic figures must act. The inner play of psychic characters and the outer representation of ourselves in various roles are not our concern so long as they do not contradict the moral and ethical conditions derivable from communicative rationality.

Samuels approach is in danger of not providing us with any means of differentiating a 'healthy' psychic plurality from 'psychopathology':

> The corrosive emptiness that is so voracious that it has had to be sated by sex, food, drugs, work, giving, is often found to be not so much an emptiness – for emptiness is not so hard to satisfy; it can be filled – as a black hole which conceals a sense of disintegration, a dispersing of self. The atomized bits can't seem to connect in a sufficiently meaningful way to generate a sense of sustainable self. The bits can't connect because they themselves make up a gossamer-like shield, covering not an empty core, but a core infected with a sense of its own badness. (Orbach 1996: 6)

My notion of a decentred self is more compatible with theorists who have seriously taken into account the positive aspect of the postmodern outlook whilst finding it an inadequate conception unless it is complemented with a notion of a reflexive self-identity. Taylor (1996: 480) recognizes the limitations of the unitary self model and the need to except that we live on many levels. That life is multilevelled necessarily involves a reflexive turn towards inwardness and depth. He is critical, however, of the postmodern turn whereby all subjectivism is rejected in favour of structures outside the self. With Kegan's (1981: 228–9) work we have already seen how it is possible to have a decentred sense of self which enables us to work through the competing demands of connection and separation without this self becoming fragmented; rather this self can maintain paradox. Maranhao (1986) reminds us that an endless decentring of the self is held in check by the mechanisms of guilt and shame. Bauman worries that the postmodern 'dis-encumbering' of the self makes it 'all too easy to choose identity, but no longer possible to hold it' (1996: 50). He characterizes the postmodern self as that of a 'vagabond' or a 'tourist' and: 'One thing that the vagabond's and the tourist's lives are not designed to contain, and most often are excused from containing, is cumbersome, incapacitating, joy-killing, insomniogenic moral responsibility' (1996: 54). Benhabib attacks postmodernism for its celebration of heterogeneity, opacity and difference whilst belittling the importance of a coherent self-identity. She reminds us that not all difference is empowering and not all opacity leads to a sense of a self that is flourishing. A coherent self-identity does not have to be monolithic, rather we can see this coherence as a narrative unity. 'The self is both the teller of the tales' she writes 'and that about whom tales are told. The individual with a coherent sense of self-identity is the one who succeeds in integrating the tales and perspectives into a meaningful life history' (1994: 198–200). The fact that individuals may have to act differently in different contexts has:

led some authors to suppose that the self essentially becomes broken up – that individuals tend to develop multiple selves in which there is no inner core of self-identity. Yet surely, as an abundance of studies of self-identity show, this is plainly not the case. The maintaining of constants of demeanour across varying settings of interaction is one of the prime means whereby coherence of self-identity is ordinarily preserved. (Giddens 1991: 100)

Returning to Habermas we may recall that, in the first chapter, I outlined that the subject has three ways of orienting itself to the world. In scientific mode the subject relates to an 'objective' world; she relates to the social world as a person in interpersonal relations regarded as legitimate in terms of morals and ethics; finally she relates to her own subjective world. This is also a form of decentred self in which the self is able to maintain its identity across three different orientations to the world. For Habermas the self can also maintain itself over time:

> The ego-identity of the adult proves its worth in the ability to build up new identities from shattered or superseded identities, and to integrate them with old identities in such a way that the fabric in of one's interactions is organized into the unity of a life history that is both unmistakable and accountable. (1998a: 98)

As a summary I take the decentred self to have the following features. The inner core of the self is able to maintain its identity when enacting various roles. It does not lose itself in the role (therefore prey to 'acting out' and unconscious projections), but is also not aloof from the role (analytically distanced, censorious or overly self-conscious). There is an element of authentic core self in the roles and this can be observed by others. The self can move in and out of role. This level of reflexivity is loose and not controlling. Through self-awareness the individual can move between roles; reveal to others that self and role are not identical. On the other hand, it can knowingly act roles and perform duties and obligations. This self knows that it is constituted through interaction and thereby must honour links with others and reciprocate. It loses the narcissism of the self-centred 'I'. It is confident but knows its own fragility and fallibility. It is beyond the desperate narcissism of finding some pure 'authenticity' – it is authentic enough to need less affirmation from others, hold tension and conflict and move towards the universality of moral consciousness.

A self that has failed to become decentred or has not yet reached this stage can take one of at least two general positions. It can be a *fragmented* self in which the inner core is less developed such that the person cannot easily hold the tension between identity and role. This self tends to *become the role* and be unable to hold a reflexive perspective on the role. Anger, and other emotions, become acted-out on the false assumption that authenticity is characterized by 'being-the-role' – 'authentically' expressing an unmediated emotion. This self cannot display simultaneously role enactment and role distance – it cannot hold the tension of being in the role and yet being accessible to be called out of role. The act of communication as a reciprocal event (illocutionary rather than perlocutionary) collapses into manipulation – 'this is my feeling and you are going to experience it'. The fragmented self suffers from an insecurity about self and role – it hides in the role. The opposite of this position is the *unitary* self. Here the tension between self and role is solved by denying any difference between them. This person is anxious to maintain a uniform authenticity by not acting any roles at all. The unitary self wants to remain identical in all situations.

I believe that the conception of moral character development[12] outlined here is of great benefit to us in understanding the purpose of counselling and psychotherapy. To comprehend how the interactions of socialization generate a *moral* self is to understand that this moral process continues in the dialectical interaction inside the counselling room. The therapeutic process is an intervention designed to remedy the failed socialization dynamics of the family, the education system and the culture in general. The logic of the process of mutual recognition enables us to understand that a breakdown in this dialectic leads to domination, the damaging results of which counselling is at pains to unpick. The psychotherapist who is able to understand the specific nature of moral emotions will be able to see how they are constituted through self-identity and therefore avoid reifying them as natural or primary forces. The theory of evolutionary development provides the therapist with a diagnostic tool that can reveal both the current stage of development and the goals of postconventional moral consciousness and autonomy. In seeking to rescue the concept of the decentred self from some of its fashionable excesses I have attempted to articulate a form of reflexive self-identity robust enough to act autonomously.

In so doing I have, indirectly, outlined the type of self-identity that is required of a counsellor or therapist. This model of the counsellor, possessing a decentred self which is able to maintain itself across time and context and maintaining a reflexive relation to itself such that it holds itself accountable, is able to act authentically, morally and autonomously. Moreover, such a self would freely place itself under the obligation to achieve this behaviour *both in and out of the counselling room*. This is not as unrealistic as it sounds.[13] We might devote more attention to the character that we require of a counsellor rather than hoping that the correct behaviour will be guaranteed by codes of professional ethics and loose concepts like 'congruence'. Our failure to sufficiently understand and assess the counsellor's own actions in terms of morals, authenticity and autonomy makes us blind to the negative effects of some of the behaviour of counsellors not only on their clients, but on the organizations within which they work. Wasdell perceptively outlines the way in which counsellors who interact in group settings become prey to unconscious group dynamics:

Individuals professionally involved in one-to-one relationships find themselves at the mercy of unconscious, irrational and often destructive forces being acted out at the corporate dynamic level of those organizations which bring psychotherapists, counsellors and analysts into organizational relationships. (1992: 9)

Issues arise of power and powerlessness, omnipotence. There are fears about survival or destruction, blaming, scapegoating, inappropriate struggle for resources and irrational anxieties about implosion, chaos, fragmentation and annihilation. Patterns of splitting from this primitive level of defence are absolutized. Issues tend to be polarized into black and white, good and bad, us and them, inside and outside. As the dynamics build-up in intensity, so inter-group negotiation becomes more and more fraught. (1992: 11)

With this kind of behaviour being very possible in the psychotherapeutic community we may well derive great benefit from a general understanding of the kind of authentic decentred self we have described as being very relevant to both client and counsellor.

CHAPTER 4

Communicative Action and Counselling

I have so far used the theory of communicative action to try to help understand the purpose of counselling and psychotherapy in three broad ways. I began by outlining a philosophical basis that suggests to us the generation of a notion of universal valuation in the face of relativism. This was followed by an analysis of the six validity claims and values that can be found in all communications intended to reach a mutual understanding. These values provide us with a conceptual framework with which we can understand the purpose of psychotherapy and counselling. By moving to an analysis of the development of moral character within socialization processes of mutual recognition I believe I have outlined how the framework of communicative action can help explain the process of identity formation. In so doing, counselling and psychotherapy can be understood as agents of socialization which become relevant when conventional socialization processes fail because either they are inherently inadequate, or they are undermined by wider social, economic and cultural factors which privilege strategic action over communicative action. In these circumstances therapeutic interventions have the purpose of regenerating the individuals' striving for autonomy (as I have defined autonomy) through communicative action that successfully works in accordance with the relevant validity claims, particularly those of justice and personal authenticity.

It seems reasonably plausible to me that the theory of communicative action could go a long way to providing a general theoretical framework which could unite the often competing psychotherapeutic traditions whilst avoiding the current position of ad hoc eclecticism[1] found at the organizational and individual practitioner level. At the moment we seem to lack a general model against which the random shopping basket of theoretical models can be assessed. However that is a project in its own right and is not my objective here. Nevertheless, whilst in no way attempting to address all the issues arising out of the theory of communicative action that pertain to the theory and practice of counselling and psychotherapy, I do wish to make some excursions into this area that will hopefully prove fruitful.

Communicative Action and Counselling

We can gain some useful insights in understanding the conditions and symptoms that people bring to counsellors by reframing these phenomena in terms of language and communication. (The usage of the term 'symptoms' carries the same problem of 'medicalizing' socially induced phenomenon that I have already outlined with the usage of the term 'psychopathology'; however, I shall continue to use it for similar reasons.) Communicative theory is not limited to the verbal dimension and includes all forms of symbolic expression including body-language. This approach is not new but does provide a different perspective when brought to bear upon psychotherapy. Thus viewed clients inhabit and bring with them a system of distorted communication characterized by a discrepancy between the levels of communication such that the congruence between linguistic symbols, forms of expression and action has disintegrated. These can vary from minor slips and confusions to the most intractable of symptoms that give people distress. The key concept that Habermas uses is the distinction between public and private communication. The former does not simply mean talking with other people; it is a much deeper concept drawing on his theory of universal pragmatics and the necessary rules and validity claims inherent in all communication aimed at reaching an understanding. In contradistinction a private communication is one which fails to perform in accordance with these pragmatics such that validity claims are broken and, to varying degrees, the sufferer is condemned not to be understood, with the associated problems of a reduction in mutual recognition and damaged identity formation.

> No matter on what level of communication the symptoms appear . . . it is always the case that a content, which has been excommunicated from its public usage, assumes independence. This content expresses an intention which remains incomprehensible according to the rules of public communication, and is, in this sense privatized; but it also remains inaccessible to its author. (Habermas 1980: 192)

The consequence is that there exists within the self a barrier between that part which can communicate publicly and a distorted aspect of self that is subject to a private symbolic system.

During childhood defence mechanisms are generated in the psyche to separate the unconscious or strategic aspect of action from conscious intentional actions that aim at reaching understanding. These defences explain why a person can deceive himself about the fact that he is 'objectively' contradicting the inherent presuppositions of communicative action. Consequently, actions that appear to be unconsciously driven can be understood as a reversal of the differentiation previously established between strategic and communicative action. This fusing of previously differentiated types of communication is hidden from the subject and is a form of self-deception which is interpreted by Habermas to reflect an intrapsychic disturbance of communication. Communicative theory enables us to understand self-deception as a form of systematically distorted communication that can be found at both the interpersonal and intrapsychic levels. For example, a child may suffer a terrible conflict which is then subject to repression (a 12-year-old boy witnesses his mother in an illicit relationship with another man whilst they are in a taxi). The movement of repression is the process whereby 'normal' symbolic structures are de-symbolized, that is, they cease to make sense in a way that is readily accessible such that this distortion may well lead to the formation of a symptom. The child excludes this disturbing experience of conflict from public communication (language that carries an accessible meaning) because it is too troublesome and thereby renders it invisible to himself. The object, or part thereof, that carries the projection of conflict is subject to splitting such that the troublesome aspect of the object is de-symbolized. In this case he develops a phobia about taxis. The meaning attached to the object has now become incomplete because of this splitting and subsequent repression – the image of the taxi now carries the conflict thereby enabling a repression or 'forgetting' of the real problem which is his knowledge of his mother's affair. This gap is filled by a symptom (the phobia about taxis), an unsuspicious symptom that safely replaces the symbolic content that has been removed thereby protecting the child from future repetitions of the original disturbing conflict. The substitute symptom is a safe symbol because it only carries a private meaning and cannot be decoded in terms of the rules of public language. Disturbed behaviour patterns (the phobia) that apparently are incoherent to the observer carry a private, coded meaning to the sufferer.

This mode of interpretation is based on making a differentiation between pre-linguistic and linguistic organization of symbols which needs explaining. The realm of the pre-linguistic is inhabited by paleo-symbols whose contents cannot be translated into public communication. We only know of them through the study of dreams and distorted speech. These paleo-symbols are devoid of the properties of normal speech, and do not exist within a system that can be subject to rules of grammar. This, notes Habermas, is because such symbols have a low constancy of meaning such that the same symbol can mean different things – these symbols have a high proportion of private meanings. They are therefore unable to provide a common identity of meaning. There are several reasons for this: the distinction between symbolic sign, semantic content and referent has not yet developed; there is an absence of the necessary distance between self and other; there is no clear distinction between the level of reality and that of appearance; and the public and private spheres have not been sufficiently differentiated.

This concept of the organization of symbols is a theoretical construct unavailable to direct observation. It is a necessary construct for those therapies that understand confusions of normal communication in terms of a forced regression to an earlier stage of communication or as the unmotivated entry of an earlier form of communication into language. This does not mean, however, that all disturbed behaviour has a historical cause in early childhood. Socialization in a culture where some public communication is ideological or mythological results in the subject using symbols that contain levels of meaning which are normally unavailable to the subject. For example, the everyday process of marketing in western societies often contains deliberate attempts by advertisers (who represent the interests of their client) to implant branded images that lodge in our psyches at a level below that of public communication. Various religious and political ideologies operate in the same way. The function of a therapeutic intervention is to reintegrate split-off symbolic contents through a process of re-symbolization which retraces the original process of repression into a private language and begins the process of healing by decoding the private language into a publicly accessible meaning. (In our example therapy would attempt to bring back to public communication the split-off and repressed meanings associated with the boy's private phobic responses to his mother's behaviour and its association with taxis.) The fact that an individual's distorted communication patterns can have currently existing social and cultural causes illuminates the limitations of many forms of therapeutic intervention which are often limited to early childhood traumas or to forms of repression typically understood as operating at the level of small-scale interactions, typically the family.

Habermas believes that this theory of distorted communication can explain much of the behaviour exhibited by those experiencing many of the psychological problems associated with anxiety, depression, addiction, compulsion and other conditions. The process of privatizing symbolic content explains why these phenomena act as pseudo-communications in so far as the subject is not aware of the distorted meaning whilst the hearer experiences a distorted communication but often cannot explain it. Behaviour can become compulsive and stereotyped because the repressed symbolic content is subject to repetition resulting from the fact that it no longer operates as a conventional symbol in a language subject to the rules of grammar. The high emotional attachment and expressive content of such symbols results from the impact of the intense feelings experienced at the moment of the repressive transformation of the symbol into a symptom. If repression is regarded as de-symbolization then we can use this same mode of interpretation the other way round, that is, not as a defence mechanism directed at the self but a defence held against external reality in the form of projection and denial. In this latter case, distortion comes from the uncontrolled emergence of paleo-symbolic phenomena into language. Linguistically minded therapy in this context does not try to transform the de-symbolized contents into an articulate meaning, rather it attempts to eliminate the pre-linguistic elements.

In both instances, systematic distortion of everyday communication can be explained by reference to semantic contents which are tied to paleo-symbols and which encyst within language like alien bodies. It is the task of language analysis to dissolve these syndromes, i.e. to isolate both levels of language. (Habermas 1980: 199–200)

The alleviation of this systematic distortion involves a creative process of transferring the semantic contents from the pre-linguistic to the linguistic level. This continually expands the sphere of communicative action at the expense of unconsciously motivated action. 'The moment of successful, creative use of language is one of emancipation' (Habermas 1980: 200).

This process, which Habermas calls depth-hermeneutics, must be distinguished from conventional hermeneutics which is the school of study concerned with the problems of translation from one language or culture to another. The realm of the paleo-symbolic is not a language as such and therefore cannot simply be translated into the linguistic sphere. Consequently, the decoding of inadequate expressions requires not only the skills of translation, it also presupposes a theory of communicative competence. This is the theory that I articulated at the beginning of this work. Only if we have a sense of what constitutes an adequate communication, can we understand its deformation into distorted communication.

I would say, however, that each depth-hermeneutical interpretation of systematically distorted communication, irrespective of whether it appears in an analytic encounter or informally, implicitly relies on those demanding theoretical assumptions which can only be developed and justified within the framework of a *theory of communicative competence*. (Habermas 1980: 202–3)[2]

The fact that psychotherapy and counselling is not simply a work of translation but also relies on theoretical constructs provides some explanation for the peculiar status of the psychotherapeutic methodological model. Habermas (1980), Lobkowicz (1967), Apel (1972) and others have alluded to this fact and suggested that the psychotherapeutic method be seen as a model for certain social sciences. The social sciences in question are those which provide a critical and emancipatory analysis similar to that found in the psychotherapeutic process. This process is not merely concerned with understanding the client, but is also interested in enabling the client to transform herself out of suffering and into a more developed self-identity. Psychotherapy, therefore, is neither a natural science nor a hermeneutical science of interpretation but a blend of both. Whilst the therapist and the client are at all times relating to each other as human partners in an interactive communication, the relationship is not symmetrical. The therapist will, at different moments, also engage in a private process whereby he knowingly objectifies the behaviour and life story of the client as phenomena which have an unconscious causality on the client.[3] At these moments the therapist is drawing on theoretical constructs. These can be drawn from a wide range of traditions, the most comprehensive of which, I would argue, is the theory of communicative action. If the client is subject to driven behaviour resulting from systematically distorted communication, endless interpretations will be fruitless unless accompanied by the 'quasi-scientific' analysis of distorted communication. When drawing on such knowledge the therapist holds frames of reference that are often unavailable to the client. This must be strictly differentiated from any sense of behavioural intervention because the psychotherapist only uses this objectifying analysis as a transitory phase in the therapeutic process, and the therapist should be transparent enough to reveal the nature of this objectification to the client when appropriate. The function of this method is to enable the therapist to work jointly with the client to uncover the process of distorted communication and restore the client to the realm of fully functioning public communication within the therapeutic situation and, eventually, in everyday life. Psychotherapy might therefore see itself as neither a science nor an art form but a critical and emancipatory social science. Counsellors and counselling organizations, might, if they took this view, be more protective of the critical-emancipatory values inherent in their work and more cautious of borrowing methodologies from sectors whose interests are more strategic (as opposed to communicative), commercial and conservative.

The communicative action approach to counselling is not without its critics. Coole (1997: 226–7) believes that Habermas offers people the possibility of too much communicative access to the inner self such that, in principle, there is nothing unavailable to rational self-communication. Whitebook makes a similar point when he suggests that Habermas is solving the problem of communication between the linguistic and the pre-linguistic in advance through proposing a pre-established harmony between the two levels. 'Habermas' observes Whitebook 'is correct in arguing that "language functions as a kind of transformer" which draws the individual into the intersubjective social world. But it does not do so without a residuum of private in-itselfness – without which we would all be pre-coordinated clones – and it is this residuum that does not adequately appear in Habermas's account' (1997: 185). Whitebook continues by acknowledging the important contribution that Habermas has made to psychotherapy through his perspective of elucidating the linguistic dimension inherent in this process such that there is an element of homogeneity between the two systems which makes the translation from unconscious to conscious possible. The corresponding shortcoming, however, is that Habermas over-extends the amount of homogeneity and undervalues the level of difference between the conscious and unconscious systems.

The point of Habermas's theory, however, is that it is methodological in nature as opposed to being an attempt to define our inner being. What he is essentially doing is replacing the earlier Freudian hydraulic model of drives, instinct, energy and cathexis with the more adequate model of interpreted needs and identity formation.

In this communication-theoretical reading, inner nature is in no way vaporized into culturalistic haze. It does not determine in advance that the substratum of inner nature has to fit harmoniously into linguistic structures, and even be utterly absorbed into them. But such a categorial framework does decide in favour of the perspective of a life-world intersubjectively shared by participants. One does give up biological or physicalistic third-person descriptions of the organic substratum. This change in the perspective of description does not entail the elimination of inner nature as an extralinguistic referent. (Habermas 1985: 213)

Self-Reflection and Critique

In his earlier work, Habermas regarded disturbed psychological states in terms of the discrepancy between public and private languages. To some extent, this left him in the 'therapy as social adjustment' school. As he developed his theory of communicative action and generated the concept of the ideal speech situation (which outlines the conditions necessary for successful communication leading towards a mutual understanding) he was then able to critically compare the distorted private language of the subject experiencing psychological problems to the ideal communication of a public language. This notion of the critical element in counselling and psychotherapy becomes an important issue in our understanding of the purpose of these processes. I want to try to link the self-reflective element of counselling to its purpose as a form of critique of the conditions and symptoms that clients bring. The term 'self-reflective' is similar to the concept of 'self-awareness' but is more incisive because, with its link to communicative action, it is not just a process of 'coming to awareness' and somehow becoming a 'fully functioning person' (whatever that is), instead the concept of a public language provides a benchmark against which our distorted private language can be measured and then made open to the critique that the therapeutic process offers, enabling the possibility of emancipation from the concomitant symptoms. The term 'critique' in this context does not mean to be critical in the sense of guilt-inducing moral condemnation, rather it proffers the possibility of the client working with the counsellor to conduct a joint analysis or a joint rewriting of the client's narrative that accepts that the presenting symptoms are real, but are not a 'valid' reflection of an authentic life.

My point here should not be confused with the simple dictum that the point of counselling is in bringing the unconscious into consciousness. Many schools of therapy know that insight on its own is insufficient to release people from their distressing ailments, let alone enable them to develop towards autonomy. Two of the founding fathers were clear about this:

Informing of the patient of what he does not know because he has repressed it is only one of the necessary preliminaries to the treatment. If knowledge about the unconscious were as important for the patient as people inexperienced in psycho-analysis imagine, listening to lectures or reading books would be enough to cure him. (Freud, quoted by Habermas 1972: 209)

Mere insight into themselves is sufficient for morally sensitive persons who have enough driving force to carry them forward; for those with little imagination for moral values, however, it does not suffice. Without the spur of external necessity, self-knowledge is ineffective for them even when they are deeply convinced – to say nothing of those who have been struck by the analyst's interpretation and yet doubt it after all. These last are mentally disciplined people who grasp the truth of a 'reductive' explanation, but cannot accept it when it merely invalidates their hopes and ideals. In these cases also mere insight is insufficient. (Jung 1973: 49)

Insight is insufficient because the psychological disturbance is not merely cognitive but involves resistances on the affective level. This is why the act of counselling is not simply a translation from a distorted text to a com-prehensible text because the former is rendered inaccessible to translation by habitualized emotional blocks. As a consequence, psychotherapy is well aware that therapy also involves working with the client over a period of time such that the trust invested in the therapeutic relationship will enable the client to bring to the surface, and act out, the disturbed feelings in a way that slowly releases them from the compulsion to repeat. Habermas's concept of self-reflection incorporates these aspects of the therapeutic process. The process of critique involved in counselling and psychotherapy is not limited to the intellectual/cognitive but involves the whole identity of the client.

The benefit of using the term 'critique' is that its conventional usage is associated with power. A critique is not simply an analysis of something to show that it is incorrect or distorted, rather it shows that such distortion is the product of an imbalance in power. The phenomenon under study has therefore not been subject to distortion in an accidental or haphazard way, but is a result of a specific set of power relations. In our study of socialization as a process of mutual recognition, the work of Benjamin enables us to see how imbalances in the mutuality of recognizing the other, as a subject in his/her own right, create relationships in which one partner takes a domin-ating role.

Psychotherapy as critique is not rendering the client's biography under-standable from just any perspective, but is helping the client to rewrite her history from the assumed vantage point of the preconditions of public communication which enable past distortions to be understood as resulting from domination.

Psychotherapy as a process of self-reflection (in the sense of being conceptual and affective) is not only a process whereby distorted language becomes clear, but, as a critique, it gains an understanding of domination which enables the possibility of not only the release from symptoms, but is also a process of emancipation from historical or current domination.[4] The sources of domination are not just within the family but wider cultural and social processes which become internalized. We shall come to these later.

The psychotherapeutic method offers possibilities unavailable to other forms of knowledge and experience. Unlike science, philosophy, hermeneutics and the social sciences, the psychotherapeutic process, as critique, does offer a form of knowledge, but its 'claims to validity can be verified only in the successful process of enlightenment, and that means: in the practical discourse of those concerned' (Habermas 1974: 2).

Counselling Presupposes the Ideal Speech Situation

Implicit in the above is the idealized form of communicative action that we have variously expressed as: public communication, undistorted communication, communication conforming to the necessary validity claims or the ideal speech situation. From Freud onwards therapeutic interpretation involves working with texts that simultaneously reveal and conceal the client's self-deceptions. This notion only makes sense if we have an understanding of what an undistorted text might look like. This position leaves only two options. We either forget the notion of undistorted communication and abandon therapy to the circularity of postmodern relativism, or we endeavour to conduct the theoretical work that enables us to outline the preconditions of public communication. Following Habermas, I believe that

> the psychoanalyst must have a 'prenotion', or rough understanding, of the structure of undistorted ordinary-language communication in order to be able at all to trace systematic distortions of language back to a confusion of two developmentally distinct stages of pre-linguistic and linguistic organization; then he needs to reconstruct the conditions making *normal speech* possible. The answer to this question cannot be supplied by an objectivating science of communication. (1973b: 184)

With this conception Habermas sketches an approximate analogy between psychotherapeutic and political dialogue; between the psychotherapist and the critical social theorist. Both must have some notions of what undistorted communication and social interaction must look like. Given the preconditions of communicative action, it is clear that the corresponding political framework must be both democratic and free from domination.

Rationality and Counselling

Is there a sense in which the process of counselling and psychotherapy can be termed 'rational'? How can what often appears to be the most emotional of experiences be classified as rational? If we were to think of rationality only in terms of logic or instrumental reason then it would most certainly be an inappropriate description of the therapeutic process. However, when considered in the context of the universal pragmatics of communication, this communicative sense of rationality is germane to the purpose of counselling. If we take authenticity to be an integral aspect of successful communication, and if transparency is an essential ingredient of authenticity, then a person who is subject to self-deceptions does not act rationally when under the sway of such illusions. Vice versa, a person can be said to act rationally when he is both willing and able to free himself from self-deceptions. In this sense, congruence would be rational and is secured by the preconditions inherent in communicative action aimed at reaching understanding.

This does not deny that there are situations where a person has reason to conceal his subjective experiences from others. In these situations he is only simulating a claim to truthfulness while behaving strategically. Such expressions are deliberately not aiming at transparency or sincerity and can therefore only be judged as more or less successful in relation to their original goal. This can happen in the counselling room when the counsellor makes a statement which is intended to circumvent the client's defences and hopefully enable a change in perception. At this moment the counsellor is acting strategically rather than transparently. Such an action is ethically secured by the long-term goal of enabling the client to gain the psychological competency to conduct fully transparent communications. Thus the rationality of acting transparently only applies in the context of communication aimed at reaching an understanding.

Counselling and psychotherapy can only be defined as rational when they are free from domination and the use of force, which also means, as already suggested, that a significant purpose of these interventions is to alleviate symptoms that were engendered by the distorting effect of domination, and to restimulate the personal growth that was stalled by oppression. A communicatively achieved agreement, in or outside of the therapeutic process, has a rational basis. Such an *agreement* cannot be imposed by either party. An 'agreement' can be objectively obtained by force, but such a state of affairs cannot count subjectively as an agreement. True agreements do not solely exist objectively, but must also be experienced subjectively as such. Agreements, Habermas says, rest on common *convictions*. The process of reaching an agreement is like the dialectic of mutual recognition. Both the participants must treat each other as subjects in their own right such that mutual recognition only occurs when their different subjectivities are acknowledged. The usage of force collapses the interrelationship with one identity dominating an other. The same is true of reaching an agreement in communication; agreement is only reached if the subjects involved believe this to be the case. The use of force in counselling (notwithstanding that strategic communications can be an essential part of the process) is clearly irrational, whilst it is rational to work towards reaching an understanding or agreement. It therefore follows, I propose, that part of the rationality of counselling is its therapeutic purpose of undoing the damage to clients caused by the force of domination in their lives.

There is a more general sense in which the work of counselling and psychotherapy can be said to be rational. If we recall the validity claims that are essential to the process of communicative action, then anyone who consistently and systematically behaves in accordance with these preconditions is conducting their life in a rational manner. Thus anyone who: has the cognitive competency to judge facts; is able to act successfully in a purposive-rational manner; can act morally; behaves authentically and is practically reliable; is aesthetically sensitive and open-minded; is capable of letting himself be enlightened about his own irrationality and can integrate these various aspects across the full-spectrum of interactions and over the span of a lifetime once maturity has been reached, can be said to be conducting a rational life.

Such a conception of rationality clearly bears no relation to the narrowly defined conventional sense of rationality as logic or instrumentality. In so far as this developed definition of a rational life is indistinguishable from the concept of autonomy, and we have suggested that autonomy is the key purpose of counselling and psychotherapy, these interventions have a rational intention. Furthermore, at the political and social levels, the institutions and culture of counselling and psychotherapy should ally themselves with those social forces committed to realizing the conditions that would enable people to lead such autonomous and rational lives.

Bringing the Social Context into Knowledge

That the understanding of an expression needs to be placed in the context of the relevant background from which it came is a trivial observation. Indeed, a salient feature of therapy involves the process of coming to an understanding of the privatized language of the client in relation to the relevant contexts of early socialization, family background and current domestic arrangements. With the notion of critique I think we are more able to understand the degree to which the everyday cultural and social context that the client and counsellor share (or, more to the point, perhaps do not share) remains an unexamined factor in the therapeutic alliance and acts as a causal force in the presenting problem of the client. In order to understand linguistic expressions we unthinkingly take for granted a wide range of background knowledge though, of course, it does not carry the status of knowledge. Rather than being a publicly verifiable source of knowledge it acts implicitly; it is the wallpaper of our environment and 'it is a knowledge that does *not stand at our disposition,* in as much as we cannot make it conscious and place it into doubt as we please' (Habermas 1997b: 336). Background knowledge is deep-seated and unproblematic in its everyday usage. It is pre-consciously or unconsciously assumed and operates beneath any threshold of validity.

Cushman illustrates how different social contexts create different psychological theories and practices. He contrasts Beard's theory of neurasthenia with Freud's theory of hysteria in the nineteenth century. Freud's theory unintentionally reflected the need of the state to control a population disrupted by war and social upheaval. On the other hand, Beard's neurasthenia reflected the need of the American state to settle the continent and build an industrialized nation. 'In Europe, illness was uncontrolled sex or aggression; whereas in the United States it was the absence of initiative, the inability to work, that was considered sickness' (1995: 134). This engendered a different sense of selfhood. In Europe the need to control represents a view of the self that is inherently bad and prone to violence – it is a self that needs *dominating*. In the USA a conception of human goodness in a context of undreamed abundance induces a concept of the self as an entity that needs *liberating* not controlling. These different approaches were so embedded in their social contexts that their socially constructed nature was invisible to the participants at the time.

Ironically, it is their ability to camouflage themselves as knowledge that enables background assumptions to carry such everyday certainty despite the obvious fact that they have endured no critical assessment. My argument here is not just to revisit the well-worn mantra that counselling and psychotherapy should be more aware of the social and cultural background of their clients. Instead I wish to draw attention to the fact that the process of identity formation is such that these environmental factors are deeply constitutive of identity and reach right down to the bedrock of our being. Indeed, as we shall see later, in late modernity there are very powerful social forces that maintain social order and integration through the process of a deep internalization of unarticulated values which present themselves as everyday background knowledge. In other words, background knowledge is not neutral, naive or value-free. It is often ideological, not in the simple sense of just representing a certain class interest, but in the sense of maintaining the equilibrium and status quo of a social system that appears to be impersonal, technocratic and 'beyond ideology'. If counselling and psychotherapy fail to create a dialogue with, or an understanding of, those radical social theories (for example, postmodernism, poststructuralism, critical theory, systems theory and so on) that enable a more critical insight into the social constitution of the self, then they run the serious risk of failing to understand and diagnose client problems whilst simultaneously, and unknowingly, allying with cultural values and social processes that help create the pathologies they attempt to heal.

Non-Judgemental and Value-Free Counselling

For some time there has been a debate between those who believe that counselling is a value-free process in which the counsellor should, at all times, be non-judgemental and non-directive, and those who believe that the avoidance of values and judgements is impossible.[5] My interest here is not only to illustrate my disagreement with the former position, but to strengthen the latter position. The criticism of the non-judgemental position is often committed to a listing of a variety of personal, social and cultural values which the counsellor is unable to exclude from the counselling room. I suggest a much stronger position which is not quite so interested in issues of personal bigotry or cultural insensitivity because, in principle, with sensitive hermeneutic awareness these can be minimized; instead, the values that cannot be eliminated from the counselling process are precisely those that are a precondition of any communication aimed at reaching an understanding. That is, the validity claims that we have outlined at some length (establishing truth, comprehensibility, justice, truthfulness and authenticity, health and autonomy) cannot be made extrinsic to the counselling interaction and are instead integral to, and constitutive of, counselling and psychotherapy. Thus, not only are values an essential feature of counselling; these values are not randomly selected but are specifically generated by the communicative rationality inherent in this process. I shall not be reworking the philosophical argument in favour of communicative rationality; in so far as its validity has been established I rest this case with the argument presented earlier in this work. Here I wish to provide a critique of non-judgementalism from the vantage point of the validity claims inherent in communication.

Although he may not have been the first to be interested in the subject, Rogers, with his person-centred approach to psychotherapy, is often seen as representing the paradigm of the value-free approach.

> There is also a complete freedom from any type of moral or diagnostic evaluation, since all such evaluations are, I believe, always threatening. (Rogers 1993: 34)

> I have come to feel that the more I can keep a relationship free of judgement and evaluation, the more this will permit the other person to reach the point where he recognizes that the locus of evaluation, the centre of responsibility, lies within himself. The meaning and value of his experience is in the last analysis something which is up to him, and no amount of external judgement can alter this. So I should like to work toward a relationship in which I am not, even in my own feelings, evaluating him. (Rogers 1993: 55)

This is somewhat ironic coming from a theorist who also believes that psychotherapy should be helping the client to become a 'fully functioning person'. As Brazier points out, 'although the approach is called non-directive, we are told where it is going' (1995: 37).

Consumer Choice/Freedom of Choice

Let us consider the notion of 'value-free' in the context of client choice. In line with the characteristic developments of the social and economic spheres of western societies in late modernity, counselling and psychotherapy have become more concerned with the needs of consumers above the needs of producers. Increasingly we hear issues concerning client choice which, as counselling loses confidence in its own language and culture and naively adopts the background assumptions and language of business, almost inevitably become framed in marketing jargon as 'clients' become 'consumers'. Whilst, in the simplest sense, I am 'for' freedom of choice, when this is placed in the context of an advanced capitalist society in which a huge proportion of our interactions have become commodified then 'choice' is no longer a simple and universal benefit but takes on specific features that reflect background cultural values. Just as counsellors have difficulty in getting to grips with the background, contextual knowledge of their clients so does the counselling culture have difficulty in maintaining its own identity and values in the face of the dominating nature of the prevailing culture within which it sits a little too comfortably.

There is a strong tradition that places counselling and psychotherapy in the tradition of political liberalism such that the purpose of the therapeutic intervention is to help people find their own values:

> rather than espousing any particular set of substantive values, psychotherapy tries to expose the psychological mechanisms which underlie different moral alternatives, and so help the patient to choose between them. In this it is congruent with the liberal conception of individuality. (Holmes and Lindley 1989: 136)

> Psychotherapeutic autonomy is pluralistic in that it aims to help people to find and follow their *own* various goals and desires, without imposing any particular view of what is right upon them. Part of the process of therapy is helping people to recognize whether a particular decision on a course of action feels right for *them*. (Holmes and Lindley 1989: 129)

> Psychotherapy is, more than anything, about helping people to choose; *what* they choose (with certain exceptions...) is left to them. (Holmes and Lindley 1989: 123)

This is based on the simple conception that all values are equal and that there is no difference between personal ethics and universal morals. The issue of conceptual truth fails to register as do the values of comprehensibility and health. Even if we ignore the omissions and just concentrate on the realm of ethics, as seems to be the sole concern of the above commentators, there is still a lack of articulation of the issue. Before we can accept the validity of the proposition that the individual chooses their own goals and desires there are some essential filters that have been overlooked:

- personal values should be congruent with all the other validity claims – truth, universal morality, comprehensibility, health and autonomy;
- the realm of personal ethics, goals and values has its own validity requirements. Any values I choose should be consistent with the requirement that I act authentically in terms of being transparent, congruent and truthful, as well as maintaining these characteristics within a mature and decentred self over time;
- when considering the issue of personal choice liberal theorists all too easily concentrate on the 'free will' of the agent rather than the specific self-identity of the agent and the competency of this identity to exercise its 'will' freely in the act of choosing. In other words, free will is not an inborn right or inherent personal agency but is something that we acquire through our socialization; more specifically, we acquire it through a socialization leading to moral consciousness and our sense of autonomy. The sense of autonomy that I use defines those people who have achieved the highest stages of moral development; who have, and maintain, a coherent sense of personal authenticity; who are (and know that they are) constituted through a social process of mutual recognition, and who freely accept the duties imposed upon them by universal moral obligations. This exercise of choice by an autonomous and individuated subject should in no way be confused or conflated with that of an individual almost shopping for any set of values that happens to suit them. The simplistic liberal definition of choice becomes detached from the attributes of the self that does the choosing:

> an identity that always remains mine, namely, my self-understanding as an autonomously acting and individuated being, can stabilize itself only if I find recognition as a person, and as this person. Under the conditions of strategic action, the self of self-determination and of self-realization slips out of inter-subjective relations. The strategic actor no longer draws from an intersubjectively shared lifeworld; having himself become worldless, as it were, he stands over and against the objective world and makes decisions solely according to standards of subjective preference. He does not rely therein upon recognition by others. Autonomy is then transformed into freedom of choice, and the individuation of the socialized subject is transformed into the isolation of a liberated subject who possesses himself [and]. (Habermas 1998c: 192)

- once these conditions are fulfilled then the specific contents of the individual's value system are no longer the business of the therapist, sociologist or philosopher but are a matter for the individual concerned.

This incarnation of counselling as value-free in terms of representing the purpose of counselling as that of enabling free choice of personal values not only fails to be compatible with the validity claims inherent in communicative action, it also grants an unwarrantable privilege to that part of self-identity concerned with strategic or instrumental interests and ego-management. This is the kind of self needed and created by a consumerist society and may more appropriately be seen as a symptom rather than an achievement. *The kind of self that is assumed by the value-free approach is a current example of the unexamined nature of the background assumptions used in psychotherapy and counselling.* From this standpoint, Rose's[6] chilling interpretation of counselling and psychotherapy (as processes that take failing consumers, repackage them and restore them as effective strategic choice makers) gains a certain credence.

A different sense of the value-free position concerns freedom of choice in the act of selecting an appropriate form of counselling intervention by the client as opposed to the process of counselling enabling the client to gain a freedom of choice. It seems incongruent to choose the term freedom of choice for a state of affairs that pertains both prior to and as a consequence of counselling. The exercise of freedom in choosing to go to counselling has real pragmatic limitations. In the first place the range of therapies on offer has grown enormously and almost presents a bewildering range of choice; moreover, at the point of selection there are few, if any, criteria which enable the potential client to make comparisons and judge effectiveness. Paradoxically at this time clients are in a state of mind least able to make effective decisions, given that they are typically experiencing emotional and physical suffering, stress and confusion. When the subjects considering psychotherapy are not individuals but couples or families then the exercise of free choice by all the participants becomes a rather abstract notion. The problems of choice continue – even if the individual or group manages to select an appropriate type of counselling they are then faced with a whole set of extra choices that challenge the potential client's rational competence. Which counsellor should I choose? Male or female? Black or white? Should I choose a counsellor from: my employer, my doctor, a professional agency, a voluntary organization or a private practitioner? Finally, not only is the potential client's ability to choose made difficult by the distractions of anxiety and other emotional disturbances, but, to the extent that he is subject to unconscious motivations, he is potentially almost completely unaware of the deeper reasons that drive him to seek therapeutic help. In such circumstances how can he freely choose the most suitable form of help?

Consequently, the degree of freedom involved is massive whilst uncertainty is pervasive and information is minimal. In most cases the counsellor is in the role of selling his services and the client is the purchaser. However, the counsellor is not offering a purely technical service but is offering his self in a relationship with the client. This makes the interaction between counsellor and client quite unique and uncomfortably expressed by the market model of offering the client freedom of choice in purchasing. This position is ameliorated by the development of standards of accreditation, professional ethics, standardized training and so on. Nevertheless, the primary responsibility for the counselling process resides with the counsellor and a more honest and transparent espousal of the six validity claims would not only give the client a clearer understanding of what to expect, it would also outline those aspects of the relationship which are unequal and for which the counsellor is responsible. The counsellor is not in a value-free position with regard to this issue.

The increasingly consumerist character of counselling[7] and psychotherapy can not only have the unfortunate effect of characterizing issues of accessibility in consumerist and marketing terms, but it also, as mentioned earlier, has the effect of reinforcing a certain kind of psychological alienation that results from the commodification of our interactions. To subject the client to the forces of advertising, branding, contractual relationships and lifestyle images may present counselling in terms with which the client is familiar, yet they have the potential to reinforce some of the problematic identity issues that clients bring to the therapeutic process. The usage of branding by marketing agencies is a specific attempt to implant certain images favourable to the product or service and is often aimed at the unconscious mind of the potential consumer. For example, two-year-old children can identify different brands without having any functional understanding of the products they signify – such is the power of branding. Also, following Hoggett (1992), in learning processes the learner (client) needs humility in face of the relative ease or difficulty of that which is to be learned. Money and commodified interactions facilitate the narcissism of the purchaser/client – providing the opportunity for some to avoid the inherent difficulty in the learning process. Ideologies of consumerism and accessibility are in danger of making the purchaser/client arrogant and resistant in the face of a difficult process that demands considerable psychological change.

As counsellors and counselling organizations dip their toes in the muddy water of marketing, any criticisms of this practice are dismissed as antediluvian. Whilst some radical possibilities exist, it is more likely that the counselling culture, which has little resistance to the 'expertise' of advertisers and public relations consultants, will conform to marketing strategies that increasingly colonize our everyday life with texts, signs and images that continually seduce the minds of potential clients to collaborate in the extension, to ever deeper places, of the individual's self-management[8] through the ceaseless consumption of corporate capital's codes, images and lifestyles. As counselling becomes more comfortable with the values of the marketplace we should be aware that such values, whilst described as mere techniques, are not value-free.

The Values that Counsellors Bring

I now want to take a more pragmatic look at the way in which counsellors bring a range of values into counselling. Such values can vary from simple prejudice concerning personal taste to unconscious projections. I agree with other commentators that the elimination of values is impossible and that the situation would be dramatically improved if we were to make this issue transparent. However, I am interested in attempting to show that the level and range of values and preconceptions that counsellors import into counselling are both deeper and wider than is often portrayed, whilst maintaining that the problem becomes significantly more manageable when placed within the context of the preconditions of communicative rationality.

Having already discussed some theoretical and general concerns surrounding the claim that counselling and psychotherapy often have a poor understanding of background knowledge and social context, it might be useful to consider how this can happen in practice. It is obvious to observe that counselling takes place within a social context, but how resilient are counselling organizations and individual practitioners to changing social values when the changes may not only be faddish, but may also represent opaque (and difficult to analyze) tectonic systemic changes to the social, economic and political environment?

Almond (2001: 8) looks at the general phenomenon of the breakdown of promising and contracting in social relationships and relates it to the particular problem of the instability that this phenomenon creates in marriage and family relationships. The ease of entering such relationships, she argues, and their ready dissolubility place an intolerable strain on them. Without the security and trust engendered by an existential commitment and promise to the relationship, which can be entered into with a measure of self-awareness, the relevant parties must maintain the relationship by a constant process of managing themselves and satisfying their partner in a way that can be unremitting and oppressive. A committed promise to each other may create enough trust for each partner to reduce the level of self and other management and enable a more relaxed being with oneself and the other. The danger in this situation is that, should they seek therapeutic help, the counsellor may simply follow surface trends and make the situation worse by an easy acceptance of contemporary, and perhaps popular, 'solutions' to such problems. A relationship counsellor might easily accept the difficulty that two people face in reconciling their individual needs as a sign of their mutual incompatibility, rather than considering an alternative perspective that interprets their 'incompatibility' as resulting from their excessive individualism and narcissism which only feels 'normal' because the social context valorizes excessive individualism.

The acceptability in recent years of the generic term 'partners' reinforces the point because it symbolizes the tendency to replace a permanent contractual relationship (husband and wife in marriage) with a temporary and non-contractual one. In the attempt to distance oneself from the value of marriage, the retreat to the term 'partner' is not a value-free option but indicates an unreflective acceptance of a new norm. Similar problems adhere to the psychotherapist's involvement in parent–child relationships, particularly with regard to the abuse of children. An unreflective adopting of changing values by the psychotherapist, without being able to check them against a reliable set of values as can be found in communicative rationality, can have significant clinical consequences. As Almond points out in some cases the psychotherapist fails to consider the validity claim of truth: 'Here philosophical notions of truth and knowledge are conspicuously involved – the past cannot be re-visited and the limitations of trying to recreate it from the present should be recognized' (2001: 8).

Masson (1989: 251) finds family therapists frequently guilty of these charges. Seeing themselves as pragmatists with a firm grasp of social realities many believe that their approach could be extended into society as a whole. Masson contends, as does Maranhao (1986), that their understanding of social dynamics is limited and often just reflects the surface realities that have been engendered in them by their culture. He is also concerned that the psychotherapist's concentration on the client's past can have a damaging effect on the client because the act of ignoring some of the present social causes of the client's condition prevents the client from a full understanding of his condition and its causes and thereby limits possibilities for enlightenment and development. Behavioural approaches in some disciplines like psychosexual therapy can steer the client into specifically resolving the immediate sexual dysfunction without reaching an understanding of its genesis. For example, a middle-aged man who has been brought up on the notion that it is his task to provide a sexual performance for his female partner can sometimes lose the pleasure to be found in sexual experience. He may become distanced from himself and his own sexual needs and desire which, in turn, can reduce mutual sexual satisfaction. The success in returning the man to satisfactory sexual relations through a behavioural intervention should not blind us to the fact that such a process can deprive him of an understanding of the social definition of masculinity that helped create the problem in the first place. Without this understanding his development will be limited.

Bellah *et al.* analyze the therapeutic culture as a whole and illustrate how the 'new' norms and culture of therapy become ossified to create a new layer of un-deconstructed background assumptions:

> In asserting a radical pluralism and the uniqueness of each individual, they conclude that there is no moral common ground and therefore no public relevance of morality outside the sphere of minimal procedural rules and obligations not to injure. . . . In thinking they have freed themselves from tradition in the pursuit of rationality and personal authenticity, they do not understand the degree to which their views are themselves traditional. Even being anti-tradition is part of the individualist tradition... Indeed, by not seeing the extent to which their own beliefs are part of a pervasive common culture, they run the risk of doing just what they attack in the older moral traditions – that is, accepting as literally true what is merely a cultural convention

and then refusing to open their position to discussion. Since their views are to them so self-evident, they are even tempted on occasion to force them on others. (1988: 141)

Samuels (1993) reacts to the proposition that there should be no politics in psychotherapy. This supposedly 'value-free' approach is advanced as if any discussion of politics was completely out of the question in psychotherapy, whereas the introduction of topics like sex and aggression, which are remarkably value-laden, do not seem to raise an eyebrow. This does not mean that proselytizing or discipleship is acceptable. Nevertheless, the psychotherapist and the client are subject to the same social forces, some of which are repressive. 'There is no personal outside the political; the political is itself a precondition for subjectivity. That is perhaps why there is so much politics in depth psychology, the profession of the subjective' (Samuels 1993: 55). It is not a source of worry that the positivistic project of a value-free counselling and psychotherapy must be abandoned; neither is it a problem that the therapeutic process must inherently involve values;[9] what is very worrying and prevalent is the failure by counselling institutions and individual practitioners to subject values to rational discourse and philosophical debate.[10]

In the above section I have attempted to show how background cultural values can have a general effect on counselling. Shortly I shall attempt to show how these and other values are brought by counsellors into the counselling process. Before that I wish to look at some values that are *intrinsic* to the process itself. Whilst trying to draw these analytic distinctions the nature of the subject may well result in some overlapping.

Habermas articulates a fascinating analysis illustrating how the process of reaching an understanding necessarily involves making judgements. In order to understand an expression I must bring to conscious awareness in my mind the reasons with which the speaker would, if necessary, defend its validity. I am therefore brought into the process of assessing validity claims. This is because it is in the nature of reasons that they cannot be described or understood in the mental attitude of a third person – to understand an expression the reasons on which it claims validity must be comprehendible to me for myself. 'The interpreter would not have understood what a "reason" is if he did not reconstruct it with its claims to provide grounds; that is, if he did not give it a *rational interpretation*...' (Habermas 1997b: 116). The description of reasons demands an evaluation. I can understand reasons only to the extent that I understand *why* they are or are not cogent.

An interpreter cannot, therefore, interpret expressions connected through criticisable validity claims with a potential of reasons (and thus represent knowledge) without taking a position on them. And he cannot take a position without applying his *own* standards of judgment, at any rate standards that he has made his own. (Habermas 1997b: 116)

As counselling and psychotherapy are inherently processes involved in reaching understandings it is an unavoidable fact that the practitioner cannot avoid making evaluations.

When discussing marketing a little earlier I was concerned about its possible effects of increasing the colonization of our very selfhood in forms of self-mastery or control in order to increase the exercise of choice from a range of consumables in a consumer society. Giddens puts a slightly different slant on this insight. As counselling and psychotherapy continually fail to grapple with the issues of morals and ethics (other than in the extremely narrowly defined concern with confidentiality[11]), they become increasingly absorbed with skills and technique so, as Giddens puts it, 'mastery, in other words, substitutes for morality...' (1991: 202). Therapy mimics management.[12] Just as managers control an organization, then, through therapy, the self is trained in techniques of self-control. Issues of why this is taking place and its relation to social values fade away. 'Even therapy,' observes Giddens 'as the exemplary form of the reflexive project of the self, can become a phenomenon of control – an internally referential system in itself' (1991: 202).

Bond seems a little ambivalent on the issue that values are intrinsic to the counselling process. On the one hand, he states:

> Counselling is not a neutral activity in the way 'non-directive' seems to imply. The values of counselling, namely respect, integrity and impartiality mean that there is an implicit tendency to direct clients towards taking personal responsibility for their own lives and there are times when this may even the explicit. Counsellors are in the business of influencing people towards relating to each other as autonomous individuals on an adult/adult basis. (1997: 62)

Unfortunately Bond does not inform us of: where the values of respect, integrity and impartiality come from; how they are related; or how they are to be philosophically justified. This is the difficulty with just about every commentator on values in counselling and psychotherapy. Nevertheless, he is clear that the theory of non-directiveness is redundant. Yet this lack of philosophical justification and conceptual clarity leads him into difficult terrain. For example, he goes on to say that: 'The onus is on the counsellor to provide the client with sufficient space to work within her own value system with the counsellor's own value system validating this relationship and avoiding the imposition of the counsellor's own personal values' (1997: 72). We have three different value systems operating here – the client's, the counsellor's and the counsellor's personal values. It is in contexts like this that I think the concept of validity claims is very useful. It provides us with a viewpoint from which morals claim universal validity and cannot be made relative to an individual's 'value system'. Validity claims also enable an understanding that personal authenticity is not simply a matter of individuals expressing their own values and lifestyle.

In fairness, Bond is willing to tackle the issue of counselling and religion. He asks the question whether or not counselling is fundamentally a secular activity. His answer is interesting:

> It is sometimes suggested that counselling...is fundamentally based on humanist values and is therefore exclusively secular in character. This is also a misunderstanding if it is being implied that counselling seeks to promote a humanist view of life. It is more accurate to think of counselling as a humanitarian activity in the sense of promoting general well-being, regardless of the recipient's belief system. (1997: 73–4)

Without an articulated philosophical basis the purpose of counselling gets reduced to 'promoting well-being'. I have already suggested that the concept of 'well-being' is inadequate. More importantly, however, we should not be afraid of challenging religious assumptions. At the beginning of this work I outlined how the ontological assumptions inherent in religious claims are incompatible with a deontological ethics and communicative rationality. We cannot have our cake and eat it. Counselling and psychotherapy are, I believe, secular activities. In so far as the person holding a religious position can operate within the secular realm of rational discourse, they are open to the therapeutic process. To the extent that they introduce fixed, ontological religious beliefs into a communicative process towards reaching an understanding it is not possible to create a decentred moral consciousness or conduct a true process of argumentation. This is particularly true of those subscribing to a religious fundamentalism, regardless of the particular faith system involved:

> As the Rushdie case reminded us, a fundamentalism that leads to a practice of intolerance is incompatible with constitutional democracy. Such a practice is based on religious or historico-philosophical interpretations of the world that claim exclusiveness for a privileged way of life. Such conceptions lack an awareness of the fallibility of their claims, as well as a respect for the 'burdens of reason' (Rawls). Of course, religious convictions and global interpretations of the world are not obliged to subscribe to the kind of fallibilism that currently accompanies hypothetical knowledge in the experimental sciences. But fundamentalist worldviews are dogmatic in a different sense: they leave no room for reflection on their relationship with the other worldviews with which they share the same universe of discourse and against whose competing validity claims they can advance their positions only on the basis of reasons. They leave no room for 'reasonable disagreement.' (Habermas 1999: 224; see also Habermas 2003b: 31–2)

Kegan is mindful of the fact that the value which is undeniably at the heart of the therapeutic endeavour is that of truth – which, in my terms, is communicative rationality. It may well be that counselling may help a person to become more loving, spontaneous, kind and caring and so on, but this is not the main purpose. Kegan warns counsellors and psychotherapists that the 'career of truth' may not always include this attractive range of aspirations and they should therefore above all understand that 'much of human personality is none of their business' (1981: 296).

Finally, in our survey of values intrinsic to the therapeutic process, there is an another basic reality, rarely mentioned, which trumps even communicative rationality. White (1960: 173–4) reminds us that the end of all men and women is everywhere the same. Regardless of individuality and cultural differentiation we all die. White believes that if psychotherapy is to be more than a routine technique then the therapist has to orientate the client in the direction in which they are already facing, that is towards the future and the suffering of eventual death.

It might now be useful to change our orientation and look at the value-free issue from the perspective of what the counsellor brings to the act of counselling. The illustration of the depth and range of values that counsellors are likely to bring is not an attempt to so thoroughly deconstruct the value free ideology that we descend into the complete relativism that we have been challenging throughout. Communicative rationality remains a moral and ethical framework that will assist us, just as the process of individuation creates a self-awareness that enables mature counsellors to gain a reflective understanding of the needs and values that they bring. Hillman lists a variety of needs that counsellors bring to their work, or as he puts it: 'In analysis we would say that the countertransference is there before the transference begins. My expectations are there with me as I wait for the knock on the door' (1991: 17).

First, there is a countertransference before one even becomes the counsellor – something impels the counsellor to do this kind of activity. The counsellor could not do this demanding kind of work if she did not *need* to do it. She may bring a need to heal or redeem her wounded inner child, or she may need the client to help her express her ability to give help. The helper and the needy go together. Secondly, Hillman argues, the counsellor's relationship with the client expresses a need that is more than personal. Her need to be with the client may not simply be a personal need but reflects an objective requirement of the relationship between counsellor and client. Both need to affirm the voice of mutual love and recognition. Moreover, not everybody would be comfortable with the personal revelations and sharing that occurs in counselling and psychotherapy. If the therapist is not conscious of her need for intimacy and she is not satisfying this need in other aspects of her life, it may turn into a demand on the client and herself. The therapist may then become over-revealing and the session becomes a mutual confessional. Fourthly, the practitioner may be drawn by her need for fame and power and become a celebrity therapist concentrating on the needs of 'important' people. Other counsellors may be drawn into the archetype of therapist as scientist, or detective or technocrat such that they are absorbed by the details of the case and the need to solve puzzles.

Finally, a fairly common need for counsellors, particularly during recruitment and training, is their need for self-worth. As potential clients themselves they are attracted to the therapeutic environment as a means of finding out their own identity and possibly improving their own social status – particularly the status of being a 'professional'.

Needs in themselves are not harmful. They become so when they are repressed and denied and eventually transform themselves into demands. Demands ask for fulfilment and cannot help but intrude upon the client, whereas needs only require expression. Needs cease to be a negative input into the counselling process when I become conscious of them.

> My needs and the style in which I work cannot be purified out by means of a pseudo-openness and impersonal detachment. The less I am aware of my personal needs and how they filter the forces playing through me, the more the archetypal aspects appear directly and impersonally . . . No one can control the psyche and keep these forces out, but one can know something of them beforehand and hold to the human side of the line by admitting from the beginning the needs of one's own personal equation. This may mean at times admitting these needs to the other person, which helps to keep the human side. (Hillman 1991: 19–20)

Psychotherapist and counsellors bring more than needs, they also bring several levels of preconceptions which are harmful if unconsciously held and unmediated by communicative rationality. For example:

- No feelings or thoughts are detachable from the theories or world-views which give them meaning. We must therefore be aware of the overarching worldview or theoretical frame with which we approach the world.
- The counsellor himself has an inherent ethical and moral interest in developing himself and the client towards the values involved in all communication aimed at reaching an understanding.
- Various preconceptions about theoretical models of psychotherapy will orientate the therapist in ways that are specific to the models.
- To the extent that the counsellor has not achieved congruence he is likely to be involved in unconscious attachments, identifications and projections resulting from his personal narrative.
- The counsellor may also consciously bring a set of personal values, ranging from bigotry to religious beliefs. Some of these are impossible to prevent. The clothes you wear, as well as their colour, quality and tidiness reveal a great deal about you: as do your car, the pictures in your counselling room, your jewellery, your furniture and so on.
- In so far as they identify with a professional status, practitioners will bring a set of values and behaviours in line with the professional culture and codes. Such values may benefit the counsellor more than they benefit the client.

- Those counsellors that work within organizations will be subject to organizational imperatives. Those working in a corporate setting are likely to have an outlook different from that of those working in the voluntary sector.
- The practitioner may identify with various sectional interests of which they are unaware; for instance, social groups defined by gender, wealth, ethnicity and so on.

The contradictions and paradoxes involved in the attempt to be value-free and non-judgemental can induce the practitioners into taking very convoluted psychological positions. Halmos clearly observes how the attempt to be non-judgemental almost encourages the practitioner to strive for 'objectivity' and to dis-identify from any appearance of 'doing good' or 'benevolence'.

> At its lowest estimate, the counsellor cannot sustain the activity of healing another or helping another with perseverance, and scrupulously avoid communicating the idea that concern for the welfare of others is worthwhile! The therapeutic attention is a moral stance, no matter how much effort is expended on the most cautious non-directive self-control. And indeed even this, the conscientiousness of it, the painstaking tactfulness of it, and so on, will hardly escape the attention, no matter how unconscious and intuitive, of those who are helped. The whole performance is inevitably personal, and biased in some most important sense. The truth lies not in disowning this bias but rather acting on it with full awareness and frank admission. The real bias is to think that we can care and remain unbiased, that we ought to be unbiased even in the 'I and Thou' relationship of persons, or that counselling does not need that kind of relationship. (Halmos 1965: 104)

One unfortunate consequence of this phenomenon is that counsellors and psychotherapists retreat to the safe citadel of technique. This can mean camouflaging the emotional involvement with the client behind the exercise of their practical skills, an over-elaborate professional etiquette and clever manipulations of presentation of self.

Finally, counselling and psychotherapeutic organizations can bring a set of values into the domain of the practice. Or, what is more accurately the case, they can become paralyzed by the fear and responsibility of so doing and retreat behind value-free. The environment of counselling organizations in the voluntary sector becomes increasingly difficult to manage. In times of fuller employment and the rapid increase in the number of women entering employment, the supply of volunteer counsellors has reduced. This increases the cost base of these charities at a time when there is an increase in the number of organizations seeking funding and a reduction in the amount of funding available. Moreover, whatever funding is available becomes increasingly tied to the requirements of the funder. This leads to a real conflict of values. Grants from charitable trusts become increasingly

targeted and project-based obliging counselling organizations to sometimes move away from their values in the search for income. Local government
funding is declining and increasingly focused on a limited set of values and
targets defined by central government. The latter, disguising itself behind
pseudo-claims to represent the democratic will, obliges funded organizations
to work in the interests of the state, government or political party. This
creeping invasion of civil society by the state is a serious threat to the
integrity of the independent nature of the voluntary sector.[13] A classic
example of this, in Britain, is the direct dependence of Relate, the largest
counselling charity, on government money. The power of government
patronage creates a conflict between the competing values of the state and
the charity with the sad result that the charity compromises its independent
voice such that the notion of counselling as critique is all but lost. In this
context non-judgementalism and value-free can become ideological
smokescreens.

> In this discussion of the development of the technical aspects of marital work in the
> organization, the question of such values has mainly been kept at arm's length. This
> is legitimate for heuristic purposes, but it is not a useful guide to action. The organ-
> ization is concerned to offer help to those experiencing difficulties within the intimate
> domain of marital relationships. In doing this it cannot ignore the many public ways
> in which these relationships are constructed and disputed. Marriage, as relationship
> or institution, is conflicted territory. Intervention in marriage cannot therefore be
> regarded as a neutral activity, merely constrained by limitations in the technical
> aspects of counselling and therapy. It remains an open question whether Relate, in
> its future thinking and development, will be prepared to grasp this nettle. (Lewis
> *et al.* 1992: 265)

The Moral and Ethical Responsibility of the Counsellor

At this juncture I do not wish to get involved in the details of codes of
ethics and confidentiality. Keeping to our theme of offering a critique of
non-judgementalism I want to investigate the issue that the inequality
between the therapist and the client creates a special duty of moral and
ethical care on the therapist. There is no doubt that the client is equal to
the counsellor (and anybody else) in the sense that we are all beings of
worth and should be valued as such. However, as moral consciousness is a
competence, we should expect that the counsellor or psychotherapist
should be operating at a more developed level than the client. Linked to
this should be the expectation that the practitioner is more self-aware than
the client and therefore less subject to unconscious determinations. This
leaves the practitioner with the classic question of whether or not he
should make judgements about the authenticity and morality of the client,
as presented by the client, in line with an assessment of the client's 'real

interests' irrespective of the client's avowal of such interests. Given certain caveats, I believe that the practitioner is bound by the telos of the counselling process to make such judgements and that the criteria used are the validity claims inherent in communication aimed at reaching an understanding. The counsellor has the duty of care to try to develop a client to full autonomy as understood in the full sense that I have already outlined. Hillman reminds us that the Greek word *therapia* is linked to caring. The root is *dher* which means to carry support or hold. 'The therapist is one who carries and takes care as does a servant.... The psychotherapist is literally the attendant of the soul' (Hillman 1989: 73).

As a tenet of methodology it is understandable that the psychotherapist will, at times throughout the process until the end is in sight, withhold expressing judgement on the moral or ethical statements of the client. Since the therapist is dealing with the systematically distorted language of the client and the authenticity of the client is itself in doubt, it would be inappropriate to make judgements on statements that may not represent the 'real interest' or 'core identity' of the client. Given that the therapeutic intervention is characterized by the phenomenon of transference, counter-transference, projection, denial, splitting and other dynamics, the precipitate introduction of moral and ethical judgements would be self-defeating. The counselling room is not the right setting for moral didacticism, nevertheless the counselling process has the purpose of enabling the client to experience moral and ethical development in such a way that they can adopt it for themselves. It is therefore necessary for the counsellor to hold the moral frame. So, although counselling involves accepting this person as she or he is, it does not mean that '... it would be good for the client and for society if they were to carry on in the same way. In other words, it does not mean seeing behaviour, lifestyle or the attitudes behind them as morally unprob-lematic' (Almond 2001: 6). Similarly, to liberate clients from all guilt feelings associated with any transgressions in a value-free flurry of compassion may only result in the accompanying guilt-sense being repressed back into the unconscious and therefore ever more likely to be subject to repetition.

In the late stages of psychotherapy the therapist is helping the client to develop a critique of the client's rewritten narrative of the self. The therapist helps the client evaluate the new story in terms of its coherence, truth, authenticity and morality. Inconsistencies, gaps and blind spots are challenged. The thoughts of Kegan may be able to help us at this point. From his constructive-developmental point of view the therapist is trying to join another person in a pivotally intimate way; she is trying to become a helpful guide to the person's very evolution. Whether you call this the process of meaning-evolution (Kegan) or moral consciousness (Habermas) is not important at this juncture; it involves the evolution to full, non-individualistic autonomy through an increasing competence in the validity claims of truth, justice, comprehensibility, authenticity and health. This evolutionary process is not usually brought to awareness whilst the person is developing in a balanced manner. The presenting problem that the client brings represents a break in his ability to maintain equilibrium and development. From the client's point of view this rupture is a source of suffering; from the therapist's point of view this is an opportunity to protect the unseen evolutionary process. This is a primary purpose of counselling and psychotherapy and it entails the counsellor holding a fundamental moral and ethical position on behalf of the client, with or without the client's knowledge or permission. 'If "the problem" is the way into this work for both of them, it should be acknowledged that 'this work' at the start is more the counsellor's agenda than the client's...We both know that she has come not for a "valuable learning experience" but to get herself out of this mess' (Kegan 1981: 278).

The counsellor is not seeking to 'get' the client to do anything; he is not seeking to manipulate or use rhetorical devices on the client – the choice in the end will always be the client's; the counsellor is seeking to make that choice available to him. The pain and suffering embedded in the presenting problem represent a resource to both the counsellor and client. The counsellor is trying to protect the choice that is hidden in the problem and hold open the possibility for evolutionary change. He is trying to understand and feel the experience that having such a problem may entail. But the counsellor is not trying to help '...solve the problem, or try to make the experience less painful. He chooses the phenomenological perspective because his loyalty is to *the person in her meaning-making*, rather than to her stage or balance. He is seeking to join the process of meaning-evolution, rather than solve the problems which are reflective of the process...' (Kegan 1981: 274). It is quite natural for the client to want to go in the opposite direction and try to solve the problem as quickly as possible by attempting to contain it rather than spread it into the whole of her life. As we shall consider later, the moral requirement that the counsellor be the guardian of this process, often in spite of the client's desires, can pose real problems for the rapidly expanding practice of brief therapy. Whilst it is not intrinsic to the brief therapeutic encounter that it ignores this requirement, in practice it may all too often be the case. Under attack from, on the one hand, relativists, postmodernists and multiculturalists, and, on the other, the behaviourists, pragmatists and rationalists, the counsellor's confidence in holding this line is diminishing. Similarly, the increasing consumer consciousness in the client for quick results creates an uncomfortable alliance with the prevalent practice of organizations purchasing counselling for their staff on the basis that the number of sessions purchased will be limited and that the counselling methodology involved will be targeted, focused and aimed at symptom relief.

Counsellors and psychotherapists have great difficulty in separating and distinguishing between *tolerance and respect* for the fact that each person is an individual *meaning-maker*, and the usage of *discernment and judgement* on the *validity of the meanings made*. This is to confuse integrity with validity. The failure of counselling theory is its inability to offer a critique of the dominant relativist worldview. This is a product of its inward looking culture:

> The conviction that there are no non-arbitrary bases upon which to consider one state of meaning-making as better than another is, in a therapist, at once a philosophical confusion and a psychological confusion. Philosophically, it confuses the inevitability of subjectivity (that there is no absolute truth; that each of us is making our own truth) with what I believe is the false notion of the impossibility of thereby non-arbitrarily comparing these subjectivities. The second does not follow from the first. Psychologically, the conviction confuses the need for the clinician's unconditional positive regard for the integrity of another's meaning-making activity with what I believe is the false sense that the clinician must regard all made meanings as equally valid. Again, the second does not follow from the first. I do not judge a person's meaning-making activity, but I must admit that in an indirect way I do judge a person's made meanings. Persons cannot be more or less good than each other; the *person* has an unqualified integrity. But stages or the evolutionary balances (the structure of made meanings) can be more or less good than each other; stages have a qualified validity. It is, in fact, the unequal validity of the various evolutionary truces that actually provides the basis for my sense that counselling is proceeding. In trying to avoid the traps discussed earlier, for example, I am making a judgement on behalf of one stage over another. I never voice my judgement, but not because I believe the judgement is itself unjustified; I never voice it because I do not think that is doing so will be of any use. But I *exercise* my judgement in my address to the experience of the new voice emerging, and I judge our mutual process according to whether or not the person is being presented the opportunity to move from a less evolved to a more evolved state. (Kegan 1981: 292)

Acting in someone's 'best interests' is problematic. We are often suspicious of people who think they know our 'real interests' and with good reason. There is a long history of genocide, war and repression resulting from ruling classes, religions and political beliefs telling us what our real interests are. We are right to be suspicious but some of these worries are unfounded. The pith of the question of real interests centres around the phenomenon of a person who will not believe something that he rationally should believe. Williams (1993) considers the case of someone contemplating suicide. The person involved in a suicide attempt does not believe that things will look different at some point in the future. For those who know this person and believe that the current dire circumstances can be alleviated, are they not acting in his best interests by preventing him from committing suicide? We would make this intervention on the assumption that his lack of desire to live and disbelief in a better future is itself part of the problem that can be cured. However, we cannot justify such an intervention by using the argument that by acting in someone's real interest this will be verified by the fact that when 'cured' this person will acknowledge that we were indeed acting in his interest. As Williams points out people who are subject to brainwashing, perhaps by a religious sect, often fully embrace their new condition. At this point some will abandon the argument and accept that the notion of real interest is incurably subjective. If we are to move beyond the dead-end of justifying change via the self-validation of the brainwashing type we need to change the direction. If someone at the moment does not acknowledge that a certain change would be in his interest but, following the change, he accepts that it was in his interest this will show '...that the change was really in his interest only on condition that the alteration in his outlook is explained in terms of some *general incapacity* from which he suffered in his original state, and which has been removed or alleviated by the change' (1993: 42–3). Williams defines 'general incapacity' in two ways. First, it cannot simply represent the fact that his alleged inability to recognize his real interest before the change is simply tailor-made to the requirements of the recommended change; in other words, it must have general implications. Secondly, the problem in question must be a genuine incapacity. His failure to acknowledge his best interest is seen to be an incapacity because it is understood and defined as something that is essentially constitutive of being a human being.

> The answer is that not everything in someone's interests is necessary to his human functioning, or is something that he *needs*. What he does need are the capacities, including the basic patterns of motivation, to pursue some of the things that are in his interests. If it is not to be purely ideological, the idea of real interests needs to be provided with a theory of error, a substantive account of how people may fail to recognize their real interests. (Williams 1993: 43)

Psychotherapy and counselling, firmly based on the theory of communicative rationality, provide such a theoretical framework.

CHAPTER 5

Issues in Psychotherapy and Counselling

Transference, Countertransference and Eros

In the therapeutic process the client's development is dependent upon the disturbed experiences and feelings being expressed, brought to consciousness, recognized and then worked with in the secure environment of the counselling room. However, these experiences can become subject to repression which channels their expression through privatized symbols and symptoms which are not readily understood and which operate in a closed loop of repetition. The client continually repeats the symptoms. The psychotherapist or counsellor endeavours to gain the trust of the client such that the client will then repeat the symptoms towards him. When this special relationship has been created, transference is possible, that is, the client 'transfers' or projects the symptoms on to the therapist. The client switches the irrational and distorted aspects of his behaviour on to the therapist. The therapeutic process is not only a matter of analyzing the genesis of the symptoms and giving the patient insight, it is also contained in the real and living relationship between the therapist and the client. Over time the client repeatedly tests the therapist by projecting aspects of her shadow self on to him just as the therapist repeatedly demonstrates that the client's projections are false. Through this dynamic process the client is able to make a step-by-step progress (punctuated by resistances and the odd step backwards) as the therapist 'withdraws' the projection. Rather than attempting to be non-judgemental the therapist does not bracket or exclude his subjectivity; with its controlled employment the therapist's subjectivity becomes the vehicle of change. Once the therapist's own identity is involved, this intersubjective connection with the client has its own transferential qualities and is known as the countertransference.

We can identify at least four aspects of the countertransference: first, there are the feelings and thoughts that the counsellor has for the client, which may well be in place before the client engages in her transference; secondly, it involves the experiences the counsellor has as a result of playing the role projected on to him by the client; thirdly, the thoughts and feelings of the therapist associated with resisting and withdrawing the transference; and finally, the counsellor may end up adopting some of the material projected by the client.

For example, it would not be hard to imagine a circumstance where a white counsellor discovers that the new client she will meet the next day is black. The counsellor is at one level quite convinced that she does not have any feelings of racial prejudice, but, at another level, this will be her first ever black client and some doubts about her 'pure non-judgementalism' gnaw at the deeper recesses of her psyche. So before she has even seen the client some countertransference is in place. On the day of the first session the counsellor experiences another surprise, the black client is none too happy to be seeing a white counsellor. This particular client, it transpires, has developed a very cogent political understanding of the psychological issues he is bringing to counselling. From his perspective, the history of slavery, colonialism and racism have created the very social environment that is conducive to creating the symptoms that he experiences. He transfers some of this resentment on to the counsellor and her antennae pick it up very quickly. The second stage of the countertransference relates to the uncomfortable feelings that the counsellor now has with regard to the client's projection on to her relating to her part in white cultural dominance or racism. She may now be feeling a certain guilt or shame or, on the other hand, she may feel resentment at the inaccuracy of these projections. During the process of withdrawing the countertransference the counsellor has to rise to the challenge of repeatedly showing the client that, in this case, his projections about the counsellor were false. Or, in the final stage, the counsellor may admit to the client that, in some small ways, his projections were accurate and, as a result of the fact that counselling is an interactive process, she has learned from the client and endeavours to alter her behaviour accordingly. Imagine how much more complicated this would be if the transference and countertransference were suffused with a sexual chemistry!

The concept of countertransference carries more ambivalence than that of transference. Because of its Freudian roots and the dogma of non-judgementalism there can still be a sense that the counsellor 'should not' have such feelings, and when the feelings do exist they can be reduced to being merely a reaction to the client's material thereby overlooking the fact that counsellors have their own emotional and fantasy life. Indeed, if the counsellors did not have any emotional or imaginal interest in the clients, whence would they generate the motivation to do this most diffi-cult work?

Fundamentally I believe that it is important to understand the issue of transference and countertransference as being an erotic connection between counsellor and client. The therapeutic relationship is an intersubjective process whereby the internal worlds of the client and the counsellor meet and dynamically interact. As erotic desire is an element of both their psychic worlds it would be very surprising if it did not feature during therapy. Indeed, it is as old as the hills.

What happens is what is called in its most common appearance the *transference effect*. This effect is love. (Lacan 1988: 253)

The transference is a phenomenon in which subject and psycho-analyst are both included. To divide it in terms of transference and counter-transference – however bold, however confident what is said on this theme may be – is never more than a way of avoiding the essence of the matter.

The transference is an essential phenomenon, bound up with desire as the nodal phenomenon of the human being – and it was discovered long before Freud. It was perfectly articulated ... with the most extreme rigour, in a text in which the subject of love is discussed, namely, Plato's *Symposium*. (Lacan 1988: 231)

Hillman (1991) is equally clear that we should not shrink from understanding the true nature of the force at work in the transference and countertransference situation.

Alone in the room, face to face, in secrecy, the soul laid bare, the future at stake – does this not constellate the archetypal experience of human love? We come no further in our understanding by pejoratively naming the experience 'projection' or denigrating it as 'transference.' Two people committed to each other and to the course of their involvement in the sufferings of the psyche are at once played through by the archetypal force of love. This is yet stronger when they together hope through their encounters to create a new life as a result of their union. (1991: 35)[1]

Samuels (1989) sees himself as working towards the idea that eros is something that we should expect in psychotherapy and we should be concerned about its absence. Without the presence of eros Mann (1997) finds it hard to imagine whence does the client develop a deeper and richer connection to life. Rather than happening outside the counselling room it is an inevitable part of the process. 'It is the medium through which transformation occurs' (Mann 1997: 25). Just as eros is not excluded from the counselling room neither is it confined to it. Both counsellor and client carry a profile of erotic connections generated through their life and conditioned by general social and cultural constructions of eros. Working with the erotic in transference is not limited to the immediate connection between the counsellor and the client, but also includes the background assumptions.

The term 'eros' has many associated meanings dependent on whether the context is psychological, philosophical, sociological or religious. The definition that I am most interested in is the Jungian sense of eros as an archetypal feature of psychological functioning, that is, connectedness, linking and relatedness. Secondary, but also of interest, are the sexual connotations of eros, in either the sense of reproduction or eroticism, as a rich and powerful source of sexual attraction, be they heterosexual or homosexual. All of these can occur in counselling with differing levels of emphasis and importance depending on the particular chemistry between counsellor and client and the stage which the counselling has reached. Thus, whilst I am primarily interested in a theoretical psychological understanding of eros, this does not detract from the enormous immediacy and power it carries in therapy. The erotic interpersonal connection can be expressed in such states as sexual arousal, passion, love and frustration.

The classical Freudian school, which was later represented by Lacan, denies the positive construct of the role of eros in psychotherapy. Love, they say, does have a transference effect but it results in a resistance to therapy. From this viewpoint the transference is the means by which the communication of the unconscious is blocked, so that rather than opening the door to the unconscious the transference closes it. The transference makes the client resistant to the therapist's interpretation. I feel that Mann and Hillman offer a constructive critique of this position. Mann (1997) acknowledges that the classical interpretation will work in some cases, although the resistance is more likely to be a feature of the therapist's own anxiety about dealing with the erotic and containing it. Indeed, many of Freud's evolving techniques in psychoanalysis were designed to prevent the client from becoming erotically excited and to avoid the analyst's own countertransference. Freud abandoned touching the patient's head and any other form of physical contact; the analyst's chair was moved behind the client, and the analyst was to maintain an objective neutrality.

Hillman (1972) is more radical. The process by which the power of eros is overcome is analytic reflection – the act of interpretation that Lacan demands. This 'withdrawing of the projection' is essential if we are to work through the transference but it can be a virtue that becomes a vice when the production of interpreted meaning is favoured above the value of the erotic experience. The rush to interpretation with the hope of the 'solving the problem' can be a defensive measure by the therapist to gain control, and ignores the importance of the transference. Eros must not be enslaved to Apollo. The therapist must let the withdrawal of the projection ensue from a radical immersion in the transference and countertransference such that reflective interpretations of the client's behaviour occur through the therapeutic interaction rather than from the therapist drawing on a fixed, external theoretical framework which is mechanically imposed. This enables the therapist to keep the process alive and allays Hillman's fear: 'We went for soul-making only to have the actual erotic process which makes soul negated by psychological language' (1972: 297). Indeed, clients have become increasingly aware of the nature of counselling and many will already know that it stimulates transference. It therefore makes sense for the counsellor to invest in this process rather than the resistances.

Right in the heart of the therapeutic process, and central to it, is this movement of eros. This reaching out from one psyche to another; back and forth, connecting and making meaning, disconnecting and finding anomie, reconnecting in the yearning to be known, revealed and loved – is this anything other than the dialectic of mutual recognition that Benjamin, Kegan and others identified as the psychologically generative power of interaction? Clients are coming to have their inadequate socialization completed and brought to realization and it requires the same need, drive and yearning to mutually connect with the other. If the process is successful then the therapist will have helped to render the client's self-identity authentic not just by assisting it through the hurdles of the validity claims, but also by conferring on this identity the crowning glory of the legitimating and valorizing love of the therapist. Psyche needs eros.[2] The psychological labour of personal growth needs the stimulus and motive provided by desire, attraction and love.

The view of psychotherapy and counselling as involving an essentially erotic relationship that connects two psyches in a development that is mutual, albeit not equally mutual, also connects centrally with the themes I have been drawing from the work of Habermas. In investigating the purpose of counselling in psychotherapy I have utilized his concept of communicative rationality. Inherent in communicative rationality, and therefore directly related to the six validity claims I have used to provide a basis for our understanding of the purpose of counselling, is the idea that the process of reaching an understanding must involve the subjectivities of the participants. In argumentation, which is the specific, higher-level discourse concerned with reaching an understanding, an agreement must express the common will which, in turn, must express each individual's will. In coming to an agreement, in discourse and in everyday life, the passive assent of the individual is insufficient. A real agreement can only be said to occur when the internal subjectivity or psyche of each participant has experienced real psychological change so that the individual agreement represents a true expression of a self acting authentically and morally. Consequently, all communication intending to reaching an agreement and an understanding involves the internal psychological participation of those concerned in the process of mutual recognition. As we have seen for the phenomenon of transference the nature of the connection between those involved is necessarily (though not exclusively) erotic. Whilst in counselling we can expect the nature of this eroticism to include the full range of erotic feelings and projections including sexual arousal, passion, lust, soulful yearning and so on, in less intense communications the erotic may be experienced as care, concern, affection, dislike and so on. I have already argued that the moral concern for justice is an inherent feature of such communication and that it inevitably leads to (as its reverse side) solidarity – a concern for the welfare of members of the community. Each individual can only individuate through association with others which makes them vulnerable to, and dependent on, other members of the community. In the mundanity of our everyday lives, whenever we communicate with others to reach an understanding the connecting force of the erotic, however low-level, is at work just as our psyches labour to make the transaction more authentic and autonomous. Communicative rationality, eros and counselling are inextricably interconnected. The erotic helps define the purpose.

Psyche and eros, self-identity and love, need each other. Psyche, our sense of self, needs the mutual recognition and affirmation that is provided by the erotic attraction supplied by another psyche in order to have sufficient motive and desire to transform itself. On the other hand, the fire of eros that burns within us needs the psychological labour (self-reflection and understanding) provided by our psyche in order to contain itself. The purpose of the erotic transference and countertransference in therapy is to 'open up' the psyche of the client to be receptive to the transformative power of the recognition provided by the therapist in a process that involves the therapist, also developing the ability of the client's psyche to hold and contain the erotic. This provides the energy and dynamism that engenders the psychological change towards the moral consciousness of an autonomous decentred self that is able to act in line with a healthy balance between the communicatively necessary validity claims of comprehensibility, truth, authenticity and justice.

The erotic transference is the client's way of forming a relationship – this may be the only way available to him or her at the time. Unknowingly the client has found a means of relating that is psychically binding and transformative.

> [T]he emergence of the erotic transference signifies the patient's deepest wish for growth. Like those in love, patients wish to be known and understood, to change what they do not like about themselves, to alter what makes them unlovable. Through the erotic, light is shone on the deepest recesses of the psyche. The fundamental nature of the erotic is that it is psychically binding and connects individuals at the most intimate and deepest levels. The erotic transference, therefore, is potentially the most powerful and positive quality in the therapeutic process. The development of the erotic transference is a major transitional stage in which the repetitive and transformational desire of the patient's unconscious meet at a passionate junction. The heart of the unconscious is visible in all its 'elemental passion', and in so opening allows for the prospect of transformation and psychic growth. (Mann 1997: 9–10)

The therapist cannot exclude herself from this erotic interaction. Even though she may subject the transference to analysis and interpretation, she cannot help but be affected by it and the accompanying countertransference. Rather than being in control of the process the therapist might be better seen as its servant who aims to stop it getting out of control. The less the therapist can reveal the erotic desire within her the more the client will demand it because how else can the client's process be ignited? The client's desire for psyche (psychological growth and awareness) represents a reaching out for individuation. In fact, any therapist or counsellor who understands and works from this model brings eros into the counselling

encounter such that the countertransference is already there prior to transference. The therapist already knows that the client's psyche will need the
spark of eros to open up to the therapist's own psyche. Underlining the
rejection of the myth of non-judgementalism is the fact that rather than
the therapist being subject to the projections of the client, the therapist
has already sided in favour of the link between eros and psyche and brings
them into the counselling room.

Naturally, erotic connections in the counselling room are not without
difficulties. The counsellor needs to be able to differentiate the level at
which the client's psyche is able to handle the erotic attraction. The
client's spontaneous defences must be respected. This is because the tentative growth of psychological development, rather than being under the
control of the client's ego (the familiar pattern), is instead being teased
out from underneath the ego by the erotic charm of the transference/
countertransference, operating on the horizontal dimension of the therapeutic relationship. Therefore early defences are a response from the growing
psyche to protect itself through shyness, secrecy and coolness until the vertical dimension of growth, created by psychological labour, is sufficiently
able to provide understandings and explanations to the client. As the client
becomes more authentic and able to maintain his own genuine self-identity
he is able to separate the erotic from the sexual in the transference relationship. For the psyches of the client and counsellor to come together
the client needs to experience the loss of primordial and compulsive love,
the love or erotic mania characterized by enthralment, servility and pain.
Through the development of psyche the compulsive aspect of love is overcome.

The erotic transference is neither a construct of the therapeutic situation
nor is it limited to it. It is real love, as real as any love experienced outside
the transference. It is because it is real that something genuinely creative
and dynamic can be generated out of it. Psychic growth cannot be fashioned
out of inauthentic experience. Transference can therefore be a feature of
all relationships. 'We are in transference wherever we go, wherever a connection means something to the soul' (Hillman 1972: 107–8).

The role of the therapist and counsellor is to be able to experience the
erotic desires and yet contain them. It is this containing function that
the client needs to internalize through his psychological efforts so that
feelings, especially some tabooed feelings like incest, can be experienced
without being repressed or acted upon. As Mann argues, the erotic in psychotherapy can be destructive[3] if the therapist is tempted to concretize the
material and fails to treat it as symbolic and consequently attempts to act
on her feelings by developing a sexual relationship with the client. This is
why the movement of eros can be torture to the therapist. 'The torture of
the soul seems unavoidable in every close involvement, of which the transference of an analysis is one example. Despite all one does to avoid and to
alleviate suffering, it would seem that the process in which the people find
themselves arranges it . . .' (Hillman 1972: 93–4). Once Eros has been

supplanted by Venus the therapist has lost control and is in deep trouble. It is therefore essential that the therapist consciously sacrifices the acting-out of desire in the full knowledge that this is indeed the torture of love.

In Chapter 2, when discussing morals and ethics, I considered the problem of motivation. Why should we act morally or ethically? One of my answers concerned the role of eros in relationships, I now wish to address this a little further. I have developed the notion of the importance of the erotic in psychological development which, in turn, links it to the purpose of counselling and psychotherapy. The same phenomenon perceived from a different angle enables us to see eros as an important motive in therapy and in general moral and ethical actions.

Mann reminds us that the erotic implies both the transgression of taboos and the making of connections that can be both sublime (romantic love) and profane (sensual desire). Both take us into the most intimate forms of relating. It therefore takes us from a place of safety and security into one that is exciting and dangerous. It is an area of the unknown where new possibilities and ideas are given birth and old shackles can be abandoned. Sexualized erotic desire can lead to the birth of a new being from the intercourse of two people; in counselling there is a psychological parallel. The power of erotic attraction can motivate us to attain better and more developed psychological states in which we can acquire a mature awareness of our authenticity and autonomy. Unless the erotic is experienced as a feeling or a passion in counselling it is difficult to see how the client would gain a more creative erotic and imaginative life. It is as if, through the transference, love has the purpose of igniting, educating and converting. The awakening of psyche is dependent upon eros – through eros psyche is transformed out of her chrysalis.

Once we have introduced eros, we cannot really ignore the role of beauty uncomfortable as we are with this subject. Socrates, of course, had no such discomfort:

> When a man, starting from this sensible world and making his way upward by a right use of his feeling of love for boys, begins to catch sight of that beauty, he is very near his goal. This is the right way of approaching or being initiated into the mysteries of love, to begin with examples of beauty in this world, and using them as steps to ascend continually with that absolute beauty as one's aim, from one instance of physical beauty to two and from two to all, then from physical beauty to moral beauty . . . (Plato 1951: 94)

Beauty, through the attractive power of its images, helps provide the motive for erotic connection. But, more importantly, the beauty of psyche links a sense of the beautiful (aesthetic) to psychological events. Being affected, moved and opened through the experience of erotic connection is not only interesting and meaningful but also attractive, lovable and beautiful.

Psychological perceptions informed by eros are life-giving, vivifying. Something new comes into being in oneself or the other. Love blinds only the usual outlook; it opens a new way of perceiving, because one can be fully revealed only to the sight of love…To meet you, I must risk myself as I am. The naked human is challenged… And even the favourite dictum of reflective psychology – a psychology which has consciousness rather than love as its main goal – 'Know Thyself,' will be insufficient for a creative psychology. Not 'Know Thyself' through reflection, but 'Reveal Thyself,' which is the same as the commandment to love, since nowhere are we more revealed than in our loving. (Hillman 1972: 90–1)

We will struggle to find a more powerful source of motivation. That which attracts us most of all is not Aphrodite, the goddess of beauty, nor is it Venus, rather it is the mortal Psyche embodied in the human psyche.

Brief Counselling

In recent years, particularly in institutional settings, there has been a strong trend towards reducing the length of time spent by a client in psychotherapy or counselling. The reasons for this can be both practical (shorter interventions are cheaper and reduce waiting lists faster) and theoretical as rational-cognitive and behavioural approaches gain in popularity. At the same time there has also been something of a cultural backlash against the 'self involvement' of interminable therapy. How brief is 'brief therapy'. Windy Dryden, who acts as an editor in a series of books concerning brief counselling, defines 'brief' as 25 sessions or less. But I think this underestimates the extent to which the length of counselling and psychotherapy has been curtailed because in most of the institutions in which counselling takes place the average length of a case is, I believe, about six sessions.

There has been a proliferation of different therapeutic schools some of which openly espouse briefer interventions. The real growth in therapeutic culture and brief interventions, however, has been in the number of situations in which some sort of therapeutic intervention takes place without this necessarily being conventional face-to-face counselling. The following list shows the range of counselling-type interventions which are usually brief in nature: social work, victim support, the Samaritans, primary health care counselling, drama therapy, bereavement counselling, radio phone-in programmes, telephone counselling, counselling financed by insurance companies, post-traumatic distress therapy, clinical psychologists, support groups, relationship counselling, alcohol counselling, drug therapy, probation work, TV programmes, student counselling, personnel management, employee assisted schemes, e-mail counselling, art therapy and magazines and so on.

Not mentioned is the enormous library of self-help books (which often have the same function that etiquette books had in the nineteenth century) that guide us with our public performances. The difference is that now 'manners' are lodged deep in the psyche. We are no longer instructed as to how to *behave*; now we are instructed as to how we should *be*. That is, how we should psychologically perform and manage our self-identity and relationships.

There are many features of this trend towards briefer work that raise concerns, but in providing something of a critique of brief counselling I am not saying that it cannot be useful nor am I saying that all counselling has to be long-term. Brief interventions can have at least the following uses: some people will have already experienced longer-term therapy and may require a brief 'top-up'; it can act as a 'taster' to those who may be fearful and anxious about long-term work; it can be a quick response to a sudden and specific need; many people may not be able to afford long-term psychotherapy; some argue that the more disturbed patients in psychiatric care respond better to the partial focus of brief work. Moreover, all forms of brief intervention need not be classic counselling in the form of weekly sessions. There is much work to be done in offering clients a combination of counselling/psychotherapy and other interventions like group work, group discussions, educational sessions, plus using other resources like video recordings, compact discs, internet interactions and so on.

My aim therefore is not to deny that short-term work can be beneficial, but that the almost relentless drive in this direction has serious implications for our understanding of the purpose of counselling and psychotherapy. My argument is not simply an adaptation of the approach that says that short-term work simply adapts people to a dysfunctional society – although this is still a powerful argument. We should be concerned for other reasons that are less visible but still important such as: brief work becomes more skills-based, 'technicized' and directive than other therapeutic interventions; the erotic component diminishes; it cannot address broader political, cultural and moral issues effectively; it tends to create and support a self-managing, adaptive kind of identity and lifestyle.

My first concern is with the 'technicizing' side-effect of brief interventions. By definition short-term work provides less time in which to achieve the purposes I have outlined for psychotherapy. Later we will consider how this inevitably influences the objective to be reduced from developmental work to symptom management or social adaptation. Given that the counsellor may only have six sessions, she will not only need to reduce the developmental side but she will also be obliged to adopt a more directive and strategic approach. This will necessarily influence the counsellor to give a higher profile to her personal intervention and technical skills used to achieve this at the expense of limiting the development of the therapeutic relationship. The counsellor is forced into a more cognitive, rationalist and distanced stance with the result that the detective work undertaken in the initial assessment sets the tone of the whole interaction:

> Assessment is like anatomy where careful dissection of the body, the search for the probable cause of the illness, leads to the making of a diagnosis on the basis of the symptoms and morbidity discovered. Scanning of the client's story systematically to find the cause for the psychic turbulence and discomfort that has made them seek help, the counsellor becomes the anatomist/investigator, who tracks down a core problem, tries to read its symptoms in the light of their professional knowledge and experience of pathology, and makes a quick decision about how to contain and tackle the disturbance, and how to involve the client in the task for the short period of time at their disposal. The counsellor will also test the client's suitability for counselling, their ego strength, ability to relate, to cope with strong feelings, to sustain the intense experience of exploring a dilemma that has seemed insoluble and to separate at the end of this endeavour without harm to either participant. (Mander 1998: 302)

Note all the caveats in the last sentence. Ironically, wouldn't counselling (if more time were available) be of great benefit to those with insufficient ego strength, poor relational ability and limited capacity to experience strong feelings?

Coren (1996) reminds us that the modern brief therapist's confidence in a set of techniques and interventions whereby resistances are challenged directly is similar to the early work of Freud. What changed Freud's view was the problem of resistance and transference, the solutions to which resulted in longer-term work. Also, to the extent that brief interventions become behaviouristic or draw on elements of behaviourism, we need to beware of false objectivism when using concepts derived from instinct or drive theories. The concept of instinct still has meaning, but is still over-used in our explanations and understandings of psychological behaviour. However, these 'natural' forces are, in psychological terms, often the result of conscious motives and collective action that have been repressed from the realm of consciousness back into the causality of nature. 'This is the causality of fate, and not of nature, because it prevails through the symbolic means of the mind. Only for this reason can it be compelled by the power of reflection' (Habermas 1972: 256). For example, as Cushman (1995) illustrates, the symptoms of hysteria of the late nineteenth century seemed engraved in human nature but were in fact historical constructs.

Behaviourist and cognitive behaviourist approaches may well get an 'outcome', but this may leave the subject in a strategic action-type relation to the new learned behavioural response rather than a communicative action-type relation. The former remains external to our self-identity – it is as if the ego separates itself out of the rest of our identity and then manipulates it in the manner of an internalized therapist. Indeed, inasmuch as our therapeutic work is related to the reconstruction of a lost fragment of the client's life history, technical and skills-based interventions will not necessarily enable the client to reintegrate the lost fragment. Only through the client's own understanding, reflection and application in the counselling setting can this objectified element of the client's biography become consciously reintegrated into his reconstructed identity. If my ambivalent relation to anger is related to the oppressive nature of my father's relationship to me then no end of behavioural interventions will enable me to supply for myself a new understanding of this and enable me to construct a new sense of my personhood. Only the client can do this. The more privatized or distorted the client's language is surrounding this issue the less six sessions are likely to decode it and the more likely is the case that the therapeutic response will be behaviouristic. The subtle irony here is that the more economically disadvantaged the clients are the more likely they are to receive brief treatment – the adaptive nature of which is designed to try to help them adapt to a social environment that alienated them in the first place.

Moreover the client who acquires skills that improve his 'success' in interactions may be left with the problem of a distanced and managed self. The newly acquired skills are in a sense external to his identity and are manipulated by the ego to achieve strategic goals. Outcomes left at this level do not necessarily promote the development of a self-identity that is able to interpret such behaviour in terms of an authentic and autonomous life project. The strategic and technical interventions may leave us with people insufficiently developed to operate at the communicative level required by a democratic society in late modernity.

Following the connection between brief counselling and the increased usage of technical and skills-based interventions I wish to pursue this idea of a self that is characterized by ego management, technical competencies and skilled performances. That is, brief counselling is more likely to be constitutive of this kind of self which may not be conducive to the kind of self proposed by the purpose of counselling that I have outlined. The therapeutic culture in general has created an enormous range of interventions based on helping clients acquire skills. We can learn the steps to the 'dance of anger'; manage anxiety in one or two easy lessons; quit smoking and become more assertive in six weeks. All are available in a wide range of settings from evening classes to prison workshops. Brief counselling sits quite comfortably alongside these processes. The counsellor helps us to conduct life as a skilled performance. We can learn how to: relax, influence others, manage ourselves, listen to others, be more vulnerable and so on. Taken singly this feels fairly harmless, but a self-identity that accumulates such skills is in danger of perceiving all forms of social action as the expression and manipulation of psychological and social skills rather than being an authentic expression of an autonomous individuated being.

Rose (1999) develops the argument. The managed self has, as a shadow side to social success, a constant self-doubt and a nagging scrutiny and evaluation of how one performs. Hounded by the mantras of self-help manuals and magazine gurus the managed self feels obliged to calibrate and monitor its performance. Even pleasure becomes a form of work[4] requiring professional expertise, scientific knowledge and the latest technology. 'The self becomes the target of a reflexive objectifying gaze, committed not only to its own technical perfection but also to the belief that "success" and "failure" should be construed in the vocabulary of happiness, wealth, style, and fulfilment and interpreted as consequent upon the self-managed capacities of the self' (Rose 1999: 243). Brief counselling cannot be held responsible for all of this but it is symptomatic and indicative of these phenomena when it is not placed within the wider frame of the purpose of counselling and psychotherapy. The managed self that brief counselling can help to create and maintain has difficulty in grounding itself in the fabric of real life or, as Giddens describes it, the hard existential realities that frame our lives are subject to 'sequestration'.[5] Life is reduced to the imitation of life. Intimacy and success become restricted to their presentations in marketing material, advertisements, soap operas, chat shows and the amenable conviviality of media celebrities. Many will shed more tears for a dying princess than they will for the pain of those close to them. In the absence of a deeper and wider moral framework (a culture-wide problem which is reflected in brief therapy), these hyper-glossed images become the benchmark against which we measure our humble failures.

Self-help books, psychological guides, advice columnists, soap operas and magazines are full of social vignettes designed to help us improve our social performance. Through these scenes:

> An interiority has opened up behind our conduct, but it is a shallow interiority, occupied by the simple, wholesome needs. Love, perfection, sex, dependency, attention and rejection operate here, but not rage, hate, self-loading, guilt, envy, fantasy and self-abasement, let alone the earlier moral imperatives of duty, obligation, social responsibility, conscience, grace, good, and evil. (Rose 1999: 256)

Rather than trying to make ourselves congruent through the reappropriation and rewriting of our biography through psychological labour in order to achieve a decentred self able to act with authenticity and autonomy, we strengthen our ego's ability to manage our identity through the application of learned skills and techniques in a process helped and motivated by our identification with both the narrow range of emotions on offer and the celebrities who embody them.

The more traditional concerns about counselling being socially adaptive still apply. Maslow (1968), long before brief counselling made the situation even more problematic, was concerned that counselling was wedded to an identification with psychological health and adjustment – adjustment to 'reality', society and other people such that the individual would be judged not so much in her own autonomy, but in relation to her competency in doing a good job, maintaining relationships and being generally adequate. Moore identifies another consequence of short-term work, which is that the client may now enter the counselling room with 'a problem to be fixed', '…where the assumption is that the psyche has spare parts, an owner's manual, and well-trained mechanics called therapists' (1992: 206–7). Mander (1997) is anxious about the fact that brief counselling registers a return to symptom control, and emphasizes behavioural change to the neglect of internal psychic causes. The search for instant cures leads to a more concrete and less symbolic kind of thinking.

There are other simple and practical problems with brief interventions.

- Brief work requires experience and skill – the counsellor must be able to think quickly, adroitly, make quick decisions and let go. Not all will have the skills.
- There is a real danger of opening up wounds which cannot be closed, promises that cannot be fulfilled.
- The client's often quick recovery may be mistakenly taken for a genuine change. Frequently clients that have been quite seriously disturbed may feel an enormous sense of relief in the early parts of counselling. For a little while the problem seems solved when their isolation is shared with the sympathetic care of the counsellor. However, the problems that brought them into counselling soon reappear.
- Brief therapy does not allow for the difficulties that arise when the client feels stuck – there is no time for the necessary work involved in dealing with difficult problems.
- Counsellors working in this field can often become dissatisfied with the lack of depth in their work.
- 'The maxim in short work is that there is only one chance' (Mander 1998: 304).
- There is an inevitable process of condensing. The counsellor has to find out as much as possible in the first session including: the client's problem, her expectations for its solution, her level of belief in the possibility of being helped, her level of fear and anxiety about the process, her willingness to engage, etc. In order to choose the right direction in the limited time available the counsellor needs to make the best possible assessment and start immediately on the work in hand. This increases the importance of the level of analytic assessment and the usage of techniques and skills making the whole process more directive and less interactive.

Given my definition of the purpose of psychotherapy and counselling, brief interventions can militate against this purpose. Notwithstanding that there can be positive applications of brief counselling, the problem, given the adaptive context in which it often takes place, is that short-term work can block or prevent the real benefits that may be obtained by a more thorough therapeutic process. The skills-and-technique-based model may actively prevent the client from ever getting deeply enough involved in the transference to enable her to witness, let alone work through, what may be serious internal psychic difficulties. Brief counsellors can be seduced into trying to be directly helpful, a strategy which may too often leave them operating at the level of symptoms. Brazier (1995) compares this issue with the paradox of the koan in Zen culture. The client brings an insoluble problem to the therapist half-hoping that the therapist can take the problem away. 'In Zen, however, we say that it is not compassionate to take such problems away since a koan is actually the means by which a person can get to our new stage' (Brazier 1995: 46–7). If therapy and counselling is essentially involved in facilitating the client's development towards autonomy through the validity claims of truth, authenticity, health, comprehensibility and justice it would be surprising if quick interventions could achieve such goals. Elements of frustration are intrinsic to this process such that the premature search for solutions to 'problems' may be an avoidance of the growth required.[6]

The earlier distinction we made between the concepts of translation and transformation may help us at this point. With translation we are concerned with helping clients make sense of the stage they are currently at, whereas transformation holds the interest of moving clients on to more developed stages of personhood.[7] Brief therapy is primarily concerned with translation and, seen in this light, is appropriate. It becomes seriously inappropriate when the issue of transformation is either forgotten or is marginalized by a culture and institutional framework that works to a political and social agenda that is distinctly 'adaptive' in outlook. Later we will consider just how endemic the adaptive outlook has become. As mentioned earlier, Kegan (1981) reminds us that the counsellor is trying to resonate with the experience that the client's problem entails rather than necessarily help solve the problem or reduce the pain:

> this can seem like just the opposite direction from the one the client wants to go. Indeed, the client may keep returning to a focus on the problem if she experiences the counsellor's invitations as a *spreading out* of the problem itself; she, after all, may want to contain it, precisely to keep it from spreading into her whole life. (1981: 274)

There is another concern. Is brief therapy suitable for all client groups or are we indirectly excluding some? Coren (1996) catalogues the ideal client for brief counselling. He should be: presenting a circumscribed problem, motivated, psychologically minded, able to establish relationships, flexible in his defences, reflective, able to recognize that problems have an emotional content, and having the capacity to tolerate frustration and anxiety. 'So what we are left with is a patient who is relatively healthy, well-functioning, with a well-defined and circumscribed area of difficulty, who is intelligent, psychologically minded and well motivated for a change. Where are they?' (Coren 1996: 26). Wouldn't all counsellors wish their clients were like this! Coren does indeed identify students as possibly being such a group for whom, at this early stage in their lives, it would be inappropriate, other than in exceptional cases, to expose them to long-term psychotherapy. If this is the case, then such discreet groups are rare.

Of greater concern is the fact that there is a growing gulf between those that can afford private counselling over an extended period of time, and those who cannot and whose only access to counselling and therapy is the publicly funded services which are overwhelmingly short-term. In the public domain lack of funding and the pressure of demand produce long waiting lists with the result that clients get brief, solution-focused counselling. The danger is that through this process the client is being made to fit into the counselling model on offer rather than vice versa, which reinforces the belief that the client is not getting the best service. Organizations that provide such brief interventions have a tendency to compound the problem by justifying their practice using arguments borrowed from consumerism – 'if the client wants a quick fix then it is our job to do what the client wants'. Superficial as this response may be it enables such hard-pressed organizations to turn away from this issue and attend to the problem of output and accessibility which respond more easily to a managerial approach. Brief counselling and the professionalized managerialism of service providers are comfortable bedfellows.

Holmes and Lindley (1989) acknowledge that clients on low incomes may have difficulties with some of the features of longer-term psychotherapy – for example, working with transference, the exploration of feelings and the elaborated codes of language. Moreover, such people are more exposed to the stresses and strains of everyday living such that they may have a greater need of the kind of symptoms alleviation that brief counselling offers. However, it is precisely such people who would benefit most from the development of the emotional autonomy that is only achievable after symptom relief. Such people are most at risk from the dangers outlined by some of the severest critics of counselling and psychotherapy. If society is dysfunctional then adapting people to it merely reinforces the dysfunction in both.

> There is a dysfunction in society that is affecting us . . . I cannot repair it in myself in my own relationships alone, because my problem is social dysfunction. So how is settling things with my wife going to repair the dysfunction of the general situation? That's a romantic delusion – that if we could just get our sex right, our conversations right, 'if I could just find the right relationship.' (Hillman 1993: 219)

A 'managed' self and a 'fixed' relationship may be poor consolations for the experience of social injustice and a loss of meaning.

Outcomes

During the 1990s counselling, particularly in an institutional context, has been put under enormous pressure to prove its usefulness. This pressure has principally come from purchasers and funders of counselling services, primarily this means local government, central government, charitable trusts, insurance companies[8] and the business sector. Counselling and psychotherapy are being forced to prove their worth in terms that are extrinsic to their own value system. They are now subject to cost–benefit analysis, scientific evaluation, market rationality and outcome measurement. This has been a significant factor in the movement of counselling towards briefer interventions which are surface-oriented and symptom-focused. A clear example of this in the UK is where the central government hamstrings the largest counselling agency (Relate) with severe underfunding linked to a clear policy programme of forcing this agency into greater outcome measurement and symptom relief, whilst providing short-term project funding for issues that comply with the government's political platform. Here we have a government using the apparatus of the state to compromise the value structure of an independent counselling charity using the ideology of positivism in a sector where it is clearly inappropriate. In these conditions it is of little surprise that the framework of civil society is withering away. The adoption of quasi-scientific criteria inevitably pushes the framing of counselling and psychotherapy into the health paradigm thereby predefining its purpose in terms of symptom relief and cure.

This creates an interesting paradox. Despite the fact that the behavioural proof for the benefit of counselling is ambiguous, there is a continual surge in the demand for counselling and psychotherapy from the general public. The state and associated bodies have not yet discovered what is obvious to the public and therefore see fit to place themselves in the role of scientific observer of the population, thereby replicating, as we shall soon see, the fallacy inherent in the unmediated application of behaviourism and outcome measurement to therapeutic processes. This is akin to reducing communicative action to strategic action. The paradox is produced by the erroneous epistemological assumptions made by behaviourists and the cultural infrastructure that rests on them. Put these assumptions to the test of critique then it becomes clear that as long as we assume that counselling and psychotherapy are simply about changing behaviour the nature of therapeutic processes will be misunderstood and open to misappropriation by those with financial muscle. When we understand these processes in terms of the purpose that we have outlined then it becomes subject to a very different form of evaluation. The threat posed by this phenomenon should not be underestimated, for when the very survival of counselling agencies is constantly at stake the resigned acceptance of embracing antithetical values may be irresistible. 'One of the greatest dangers' notes House 'of predominantly or exclusively quantitative research is that we end up knowing the *price* (or numerical value) of everything and the *value* of nothing' (1997: 201). In these circumstances the purpose of counselling becomes a side issue to the scramble to measure things that cannot be quantified and to please funders who should not be mollified. The fact that cognitive-behaviourist models are more conducive to measurement and evaluation does not in any necessary way make them more therapeutically effective.

A critical understanding of counselling and psychotherapy would draw to itself the robust and powerful critique of positivism that absorbed much critical thought in the second half of the twentieth century. We should always be highly sceptical of any claim to knowledge that reduces intentional action to behaviour. A scientific body of knowledge must be appropriate to the object of its knowledge. When this object is a human being constituted by, and operating with, symbolically structured processes the scientific process used must be sensitive towards the linguistic communications that define the humanity being observed. Therefore access to the object of study via the understanding of meanings (that is, communication) must be included. It is this phenomenon, Habermas reminds us, which creates the problem of measurement in the social sciences. In the place of the practice of controlled observation that is typical of behaviourist approaches (which guarantees the anonymity and exchangeability of the observing scientist) there is a participatory relation of understanding between the subject doing the understanding (counsellor) and the subject being understood (client).

> The paradigm is no longer the observation but the dialogue – thus, a communication in which the understanding subject must invest a part of his subjectivity, no matter in what manner this may be uncontrollable, in order to be able to meet confronting subjects at all on the intersubjective level which makes understanding possible. (Habermas 1974: 11)

This critical epistemological shift is indirectly recognized by a fundamental requirement of therapeutic practice. Precisely because the practitioner is in a participative and dialogical relationship with the client, the practitioner is required to be a client in her own psychotherapy. This is partly to free the practitioner, as far as is possible, from the typical conditions that clients bring, but it is also related to the fact that in the transference the practitioner deliberately uses her own subjectivity. There is a further twist. With the empirical sciences, observations and statements remain external to the object of knowledge, in psychotherapy and counselling the validity of the interpretations that are generated is subject to the 'object's' (that is, the client's) participation in the generation of the interpretations, accepting them and internalising them. In behaviourist approaches, techniques are *applied* to the client whereas the validity of therapeutic interpretations is dependent upon meeting the acceptance of the client.

> When valid, general interpretations hold for the inquiring subject and all who can adopt its position only to the degree that those who were made the object of individual interpretations *know and recognize themselves* in these interpretations. The subject cannot obtain knowledge of the object unless it becomes knowledge for the object – and unless the latter thereby emancipates itself by becoming a subject. (Habermas 1972: 261–2)

General interpretations generated in the practices of psychotherapy and counselling operate quite differently to general theories held by empirical sciences. They are not subject to the same rules of falsification. If, in empirical science, a prediction deduced from a law-like hypothesis is falsified then the hypothesis is refuted. The process of refuting an interpretation of a client is different. If it is correct the client will gain access to certain memories, gain insight into lost or distorted aspects of biography, and overcome disturbed communication and action. However, whilst this is only possible if the client accepts the interpretation, the rejection of an interpretation is not necessarily its refutation.

Here we have another paradox. The failure or corroboration of an interpretation is only possible when the client is able to operate reflectively. But the precondition of the psychotherapeutic process is that such reflectiveness is either found to be wanting or suspended. Consequently, the client's rejection of an interpretation can be considered sound because the interpretation is false, or unsound because the interpretation has met strong resistance. Even the disappearance of symptoms is not compelling evidence because they may have been replaced by other symptoms less resistant to initial observation. New symptoms carry a meaning for the client in the act of reaching a different level of psychic defence. 'The interpretation of a case is corroborated only by the successful continuation of a self-formative process, that is by the completion of self-reflection, and not in any unmistakable way by what the patient says or how he behaves' (Habermas 1972: 266). The therapist or counsellor is committed to helping the client progress through a process of meaning-making along a developmental path towards authenticity and autonomy. These are not measurable in any behaviouristic fashion.

This does not mean that all forms of behaviourism are outlawed. Clients with very serious disorders who have little possibility of making use of the process of insight inherent in counselling may well, in the first instance, require some behaviourist input. On the other hand, some clients who are particularly stuck in specific behavioural patterns may benefit from specific behavioural inputs *so long as they are contained within a wider context of generating explanations and interpretations that are meaningful to the client*. Much of brief therapy is not specifically behavioural but draws on skills and techniques that are not always integrated into wider interpretive frameworks and are referred not necessarily to behavioural response syndromes but to the ego that dominates and manages the internal psyche. In either case the therapeutic work is increasingly geared to meet the behaviouristic criteria involved in outcome measurement. The objectivistic epistemology of empiricist methodology will hold currency for as long as we passively accept social processes and structures that create objectified people. Counselling and psychotherapy must reject this position on the basis that immanent within their own process is the possibility of helping people enable themselves to operate at a new epistemological level where they are known in terms of their authenticity and autonomy rather than being known through the strange process of measuring their lack of fit with socially adaptive actions.

> It is only through the *experiential* task of working through and integrating the repressed and unintegrated material of early developmental experience that we will be in a position individually and collectively to heal our individual and collective psychic dis-integration and move towards a wholeness *from which it is far more likely that an epistemology and methodology which is truly humanistic in nature will organically emerge.* (House 1997: 202)

As counselling and psychotherapy have become more accepted in healthcare settings a vigorous debate has been generated between the 'soft' therapeutic approach and the 'hard' medical, behavioural and pharmacological approach. Indeed this rarely deserves being described as a 'debate', because each approach has a different purpose, but the overwhelming dominance of the medicalized model combined with the strong power base of the pharmacological industry and the medical profession oblige the aspiring counselling profession to conduct the debate in behaviourist terms. Whilst not wishing to become involved in this crossfire, Seligman's (1995) analysis provides us with a useful interpretive tool. He draws the distinction between two primary methods of assessing the outcome of psychotherapy and counselling – the *efficacy* study and the *effectiveness* study. The efficacy study is by far the most popular and works by contrasting some kind of therapy to a comparison group under well-controlled conditions – randomized controlled trials (RCTs). These have become the 'gold standard' paradigm with a sophisticated methodology. Seligman brings together the following salient features of the efficacy approach:

- the patients are randomly assigned to treatment and control conditions
- the controls are rigorous. Some patients are included who receive no treatment at all, but placebos containing potentially therapeutic ingredients credible to both the patient and the therapist are used in order to control for such influences as rapport, expectation of gain, and sympathetic attention
- patients are seen for a fixed number of sessions
- the target outcomes are well operationalized (self-report of panic attacks, percentage of fluent utterances, number of reported orgasms)

- raters and diagnosticians are blind to which root the patient comes from. (Contrary to the 'double-blind' method of drugs studies, efficacy studies of psychotherapy can at most be 'single-blind', since the patient and therapist both know what the treatment is)
- the patients meet criteria for a single diagnosed disorder, and patients with multiple disorders are typically excluded
- the patients are followed for a fixed period after termination of treatment with a thorough assessment procedure.

According to Seligman these efficacy studies do achieve some recognisable outcomes. Cognitive therapy, interpersonal therapy and medications all provide moderate relief from unipolar depressive disorder. Cognitive therapy works very well in panic disorder. Systematic desensitization relieves specific phobias. Transcendental meditation relieves anxiety. Aversion therapy produces only marginal improvement with sexual offenders. Cognitive therapy provides significant relieve from bulimia, outperforming medications alone. All these outcomes are concerned with the *relief of symptoms*. The medicalized and behavioural model has simply overwhelmed and negated the value system that is immanent to counselling and psychotherapy. Efficacy studies are the dominant paradigm that places a stranglehold on the development of psychotherapy and counselling.

Seligman challenges this model. The method of deciding whether one treatment, under highly controlled conditions, works better than another treatment or a control group is a different question from what works in psychotherapy and counselling *as it is actually practised*. Long-term psychotherapy and counselling (in all their forms) have not been subjected to efficacy studies yet they represent a significant portion of what is actually practised. However, this '. . . still leaves the average psychotherapist in an uncomfortable position, with a substantial body of literature validating a panoply of short-term therapies the psychotherapist does not perform, and with the long-term, eclectic therapy he or she does perform unproven' (Seligman 1995: 3). More to the point is the fact that the efficacy study is the wrong method for empirically validating psychotherapy as it is actually done because the narrow confines of behaviourist methodology exclude too many factors. Seligman outlines the following failures of efficacy studies. In the first place, because efficacy studies are time-limited, usually about 12 sessions, they cannot assess the improvements that clients make with longer-term work. Secondly, counselling and psychotherapy are self-correcting. If one technique fails then another can be tried. Similarly, given the importance of the therapeutic relationship, if one counsellor fails another may well succeed. In contrast, the intervention used in efficacy studies is confined to a small number of techniques which are often delivered in a fixed order.

Thirdly, clients entering therapy often get there by an *active* process of shopping around for a specific therapeutic approach and individual therapist.

Client entry into efficacy studies is *passive* – the result of random assignment to treatment and an acceptance of the treatment and practitioner on offer. The next problem is the fact that clients in efficacy studies are selected on the basis that they have only one (or two interrelated) presenting problem, whereas counselling and psychotherapy are geared to work with multiple problems interacting in complex ways. Finally, efficacy studies usually focus on specific symptoms and the relief thereof. Psychotherapy moves beyond symptom relief to the values that I have outlined. Curtis Jenkins (2002: 1999) makes a further useful distinction. The use of RCTs as a source of evidence-based healthcare is quite appropriate in relation to *cure* conditions like diabetes, heart conditions or cancer whereas it is inappropriate with *care* conditions like counselling. Hemmings makes a similar observation.[9]

Whilst using different terms of reference to those involved in communicative rationality, it is clear that studying psychotherapy and counselling in terms of the effectiveness produces 'outcomes' more in line with their intrinsic purpose.

> The advantages of long-term treatment by a mental health professional held not only for the specific problems that led to treatment, but for a variety of general functioning scores as well: ability to relate to others, coping with everyday stress, enjoying life more, personal growth and understanding, self-esteem and confidence. (Seligman 1995: 6)

Counselling and psychotherapy are in desperate need of rescue from the unproductive debate with the dominant culture about their purpose. Pushing them into behaviourist, measurable, medicalized and health agendas blinds us to the fact that they are fundamentally moral and ethical endeavours. Freud never saw psychoanalysis in these terms. Despite his clinical background, the main function of psychoanalysis for him was in knowing the truth, facing up to it and seeing reality with transparency. The drive for facts and assessment blinds us to the complexity of the narrative construction of our lives and the skill and erotic awareness required by those who help us rewrite this narrative in a way that enables us to live a more authentic and autonomous life.

> We must have a new way of grasping what goes on in our lives and in our practices, another view of the women who leave their children for a lover; the women who fall in love with youth, as the men do with beauty; the insupportable triangles and jealousies we suffer; the repetitive erotic entanglements which, because they are soulless and without psychological reflection, lead only to more despair . . . These situations, and the intense emotions flowing from them, feel central to a person's being and may mean more to working out his fate than the family problem and his conscious development on a heroic course. These events create consciousness in men and women, initiating us into life as a personal-impersonal mystery beyond problems that can be analysed. (Hillman 1972: 95–6)

Professionalism

Have we benefited from the professionalization of counselling and psychotherapy? Has this process been successful in keeping them focused on their purpose, or have they been realigned in the interests of professional counsellors and their organizations? How did we deal with personal problems before the advent of the professional counsellors? Wheeler (1999) traces the demand for help and support for personal problems back to the industrial revolution. Urbanization obliged people to move from traditional rural communities to the cities with the subsequent experience of the loss of support previously provided by extended families and village life. This created a need for personal services which was initially provided by solicitors, doctors and clergy. The clergy became most involved and experienced a shift in their own work from the theological to the pastoral. Increasingly 'nerves' and nervous problems were identified as a distinct category of complaint taken to the medical profession which developed a neurological interest. Between 1880 and 1920, neurologists were besieged by patients needing treatment; the clergy more consciously adopted a social model of intervention and Freud was developing his theories of psychoanalysis. At the same time psychiatrists began treating severe mental illness in mental hospital accommodation. During the early part of the twentieth century, psychoanalysis grew in popularity and successfully challenged the supremacy of the medical establishment when treating problems of everyday life. Demand outstripped the supply of psychoanalysts so social workers began adopting analytic techniques which in turn led to the development of psychotherapy. Counselling and psychotherapy are thus a response to increases in demand and have carved a path through social work, the clergy, psychiatry and psychoanalysis.

Generally a profession will have the following qualities and attributes: a skill that is based on theoretical knowledge; it provides training and education for its members; it tests the competence of its members; it generally provides an umbrella organization that is self-regulating; a certain level of altruistic service is expected; an articulate code of conduct; a profession usually dominates the market for the service rendered and members usually gain in income, power and prestige as a profession becomes increasingly recognized.

In recent years, counselling and psychotherapy have made strenuous efforts to fulfil many of these criteria and establish themselves as legitimate professional bodies. In terms of their desire to be seen as professionals this was a necessary step at a time when unregulated entry enabled incompetent people to call themselves 'counsellors'. It is not my concern here to judge whether or not counsellors and psychotherapists have reached the status of a profession. I am more interested in some of the ambivalences between counselling and psychotherapy as a profession and to what extent this conflicts with their moral and ethical purpose. There is a tendency for the overall ethical purpose to be reduced to the ethical problems (largely issues of confidentiality) of therapeutic practice.

Towards the end of the' twentieth century the provision of training courses on psychotherapy and counselling grew at an incredible rate. Whilst there is some very fine training on offer and the 'profession' is attempting to raise standards, some of the observations made by Reiff (1966) many years earlier still ring true. Following my suggestion that the world of therapy has distinctly failed to generate a cogent understanding of its own purpose, it is no surprise that the training bodies display the same phenomenon and have a poor overall conception of what they are trying to do with little understanding of their historical, social or political roles. There is a real danger that counselling and psychotherapy become almost lifestyle activities populated by people who do not need to work full-time or generate a self-reproducing income. Their work in private practice enables them to select their own clients and generally provide a service more tailored to their own needs than those of the community. 'Meanwhile', observes Reiff, 'the institutes have become what most of the students ardently desire them to be: trade schools preparing them for accreditation and the good life in some suburbs, without night calls from troublesome patients' (1966: 104–5). As the privatization of counselling increases[10] and the provision of training is often provided by private institutions or by public bodies hungry for the income that students bring, there is a real danger that the over-supply of counsellors reduces training standards. This pressure can threaten the professional status of psychotherapists and counsellors in other ways. A training that is tied to the needs of its purchaser can be limiting and narrowly confined. The psychotherapeutic tradition is often not placed in the context of associated subjects like sociology and psychology; students and practitioners, particularly those in private practice, rarely meet people from other disciplines. Their imagination has often been too confined to a limited rendering of the psychotherapeutic tradition. It is too easy for private practitioners, without the stimulus of mandatory requirements, to limit their development after obtaining their professional qualification. The privatization of counselling and its commercial basis are not necessary stimulants to its development as a profession.

The research output of the profession is not much more encouraging. When it is not confined to the sterile rigour of behaviourism and RCTs, it suffers from an empiricism cut off from other academic and cultural movements. If they are not measuring anxiety or depression in desperate attempts to 'prove' that counselling 'works', then there is an endless provision of case histories from which, by induction, all will be made clear. Critical thinking, theoretical insights and openness to other bodies of knowledge are resisted in a way that is antipathetic to professional aspirations. Indeed, Holmes and Lindley (1989) believe that, for some therapists, the notion of respectability and professional status represents a contradiction. The subject matter and purpose should make the practitioner subversive of, and opposed to, the dominant culture that handsomely rewards those who conform to professional status and career development.

These developments, along with many others, have led to the increasing separation of the professional aspect of counselling and psychotherapy from their vocational nature. As counselling and psychotherapy initially developed the practitioners often felt that they were entering into a vocation or a 'calling'. They felt that they were meeting a real and perceived need within their communities which was their 'obligation' to try to meet. Often they began as volunteers and only later placed their work on a commercial footing. My intention is not that we should attempt to return to a romanticized vision of the past, but that the particular path that counselling and psychotherapy have taken towards professionalization was not the only route to that destination and it was not the place we should have been travelling towards. I have already intimated some of the failings involved in the professionalization of private practice, but the journey of counselling organizations has not been altogether more successful. Counsellors in such organizations have, like their private colleagues, experienced the move from being the unpaid amateur to being the paid professional. If they have not achieved this it is a widespread aspiration. The organizations themselves have also changed from being a *social movement* to operating like a *service agency*. As a social movement they had a set of values to promote. Members joined these organizations in order to work with these values and donate their time and commitment in furthering these ideals. Over time the dissemination of values becomes a set of targeted objectives to achieve; organizational values get supplanted by individual career aspirations; donations of time are transformed into the paid and routine application of skills. The process of becoming an organization has resulted in counselling mimicking the practices of organizational development expressed by the dominant culture, with the importation of: corporate culture, functional managerialism, individual career and status aspirations. This is neither necessary nor inevitable. Providing counselling and psychotherapy within an organizational setting has distinct advantages over private practice in that, in the right circumstances, it enables: the articulation and dissemination of core values; an internal resistance to the dominant culture; mutual support and stimulation; maintenance of standards and quality control.

There is a different way to be 'professional'. Perhaps we need to rekindle our notion of professionalism more in line with a sense of vocation and calling and away from career, status and material rewards. The latter approach has a psychological impact on the professional in line with our sense of the managed self created by short-term, skills-based counselling:

> In this imagery of exchange, the self stands apart from what it does, and its commitments remained calculated and contingent on the benefits they deliver. In the calling, by contrast, one gives oneself to learning and practising activities that in turn define the self and enter into the shape of its character. Committing one's self

to becoming a 'good' carpenter, doctor, scientist or artist anchors the self within a community practising carpentry, medicine, or art. It connects the self to those who teach, exemplify and judge these skills.' (Bellah *et al.* 1988: 69)

This standing apart, scientific neutrality and professional distance is inimical to our characterization of the therapeutic process as an erotic interaction. In a paradoxical fashion, counsellors seek the neutrality of professionalism to display a studied disidentification with the sentiments of worthwhileness associated with giving personal service to others. Unable to accommodate the paradox and irony achieved by the decentred self, counsellors often feel more secure with the more managed self offered by the professional façade.

> The contemporary socially conscious individual is ashamed of postures of charity and to detect styles of the 'lady bountiful' in a social caseworker would amount to an insult to her professional sincerity and seriousness. Professionalization has proved an excellent camouflage for the counsellors' *agape* and the formal-technological jargon, the impersonal clinical manners, the social science collaterals, and so on, have all helped to reassure the counsellor that he was doing a job of work and no more. (Halmos 1965: 29–30)

The move to professionalization and the associated process of accreditation can be seen as part of the process whereby counselling and psychotherapy become normalized and lose their radical disengagement from the dominant culture which creates many of the symptoms their clients are struggling with.[11] Wasdell interestingly parallels this with the client–counsellor relationship. The client, with his sense of shame and profile of symptoms, acts as a carrier for the distortions and disturbances he has internalized from his family and wider social environment and thereby protects the latter from blame and the requirement to change by his own psychological sacrifice. Similarly in the process of the professionalization of counsellors and psychotherapists, society is protected from an obligation to critically analyze and transform the social and political determinants of individual psychological disturbance.

> It is therefore possible to interpret the psychodynamics of the profession as collusional counter-transference, maintaining the pathology of the social system, reinforcing norm patterns of neurotic and psychotic behaviour and reinforcing the stasis-maintenance dynamics of the community. Caught in this collusional dance, it is hardly surprising that the profession of therapy has so little impact on the behaviour of social systems. So the processes of professionalism and accreditation come to represent the internalization of the shadow of the social environment. (Wasdell 1990: 13–14)

From this perspective the social system as a whole is seen as the corporate client of the profession – in which case client and therapist are locked in a pattern of transference and counter transference, preserving each other's defences and blocking the progress towards maturation.

Do we really want therapists to be professional? We certainly need them to be skilled, competent, supervised and so on, but does this have to follow the conventional path of professionalization? The term 'client' is ambivalent and describes the therapeutic relationship in contractual and commercial terms rather than erotic or relational terms. The very language that we use is being colonized by the professional aspirations of the practitioners. The counselling room might be more productively envisaged as a secular church, a place of sanctuary and transition to a new community of people who are ethically authentic and morally autonomous. Rather than solving problems it enables people to emerge as citizens of a democracy. We could reverse the process of colonization. Rather than acting as an agent of the dominant culture by colonizing the psyches of its clients with coping strategies and a managed sense of self, it might act as a counter-colonial enterprise populating society within increasingly autonomous individuals who recognize their embeddedness in social solidarity, much as Christians infiltrated pagan Rome.

I wonder if the Latin root of the word voluntary (*voluntas*) might give us a different and more productive way of understanding the nature of voluntary work. An aspect of *voluntas* is a connection with the will such that a voluntary action is one that is freely chosen and is done willingly. It is closely linked to the concept of *volition*. In this sense a voluntary act is very closely associated to our concept of an autonomous act. An act that expresses our demotivated will, that is, our ability to act on our autonomous will as opposed to acts that are determined by other factors. The power and significance of a voluntary action (volunteering) is that it is an ultimate authentic and ethical act of will that expresses my moral character – that is, a truly autonomous action. Has the drive to professionalization made us so cynical that we are now more concerned with earning higher fees because 'we are worth it' (that is, we want the external world to recognize our value), as opposed to acting voluntarily because it is an expression of our inner desire to be worthy of such authentic acts? Perhaps we might define 'unpaid' work as passive voluntary acts and understand active voluntary acts as those which express the highest aspect of character – truly autonomous acts?

Codes of Ethics

If there is a particular place where we should have some confidence in finding an adequate expression of the role of morals and ethics in counselling and psychotherapy, it would be in the codes of ethics provided by the relevant professional bodies. They prove to be a disappointment.

[M]ost of the commonly available and read books on psychology, counselling and psychotherapy deal with the issues of values, social justice and ethical questions either by simply ignoring them . . . or by referring it to consensually agreed codes of ethics and personal practice – all of which are shot through with unanswered ethical dilemmas and profoundly serious questions to the profession itself. (Clarkson 2000: 51–2)

In Pattison's study (1999) of professional ethics he found an arbitrariness in the selection of morals and ethics included, together with a failure to explain (in a rationally coherent and defensible way): the nature and status of the components of the code of ethics and how these relate to each other and to wider moral and ethical themes. He finds the code for the British Association of Counselling and Psychotherapy (BACP – the principle professional body in the UK) particularly defective. These codes are a peculiar mixture of some ethical issues, few moral issues and some narrowly defined 'ethical' issues that protect the profession. Other professional bodies have codes which involve notions of citizenship, truth and justice but these are not clearly articulated in counselling codes.

With our conception of communicative rationality I have attempted to show how it might be possible to generate a cogent framework for moral and ethical behaviour out of the immanent processes of communication aimed at reaching an understanding. This anchors the purpose of counselling and psychotherapy securely within a broader philosophical, psychological and sociological setting. Just as important is the fact that this approach is open to rational debate. Not only is this perspective absent from the field of counselling, but there appears to be little attempt to provide any other framework with a similar philosophical basis that is open to rational discourse. The professional codes express this absence. Pattison agrees that a broad framework of moral principles which are open to debate would be a valuable addition to these codes of ethics if they are actually meant to promote ethical behaviour in its widest and proper sense. Given our doubts about some of the benefits of professionalization, it is not surprising that their codes of behaviour seem so limited. If counsellors and psychotherapists were obliged or motivated to place their work within a broader and deeper moral perspective it might encourage them to be less conservative, self-protective and defensive about the profession. This would also provide a built-in mechanism enabling the profession to be responsive to the arguments of those who believe that their work should be more soundly ethically based.

The lack of discussion of the moral and ethical in these codes generates an unforeseen danger. It would be natural for a practitioner to accept the professional code as an adequate ethical guideline. These codes create an implicit understanding that if people conform to the code they will be acting to all intents and purposes ethically. However, as these codes are inadequate, they can create a false sense of certainty and discourage people from exercising their own wisdom and judgement. By using unstated moral precepts these codes do not promote the independent critical judgement that is associated with moral responsibility and good professionalism. By extension this can lead to practitioners colluding with, or remaining silent about, practices that might otherwise be thought to be unethical or immoral. 'I suspect' writes Pattison 'that whatever their good effects in terms of clarifying standards, expectations, accountability, etc., codes contain considerable potential for harm and limiting ethical awareness. By failing directly to consider and include many ethical principles and dilemmas that members of the general public as well as professionals would think directly relevant to the provision of care, codes may narrow the sensibilities and responsibilities of professionals' (1999: 378–9).

The BACP updated their code of ethics in late 2001 and the outcome illustrates this theme. This 'framework for good practice' differentiates between values and principles with the former having precedence. I note the following about BACP values:

- respect for human rights and dignity is included but is nowhere defined or situated in a legal or any other context. How would a practitioner comply with this vague generality?
- counsellors should 'foster a sense of self that is meaningful to the person(s) concerned' – as if clients can choose identities that are authentic and moral like items on a supermarket shelf: No sense here of the socially constituted self;
- counsellors should appreciate 'the variety of human experience and culture' yet the problematic issues concerning cultural relativity are completely ignored;
- the value of truth is not mentioned;
- autonomy does not appear;
- authenticity does not appear;
- justice, other than the meek concern with the equal distribution of counselling, does not appear; and
- any wider social purpose that counselling and psychotherapy may have is not addressed.

No rationale is offered for the inclusion or exclusion of any values. We are simply told that these are the values of the counselling profession. It is also less than satisfactory that these ethical principles are not given any relative priority, such that small-scale issues of professional conduct rank as high as universal moral principles. Whilst the codes themselves are meant to be reasonably brief guidelines rather than a philosophical treatise, there is no reason why they should not signpost us to other, more considered, ethical and moral debates conducted by the profession. It is difficult not to reach the conclusion that the profession does not know what its purpose is, neither does it have an adequate comprehension of an appropriate moral and ethical framework. Moreover we are provided with no reason as to why we should comply with the code of ethics. It is assumed that the 'is' of the norms provided will provide sufficient 'oughts'.

CHAPTER 6

Abstract Systems and the Colonization of Self

The clarion call to counsellors and psychotherapists to take a much greater interest in social and political issues is not new. Hillman and Ventura (1993), Samuels (1993), Smail (1998) and many others have tried to raise awareness of this issue but it seems to get lost in counsellor training and everyday practice. The debate becomes sterile with a notional acceptance of the importance of social and political factors subverted by the immediacy of the client–counsellor interaction. Doubtless there are a range of projections and resistances in operation creating this phenomenon but that is not my interest here. I intend to spend some time drawing on a limited range of sociological understandings of contemporary capitalist democracies in late modernity in an attempt to show that it is no longer tenable for the counselling and psychotherapy culture to substantially ignore the proposition that the specific features of late modernity create a much greater inter-penetration between the individual psyche and social processes. The client sitting in the counselling room presents a sense of identity and self-identity that is substantially influenced and constituted by macro social and political structures; more so now then at any other period in history.

We are witnessing not only profound social change, but it is also happening with increasing velocity. Transnational corporations, with budgets larger than many countries, have created an international economy and are able to move capital and control labour with only minimal interference from nation states.[1] This, connected with global communications and transport systems, has generated the increasingly familiar concept of globalization which creates such paradoxical phenomena as massive increases in consumer choice at the supermarket necessarily linked to environmental crises that resist conventional remedies. Huge increases in female employment, and the growth of part-time and portfolio working combined with greater job insecurity are changing our perceptions about work. Warfare, which has become highly technical and remote-controlled, is no longer used as a method of direct imperial expansion, but is more likely to be an instrument of policing and managing 'civil wars' within a global imperium[2] maintained by a broad western alliance in the *pax Americana*. The mass media and communication technologies infiltrate into most aspects of our life as does the commodity structure. Large-scale political movements atrophy and give way to identity and lifestyle politics. The whole social, cultural and political landscape is being redrawn so quickly and so radically that the consequences for psychological identity are profound. My argument is that counselling and psychotherapy, in the main, fail to address these issues while simultaneously failing to understand the uniqueness and importance of their social and political roles. An inadequate comprehension of the level of mutual interpenetration between individual identity and social processes leaves the counsellor vulnerable to a serious misunderstanding of the nature of the symptoms that clients bring with the result that psychodynamic or behavioural methodologies will be imposed on socially induced psychological conditions.[3] The solution to this requires not just emotional adjustment or psychological self-management, but also a liberating process which enables clients (citizens) to understand the social, as well as the psychodynamic, sources of their distress and pathology. Only with this will they acquire the social and psychological tools required to gain that specific kind of autonomy that recognizes its debt to its own social construction and its obligation to express itself politically. Globalization has seeped into the counselling room and the walls are crumbling.

Legitimation Problems of the State in Late Modernity

Developed capitalist economies carry certain inherent structural risks. For example, the business cycle creates interruptions in the process of capital accumulation which, with the process of internationalization, is open to a wider range of positive and negative influences. These economies create disturbances at social and psychological levels which they are unable to resolve. Whilst our traditional conceptions of social class have been radically revised, capitalist economies inevitably create patterns of privilege and an unequal distribution of wealth and income. Governments, through the mechanisms of the state, have responsibilities that correspond to these risks. They must attempt to implement an economic policy that ensures growth despite systemic fluctuations. Governments must attempt to influence the economy in order to limit the damage caused to other social sectors. They may fail (and often do) to correct patterns of social equality but they must succeed in giving the impression of remedying this problem. 'The sole economic task', observes Bauman, 'which the state is allowed and expected to handle is to secure "the equilibrated budget" by policing and keeping in check the local pressures for more vigorous state intervention in the running of businesses and for the defence of the population from the more sinister consequences of market anarchy' (2000: 67).

This leaves governments with a dilemma. They have to meet these responsibilities without contradicting the precondition of a capitalist economy which resists any state intervention, whilst being entirely dependent on it. As Habermas observes, this leaves the state with a key legitimation problem. It is no longer possible for the state to hide its relationship with the capitalist economy; the problem resides in how to represent the success of this economy as being the best possible means of satisfying general interests. The state, both consciously and unconsciously, must keep the unacceptable side-effects of the capitalist economy within acceptable limits; those states that fail may not only find a new party in power but also experience a usurpation of the democratic process itself. The state is therefore obliged to provide support to a social order in a form that legitimates both the social order and a form of individualism that is nonetheless fractured by the deleterious psychological side-effects of the capitalist economy.

In late modernity the state faces substantial problems that limit its ability to provide such legitimation.

- There is a conflict between maintaining economic stability and compensating for the social costs of economic growth. As the business cycle hits a downward trajectory and social costs increase, the state may be obliged to transfer resources from the social sector (for example, the welfare and health services) to the economy. The development of 'soft landings' in the more powerful economies may only result in shifting the economic and social problems to weaker economies on the periphery.

- Increasing technological development makes it increasingly difficult for the state to maintain full employment.

- The internationalization of capital and labour weakens the power of national governments whilst also undermining their ability to validate themselves to a purely domestic constituency which is increasingly aware of this paradox.

- The erosion of citizens' identification with their national identity (either by a decreased interest in politics or the immersion of nation states in supranational bodies like the European Union) deprives governments of a once powerful source of legitimation for their actions. Judging policies to be in the 'national interest' could previously successfully divert attention from the social and individual pathologies engendered by capitalist growth.

- The state's reluctance to interfere with the canonized process of economic growth leaves it, and the environment, at the mercy of this unplanned, almost nature-like dynamic called 'economic growth'. The resultant increase in worldwide population and production creates two insurmountable material limitations for governments: a finite supply of resources (cultivatable land, fruit, water, fossil fuels and so on) and the finite ability of ecological systems to absorb pollutants.

- Although not so clearly defined, the personality system, like the ecological system, provides limits to the degree to which it can be exploited, colonized and infiltrated by the side-effects of capitalist growth. People like you and I have the potential to protect ourselves through increased self-awareness from ideological narratives (political spin) that attempt to legitimize the actions of the state. This makes it harder for the government to continually deceive us.

With the significant expansion in education to a high standard to more people a contradiction opens up between the state's capacities to engender belief in its actions from an electorate endowed with greater access to alternative views of the world. On the one hand, more areas of life become politicized and fall within either direct government control or the purview of a whole host of quasi-governmental organizations. For example, the family becomes increasingly regulated through: changes in divorce and marriage laws; domestic violence and child abuse interventions; the tightening of adoption and fostering procedures; legal control over the financial arrangements for children after divorce and separation. Similarly, in education, issues of curriculum choice become increasingly codified under state regulation. Whilst these developments may bring some benefits, the state still has the problem of disguising the link between its intervention in, say, the family, and the systemic causes of family dysfunctions which often reside within the economic system; for example, the extension of working hours to evenings and weekends means that parents spend less time with their children. This creates greater demands on the state to provide greater participation and consultation hence its appropriation and redefinition of key words and concepts to suit its own ends. Such terms as 'partnership', 'community', 'consultation' and many others are cast like confetti through governmental documents and pronouncements.

On the other hand, socialization processes, including the expansion of education and counselling services, have the potential to create a public whose identities are generated in processes of linguistic intersubjectivity which work in accordance with communicative rationality and its immanent validity claims. As our identities become more reflexive (self-aware) and establish their authenticity by providing reasons for actions the state is faced with a citizenry which has an increased intellectual, psychological and moral capacity to subject to critique the processes of legitimation that the state relies on. In other words it gets harder for the government to disguise its vested interest in certain sectors of the society (for example, by reducing taxes on the wealthy) by calls to the 'national interest' or by subscribing to a view of the world that justifies inequality. Governments are increasingly forced to give reasons for actions to citizens who are increasingly empowered to question them, through not only the exercize of their own critical faculties but also through the opening up of new communications technologies, such as the Internet and mobile phones, which provide them with potentially subversive communicative media.

The greater the activity of the state and its various delegated organizations, the greater the opportunity that its uncomfortable relationship with capitalism will be revealed. The state cannot ignore this threat without undermining its democratic legitimation. How is this managed? The full answer to this question is beyond the scope of this work although I shall shortly discuss the issue of abstract systems which does have a bearing on this issue. For now, one or two factors do have some salience.

One means of suppressing the validity of critiques of the current uneasy balance between democracy and capitalism (and thereby obtain a mass loyalty) is to functionally detach, as far as possible, the process of political decision-making from the interest of the citizenry. I am not talking here of totalitarianism or conspiracies but of largely systemic processes over which political and economic elites have only a shaky control. This detachment of the political, and other value systems, can be achieved by, on the one hand, proclaiming the 'end of ideology and history' – this vision suggests that all values are pretty much relative, with no one ideology being better than any other with the consequent philosophy that the government should keep clear of all value statements.[4] This leaves the other hand free to get on with the practical implementation of policy as if it were merely a technical issue to be left to the executive elites. Political decisions about how we should live become technical issues of implementation. This is only possible when processes of legitimation are successful enough in convincing the electorate that the current political and economic arrangements are immutable, natural, obvious and so 'taken-for-granted'[5] that the only relevant discussions are those centred around the technical issues concerned with improving consumption.

> What is wrong with the society we live in, said Cornelius Castoriadis, is that it stopped questioning itself. This is a kind of society which no longer recognizes any alternative to itself and thereby feels absolved from the duty to examine, justify (let alone prove) the validity of its outspoken and tacit assumptions. (Bauman 2001: 22–3)

> [S]uch questions relevant to legitimation need not even be allowed if the powers that be are successful in further redefining practical questions into technical questions, if they are successful in preventing questions that radicalize the value-universalism of bourgeois society from even arising. (Habermas 1995a: 198)

This kind of managerialization of everything in sight is uncomfortably close to the managerial and technicizing processes in counselling and psychotherapy (in some ways characterized by the ascendancy of brief therapy) that I discussed earlier.

Legitimation is also achieved by keeping democratic procedures formal rather than substantive. Formal democratic institutions and procedures enable the executive decisions of the state (or any other kind of organization) to be made largely independent of the specific motives and desires of its voting members. General elections, political parties and parliamentary processes generate a diffuse loyalty but avoid participation. Significant amounts of power are shifted to media moguls owning huge corporate communications empires with the result that ministers of state are often observed visiting newspaper editors prior to announcing policy decisions. The citizenry, as observed by Habermas, is thereby often reduced to 'the status of passive citizens with only the right to withhold acclamation' (1973a: 37). This democratic deficit is accompanied, and made palatable by, the tandem process of civic privatism. The citizen is not subjected to any kind of despotism, but is educated and seduced into replacing public ambitions with privatized and individualized personal goals centred on career, leisure, personal identity, lifestyle and consumption. To maintain legitimacy the government must support the capitalist economy which delivers the services that enable citizens to enact these lifestyle choices whilst also ' "acting at a distance" upon these choices, forging a symmetry between the attempts of individuals to make life worthwhile for themselves, and the political values of consumption, profitability, efficiency, and social order. Contemporary government, that is to say, operates through the delicate and minute infiltration of the ambitions of regulation into the very interior of our existence and experience as subjects' (Rose 1999: 10–11).

Other legitimating factors maintaining a level of social solidarity in a society which is systemically fractured include fragmentation, individualization and individualized pathology. Held (1982: 190) holds that stability is also related to the fragmentation of culture and to the fragmentation of people's daily lives and subjectivities. This prevents people from seeing the total picture. Bauman (2001: 36) convincingly argues that the concept of citizenship itself is undermined by the process of individualization (which is not to be confused with *individuation*). The *individual* is the *citizen's* worst enemy. The *citizen* seeks her own welfare through the well-being of the city/society – she realizes that personal fulfilment is necessarily and dialectically connected to the fulfilment of one's fellow citizens. Whereas the *individual* is sceptical and wary about commonality and community as expressed in the 'common good' or the 'just society'. For the privatized individual the common interest is reduced to the minimum level necessary to protect individual rights both legally and physically through the state control of violence. The third of these factors (which I shall shortly address in greater detail) is concerned with how problems caused at the system or structural level get diverted and percolate through to the level of individual pathology. 'As Beck aptly and poignantly puts it , "how one lives becomes a biographical solution to systemic contradictions". Risks and contradictions go on being socially produced; it is just the duty and the necessity to cope with them which are being individualized' (Bauman 2001: 34).

Yet, despite the fact that socialization is achieved through communicative action with its attendant validity claims, there is always the possibility for the individual to gain insight and see through the fog of the taken-for-grantedness of an everyday life that prevents him from becoming a citizen. An important feature of Habermas's theory of communicative rationality is its deontological approach to truth, morals and ethics as outlined in Chapter 1. With this approach I have tried to show how it is possible to find grounds from which valid moral and ethical statements can be made. A political process that operates without any such claims to legitimacy has to base its value statements solely on the psychological effect and impact (sometimes called 'spin') they induce – that is, it is much closer to rhetoric than truth. This gives us little leverage to articulate the difference between an individual and a citizen.

This feels like a long way from counselling and psychotherapy. But this sense of distance is symptomatic of the difficulty these practices have in understanding the level of interpenetration between the psychological and the social as found in the subjectivities presented to them by their clients. This is barely recognized in their theoretical and methodological responses which leave the counsellor with a confused and minimal sense of purpose. This almost inevitably results in them being enthralled and bedazzled by the legitimized construction of the 'individual', such that the 'citizen' never comes into view. The ethical (operating at the level of the individual) trumps the moral (operating at the level of the social), and the ethical itself is no longer dependent on achieving an authenticity which demands mutual recognition and validity testing from significant others; instead, personal authenticity is reduced to lifestyle choices based on values that require no justification other than the fact that I chose them. As I shall argue later, counselling and psychotherapy provide one of the very few platforms from which people can not only reconstruct and reframe their own biography but also (and true biographical rewriting is dependent upon this) understand how their individual difficulties are directly related to disruptions operating at the economic and societal level. A therapeutic process linked to the validity claims of truth, justice and authenticity not only is dedicated to enabling people to achieve transparency and autonomy, but also understands that such people cannot tolerate the social obfuscations created by the processes of legitimation and they therefore acknowledge that achieving their own autonomy is dependent upon creating the conditions for others to achieve theirs. The individual who became a client becomes a citizen. By this process they claim not only their psyche but their *political* psyche, not only their story but *history* itself.

Abstract Systems

The current claim to the 'end of ideology and history' not only closes down the debate concerning political values, it also undermines analytical understanding of current systemic and structural social processes. Through a brief understanding of some aspects of these processes I wish to illustrate how the identity structures and presenting problems that clients bring to counselling and psychotherapy are deeply socially constituted and are not susceptible to remedial action operating only at the level of the individual psyche.

Many social observers have drawn our attention to rationalization as a fundamental feature of western societies in late modernity. On the one hand, we have systemic rationalization whereby what would otherwise be massively over-complex social interactions are simplified and rendered more workable by being mediated by money and bureaucratic systems. On the other hand, communicative interactions are rendered more rational in so far as the operation of validity claims create the possibility of much greater success in achieving understanding. These are very different kinds of rationality. While it is easy to forget that money, for example, symbolizes a social interaction and is constantly open to reification (that is, we make it into a thing and ignore that it is a relationship between real people who are exchanging value), it allows us to conduct social interactions with great speed over huge distances without the need for each of such social interactions to be subject to the lengthy and complex process of assessing all the validity claims inherent in any active communication. Without such system processes it is difficult to imagine how over-complex late modern societies would cohere. Communicative action is too fragile a mechanism to sustain social integration at this level. Although I have constantly asserted the primacy of communicative action over strategic, instrumental or systemic forms of action, this in no way means that we can abandon the latter.

In very broad terms, a society holds together by striking a balance between lifeworld processes (those in which communicative rationality dominates, such as the family, education, socialization processes, religion, art, cultural expressions individual self-identities and so on) which create and maintain *social integration* and those processes of the economy, bureaucracy and administration which act through functional interconnections. The latter operate as quasi-autonomous abstract systems that are dominated by strategic and instrumental actions which create and maintain a *system integration* geared to achieve goals rather than reach understandings. The history of capitalism has been one in which the forces of system rationalization have proved dramatically superior to those of communicative rationalization. This interpretation of historical development, developed by Habermas, sees the lifeworld as being threatened by the dominating power of economic and bureaucratic processes to the point that the lifeworld is being 'colonized'. This colonization works its way through to the individual psyche.

It is no accident that the system perspective has come to dominate since '. . . it was not the theorist who objectified, reified interpersonal activity but capital itself. The logic of capital works behind the backs of the agents of capital, and its comprehension therefore necessarily invokes the perspective of the thinker–observer' (Bernstein 1987: 22). The notion of the increasing dominance of system integration through abstract systems is represented by the transformation of the character of the forces that try to resist it. Until the 1970s the force of resistance to the dominance of capital and economic factors was channelled through traditional workers' movements. From then on the fear of the dominance of economic, strategic and technical issues was no longer limited just to the workplace, instead the fear was extended to a concern that the whole of the lifeworld would become absorbed by these issues. This led to the development of new social movements committed to the defence of the integrity of the lifeworld and personal identity against colonization, for example: the protection of minority issues (the elderly, ethnic groups, gay and disabled issues), new age groups, the whole psycho-scene (counselling, alternative therapies and so on), vegetarianism, animal rights and so on. These groups are trying to protect a whole way of life and a sense of identity and not just economic and employment issues.

Before continuing to develop an understanding of the importance of the extent of the penetration of the individual psyche by abstract social systems, it is important to understand that the historical process that has privileged system integration is neither necessary nor inevitable. It could have been, and still can be, different. My position is that the historic task before us is to make processes of system integration subordinate to those of social integration and that an important agent for such change is the means by which individual subjectivities are constructed or reconstructed. Counselling and psychotherapy represent one of the most important social forces that enable the consensual reconstruction of subjectivities – unfortunately, their practitioners and institutions usually fail to understand their social purpose. In so doing, they fail, to varying degrees, their clients at the individual level.

In a society dominated by systemic imperatives the way people interact becomes detached from the communicative processes of the lifeworld. My view of a more emancipated society is not a utopian vision – and therefore it does not assume that we can dispense with systemic forces of integration any more than we can expect individual pathologies to disappear. Rather, it is not unreasonable to anticipate and work towards a society where the abstract processes of system integration are subordinated to and consensually determined by the individual and collective needs of people acting communicatively in the lifeworld. This would clearly need subjecting our concepts of economic growth, democracy, institutional and socialization processes to radical critique, but this is not my present concern.

Steering Media

With the increasing complexity in social interactions and their increasing detachment from any moral, religious or shared tradition, social interactions fail to find any solid framework. With this kind of development, reaching an understanding becomes more difficult and the risk of disagreement is increased. Therefore a need is created whereby these actions can be coordinated in a different way. Mechanisms emerge in the form of a symbolic communicative interaction that is limited to specific contexts and which condense or replace the need for mutual understanding. Money is such a mechanism. Within the abstract system of a market economy money acts as a steering medium enabling economic interactions between individuals (the buying and selling of goods and services), and also facilitating the management of the total economic and financial system itself. Money is a symbol promising the experience of meaning ('I promise the bearer on demand...') which carries the high statistical probability that the partner in the exchange will honour the promise. Although not a fail-safe device (theft, bankruptcy, inflation all serve to devalue the promise), the pre-understanding involved generally creates a successful exchange that is free from the burden of employing the whole range of validity claims involved in communicative action. This reduces the expenditure of interpretive energy and limits the risk of the action sequence collapsing. Money therefore acts as a substitute for special functions of language. It is a code through which information can be transmitted from a sender to a receiver. The money economy is an extraordinarily complex and sophisticated abstract system enabling the provision of goods and services for everyday life. Markets operate without any regard for value-based forms of behaviour – ethics, moralities, traditions and religions only represent obstacles in the way of unfettered exchange. In late modernity capitalist enterprise shapes not only production, but the process of capital accumulation necessarily requires capital to shape consumption and, by extension, the very identity of the consumer.

Bureaucracies[6] (like the tax office, local and central government, the NHS, large corporations and so on) form another abstract system wherein power acts as the steering medium. Although not as pure an example as money, in bureaucracies (be they state or corporate) members of the bureaucratic system act communicatively only in a restrictive sense. Clearly no bureaucracy could function if social interactions were completely depersonalized, as is the case with money. Communicative action is not replaced but it is disempowered. In order to maintain maximum flexibility in achieving instrumental and operational goals, making decisions through reaching consent via communicative validity claims is restricted to the barest minimum. Bureaucratic processes therefore establish an abstract system which is maintained by formally regularized patterns of interaction governed by fixed rules, habitual interactions and strategic communication towards fixed, but not consensually agreed goals. Completing tax forms or claims for state benefit exemplifies the rigidity of communications in bureaucracies.

In such systems, social interaction becomes instrumentally reified and is distanced from the identity of the people involved. A contradiction arises between the instrumental/strategic imperatives of the organization and the subjective meaning contexts of the individuals involved such that there is a distinct lack of fit. This is why people working in bureaucracies and those served by them often feel quite alienated by, and from, them. The need of these systems to achieve targets and goals forces their employees to work in a purely instrumental way, such that the wider communicative needs (truth, authenticity and so on) of both the employees and service users are largely ignored.

Our understanding of abstract systems and their maintenance requires a cadre of 'experts' who mediate between the individual and the system. Because, for example, financial matters can be so complex, we need financial advisers, accountants, bankers and economists to explain our individual and societal monetary systems. Without these purveyors of highly technical knowledge the lay person is in a poor position to understand the mechanisms of abstract systems and thereby protect his own interests. Whilst essential on the one hand, the need for such experts symbolizes the degree of the alienation and distance of the individual from processes that have a profound effect on his life.

The Colonization of the Lifeworld

The development of complex abstract systems in late modernity results in, what Habermas calls, the colonization of the lifeworld with the instrumental and strategic values which dominate the processes of system integration. In the lifeworld (our everyday life in the family, friendships, socialization processes and cultural activities) we interact through processes of communicative action. However, the sheer power and scale of abstract systems like the economy, science and technology, corporate and bureaucratic working environments results in these predominantly strategic and instrumental forms of social interaction being exported into lifeworld systems of social integration and colonizing them with their non-communicative and non-consensual forms of interaction. The lifeworld therefore becomes instrumentalized and technicized. Hoggett captures a taste of this instrumentalization of everyday life.

> A friend of mine, recently returning from the USA, remarked on the perplexity she felt in experiencing the exhausting weekend leisure routine of her American hosts, a ceaseless round of activities geared to body maintenance and the accumulation of new skills and experiences and an attitude towards the self which precedes no value in leaving it to be, only in putting it 'to use'. (1992: 107)

The colonization of our everyday life by instrumental values has the peculiar effect of making abstract systems appear immutable. Money and power seem to operate 'behind our backs' without we apparently having to do anything. This, in turn, encourages a kind of self that has a reduced arena for real, autonomous action – if abstract systems look after themselves then we need feel little responsibility for them.

The colonization thesis is not the only one available, nor the only one to be concerned with the kind of negative effects created by the dominance of system integration such as: anomie, loss of meaning, insecurity, motivational deficit, and the trials and tribulations of modern self-identity. A whole host of theoretical perspectives (including the postmoderns, poststructuralism, critical theory) are concerned with these issues though their approach may vary. They all reflect a major concern with the great increase in the extent to which the social penetrates (and, to some extent, vice versa) the realm of everyday life and the individual psyche. This phenomenon creates powerful and disturbing influences on the individual psyche which are, in relation to communicative action, pathological. If counsellors and psychotherapist are to interact successfully with their clients, psychodynamic, behavioural and systems approaches will not be sufficient. Psychological disturbances which are deeply socially engendered cannot be undone without an understanding of this fact and the creation of different methodologies:

> The individual's feelings and thoughts, because they were located by psychotherapy *inside* the bounded, masterful self, were considered to be the products of intrapsychic processes, and not the products of culture, history, or interpersonal interactions. Psychological problems have been interpreted as illnesses that are conceptualized as residing within the person and caused by intrapsychic conflicts or malfunctions. By conceiving of mental ills in this way, interpretations of deviant behaviour such as alienation, depression, and, in the post-world War II era, narcissism, were depoliticized. Because psychotherapy denied the central influence of history and culture, symptoms reflecting the frame of reference of the modern Western world – such as loneliness and alienation, extreme competitiveness, and a desire for non-essential commodities – had to be considered unnatural and unavoidable. As a result, individuals have been constructed to strive tirelessly to consume and expand, and at the same time to believe that the search is simply an aspect of universal human nature. If symptoms were considered natural and unavoidable, they were located outside of the realm of politics and history and thus could not be changed through political action: the status quo prevailed. (Cushman 1995: 157)

Moreover, the pathological consequences of colonization will not readily respond to brief interventions aimed at returning people unreflectively to the source of the alienation. Below, I outline a series of phenomenon that express the impact of abstract systems on the identities of the people who are subjected to them.

Fragmentation

Held (1982), along with others, argues that the structural conditions of work and many other activities in a complex society atomizes individuals' experience and fragments their understanding of the work process, and the societal process, as a whole. It is difficult for people to hold a coherent set of beliefs and values and it is equally difficult to imagine alternatives to the status quo. If my job is just one small component in a production line or a huge office system, it is very difficult to see the value of what I do in the context of a bigger picture or a reference system that gives it either a pragmatic or an existential context of meaning. This can lead to a pre-occupation with one's 'own lot in life' and an anxious concern with meeting this need primarily through adapting to contemporary society. The social and technical division of labour in a highly commodified society engenders atomization, privatism and isolation.

Commodification

Traditionally, capital only had to produce goods – consumption ran by itself. In late modernity, capital now has to produce consumers and demand. In order to achieve this, the framework and substance of society becomes geared to sustain consumption. Seemingly private realms like the family, the household and our very identity become besieged by market forces, advertising, marketing and branding. Individual desires become heavily influenced by codes of signification that pre-pack our needs to serve the requirements of increased consumption and capital accumulation.

This process has a profound effect on our sense of self. It becomes increasingly difficult (and for some people impossible) to differentiate an authentic self from a self colonized by images and styles engendered by the engineered need to consume.

> To a greater or lesser degree, the project of the self becomes translated into one of the possession of desired goods and the pursuit of artificially framed styles of life. The consequences of this situation have often been noted. The consumption of ever-novel goods becomes in some part a substitute for the genuine development of self; appearance replaces essence as the visible signs of successful consumption come actually to outweigh the use-values of the goods and services in question them-selves. (Giddens 1991: 198)

Giddens develops the argument with the proposition that the project of the self is heavily commodified not just by lifestyles, but also that the process of 'self-actualization is packaged and distributed according to market criteria' (1991: 198). Self-help books, weekend retreats, self-styled gurus and innumerable therapists advertising their solution to just about everything (ranging from finding the 'inner flame' to working with a man who has just discovered the latest Zen therapy from the wastes of Mongolia) are in an ambivalent position to the process of commodification when they use the same process to market pre-packaged remedies and solutions concerning how to live.

Loss of Meaning

The loss of traditional values, the colonization of the lifeworld by abstract systems, the secularization of the cosmos and the technicizing of everyday life can leave the self with a pervading sense of personal meaninglessness. This depressive feeling that there is nothing worthwhile striving for becomes a fundamental problem. What Giddens calls the 'reflective project of the self' is undertaken in conditions that restrict our personal involvement with some of the deepest existential issues of human life. When a self-identity, which is already burdened with a chronic need to monitor itself and others, has to achieve a high level of technical competence in social interactions and psychological maintenance in a social atmosphere that resembles a moral desert, there is bound to be a strong underlying threat of personal meaninglessness.

This is not surprising, given the pervasiveness of abstract systems and the social imperatives they create. Everyday life becomes more calculable (even finding time to see our children can involve intricate calculations about time availability) and we are obliged to increasingly colonize our futures by a chronic scheduling of future activity through diary systems (it is strange that it can take weeks before we can arrange to meet a close friend). Calculability is also expressed through the commodity structure where everything acquires a monetary value, and through organizational management systems which measure not just our labour but our psyche (for example, psychometric testing). The self is also besieged by an endless process of self-monitoring and by the performance requirements involved in presenting itself in a wide range of different contexts. Mastery substitutes for morality, and as Bauman says: 'Moral issues tend to be increasingly compressed into the idea of "human rights" – folkloristically translated as the right to be left alone' (1996: 55). To be able to control one's life, given that we are subject to the vagaries of abstract systems which act like forces of nature, becomes a sufficient challenge before being burdened with the categorical imperatives of moral activity. As already mentioned, therapy and counselling can become co-conspirators in this process providing the self with greater control rather than greater meaning.

Meaninglessness can be held at bay by the busyness of everyday routines and practices. It tends to come to prominence when we hit those life stage and existential issues like birth, death, divorce and unemployment which break through our fragile defences. In such circumstances, our lack of moral resources, and the corresponding dissolution of familial and community ties, leaves us vulnerable to meaninglessness and psychic desolation. A project of the self confined to personal mastery leaves the self with that highly *individualized* sense of authenticity which I have already rejected in favour of an authentic self based on an *individuation* which acknowledges its social debt by adopting the mantle of the citizen. The individualized process of authenticity 'becomes both a pre-eminent value and a framework for self-actualization, but represents a morally stunted process' (Giddens 1991: 9).

Instrumentality

The capitalist imperative of economic growth results in the predominance of the economic and bureaucratic systems, with their heavy reliance on cognitive-instrumental rationality, which, in turn, results in a distortion of everyday communicative practice. The overwhelming need for instrumental action and cognition means that our everyday actions become predominantly concerned with the 'how to' questions of achieving targets and goals and much less concerned with how we value these goals. We work longer hours in order to purchase more material goods that we can then consume. These are instrumental actions that cast a shadow over our ability, time availability and level of interest in spending time deepening and broadening our interactions and understandings of our inner selves as well as our family, neighbours, friends and colleagues. Communicative action in everyday life requires a balanced interpenetration of the cognitive, moral and expressive validity claims. Communicative action, as such, cannot be instrumentalized; consequently, its colonization by the technical imperatives of the economic and bureaucratic spheres can only result in its degeneration which, itself, leads to the state of affairs in which '...consumerism and possessive individualism, motives of performance, and competition gain the force to shape behaviour. The communicative practice of everyday life is one-sidedly rationalized into a utilitarian life-style; this media-induced shift to purposive-rational action orientations calls forth the reaction of a hedonism freed from the pressures of rationality' (Habermas 1998a: 325).

   This colonization can create direct psychological conflict and contradictions for individuals in their everyday actions. In this context the benefits that I have already mentioned, accruing to the concept of the self as a decentred self and its suitability to the requirements living authentically and autonomously, become relevant. Also, associated with this is Habermas's notion of the different approaches and orientations to the world available to the individual self. It is therefore possible for the decentred self to understand external nature instrumentally (for scientific and technical purposive), aesthetically (as the source of expressive inspiration) and morally (concerning our obligations as stewards of nature). The self is therefore able to switch between these orientations or forms of rationality. The preponderance of one orientation over the others '...overburdens the personality system's average capacity for integration and leads to permanent conflicts between lifestyles' (Habermas 1997b: 245).

Colonization therefore permeates the individual psyche and creates an imbalance in the decentred self and the components of communicative action. Pathologies ensue. We should not be surprised that the overwhelming penetration of the typical male psyche with an instrumental and technical orientation to self and social action results in a male identity which: struggles with the grammar and vocabulary of emotions; experiences sex as performance; struggles hard not to relate to others in strategic terms and thereby objectify them and, far too often, when their controlling mastery fails, subjects women (and other men) to violence. The decentred self becomes fractured and uneven. It is replaced by the managed self or, as Hochschild calls it, the managed heart.

> And in their private lives – driving back home on the freeway, talking quietly with a loved one, sorting it out in the occasional intimacy of a worker-to-worker talk – they separate the company's meaning of anger from their own meaning, the company rules of feeling from their own. They try to reclaim the managed heart. These struggles, like the costs that make them necessary, remain largely invisible because the kind of labour that gives rise to them – emotional labour – is seldom recognized by those who tell us what labour is. (Hochschild 1982: 197)

Community as Carnival or Spectacle

Bauman (2001) develops a theme concerning the difference, in late modernity (what he calls liquid modernity), between *de jure* individuality and *de facto* individuality. This idea is linked to the difference between an *individual* and a *citizen* but views this phenomenon from a different perspective. The individualism which people seek so assiduously is merely *de jure*. It is the formal shell of an individuality as recognized in the legal framework. It is the possessive individualism of an atomized world where the weave of the social fabric has become torn and frayed. *De facto* individuality is one in which the formal shell has been filled by the concrete psychological activity of individuation and the social activity of citizenship. How do the *de jure* individuals in late modernity gain any sense of community? A new kind of temporary 'community' has developed which gets people together for short and intense experiences. Examples are: raves, street carnivals, music festivals, various flamboyant marches for marginalized groups, anti-capitalist demonstrations, clubbing and so on.

> Such communities, after all, offer temporary respite from the agonies of daily solitary struggles, from the tiresome condition of individuals *de jure* persuaded or forced to pull themselves out of their troublesome problems by their own bootstraps. Explosive communities are *events* breaking the monotony of daily solitude, and like

all carnival events they let off the pent-up steam and allow the revellers better to endure the routine to which they must return the moment the frolicking is over. (Bauman 2001: 200–1)

These communities offer, what Bauman calls, a 'virtual common purpose'. For the brief moments they share the participants experience synchronized feelings of panic (moral or otherwise) and ecstasy. These episodic carnivals are the counterweight to the atomization and solitariness of everyday life. However, not only do they fail to bridge the gap between *de jure* individualism and de facto individuation; they are symptoms and sometimes the cause of the problems they attempt to alleviate. These communities of spectacle only serve to undermine the more comprehensive and lasting communities that they seek to instantly replicate. We do not need to resurrect romantic visions of idyllic social communities in order to comprehend the shallowness of this phenomenon. The need and desire for social association becomes scattered and fragmented thereby increasing the solitude that such temporary collectivities are desperately trying to forget.

Loss of Supporting Frameworks

The personal growth industry can, as already mentioned, easily be diverted into a commodified process which is more concerned with personal mastery and has little interest in moral concerns. Linked to this phenomenon, however, is the withering away of the social supports we need when experiencing genuine self-actualization. Kegan (1981) is rightly worried that in our overemphasis of individuality and differentiation our '...culture has not found a way to respond to the destruction such growth entails or to support the new integrations such growth demands' (218). The intrusion of abstract systems and their instrumental/strategic forms of interaction into our lifeworld activity demands over-individualized subjects who are not fettered by community ties. The loss of once-available supports and the inadequacy of any replacements leave the individual vulnerable and isolated in his or her transition to adulthood and maturity. Separation from others (be it divorcing our partners, breaking all family ties, leaving communities) has become the benchmark of psychological 'growth' as opposed to a process of individuation that leads to a greater connection to community and moral bonds. As with carnival communities this process feeds on itself. The greater the individualization the greater the breakdown of external supports, which in turn increases individual isolation. Luhmann (1982) warns us that as external supports are dismantled, the internal tensions (either intrapsychic or interpersonal) become more acute. The capacity for stability, say in a marriage or committed relationship, comes to depend purely on the personal resources of the two participants. 'Personal relationships are overburdened by the expectation that one will be in tune with the person, and this often dooms such relationships to failure – which in turn only serves to intensify the quest for them…' (1982: 162). By not being adequately socially supported during life transitions we come to over-rely on intimate relationships. When they fail we are impelled to seek new ones. Maybe, suggests Kegan, the anger and shame attendant on such developments drives us to compound the problem by constantly turning to new relationships or communities where only the 'new me' will be known. Such behaviour militates against our development as an authentic and autonomous person.

Expert Systems

Abstract systems deskill people in many aspects of their life. The increased complexity of abstract systems which shape and steer large tracts of our lives necessitates the introduction of experts and professionals to aid our understanding of how these systems work and how we might find a path through them. As a consequence of professionalization the distance between expert cultures and the general public grows greater. Our ability to understand our culture and its tradition becomes more difficult and inaccessible to the average person. As a result, individuals not only lose their sense of cultural placement but have an increasing sense of being unskilled in relation to the abstract systems which permeate their life. The simple act of saving some money becomes a complicated financial puzzle requiring a significant investment of energy as well as expert advice – even our pensions are now sources of anxiety as their security is far from certain. Our computers become prone to viruses that make us dependent on the anti-virus providers – who may have a financial interest in increasing the number of viruses at large. Our cars are so complicated that we can no longer tinker with them and try to make or own repairs. This deskilling of everyday life engenders an experience of alienation and fragmentation because the intrusion of abstract systems and experts into all aspects of life undermines our sense of controlling our own lives and our ability to plot our own path in life. Despite the huge emphasis on individualism, we are peculiarly dependent on others to provide us with expert knowledge. However, as has often happened, we discover that either experts have feet of clay, or their so-called expertise is often not independent but geared towards the interests of the state or commerce. Bourdieu calls such experts the new aristocracy or state nobility: 'We must put an end to the reign of "experts" in the style of the World Bank or the IMF, who impose without discussion the verdicts of the new Leviathan, the "financial markets", and who do not seek to negotiate but to "explain" …' (2001: 25–6). This leaves us in a state of anxious attachment to professionals who often let us down. This feeling of anxiety and lack of control has fostered the notion that late modern societies are characterized by being exposed to high levels of risk over which citizens and governments have little control.

High-Risk Society

Whilst late modernity provides greater security in many aspects of day-to-day life, we pay a high price for this. We gain everyday security at the expense of high-consequence risks operating at the systemic level. The wholesale penetration of abstract systems into daily life leaves the individual uniquely prone to risk when these systems fail. Previously, individuals and local communities would have a measure of greater control of their lives which would leave them better protected against failures at the systemic level. Because we have integrated electricity into national grid systems, a power-failure in one power station in the USA in 2003 left virtually the whole of the north-east of the USA and large parts of Canada without power for days. Highly integrated agricultural systems quickly collapse when penetrated by animal diseases which spread rapidly through integrated distribution networks as happened in the UK in 2001. The terrorist attacks on New York and Washington in 2001 were a vivid example of how highly targeted yet small-scale disruptions can create massive panic, huge international financial losses and war. These high-risk affects seem endless: for example, nuclear waste, genetic engineering, the arms race, environmental disasters, drug resistant viruses, dramatic swings in financial markets, fundamentalist movements and so on. Whilst everyday services seem to improve, we become more at risk from random, dramatic, dangerous and high-speed disruptions to our daily lives.

This phenomenon has several important psychological consequences and illustrates how social factors can penetrate deeply into psychological conditions leaving them resistant to the remedial intervention of psycho-therapy and counselling. Habermas (1998a), for example, shows how these high-level risks act as catalysts for a feeling of being overwhelmed by the fear of the possible consequences attendant on the failure of abstract systems. Not only do we fear the consequences; we have a sense of moral failure. We know these processes are a result, however indirect, of our actions but we can no longer take responsibility for these abstract systems because their sheer size has placed them beyond our effective control. Sennett (1998) sees this in terms of an erosion of our moral character. Being at risk, he observes, is inherently more depressing than promising. Risk, for Sennett, not only is limited to these high-consequence situations but also includes less visible consequences of the impact of abstract systems on our working lives in the form of short-term contracts of work, down-sizing, part-time working, shift-work and other, so-called, flexible working arrangements.[7] Each element of risk, in this context, is like the random rolling of a dice. The next little adjustment or role of the dice is as random and unpredictable as the last. Continual risk-taking lacks the quality of a narrative in which one event leads to and has an effect on the next. 'Being continually exposed to risk can thus eat away at your sense of character. There is no narrative which can overcome regression to the mean, you are always "always starting over"' (Sennett 1998: 84).

Many theorists have tried to grapple with this relatively new social and psychological phenomenon. What they all have in common is a concern that contemporary social arrangements lead to the creation of states of anxiety, depression and short-term expectations resulting from peoples experience of: insecurity (as relating to their position and livelihood); uncertainty; and danger to their own body, selfhood and community. Bauman develops this theory to show how it leads people to a greater self-concern and self-interest. In a world where the future is unclear and full of risks and dangers setting distant long-term goals has little attraction. Similarly, sacrificing personal interests in order to increase group power and thereby collectively influence the future is equally forlorn when abstract systems appear to be impervious to social control and influence. 'Any chance not taken here and now is a chance missed; not taking it is thus unforgivable and cannot be easily excused, let alone vindicated. Since the present-day commitments stand in the way of the next-day opportunities, the lighter and more superficial they are, the less likely is the damage. "Now" is the keyword of life strategy, whatever that strategy applies to and whatever else it may suggest' (Bauman 2001: 163).

Lifelong commitments, like 'till death us do part', lose meaning and, Bauman suggests, become transient contracts 'until satisfaction lasts'.[8] Relationships are prone to be broken unilaterally whenever one partner discovers the possibility of a better opportunity elsewhere. Bonds, partnerships and relationships come to be viewed as things meant to be consumed rather than produced – purchased for a trial period, relationships can be returned or abandoned if the purchasers are less than satisfied. Relationships become less a matter of something on which we work together; instead we shop around for the right partner in order to obtain ready-made satisfaction.

Hedonism and Intolerance

With the closing down of the future the concentration on the 'now', in the context of a capitalist society, results in material and experiential consumerism. When gratification can no longer be deferred the link between desire and its fulfilment meets in the experience of ecstasy. The hunt for ecstatic experiences becomes consuming because such experiences need to be constantly available, diversionary and increasing in amplitude. The state's growing indifference to the psychological and sociological impact of soft drugs seems to me less a result of a flirtation with libertarianism rather than a serious failure of imagination in understanding the subtle way in which they corrode character.

> To stay alive and fresh, desire must be time and again, and quite often, gratified – yet gratification spells the end of the desire. A society ruled by the aesthetic of consumption therefore needs a very special kind of gratification – akin to the Derridean *pharmakon*, the healing drug and a poison at the same time, or rather a drug which needs to be apportioned sparingly, never in the full – murderous – dosage. A gratification-not-really-gratifying, never drunk to the bottom, always abandoned halfway . . . (Bauman 2001: 160)

Such an imperative militates against those most treasured components of therapeutic interventions – patience, reflection, authenticity and autonomy. Without an understanding of such phenomena, counselling and psychotherapy seem doomed to make little headway with this aspect of our culture and those people who embody them. By an interesting turn, Bauman links this hedonism to intolerance. People in an urgent search for their next gratification are intolerant of anything standing in their way. Since quite a few of their desires are bound to be frustrated, there is no shortage of things and people to be intolerant of. If the uncertainties and anxieties created by insecure abstract systems are ameliorated by instant gratifications then we are less likely to be tolerant towards things or people that obstruct our desire's satisfaction.

The Sequestration of Experience

Closely allied, yet distinct, to our understanding of the high-risk society is Giddens's (1991 and 1992) theory of the sequestration of experience. Through abstract systems the background services of everyday life which are particularly fundamental, existential, unpleasant and morally challenging become concealed from our gaze. Sequestered, or set apart, from the routines of ordinary life, we are shielded from the shadow side of our existence. Madness, death, sickness, old age, criminality, animal testing and meat production are subject to, and screened by, organizational systems – the asylum, hospital, nursing home, prison, laboratory and abattoir. As previously mentioned, even eroticism becomes replaced by sexuality which seems less threatening and more manageable. The ontological everyday security which abstract systems provide is obtained at the expense of the sequestration or exclusion of fundamental existential concerns.

This sequestration can be seen as both a conscious and an unintended consequence of the process of colonization. The moral and aesthetic domains linked to communicative action become permeated by the imperatives, and consequent abstract systems, of the dominating economic forces of instrumentality, strategic action and system integration. Identities truly concerned about these existential issues would be insufficiently mobile and flexible to be passive producers and diligent consumers. There would be insufficient time to discuss the meaning of these issues. The effect of sequestration is to '*repress a cluster of basic moral and existential components of human life* that are, as it were, squeezed to the sidelines' (Giddens 1991: 167). This mechanism is not a psychological repression in that it relies on the internalization of conscience and produces guilt. It is an organizational and psychological process which has the psychological consequence of limiting the possibility of self-realization and authenticity by hiding from view of those moral dilemmas which we must face if we are to mature.

Everyday ontological security is maintained by the routines and predictable practices provided by abstract systems. But the very routines,[9] which are largely instrumental and technical in nature, lack moral meaning and are unable to provide a context within which we can construct a meaningful personal narrative. These routines can generate feelings of emptiness (they have no bigger purpose) or feelings of anxiety as their volume and speed threaten to overwhelm us. When these routines break down, as a result of either system failure or personal psychodynamic disruptions, we are likely to experience existential crisis. 'An individual might feel particularly bereft at fateful moments, because at such moments moral and existential dilemmas present themselves in pressing form. The individual, faces a return of the repressed, as it were, but is likely to lack the psychic and social resources to cope with the issues thus posed' (Giddens 1991: 167).

Such life-transition moments (like divorce, death of a loved one, unemployment) are likely to create greater psychological damage and disturbance than is strictly necessary.[10] Consumerist substitutes in the form of monetary compensations fail to satisfy and fill the vacuum that remains when moral and existential issues are both camouflaged by technicity and organizationally hidden from view. The process of dying, without any cosmological, existential or personal framework of meaning attached, breaks through the comfortable veneer of technical competence because it cannot be seen as anything other than loss of control and is unintelligible from a technical point of view.

The sequestration of experience can therefore be seen to generate only a specious control over the demands of our lives. The trust in abstract systems becomes ambivalent when they are prone to high-consequence breakdown and when they embody little of moral significance – they offer little motive or psychological reward for the individual. Sequestration is therefore associated with enduring forms of psychological tension. 'The loss of anchoring reference points deriving from the development of internally referential systems creates moral disquiet that individuals can never fully overcome' (Giddens 1991: 185). It is not surprising therefore that during life-transition phases people seek to reshape their self-identity through counselling or psychotherapy. The fundamental question for the latter is their ability to understand the social composition of these psychological phenomena. Bauman reminds us of our tendency to divert our attention away from the social space (where the contradictions of individual existence are collectively produced) to the biographical in an attempt to reduce their complexity and render 'the causes of misery intelligible and so tractable and amenable to remedial action'. But '...there are, simply no effective "biographical solutions to systemic contradictions"...' (2001: 38).

In this summary I have been particularly interested in trying to illustrate how, through abstract systems and associated phenomena, the colonization of the lifeworld creates a powerful set of factors that produce damaging and debilitating psychological effects. Without in any way denying the importance of intrapsychic factors produced through socialization, I have attempted to show that in late modernity the social constitutes the psychological. Indeed, I have only scratched the surface, for I have consciously ignored those conditioning processes with which we are more readily familiar: poverty,[11] huge inequalities in the distribution of wealth, crime, housing, racism, sexism, gender, drugs and religion.

My worry is that counselling and psychotherapy have not sufficiently taken on board the extent of the social constitution of the self which begs the question: To what extent are socially induced psychopathologies being addressed as individual psychopathologies? Is it not the case that counselling and psychotherapy should be a much more critical voice in defence of their clients?

Before I move on to consider the type of self that late modernity induces I wish to stress that the above critique of the deleterious effects of colonization, abstract systems and other associated factors does not mean that there are no positive benefits which accrue from this process of capitalist development. Also, as Martin (1991: 62) points out, and Habermas (1991) agrees, the lifeworld itself is not a virgin terrain spoilt only by the colonizing influence of abstract systems. There were family and socialization problems before abstract systems. Rather, the point is that it is the lifeworld that carries the burden of maintaining communicative action and it is the latter that carries the potential for social action without domination. I concur with Habermas in his abandonment of idealistic notions of the withering away of the state.[12]

Bauman (2001) takes the argument a step further. He invites us to consider the proposition that, more recently, the question of colonization has, to some degree, reversed. It is not so much the case that the 'public' is colonizing the 'private', but that the private is colonizing public space and squeezing out those concerns that cannot be expressed in terms of individualism. Whilst he overstates the case, there is a truth in his observation. There has developed a whole host of media formats whose main interest, in the search for higher ratings, is in revealing very personal and private emotions and experiences to a wider audience of millions. Chat shows, elimination competitions, families relocating to exotic environments, decorating people's homes and redesigning their gardens are all scenes in which private dramas are staged, put on display and revealed to enormous audiences. From this viewpoint the public domain becomes infiltrated by widely accepted media events whose purpose is to play out very private dramas on a public stage with the whole world as a witness. Whilst it is encouraging that many previously hidden experiences can be shared, it is a matter of concern that the motive for so doing is often material gain and that it is almost impossible to generate any collective understanding or action from what is a mere aggregate of unconnected individual experiences.

The thesis of colonization should not blind us to the fact that although individual life is impoverished, people are not just passive recipients of abstract systems. Human beings react against oppressive conditions and are able, to a degree, to appropriate them in their own way and create new possibilities. Notwithstanding, therefore, the power of large-scale social forces people often reject a passive acceptance and continually reshape and reconstitute their lives in the face of macro processes. It is an open possibility for individuals and communities to resist the powers of colonization and steer their own personal paths. Giddens (1991) points out that, although many people feel beleaguered, they are, for example, creating new forms of gender and family relations from the broken pieces of more traditional family life. This is not an isolated phenomenon but creates a much larger social process with the result that families have been 'reconstituted' or 'recombined' in a variety of ways. The fact of divorce becomes a stimulant to create new family networks including new partners, old partners, stepchildren, biological children and friends.

Giddens also describes how the expansion of abstract systems can simultaneously increase the power of individuals and groups. Whilst lay people (and all experts become lay mortals outside their own field) become deskilled in many aspects of their life, they can also become skilled at manipulating the opportunities that abstract systems create. The Internet is an obvious example of how individuals can obtain expert knowledge for themselves. Giddens gives the example of an individual with a back problem. She can either 'passively' accept and receive the prescribed treatment from the state health system or, if she learns how to exploit the new opportunities offered by abstract systems, she can find all sorts of other treatment options. It is as if abstract systems create the conditions for their own transcendence. Is this not also an essential feature of counselling and psychotherapy? These paradigmatic creations of modernity are not essentially doomed to the Foucauldian scenario of being the techniques by which the surveillance society of (post)modernity maintains social integration through the re-engineering of subjectivities in line with the requirements of capital; they are also radical and revolutionary opportunities for individuals and societies to reshape themselves in line with the democratic values of communicative action.

Selfhood in Late Modernity

In earlier, more industrialized, phases of modernity the types of selfhood or subjectivity produced were akin to the standardized parts produced in factories. People were very much limited to their role (worker, mother, soldier, servant) and, like parts on an assembly line, were easily replaceable by another person in that role. Eventually, however, this psychological rigidity became an obstacle. Working patterns required people that were more mobile and flexible with the consequence that socialization processes produced people with a more complex psychology. Late modernity requires people with a more hybrid sense of self; able to move in and out of different aspects of their identity; not too committed to personal and communal ties that they cannot move on; able to reinvent themselves in new contexts and maintain a superficial co-operativeness. Whilst the move from a rigid definition of self is most definitely welcome, as we have seen, in our critique of the impact of abstract systems on subjectivity, the particular shape that this change has taken has serious damaging consequences. To this extent I agree with Elliott when he advises us to

> be careful to avoid a naïve celebration of the multiplicity of selves, fragmented identities, narcissistic personality disorders and schizophrenia as possible subjective sources for alternative social arrangements. In espousing the need to free the self from any psychological, social or historical conceptions and idioms, this apparently 'radical' conversion of the postmodernist critique promotes a standpoint insensitive to the emotional costs of mental illness, as well as indifferent to the social harm of fragmentation. (2001: 139)

Indeed, the development of counselling and psychotherapy can be seen as a corrective and healing response to the debilitating effects of abstract systems on our experience of our emotions and our own identities. But this is to view this development only from a negative standpoint. Although this position holds considerable value, the effects of modernity on self-identity also take a positive turn. The emergence of therapeutic interventions not only reflects the new anxieties and threats to self-identity but also symbolizes the development of a reflexive and decentred selfhood which not only has the power to create a more authentic and autonomous life for itself, but also has within it the potential to generate a society that is democratic in substance as well as form. Democratic societies require authentic and autonomous citizens. It is this potential that has opened up in late modernity. It is now time to take a look at these new forms of self-identity and their intimate connection with counselling and psychotherapy.

Pure Relationships

At the opposite pole to the process of globalization is, what Giddens calls, the 'transformation of intimacy'. Viewed negatively this phenomenon can be seen as the consequence of the inherent fragility of the kind of self-identity produced in late modernity. Each of us has to continually create and recreate a sense of self in the face of the colonization, by abstract systems, of the very lifeworld within which this self is maintained. The self as a project or narrative that is reflexive (aware of itself) has certain benefits but is also a burden given the laborious and isolating labour of self-presentation and self-maintenance. For Giddens the pure relationship becomes the natural counterpart and sanctuary for the reflexive self. In the pure relationship formal, external and traditional obligations and criteria fade away. This is not a relationship characterized by external duties and obligations. The pure relationship stands alone and survives or falls on the basis of whatever rewards and benefits it can deliver to each participant. Trust is secured not by reference to cultural values systems but by the reflexive process of mutual disclosure. In this sense the pure relationship is only possible in a society where self-identity has become reflexive. The internal self-awareness of each individual is mirrored in a mutual trust that can only be secured when each participant has a level of transparency concerning their own biography *and* when each participant undertakes to reveal their biography to their partner. It is therefore not surprising that when trying to understand current forms of self-identity we should begin by looking at how they are linked to new kinds of relationships. The reflexive self and the pure relationship demand each other. Like the self the pure relationship has to be mutually and reflexively managed over the duration of the relationship in the context of an ever-changing external social world. In this sense both are closely linked to the therapeutic culture. A relationship, just like the individual self, requires a deep level of understanding in order to generate the level of transparency required to secure and maintain trust. Couples will turn to counselling and therapy when this process is disrupted. Relationship counselling therefore is not merely a process to remedy relationship failures, but a vital component in the maintenance and development of the pure relationship itself.

There are many attractive features of this kind of relationship: a deep and close intimacy, equality, sexual openness, trust and democratic practices. It is qualities like these that enable us to move from the position of interpreting pure relationships as a mere reaction to negative features of social interaction in late modernity, and to see them in the positive light of providing the foundations for a more developed sense of self which is sustained by deeper and better intimate relationships. Such relationships can be either heterosexual or homosexual and are not limited to pair-bonding. Intimacy is also central in modern forms of friendship[13] and is a growing feature in relationships between parents and children.

Whilst all the external anchors and supports for relationships fade away, pure relationships find a new way to secure themselves. The participants create and maintain trust through 'commitment'. This commitment works in three ways. First, there is a commitment to the other person; secondly, each person must be committed to the joint venture of the relationship; and finally, each person must be committed to the reflexive project of their own self-development. This last feature may seem contradictory, but is essential. Commitment must be based on trust; trust, as I have previously mentioned, is not something that can be taken for granted in late modernity but requires each to be transparent to the other, and each to be transparent to themselves. This is the radical and innovative feature of these relationships. The social commitment in the relationship is conditional upon the existential commitment to live an authentic life. When the possibilities inherent in this phenomenon are understood we may, I trust, take more seriously the importance of preserving lifeworld actions for the domain of communicative rationality and protecting them from the intrusion of an instrumental rationality. It is in this light that we may come to see that counselling and psychotherapy are social forces of great significance because it is these processes that can help attain and sustain authentic lives and relationships. In so doing, counselling and psychotherapy, largely unknowingly, are helping to create the conditions for a more just and authentic society.

This is a historically new phenomenon.[14] Tradition, religion and state inducements would all, previously, be geared to maintaining long-term commitment in relationships. Contemporary romantic love, Giddens reminds us, is a form of commitment but is, in fact, only a secondary tie within a larger context of trust and commitment in a pure relationship. Love may come and go, but a committed person makes a serious undertaking to do the psychological 'labour' required to make the relationship 'work' in the long term regardless of the transient moods of romantic love. In this sense the commitment involved is harder and deeper than in previous intimate arrangements because the bonding is freely chosen rather than externally sanctioned. The partners commit themselves to provide mutual emotional support and to undertake personal self-examination in the attempt to make the bonding strong enough to stay afloat through the inevitable storms of intimacy. Romantic love may develop into the confluent love required by pure relationships, but this is not inevitable and it does not supply connections of sufficient durability. Romantic love, with its inevitable projections, transference and countertransference, is insufficiently reflexive and transparent to anchor a pure relationship. The blindness of romantic love, in the long-term, will be of little use to a type of relationship that is based on insight, self-knowledge, autonomy, self-worth, mutual respect and authenticity.

> What matters in the building of trust in the pure relationship is that each person should know the other's personality, and be able to rely on regularly eliciting certain

sorts of desire responses from the other. This is one reason (not the only one) why authenticity has such an important place in self-actualization. What matters is that one can rely on what the other says and does. In so far as the capacity to achieve intimacy with others is a prominent part of the reflexive project of the self – and it is – self-mastery is a necessary condition for authenticity. (Giddens 1991: 96)

These qualities are as inimical to romantic love as they are to transference and countertransference in the therapeutic process. The parallels between current forms of intimate relationships and the therapeutic culture are not accidental and remind us of our underestimation of the social importance of the latter.

The next step is critical. Giddens and Habermas, in their different ways, show how the attributes of these relationships and the kind of psyche required to live in them are also the personal qualities required to create and maintain a democratic society. I shall develop this theme a little later but, in anticipation, Habermas's understanding of the kind of self-identity required by democracy is something that I have already outlined when discussing his discourse theory as epitomized in the preconditions of the ideal speech situation. Giddens, on the other hand, in his *Reith Lecture* of 1999 suggests that, in several ways, pure relationships mirror the conditions of democracy. Notwithstanding that all ordinary relationships fail to be 'pure' all of the time and often involve conflict and confusion, the salient features of pure relationships are democratic:

- they are relationships of equals and based on mutual respect;
- good communication, free from distortion, is essential in under- standing the other person's point of view. Pure relationships are essentially dialogical;
- relationships, like democracies, require transparency and mutual disclosure to maintain trust; and
- intimate relationships and democracies must be free from arbitrary power and violence.

Giddens is right when he observes that 'we are talking of something very important: the possible emergence of what I shall call a democracy of the emotions in everyday life. A democracy of the emotions, it seems to me, is as important as public democracy in improving the quality of our lives' (Giddens 1999).

I am running ahead of myself. The pure relationship, as described, is an insufficient basis for democracy. The pure relationship contains a con- tradiction. Its attempt to be permanent is undermined by the recognition that it can be terminated, by either partner, whenever they so decide. The relationship is only maintained to the extent that it provides each partner with sufficient emotional and psychological reward and the threat of termination is a subterranean theme that continually haunts it. This shadow can, almost perversely, react back into the relationship and the fear it generates becomes an extra destabilizing factor. The pure relationship is therefore in danger of creating impossible psychological demands on the participants. The relentless insistence on self-awareness and reflexivity and the associated continual examination of self and other creates a burden whereby the participants are regularly weighing the ever-changing costs and benefits of the relationship. The relationship becomes subject to a variant of the Protestant work ethic creating a form of asceticism that is in danger of importing the very form of rationality or worldview (instrumentalism/ utilitarian) against which the relationship is meant to provide protection.

In so far as pure relationships lack external sources of validation the moral climate that it experiences is limited to the ethical axis of authenticity and excludes the universe of moral values. The search for personal and interpersonal authenticity is entirely valid, but insufficient. Dyadic mutual support, trust and respect are extremely important but, if they are not based on extrinsic moral values, they provide insufficient solidarity and security when the relationship, or the individual participants, are subject to traumas, life crises and social upheaval.[15]

The Social Constitution of the Self-Morality

We need to heed Rose's apocalyptic warnings about modern self-identity.

> It is the self free from all moral obligations but the obligation to construct a life of its own choosing... Life is to be measured by the standards of personal fulfilment rather than community welfare or moral fidelity, given purpose through the accumulation of choices and experiences, the accretion of personal pleasures, the triumphs and tragedies of love, sex, and happiness. (1999: 258)

> An age, perhaps where anyone can be anyone, by adopting the outward signs, the style of dress, the mode of speech, accoutrements and so forth that announce an identity now understood only in terms of the emitting of carefully chosen and assembled external signs ... conduct would cease to be the external expression of an inner truth and become a matter of learned skills, of acquired competences of... self-management and self-presentation. (1999: 271–2)

Through the discussion on discourse ethics and moral consciousness I have tried to show how we might generate a philosophical basis for moral action. We are not doomed to enact Rose's anxious vision but his insights are useful because they stimulate the need to provide the moral basis that he neglects. He also serves to remind us that self-identity in late modernity is socially constituted – a fact which provides the self with a moral and political dimension. The truly individuated, as opposed to individualized, subject is one who has attained autonomy through the internalized awareness that its self-identity owes a constitutive debt to the community. Bauman has captured this in his idea of the difference between individuality *de jure* and *de facto*. The former is an individual in form only. It is an empty shell of individuality anxiously claimed and protected by legal rights. The latter is an autonomous, self-sustaining person who is impelled to act as if individuation had been achieved, even if not actually attained. Consequently, the self-assertion of *individualized* men and women (*de jure*) fails to reach the authentic and autonomous self-constitution of the *individuated* (*de facto*) person. Bridging that gap is a political act: 'The gap, however, cannot be bridged by individual efforts alone: not by the means and resources available within self-managed life-politics. Bridging that gap is the matter of Politics – with a capital "P"' (Bauman 2001: 39).

It is also a moral act. The process of individuation is not the self-realization of an isolated subject acting independently but embedded in a socialization process that is linguistically, and therefore interpersonally, mediated. An 'individual' identity is simultaneously a socialized identity that constitutes itself in the process of coming to an understanding with others in language and, as Habermas (1998c: 170) indicates, comes to understand itself through the recognition and acknowledgement provided by external, concrete others. We have already noted how the process of authenticity is dependent on the confirmation provided by others. I am therefore what I have become through the process of living together with others who contribute accountability and agency to me. 'The ego, which seems to me to be given in my self-consciousness as what is purely my own, cannot be maintained by me solely through my own power, as it were for me alone – it does not "belong" to me' (Habermas 1998c: 170). Because the process of individuation is permeated with linguistically mediated relationships, the self-identity which is produced retains an intersubjective core. I can only be myself because of my bonds with others. I am inextricably morally connected to every other human being. Individuation is the flip side of universalism. The reflective project of my life history, and the search for personal authenticity and integrity would have no meaning 'as long as I could not encounter myself before the eyes of all, i.e., before the forum of an unlimited communication community' (Habermas 1998c: 186). Rose's fears are too anxious. The social processes and abstract systems of late modernity do create a rampant and narcissistic individualism, but they also latently enable a new form of self-identity that has the potential to develop itself and society in a more authentic and autonomous fashion. Indeed, this needs to happen because the stereotypical self-identity created by capitalism in late modernity takes us down the role of self-destruction. What benefit accrues from 'possessive individualism' when the self-asserted rights of such individuals can only result in ecological crises because they are unable to act collectively to save themselves? How useful are individual identities which are closely attached to national identities when warfare, the movement of capital and system breakdowns occur at a global level?

The moral dimension of selfhood in late modernity can also be understood as being essentially present within the world of psychotherapy and counselling. Hillman (1996) articulates four kinds of freedom. There is freedom *from* such things as fear and oppression. Secondly, the idea of freedom *to* do something gives us a sense of agency and enables us to do as we like and go where we want. With freedom *of* choice we have access to a range of opportunities. 'Freedom *in*', however, is a form of freedom that is limited by, and dependent on, the constraints of place, time and situation. 'Freedom *in*' is the act of living fully in the concrete situation I happen to be in – 'freed' from the obsessive desire to be elsewhere I am free to enjoy the fruits of living in the present. To live within the constraints of a fruitful marriage is to be rewarded with the freedom that ensues from being committed to this situation as opposed to the 'unfreedom' of having to negotiate my world afresh everyday with relationships that are constantly new and 'free'. The security and sense of identity I feel when I am free to walk the streets without the fear of violence is the freedom I gain from living *within* the constraints of a community backed by a codified system of laws.

Freedom *from, of* and *to* depend on having freedom in the *polis.*

> Participation in the collective affirms your actual self which I have defined elsewhere as the internalization of community. You are your city. So, collective participation, *pace* Jung, is not the price of freedom but its true ground. Freedom is assured less by exercising your individual will in distinction to all others and more by belonging to the other. Myths express this innate belonging as brother–sister marriage; for instance, Zeus and Hera. Our marriage ceremony calls it 'cleaving,' 'till death us do part.' (Hillman 1996: 5)

Hillman also argues that moral codes are essential for the development of self. Quite apart from the social need for morality, there are two essential psychological moral functions. Morals intensify conflicts, without which consciousness would not develop, and morals are conducive to the process of internalization. The development of love and eros is not favoured by an uninhibited acting-out just as it is not helped by repression. Neither repression nor acting-out is beneficial to individuation. A more constructive path, according to Hillman, is internalization or symbolization. Eros is cultivated through the psychological labour of internalization. This process is not the product of sublimations imposed by external social ethics, but is the self-inhibiting moral activity of a self-governing and autonomous self that works with conscience, ritual and fantasy.

The Reflexive Self

A further characteristic of the self in late modernity is its reflexivity. This reflexivity is to be distinguished from the reflexivity inherent in all human activity. In late modernity, reflexivity penetrates into the deepest layers of the self and is characteristic of all social activities. I have already covered this ground when discussing socialization processes and the development of the self so I will only briefly touch on the different forms the reflexivity of the self takes.

- *Self as reflexive project*: the sense of selfhood turns inward and moves from the 'me' to the 'I'. The 'I' or self becomes something that we maintain in different contexts.
- *The self spans the past and the future*: the self becomes conscious of its own lifespan which involves a past and a future. It develops a biography and a history.
- *Reflexivity is pervasive*: the self is no longer a discreet part of identity but permeates all aspects of conscious life.
- *The embodied self*: the reflexive management of the self is extended to the management of the body.
- *Opportunity and risk*: the reflexive self becomes self-constituting, creating itself through a delicate balance of managing opportunities and risks.
- *Authenticity*: the self needs to know that it is a genuine self. It therefore needs the recognition and acknowledgement of others to confirm that the self is being true to itself.
- *Life course*: major life transitions are reflexively understood as constituent factors for the development of self.

The Narrative of Self

Despite the postmodern celebration of the fractured self, it seems clear to many observers that the self requires a narrative structure. The self of late modernity, operating in the shadow of colonization from abstract systems, sustains its own meaning by seeing itself as the author of a sustained biographical narrative which, although open to editing, encompasses the story and destiny of its life. Self-identity thus forms a trajectory, to use Giddens' term, across the lifespan 'in the which the question, "How shall I live?" has to be answered in the day-to-day decisions about how to behave, what to wear and what to eat – and many other things – as well as interpreted within the temporal unfolding of self-identity' (1991: 14). The idea of an individual life having a narrative structure came from romantic love which itself is linked to the 'romances' or stories of medieval troubadours.

In Sennett's (1988) study of the corrosive effect of work patterns on character he expresses his grave concern about the impact of short-term, highly mobile and insecure patterns of employment. What he finds missing in the sense of drift, flexibility and flux that is characteristic of the situation where companies break up or merge, and jobs appear and disappear, is a sense of events having any connection or narrative structure which gives shape to the forward movement of time, suggesting reasons why things happen and showing their consequences. Current employment practice

> requires people at ease about not reckoning the consequences of change, or not knowing what comes next. Most people, though, are not at ease with change in this nonchalant, negligent way.... The conditions of time in the new capitalism have created a conflict between character and experience, the experience of disjointed time threatening the ability of people to form their characters into sustained narratives. (1988: 30–1)

The Failed Self

A self which has become committed to its own reflexive project of itself and seeks an authentic self trajectory is open to the possibility that the recognition received from others, which is essential in confirming the authenticity of its actions, may be withheld. In this sense the self has failed. Earlier I mentioned how this can take the form of either a fragmented or a unitary self. In the former the reflexive inner core is underdeveloped and has difficulty in managing a self-identity that remains sufficiently consistent and recognizable in different contexts and roles. The fragmented self will oscillate between complete absorption in the role or an inability to adopt appropriate roles. This will often take the form of acting-out or repression. This self will find it difficult to hold the tension and ambivalence between being in role and simultaneously being accessible to step out of role because, in order to achieve this, the self must have available to it a core identity sufficiently robust to remain in operation despite the tension. A unitary self takes the opposite track. Rather than becoming dispersed in various roles and contexts it seeks to maintain a rigid identity by staying identical in each situation. It maintains itself by being monolithic and fails to be context-sensitive and recognizes no difference between self and role.

Giddens has observed how the negative side of the reflexive project of self in late modernity takes the form of addictions. The process of self-realization is only partially achieved. An addiction leaves the self incapable of colonizing the future and incapable of living an authentic life. Because they are closely tied to the reflexive self they are a common feature of the failed self and reveal themselves in such addictive patterns as: anorexia, bulimia, drugs, co-dependency, alcohol, obesity, addictive sexual behaviour and so on. Giddens provides us with the salient features of the addictive self: it is not able to monitor itself successfully; self-identity becomes submerged in the other, phantoms or substances; it is unable to open out to the other; and, it leans to gender and sexual practices that are dominant/submissive.

Whilst psychotherapy and counselling would clearly identify these issues as directly relevant to their purpose, if they limit themselves to this outlook they are a real danger of being an emergency first-aid service for the casualties of capitalism in late modernity. In so doing, they ironically support the damaging status quo by 'healing' people in order to return them to the cause of the dis-ease from which they sheltered when occupying their fragmented, unitary or addictive selves. The higher purpose for counselling and psychotherapy is, I suggest, to enable people to move on to the decentred self which not only is capable of acting authentically, morally and autonomously but also has the ability and freely chosen obligation to build a society that will support and sustain such a decentred self.

The Decentred Self

The decentred self has the ability to embody all the positive forms of selfhood already mentioned whilst avoiding most of the failures. Only this kind of self can live in accordance with the validity claims that are inherent in communicative action. While acknowledging that the decentred self is able to accommodate itself in a variety of roles, contexts, self-images and fantasy figures, it is not to be confused with the emptiness of the postmodern self which is lost in the pure surface of a succession of disconnected, narcissistic and ephemeral selves.[16] The decentred or postconventional self knows its own limit. It cannot contradict moral imperatives or act inauthentically without paying a price. Of course, in everyday life we all will make a range of transgressions which can be accommodated if the audience is forgiving and we have previously established our value. But the decentred self will struggle with itself if the moral transgression is too high or if the ethical failure occurs repeatedly. Overall, successful and meaningful social interactions require a self-identity able to autonomously follow moral codes and represent itself authentically over space and time. Such interactions also require the creation and maintenance of democratic social processes that sustain them.

The decentred self is able to maintain its identity throughout the various roles that it performs. It is neither lost in role nor role-distant but is able to maintain an element of the core self that others can recognize when in role.

> Carlos didn't need to come to therapy. He had, over the years, developed for himself a whole cast of characters that he could play – Carlos as tetchy, Carlos as seductive, Carlos as: witty, intimate, angry, a touch depressed, joyful and in pain. What connected these was his ability to be a multiple of selves in these roles whilst simultaneously being recognized, by those who knew him, as a consistent identity throughout the roles. His friends were confident that, if necessary, they could 'call him out' of role and reconnect with a core self.

Reflexivity is loose rather than rigid and is flexible enough to take the risk of exposing the self to new and possibly disturbing experiences. The decentred self will resist the simplicities involved in skills-based counselling interventions because it correctly recognizes these as the legacy of an ego psychology and understands that the instrumental manipulation of self through skills is alienating and self-defeating. The ambivalence of self and role becomes a source of joy and playfulness to the decentred self. If you are trusted and honour this trust then you gain enormous freedom *in* this trust to act as you wish. At the same time, duties and obligations are equally representative of the self because the decentred self knows that it is constituted in, and sustained by, the solidarity of others in the community. It is only the decentred self that has the potential to act autonomously and has the capacity to know that individual autonomy is impossible unless available to everyone and achieved by everyone.[17]

Counselling and psychotherapy therefore have the most noble of purposes. It is their function to assist and enable the individuals that they work with to work through a process of psychological development with the intention of achieving autonomy. It is also their function to do whatever they can to enable change at the social, economic and political levels which will create a democratic society which is conducive to autonomous action.[18] For many this will create considerable discomfort in their self image as a professional as the mask of professionalism prevents them from seeing that their 'private' actions are often more likely to support a status quo that most definitely militates against the ultimate purpose of their therapeutic work. Counselling and psychotherapy are a way of life.

CHAPTER 7

Critique, Resistance and Transformation

I have discussed how counselling and psychotherapy not only attempt to heal the pathologies created by capitalism, but also have a significant part to play in the creation of a form of self that, ironically, is not just an adjustment to capitalist society in late modernity but also creates the possibility of a new kind of self able to act authentically, morally and autonomously. This form of self has the potential to create a new democratic social order that is congruent with its own decentred identity.[1] In other words we have the potential to enable individuals to create themselves into citizens who are able to act democratically-intrapsychically, intersubjectively and politically. The autonomous person who knows that her autonomy is constituted through her solidarity with fellow citizens brings a democratic substance to the rather empty and formal democratic structure that currently exists.

What is this democratic social order? My intention here is to address this briefly with the purpose of attempting to show how the autonomous, reflexive, decentred self and the types of relationships he or she keeps have a congruence with the requirements of a democratic society. I have already argued that counselling and psychotherapy have an important remedial and developmental role in the genesis of this kind of self and associated intimate relationships. I shall, at a later stage, return to this theme and consider how effective counselling and psychotherapy (in terms of the culture, organizations and practitioners) can be in achieving their social purpose of enabling the development of clients into citizens able and willing to work for a democratic social order.

Utopias and blueprints for democracy are most definitely out. All we can productively do is consider to what extent the formal requirements of a democracy fit with the kinds of democratic selfhood that I have already outlined. The democratic principle is quite separate from the moral principle. In other words 'this principle explains the performative meaning of the practice of self-determination on the part of legal consociates who recognize one another as free and equal members of an association they have joined voluntarily' (Habermas 1998b: 110). The principle of democracy already presupposes the possibility of valid moral judgements already facilitated by the theory of argumentation encompassed in Habermas's concept of communicative rationality. Assuming that rational political opinion-formation

196

and will-formation are possible, democracy has the limited role of telling us how this can be institutionalized in procedures that enable all members to participate equally. I touched on this earlier when outlining Habermas's conception of the 'ideal speech situation' which provides the outline for an idealized democratic communicative process. Drawing from Habermas and Giddens I outline below the key rights and freedoms that characterize democratic processes.

1. Each participant must say what he really believes and act transparently. They must represent themselves sincerely and authentically in their attitudes, feelings, intentions and statements. They must therefore be free from internal repression. Only when this condition is operative can we accept that the judgement of others is reasoned and authentic.
2. All participants must have an equal chance to participate in democratic processes, be it formal voting or informal debate.
3. The process must be rational. Anyone who proposes or contests a proposition must be able to provide reasons and justifications.
4. All participants must be free from external domination and coercion in exercising their democratic rights.
5. The only valid norms or morals are ones that regulate common interests and protect the democratic process.
6. Social and economic conditions should be managed in such a way as to facilitate the creation and socialization of individuals that are capable of acting in accordance with democratic rights and obligations.

Whilst the above rights and freedoms are rarely fully present in the real world, members of a society that claims to be 'democratic' must aspire to achieve them.[2]

This understanding of democracy bears a remarkable resemblance to: what we expect from an autonomous person; what is found in the pure relationship and what is anticipated at the end of the psychotherapeutic process. What we are witnessing in late modernity is what Giddens calls the *radical democratization* of the personal. Decentred selfhood embedded in intimate relationships carries the promise of democracy not only in the workings of self and other in the relationships of everyday life, but also in the creation of a social fabric that facilitates the participation of citizens in social democratic processes. Our concept of autonomy describes people with immanent democratic qualities.

> The principle of autonomy provides the guiding thread and the most important substantive component of these processes. In the arena of personal life, autonomy means the successful realization of the reflexive project of self – the condition of relating to others in an egalitarian way. The reflexive project of self must be developed in such a fashion as to permit autonomy in relation to the past, this in turn facilitating a colonising of the future. Thus conceived, self-autonomy permits

that respect for others' capabilities which is intrinsic to a democratic order. The autonomous individual is able to treat others as such and to recognize that the development of their separate potentialities is not a threat. Autonomy also helps to provide the personal boundaries needed for the successful management of relationships. Such boundaries are transgressed whenever one person uses another as a means of playing out old psychological dispositions, or where a reciprocal compulsiveness, as in the case of codependence, is built up. (Giddens 1992: 189)

The transparency that enables personal authenticity and confluent love also facilitates the trust and respect for others that is essential in democracy. The concealing of real intentions not only creates insincerity and undermines intimate relationships, but also prevents probity and accountability at the public and political levels. In a democracy, public accountability can never be fully guaranteed by formal monitoring and so it must, in the end, rely on trust. We can only trust people who act authentically and autonomously.

The autonomous person, who recognizes his social constitution, has internalized a sense of duty that ensues from universal moral codes. Whilst recognizing the rights that enable him to represent his needs, he also understands the obligations and duties that are required to guarantee the same rights to others. What he owes to his intimate partner, he owes to his fellow citizens. Similarly, just as social democracy purports to exercise power equally and without domination, the democratization of interpersonal relationships recognizes, and outlaws, violence as a form of personal domination. Finally, Giddens reminds us that the conduct of open and rational debate that is so characteristic of democratic institutions requires autonomous participants that are able to reason by providing justifications as opposed to simple polemics and emotional outbursts.

Although power is initially unevenly distributed in psychotherapy and counselling, the purpose of the interaction is to create a balanced democracy of two (or more) between the counsellor and the client. The internal process of therapeutic interaction is intended to create autonomous individuals empowered to recreate democratic relations externally. In so doing, it makes concrete the conditions necessary for mutual understanding that reside within communicative rationality and which give counselling and psychotherapy their social purpose.

> The analysis of the necessary conditions for mutual understanding in general at least allows us to develop the idea of an intact intersubjectivity, which makes possible both a mutual and constraint-free understanding among individuals in their dealings with one another and the identity of individuals who come to a compulsion-free understanding with themselves. This intact intersubjectivity is a glimmer of symmetrical relations marked by free, reciprocal recognition. But this idea must not be filled in as the totality of a reconciled form of life and projected into the future as a utopia. It contains no more, but also no less, than the formal characterization of the necessary conditions for the unforeseeable forms adopted by a life that is not misspent. No

prospect of such forms of life can be given to us, not even in the abstract, this side of prophetic teachings. All we know of them is that if they could be realized at all, they would have to be produced through our own combined effort and be marked by solidarity, though they need not necessarily be free of conflict. Of course, 'producing' does not mean manufacturing according to the model of realising intended ends. Rather, it signifies a type of emergence that cannot be intended, an emergence out of a cooperative endeavour to moderate, abolish, or prevent the suffering of vulnerable creatures. This endeavour is fallible, and it does fail over and over again. This type of producing or self-bringing-forth places the responsibility on our shoulders without making us less dependent upon the 'luck of the moment.' Connected with this is the modern meaning of humanism, long expressed in the ideas of a self-conscious life, of authentic self-realization, and of autonomy – a humanism that is not bent on self-assertion. This project, like the communicative reason that inspires it, is historically situated. It has not been made, it has taken shape – and it can be pursued further, or be abandoned out of discouragement. (Habermas 1998c: 145–6)[3]

Critique, Resistance and Transformation

How fit are counselling and psychotherapy to rise to this challenge? For some the prospects seem so daunting that any action seems to face hopeless obstacles. Bauman (2000) is clear that the path from the individual *de jure* to the individual *de facto* must involve the individual becoming a *citizen*. He correctly observes that autonomous individuals are impossible without an autonomous society. Yet for him the prospect of the individual becoming autonomous, given the immensity of the factors pressurizing the individual towards individualization as opposed to individuation and citizenship, seems increasingly remote.

In a number of contexts, including the pathological consequences of the impact of abstract systems on self-identity, I have expressed similar doubts about the ability of counselling and psychotherapy to understand the impact of the changing external social world and to understand their own purpose. Two further issues extend this doubt. First, there is a structural feature at the heart of the current practice of service delivery that is problematic. It has become a transparent feature of late modernity that a large proportion of our social interactions is mediated by contracts. They become necessary when the bonds provided by community, tradition and religion fail to generate sufficient commonality and trust. The very nature of contracting leaves every commitment unsure and unstable. Parties contracted to each other remain free to walk away so long as they are prepared to pay the price for breaking the contract. We have already seen that, despite its many advantageous qualities, the pure relationship is undermined by its contractual nature. Yet, is not the therapeutic process, at its core, regimented like a contractual relationship? This has become quite explicit with many practitioners openly describing the first few weeks of counselling as a contract. The problem is that too much of the contractual nature of the external legal, economic and bureaucratic environment becomes, within psychotherapy, the model for personal life and relationships. 'It etches the social contract into our intimacy. It echoes in our hearts the "go a long to get along" idea of procedurally regulated cooperation with others for the sake of utilities with which to purchase our private pleasures' (Bellah *et al.* 1988: 127).

My second worry is that counselling and psychotherapy, and the models provided by its practitioners, may merely serve to reinforce the message of individualism (*de jure*) as opposed to autonomy, individuation and citizenship (*de facto*). Whilst we cannot hold practitioners responsible for all the problems of society, we should hold them to account for their theoretical and methodological failure to understand the social content of their work. They must take responsibility for gaining an understanding of the purpose of their work, just as they need to take responsibility for the effects of the rush into professionalization which gives a dubious legitimacy to a practice that results in the significant failure of counselling and counsellors to become involved in social issues. Hiding behind worn-out concepts concerning 'neutrality' and 'value-free', their preoccupation with accreditation turns their attention away from the problems that people face in the real world. The psychological move inward by clients is valuable and necessary; just as necessary, but not often practiced, is the move back outward and forward into remedial *social* action.[4] As people increasingly consult counsellors and therapists for their everyday problems concerning work, relationships, sexuality and so on, it may be that they become less practised and skilful in social and collective solutions to the causes of their psychological distress. Once the social is excluded and the problem deemed to be internal, the solution is increasingly focused on better therapies rather than social action. The spiral can be never-ending. The danger is that

> the interiority or unhealthy narcissism of psychotherapy has led to a *false and destructive rupture of the inevitable* and morally and ecologically necessary interconnectedness between the individual, society and the planet. If neither therapist nor client is explicitly acting on their values they are being complicit with evil and social injustice despite the fact that they may in other settings claim to be against it. (Clarkson 2000: 67)

The fragmentation of the therapeutic workforce into private practice can, on the one hand, seem fashionably postmodern with a portfolio style of working that suits the lifestyle needs of a predominantly female workforce.[5] On the other hand, however, this process inhibits theoretical, methodological and service developments because these practitioners play little or no constructive role in the infrastructure that trained them. It also limits the extension of the service to those in greatest need who are unable to afford the fees charged, while this fragmentation undermines the ability of the few remaining counselling organizations to offer a credible and critical public voice.

Counselling and Psychotherapy as Social Critique

Enough already. It is now time to consider the very positive social and political role that counselling and psychotherapy could and should play in order to fulfil its purpose at the individual, group and social levels.

Whilst not ignoring the potential for art to degenerate into propagandistic or commercialized mass art, Habermas (1973a) recognizes that bourgeois art was one of the few cultural movements that attempted to keep itself separate from the dominant processes of rationalization, instrumentalization and materialism. Art attempted to keep alive forms of communication and spontaneity that were being marginalized by the commodification of social interactions and the hegemony of purposive rationality. 'Bourgeois art, unlike privatized religion, scientific philosophy, and strategic-utilitarian morality, did not take on tasks in the economic and political systems. Instead it collected residual needs that could find no satisfaction within the "system of needs"' (Habermas 1973a: 78). What Habermas ignores is the radical potential within counselling and psychotherapy to similarly provide a 'free-zone for communicative action' within a hegemony of instrumentalism. Although much honoured in the breach by supporting the economic and political systems which provide adjustment-based psychological interventions, the purpose of counselling and psychotherapy does provide these practices with the potential for creating a radical social critique.

There is a well-developed school of Critical Theory (which developed out of the Frankfurt School of western Marxism) which has incorporated many critical elements from other schools such as psychoanalysis, post-structuralism and postmodernism. The function of this tradition is to provide a continual critique of developing societies. A critique is not just a negative commentary, but looks to draw out the positive features inherent in current social developments so as to enable the creation of an autonomous society for autonomous people. I believe that counselling and psychotherapy should place themselves within this tradition and see themselves as movements and cultures that provide a resistance to the pathologies caused by abstract systems and also provide a haven for clients and practitioners who are struggling against the colonization of the lifeworld.

Counselling and psychotherapy that are in line with their purpose can not only provide a form of theory that enables a critical understanding, but through their practice provide the opportunity for clients to make their own 'subjective realignment' (which is quite the opposite of adjustment), regain their own repressed energy, rewrite their biography[6] and become independently minded citizens able to connect the psychological and the social.[7]

This critical understanding needs to join up the extremes of individual symptoms on the one hand, and economic growth and the ecological crisis on the other. Marcuse (1972b) was able to see, some considerable time ago, that conditioning personal and social liberation on an ever-higher standard of living only serves to justify the perpetuation of repression. Unremitting economic growth leaves us trapped in the dynamic of the 'performance principle' which I have described in terms of strategic-rational behaviour. The ecological damage that results from uncontrolled economic growth demands a coordinated global response. However, improving the environment is only possible when individuals change their lifestyles. Thus in complex societies global change requires widespread reflexivity in individuals – the personal and the global are attractively interconnected. If we require a shift in our commitment to economic growth in order to reduce environmental damage and equalize the growing chasm between rich and poor countries, we will need a widespread change at the individual level substituting personal growth, authenticity and autonomy for economic growth. The emergence and enabling of this new form of self-identity that is critical of the status quo becomes an essential component in avoiding global environmental disaster and international political conflict. Psychotherapy and counselling have an important role in enabling their clients to make their connection between the individual and the global.

The Therapeutic Link between the Personal and the Political

Connecting the personal with the political does not involve the introduction of arbitrary values into the counselling process, nor does it introduce a didacticism thereby making the counsellor a polemicist or a rhetorician. Through our understanding of communicative rationality we can comprehend how the individual is necessarily connected to the social and how issues of truth, ethics and morality are an immanent aspect of the therapeutic process. As a consequence the social and the political are already present deep inside the counselling interaction. Thus the reparative search to renew mutual recognition through the erotic transference and counter transference between client and therapist is a process of social as well as individual change.

> To attempt to recover recognition in personal life does not mean to politicize personal life relentlessly or to evade politics and give up the hope of transformation – though all these failures do happen in real life. It means to see that the personal and social are interconnected, and to understand that if we suffocate our personal longings for recognition, we will suffocate our hope for social transformation as well. (Benjamin 1988: 224)

Samuels (1993) continues this theme. He encourages us to understand therapeutic psychological transformation not so much as a 'change within' but a 'change between' moving to a 'change out there'. In the case of aggression we might understand that this is not only an intense wish for relatedness, but also involves 'equally intense wishes for participation, in a more co-operative or communal mode, in political of social activity. To be authentically aggressive, angry in the belly, and still be able to be part of social and political processes, is a psychological and ethical goal of the highest order' (1993: 56–7). From this perspective we do not get caught up in naive notions that dismiss counselling and psychotherapy as reactionary or conservative because they siphon off rage against social oppression and inequalities. A radical feature of therapy is that, on the contrary, such rage can be constructively developed and find a political platform.

Counselling and Psychotherapy as an Emergent Social Movement

Western societies in late modernity appear to have come to the end of one phase of social change and are at the margins of entering a new phase. This uncertainty is captured by a plethora of competing descriptions including: postmodernity, liquid modernity (Bauman), the second phase of modernity (Beck), late modernity (Giddens) and so on. Such transitions often spark-off the creation of new social movements. Examples of such movements in the past are socialism, feminism, racial equality and so on. Such movements become the 'leading edge' of change within the wider social context. Drawing on potentials that are already present but undeveloped, they act like new social learning processes creating new forms of socialization and personal identity formation. They also serve to stimulate public debate and revitalize existing, or create new, public institutions. For example, during the nineteenth century the extension of formal education from a small elite to the whole population had an enormous impact on social change and the creation of new subjectivities.

Reiff (1966) suggests that at times of cultural transition the dominant cultural codes experience competition from alternative symbolic structures that gather increasing support such that they continually try to elbow each other to the margins so that each may define the next stage of psychohistorical development. What was once an emancipatory moment in a culture becomes, at its close, a form of control. The creation of an ego able to rationally dominate its environment through instrumental and strategic thought and behaviour was revolutionary at the dawn of capitalist development. In its 'post', 'liquid' or 'late' phase these characteristics feel like shackles on an emergent decentred identity embedded in pure relationships based on confluent love. Bennett (1998) cautions us not to confuse the genuinely emergent social movement with the novel or fashionable. The latter is merely a side-effect of the dominant culture's need to reinvent itself continually anew in slightly different shapes and colours. The emergent culture, he notes, has to pass through a 'twilight zone before it achieves adequate and recognizable forms of expression' (1998: 99). If the world of counselling and psychotherapy could lift up its head and comprehend its relationship to the world around then it might see that it carries within itself the embryo of a new form of authentic and autonomous personal and communal identity.

Enabling a Radical Identity

> Psychoanalytic education will be taking an uninvited responsibility on itself if it proposes to mould its pupils into rebels. It will have played its part if it sends them away as healthy and efficient as possible. It itself contains enough revolutionary factors to ensure that no one educated by it will in later life take the side of reaction and suppression. (Freud 1975: 186)

If only this were the case. In Freud's time the sheer uniqueness of psychoanalysis with its somewhat shocking ideas must have seemed quite sufficient to guarantee its radical and critical nature. History proved otherwise, particularly in the American context. As psychoanalysis, and its offshoots, became absorbed into the mainstream its radical nature was steadily diluted. Indeed, the fact that the critical nature of psychotherapy and counselling is no longer obvious at all has stimulated my attempt in this work to go back to first principles in order to the secure their radical nature in communicative rationality.

Consequently, I believe that an important social function of psychotherapy and counselling is the enabling of authentic and autonomous individual identities which are immanently radical in the sense that, in order to maintain and reproduce themselves, they know that this is only possible in a conducive, revised social formation. In this sense, although largely unconsciously, social revolutionary processes are already underway in the therapeutic intervention in personal life and identity formation. 'The transformation of intimacy presses for psychic as well as social change and such change, going "from bottom up", could potentially ramify through other, more public, institutions' (Giddens 1992: 182). Not that long ago little credence was given to this sense of a slow revolution resulting from the translation of inner, intrapsychic change into external social change. Granted is the fact that such dispersed and individualized change does not generate a traditional revolutionary class with its own sense of identity and counter-culture. On the other hand, however, given the extent to which the instrumentality of the dominant culture has colonized the lifeworld and the individual psyche, it is not surprising that the process of deconstruction and consciousness-raising takes time. Social emancipation is no longer just a process of redistributing wealth and power but involves the self-liberation of persons from the very character structures that inhibit and oppress them. An important way, open to us, of protecting the lifeworld or arena of communicative action is the bottom up cumulative process of individual psychological transformation leading to social change. Our task is to enable counselling and psychotherapy to understand that it is in the realm of personal life-politics 'that the threats and the chances of individual autonomy – that autonomy which cannot fulfil itself anywhere except in the autonomous society – must be sought and located. The search for an alternative life in common must start from the examination of life-politics alternatives' (Bauman 2000: 51).

Psychotherapy and counselling need, in their theory and practice, to understand that the individual dysfunctions that they work with are necessarily heavily connected to a dysfunctional society. They need to envision not just the cure of the client but the healing of the society. 'A personal solution to the emptiness inside may not make it any easier to live in a world with so much incongruity. It may make it more discordant in a different way, drawing a line between inner dissatisfactions, restlessness and frustrations, and the alienation in and from public space' (Orbach 1996).

Counselling and Psychotherapeutic Institutions

This radical potential in therapy is not just a matter of practitioners working with their clients. Although there are exceptions, one could argue that the delivery of this form of psychological transformation through a fragmented, dispersed, self-employed cadre of private counsellors and psychotherapists is inimical to achieving its potential. On the other hand, the provision of such services through state-owned health organizations tends to have the effect of only offering the kind of therapeutic interventions which are most comfortable with the strategic rationality of the dominant culture. I have in mind here rational-cognitive therapies, behavioural work and brief counselling which are aligned to a medicalized model of health.

My scepticism of the radical credentials of private, state and commercial therapeutic practices seems to leave us with no hope – but not quite. Our concern about the lifeworld (individuals, the family, voluntary associations), which is characterized by communicative action, has been how to protect it from continual encroachment by the abstract systems of the economic and administrative. How can we police this boundary between the system and the lifeworld in order to promote the movement of values from the latter to the former rather than vice versa? Habermas identifies 'self-organized public spheres', or what we might call the voluntary sector, as institutions assigned with the critical function of policing this boundary conflict. From this perspective the general function of the voluntary sector, through the development of its power and reflexivity, is to develop practices and discourses that offer a democratic critique of the instrumental and goal-oriented practices of the state and the economy. Increasingly dependent upon the state and commerce for income, voluntary organizations are significantly at risk from losing their independence and becoming sources of legitimacy for their funders. This must be resisted at all costs because the independence of voluntary organizations is the source of their legitimacy. There also needs to be an internal struggle within voluntary organizations to keep them focused on their purpose and avoid the subsumption of values under organizational imperatives.

> Forms of self-organization strengthen the collective capacity for action. Grassroots organizations, however, may not cross the threshold to the formal organization of independent systems. Otherwise they will pay for the indisputable gain in complexity by having organizational goals detached from the orientations and attitudes of their members and dependent instead upon imperatives of maintaining and expanding organizational power. (Habermas 1987: 364)

Our earlier discussion concerning Wilber's (1990) difference between change as *transformation* and change as *translation* can now be used to generate criteria for evaluating the legitimacy and authenticity of those voluntary organizations involved in psychosocial issues. Transformation represents a change in deep structure and can be visualized in terms of moving from one level up to the next; translation is a change in surface structure and involves making changes within a level. The first represents a vertical scale and the second a horizontal scale. A psychosocial institution that validates or facilitates translation can be described as *legitimate*. A legitimate organization is measured by the degree of integration, organization, meaning and coherence it provides for its members within a given level of structural development. They must provide their members with a legitimizing world view capable of validating their existence. For psychosocial voluntary organizations this requires them to ensure that this legitimacy is based on the tenets of communicative rationality and not the values of the state or business with which is interacts. A psychosocial institution which validates or facilitates transformation upwards to higher levels can be described as *authentic*. This is the task of agents of socialization such as the family, education and therapeutic organizations. A counselling or psychotherapeutic organization can therefore be judged on the basis of its legitimacy and authenticity. Does it merely seek to confirm and validate people at the present state of growth or does it also seek to transform them to genuinely higher levels of development? These judgements can be based on an assessment of the organization's core values, public statements, theories, methodologies, organizational structure and practices.

Such organizations play an important role in social evolution. They provide what Habermas calls a 'cognitive potential'. Although I would not wish to limit it to the cognitive level, the point is that they provide society with new learning capacities which emanate from these marginal institutions.

> Learning capacities first acquired by individual members of a society or by marginal groups make their way into society's interpretive system via exemplary learning processes. Collectively shared structures of consciousness and stocks of knowledge represent a *cognitive potential* – in terms of empirical knowledge and moral-practical insight – that can be utilized for societal purposes. (Habermas 1998a: 313)

Counselling organizations mark an evolutionary advance in learning capacities and identity formation. Their role is to move these gains from the margins to the mainstream. Their rarity on any significant scale makes them something of an endangered species.

An example of such an organization in Britain is Relate, which provides relationship counselling and is the largest counselling agency in the country. Rather than focusing our attention on its task of helping couples solve their relationship problems, we might perceive it as an organization that is legitimate because it confirms for people the validity of their current stage of development, and authentic because it enables people to develop to the higher stages of personal authenticity and autonomy. In order to do the latter, it would need to provide its clients with the possibility of developing a radical understanding of current social arrangements and to achieve that it would also need to be a radically independent organization critical of the political and economic system which creates the psychopathologies which visit its counselling rooms. It fails to do either. Lewis *et al.* (1992), in their analysis of Relate, explain that, like all voluntary organizations, it must be clear about its 'why values' (the purpose and worth of its activity), and its 'how values' (the way in which its work is done). With regard to the former they find in Relate a distinct lack of clarity on values such that 'it is difficult to see how research and information can easily be harnessed to an intention to speak more publicly on matters of family policy, when no clear value position on such issues has been agreed within the organization' (1992: 264). They also found that a preoccupation with financial survival, although understandable, tends to supplant purposive values with operational goals such that concerns about 'the organization's survival was not accompanied by any thoroughgoing discussion of its purpose' (1992: 199). The situation since 1992 has only got worse. Without a coherent value base, Relate finds it impossible to make public statements of any critical significance.

Relate is not by any means alone and is representative of many voluntary organizations that have lost touch with their core values and have, without conscious direction, transformed from being a social movement to being a service agency. A social movement is characterized by: having values it wants to promote; members who affirm its beliefs; the donation of voluntary work in the furtherance of these beliefs; an amateur spirit that does not require payment. A service agency is characterized by: operational objectives to be achieved; staff who implement these objectives; the routine application of skills; and a professional outlook that seeks remuneration comparable to other professions. There is now real doubt as to whether an organization like Relate can be said to be authentic or be described as embodying a learning potential.[8]

Counsellors as Agents for Radical Social Change

What is the potential for psychotherapists and counsellors themselves to act as agents for a radical transformation of capitalist society in late modernity? If we are looking for a recognizable *revolutionary class* then the doubters have the day. Therapeutic practitioners, like the clients they work with, have to maintain their authenticity and autonomy in a consumer society that richly rewards collaboration. Resistance is possible but difficult to organize beyond loose networks which themselves are always in danger of collapsing into lifestyle choices which embody a resistance in form only.

Reiff (1966) holds the view that all previous radical social change has required a cultural elite which carries a doctrine of communal purpose as its source of motivation. The leadership power of such an elite is embodied in its capacity to express effectively a communal morality. Such elites would be hard to find in western society in late modernity – elites certainly exist but none carry an effective message about commonality. Political leaders are experiencing a crisis of legitimacy and credibility; religious leaders have been virtually sidelined, which leaves us, to some degree, with just the circus of stars and celebrities. Apart from a few well-known therapists who have their own battle with celebrity projections, therapists as a group do not form a cultural elite or revolutionary vanguard with the power to provide social and moral leadership. Indeed, as Reiff hints, the inherent democratic qualities that counselling and psychotherapy offer militate against the historical pattern of leaders and followers. Just as unlikely is the view that therapeutic work will motivate its clients to become, either singly or collectively, highly political people intent on social transformation.[9]

Counsellors, and many of their clients, do not, as a rule, live lives with strong communal links. What sometimes drives them together is not so much a search for a common cause but a strong need to share intimacies and experiences in a world that devalues both. This form of connecting

can only spawn 'communities' as fragile and short-lived as scattered and wondering emotions, shifting emphatically from one target to another and drifting in the forever inconclusive search for a secure haven: communities of shared weariness, shared anxieties or shared hatreds – but in each case 'peg' communities, a momentary gathering around a nail on which many solitary individuals hang their solitary individual fears. (Bauman 2000: 37)

Or, as Bellah *et al.* note, the social world of counsellors takes the shape of a wide range of dyadic relationships between oneself and an array of other people who are unknown to each other. Since this array of people have no articulated set of common values, 'it does not engender an angry programme to impose its values on the rest of the world' (1988: 186–7).

Yet something is happening and some potential is created. This period of rapid change, with its various appellations (modernity/postmodernity, first-/second-stage modernity, solid/liquid modernity), might have at least one thing in common with previous historical transitions like the spread of Christianity, the Renaissance or the Industrial Revolution. That is, it is neither obvious nor transparent to the participants what is going on or which way the wind is blowing. We have already noted that it is very difficult to discern emerging new social movements from what are merely stylistic re-orderings of the status quo. Nevertheless, there are some signposts around. They may not all be pointing in the same direction and the distances may vary considerably, but I believe that there are enough available to give us a sense of the way forward albeit that it may be a somewhat stumbling journey. I have spent much time bemoaning the deleterious psychological effects of abstract systems and other factors associated with capitalism in late modernity. But this disintegration of recognized social relations does have useful side-effects. Whilst eroding many things of value it does also clear away the cobwebs and dispense with many things that were oppressive (traditional, role-based relationships) and enable those which are more authentic (pure relationships and the decentred self). This process is similar to developments in electronic forms of communication which can intrude upon and limit face-to-face interactions but at the same time mobile phones, text-messaging and the Internet create new opportunities for coordinating social and political action. Anti-globalization protesters use this technology to create virtually instant congregations ready for political action. Let us finally consider some of the ways that counsellors and psychotherapists may come to understand themselves as working socially and politically towards the purpose immanent in their therapeutic endeavours.

We should celebrate the fact that we are not 'into' instant revolutions. All counsellors and psychotherapists know that true psychological trans-formation take time and, as the democratic society that I have hinted at requires psychologically competent participants, the process of social change will take time and will be predominantly evolutionary although, as with individuals, there may be occasional traumatic or 'revolutionary' transitions. The committed counsellor will not be able to prevent himself or herself from changing. Notwithstanding the ideologies of 'value-free' and 'objectivity', Halmos accurately observes that the counsellor or psychotherapist 'is an expert on moulding opinion. It is the counsellor's vocation to change people's opinion about themselves and about the world. The circumstance that their technique is personal, piecemeal, and private, merely conceals the fact of their great and lasting effectiveness

with which no advertizer or propagandist can hope to compete successfully'
(1965: 177).

The pattern of politics has radically changed. The dichotomies of 'right'
and 'left' have been pushed to the margins by a plethora of protest groups
on such issues as: anti-nuclear action, environmentalism, the peace movement, a host of single-issue and local movements, alternative movements
(squatters, travellers), minorities – elderly, ethnic, gay and disabled, animal
rights, vegetarianism, religious revivalism and fundamentalism, feminism,
anti-abortionists, regional autonomy and cultural and linguistic autonomy.

The list is almost endless but they are not completely disassociated from
each other – there are themes that bind them. They have common concerns
around the quality of life, personal identity, equal rights, self-realization and
human rights. In many ways the theoretical framework of communicative
rationality is best able to understand this phenomenon.

> From Habermas's perspective, new social movements are reacting against the
> increasing colonization of the lifeworld and cultural impoverishment. This perspective
> allows one to understand the peculiar defensive quality such movements exhibit. On
> the one hand, there is a defensive reaction against the encroachment of the state and
> economy on society, something which is similar to traditionalistic, reactive movements.
> On the other hand, the behaviour of new social movements cannot be understood
> simply as a reaction against 'the destruction of traditional forms of life,' but rather as
> a reaction against the defamation of 'post-traditional forms of life' made possible by a
> rationalized lifeworld. Protecting the conditions of possible 'communicative sociation'
> means generating space for a more autonomous construction of group identity and
> political deliberation. (White 1988: 124)

These groups are not trying to change society piecemeal but are trying to
create enough space to articulate their plural as well as their individual
identities. Counsellors and psychotherapists might find themselves increasingly able to identify themselves as *counsellors and psychotherapists* with
such movements. It is possible that their preoccupation with the very
conventional concern of being seen as 'professional' (which keeps them
well within the orbit of the dominant value set) might be shifted to a more
alternative and radical self-image that has some resonance with members
of the above-mentioned protest groups. Or they might consider the
re-interpreting of 'volunteering' along the lines of 'civil labour' as proposed
by Beck (2000).[10]

This process also operates at a more general level. It isn't just a case of
these various groups picking up on life-politics issues – there is almost a
feeling of a kind of 'spiritual' transformation taking place at what feels to be
a transition between epochs. Samuels (1993) calls this process a 'resacralization'. This represents an attempt to shift or create a sense of holiness in
a secular world. Although this may have many less than desirable spin-offs,
it is not the same as the revival of traditional gods and religions and it

certainly is not a form of religious fundamentalism. Rather, it represents an attempt to create individual, cultural and possibly metaphysical narrative structures which can enrich our lives with meaning and purpose without breaking the deontological frame that we started with. There is a desire for a new ethical basis for social and individual action which I believe will spawn new mythical narratives. It is this that makes Jungian psychotherapy attractive to many people just as Neumann's (1956) reinterpretation of the myth of Eros and Psyche can suddenly feel to be meaningful to a decentred self operating within a pure relationship.

On reading Empire by Hardt and Negri (2001) I was struck by some similarities between the potentially enormous consequences following from the slow but cumulative impact that counselling and psychotherapy have on transforming subjectivities and personal identities, and the impact of Christianity during the decline of the Roman Empire. Although the former is secular and the latter is religious, both involve the transformation of subjectivity at the individual level and the transformation of society through increasing the congregation of transformed individuals. As Hardt and Negri (2001: 21) point out, this new subjectivity claims to be qualitatively different and offers a full alternative much as Christianity challenged Imperial right. The hegemony operative today seems as total, obvious and unchallenged as the Roman imperium;[11] therefore it might only ever be successfully contested by a new ethic and vision operating at a similar level of generality. The community of authentic and autonomous people within an autonomous society is universal.

> In this regard we might take inspiration from Saint Augustine's vision of a project to contest the decadent Roman Empire. No limited community could succeed and provide an alternative to imperial rule; only a universal, catholic community bringing together all populations and all languages in a common journey could accomplish this. The divine city is a universal city of aliens, coming together, co-operating, communicating. Our pilgrimage on earth, however, in contrast to Augustine's, has no transcendent telos beyond; it is and remains absolutely immanent. Its continuous movement, gathering aliens in community, making this world its home, is both means an end, or rather a means without end. (2001: 207)

The vision that counsellors and psychotherapists can offer and spread throughout their work can indeed foster this secular pilgrimage.

Notes

1 Communicative Rationality

1. From a different perspective Castoriadis accurately describes the problem: 'given that *it is true* that at the core of the "subject" (whatever that may mean) an unconscious psyche most of the time motivates its acts (therefore, also, its pronouncements); given that *it is true* that nobody can ever jump over his times or extract himself from the society to which he belongs; given that *it is true* that any statement contains an irredeemable element of interpretation corresponding to the interpreter's position, outlook, and interests – how can it be that we are capable of any self-reflective activity, including the one leading us to the above statements and all the others?' (1991: 29). Quite differently again, the extent of the absorption of relativism into our habitual interactions is interestingly illuminated by McEwan's observation of a feature of modern accents: 'Parry had his generation's habit of making a statement on the rising inflection of a question – in humble imitation of Americans , or Australians, or, as I heard one linguist explain, too mired in relative judgements, too hesitant and apologetic to say how things were in the world' (1998b: 240).
2. In order to function as human beings we simply cannot operate with the consequences of total relativism: 'The point of view from which we might constate that all orders are equally arbitrary, in particular that all moral views are equally so, is just not available to us humans. It is a form of self-delusion to think that we do not speak from a moral orientation which we take to be right. This is a condition of being a functioning self, not a metaphysical view we can put on or off. So the meta-construal of the neo-Nietzschean philosopher – "in holding my moral position, I am imposing (or collaborating in the imposition of) a regime of truth on the chaos, and so does everyone" – is just as impossible as the meta-construal of the empiricist – "in holding my moral position, I am projecting values on a neutral world of facts, and so does everyone".... They are not construals you could actually make of your life while living it' (Taylor 1996: 99).
3. 'If language can be used as a means of communication (and the writing of this sentence assumes that this is so), certain presuppositions must be built into it... What is of supreme importance is that there is some notion of truth as such in human language. This is the cement which binds language together and stops it being fragmented into self-contained compartments, such as religious language. It is this which enables people of different views to understand each other, and allows the sentences of one language to be translated into those of another' (Trigg 1974: 153). Despite his criticism of Habermas's theory of communication holding some universal characteristics Castoriadis comes to a similar conclusion: 'and we cannot pretend to ignore that we attempt to think, to discuss and to judge irrespective of these conditions, that we intend validity for what we say irrespective of place, moment, motives, and conditions. We therefore have to recognize both the effective and the reflective point of view. And we have to face the fact that it is only in and through the social–historical (and leaning on certain capacities of the psyche) that the reflective (of which the "transcendental" is a dimension) becomes effective' (1991: 30–1).

4. House's *Therapy Beyond Modernity* (2003) provides a vigorous and stimulating deconstruction of profession-centred therapy. Despite the power of much of his critique, his whole-scale, and uncritical, adoption of a fairly radical postmodernism contains problems. The whole of the Enlightenment project is debunked without any attempt to differentiate between the various aspects of the Enlightenment and the different forms that reason takes. As Smail observes, in the Afterword (1998: 261), House twists and turns in an attempt not to create a new 'regime of truth' (a new claim to universal rationality) with his postmodernist 'New Paradigm' but for Smail and for me this proposed paradigm shift '...cannot convincingly deny that it is attempting to establish itself as just such another regime' (1998: 261). With House's emphasis that '...my own truth is inevitably a "local", subjective truth' (2003: 17) one wonders who is listening and how much they could possibly understand if the 'truth' proposed was so local. Furthermore, it is surprising that his dismissal of critiques of postmodernism is so dismissive (2003: 253) and seems to ignore Habermas and the tradition of Critical Theory entirely. Indeed, Borradori (2003), in her work *Philosophy In a Time of Terror. Dialogues With Jürgen Habermas and Jacques Derrida*, brings these two philosophical giants together within one book and draws out some of the similarities they share whilst also reminding us that postmodernism is not homogenous and that Derrida, for all the convolutions of his thought, does not simply dismiss all aspirations for universalism. For my part the postmodernists, with their work on intersubjectivity, difference and otherness, have brought great benefits to our understanding of the problems generated by a positivistic and instrumental dominant culture. The problem, of course, is that much of it is dogged by a pervasive and disempowering relativism.

5. 'The Hobbesian state of nature, in which each isolated bourgeois subject is alienated from all others, and each is as wolf to the other although real wolves live in packs – *that's* the truly *artificial* construction' (Habermas 1994: 111).

6. In the context of gender relationships, Kegan makes a similar plea to be cautious about claims to absolute contextuality. Whilst sensitivity to context, culture, tradition and gender and so on, is important, it can leave the unwary counsellor paralysed by fears of being ethnocentric, gendered and so on: 'Our differences do not radically separate us, because there *is* a single context we all share and from which both sides of the tension spring – namely, meaning-constitutive evolutionary activity, the motion of life itself. I believe East *can* talk to West and West to East, that man can talk to woman and woman to man – if neither makes its particular pole-preference ultimate; if neither forces the other to be known in its language; if each recognizes that its language is only relative to the ultimate language both share' (1981: 209).

7. The therapeutic encounter exemplifies this model of communication. That is, in the therapeutic alliance, therapist and client are in a mutually influencing communicative relationship. The mutuality at the beginning of counselling is, however, uneven as the counsellor (ideally) represents the possibility of a communicator who will only use illocutionary force (language open to rational validity claims), whereas the client has internalized the perlocutionary effects of ideological or distorted communication based on domination and closed to the possibility of rational verification. (Hence the moral doubts raised by the use of rhetorical tricks in some forms of family therapy.) From the view of a counselling case as a whole the purpose, in communicative terms, for the client is to eventually be on the same footing as the counsellor as an equal partner in a mutually constituting communicative event. At this point counselling has achieved its therapeutic purpose.

8. Castoriadis (1991: 77–8) seems to seriously misunderstand Habermas when he accuses him of portraying communicative towards reaching an understanding as a replacement for action. In fact, Habermas is quite clear that it is both an action in itself (illocutionary) and also a prelude to social action.

9. 'This thesis regarding the primacy of the communicative mode constitutes the major theoretical insight sustaining the entire edifice Habermas has built. In a very specific sense it is intended to provide a solution to the "rationality problematic".... If one can show that communicative forms are by nature prior to instrumental or strategic forms, then the earlier interpretation of modes of rationality as represented by Weber and others can be dismissed as false. Equally, one can show how this discursive form of rationality came to take the place of earlier, non-discursive, mythic forms of rationality. Further, one can demonstrate the essentially re-generative power of reason without recourse to historical argument. In other words, the thesis regarding the primacy of communicative over strategic forms functions as a hypothesis of reconstructive science. *The argument is not that communicative forms ought to be primary, the argument is that they are primary. Reason does not need to be regenerated, it is by nature regenerative in the sense that reason as communicative reason is embedded in language*' (Rasmussen 1990: 28).

10. Perhaps this term should really be socio-psychopathology. There is a danger, as House (2003) indicates, that therapy can all too easily create the psychological problems it is meant to address by its practices and language. I will continue to use the term 'psychopathology' but, as will be seen in later chapters, it is on the understanding that much psychological 'pathology' is in fact socially induced – it is not an attempt to pathologize the individual as such, indeed I am arguing quite the contrary. At the moment I feel it is more important to develop our understanding of the social causes of psychopathology rather than simply deconstruct the terminology.

11. 'The unconditionedness of truth and freedom is a necessary presupposition of our practices, but beyond the constituents of "our" form of life they lack any ontological guarantee. Similarly, the "right" ethical self-understanding is neither revealed nor "given" in some other way. It can only be won in a common endeavour. From this perspective, what makes our being-ourselves possible appears more as a transsubjective power than an absolute one' (Habermas 2003a: 10).

12. Confusion on this difference gets expressed in some of the debates on the issue of whether adult feelings and memories of childhood abuse correspond to 'actual' experiences of such abuse. The practice of always accepting the victims' account as 'true' confuses the difference between accepting the victims' claims as an authentic representation of an experience and understanding that claims to the truth of an event in the world must be open to debate or discourse. Victims' narratives may well be an authentic account of their own interpreted experience, which also make normative claims about the horror of abuse; we also know that such narratives often represent a truth about the 'facts', but this is not always the case. However, in therapeutic terms, it may make sense to promote self-esteem by supporting the victim's narrative without testing its truth content – such a challenge may inhibit the process of psychological development. Though, ultimately, I would argue that the truth could become a relevant psychological issue, just as, in a legal context, it would be a primary issue. Similarly, in the final analysis, the definition of 'abuse' cannot be monopolized by private interpretations.

13. '... we are also concerned today with the analysis of power constellations that suppress an intention intrinsic to the rationality of purposive action and linguistic

understanding – the claim to reason announced in the teleological and intersubjective structures of social reproduction themselves – and that allow it to take effect only in a distorted manner. Again and again this claim is silenced; and yet in fantasies and deeds it develops a stubbornly transcending power, because it is renewed with each act of unconstrained understanding, with each moment of living together in solidarity, of successful individuation, and of saving emancipation' (Habermas 1982: 221).

14. Working from within a therapeutic context, Maranhao comes to a similar conclusion: 'If neither knowledge, nor power, nor rhetoric can be built as absolute grounds on which to decide right from wrong, and if virtue is in the souls of all men and not only a few, how is it that some are right and commendable and others not? The answer to this question is that rightness does not reside among a group of men to the exclusion of others, but on the procedure of argumentation and counter-argumentation guided by consensus' (1986: 180).

15. Watt also catches the essence of the idea quite well when he notes about the presuppositions of the ideal speech situation that '...commitment to them is rationally inescapable, because they must, logically, be assumed if one is to engage in a mode of thought essential to any rational human life. The claim is not exactly that the principles are *true*, but that their adoption is not a result of mere social convention or free personal decision: that a mistake is involved in repudiating them while continuing to use the form of thought and discourse in question' (1975: 40). Wittgenstein also observes: 'All testing, all confirmation and disconfirmation of a hypothesis takes place already within a system. And this system is not a more or less arbitrary and doubtful point of departure for all our arguments: no, it belongs to the essence of what we call an argument. The system is not so much the point of departure, as the element in which arguments have their life' (1969: 105).

16. During the course of an argument a proponent asserts the universal validity of the principle of universalization. She is then contradicted by the radical sceptic who argues that attempts to ground this principle are strictly meaningless. If everything is fallible or relative then universalizations make no sense. However, at this point, the sceptic will have involved himself in a *performative contradiction* if '...the proponents can show that in making his argument, he has to make assumptions that are inevitable in *any* argumentation game aimed at critical examination and that the propositional content of those assumptions contradicts the principle of fallibilism' (Habermas 1995b: 80–1). This is, of course, the case because in placing his objection the radical sceptic has necessarily assumed the validity of his own argument and that it must be universally true. In taking part in the process of reasoning the radical sceptic has already accepted as valid a minimum number of unavoidable rules of criticism, which is, of course, incompatible with his scepticism and fallibilism.

The sceptic's response to this move would be to 'argue' that he does not necessarily have to engage in communicative action. He could just as easily choose to avoid communicative action and orient himself exclusively to strategic action thereby avoiding any normative obligation ensuing from the principle of universalization inherent in communicative action. Such behaviour is that of the first-person dictator or systematic free-rider. Whilst acknowledging that the systematic free-rider, in strictly logical terms, is not irrational, in terms of communicative reason he is definitely irrational. By refusing to argue, the free-rider cannot deny that he moves in a shared culture and that he was socialized in a network of communicative action and reproduces himself there. As Habermas says: '...the sceptic may reject morality, but he cannot reject the ethical substance of the life circumstances in which he spends his waking hours, not unless he is willing to take refuge in suicide or serious mental illness' (1995b: 100).

17. Bourdieu reminds us of the dangers involved in this proposition of universalism, yet, he too subscribes to the notion of differentiating between a true and false universalism. 'If it is true that one form of universalism is no more than a nationalism which invokes the universal (human rights and so on) in order to impose itself, then it becomes less easy to write off all fundamentalist reaction against it as reactionary. Scientific rationalism – the rationalism of the mathematical models which inspire the policy of the IMF or the World Bank, that of the law firms, great juridical multinationals which impose the traditions of American law on the whole planet, that of rational-action theories and so on – is both the expression and the justification of a Western arrogance, which leads people to act as if they had the monopoly of reason and could set themselves up as world policeman, in other words as self-appointed holders of the monopoly of legitimate violence, capable of applying the force of arms in the service of universal justice ... *One is still defending reason when one fights those who mask their abuses of power under the appearances of reason or who use the weapons of reason to consolidate or justify an arbitrary empire*' (2001: 19–20) (my italics).

2   Morality, Ethics and Autonomy

1. As Taylor correctly indicates, this distinction between the right and the good is crucial: '...in Habermas's case, the boundary between question of ethics, which have to do with interpersonal justice, and those of the good life is supremely important, because it is the boundary between demands of truly universal validity and goods which will differ from culture to culture. This distinction is the only bulwark, in Habermas's eyes, against chauvinistic and ethnocentric aggression in the name of one's way of life, or tradition, or culture. It is thus crucial to maintain it' (1996: 88). However, Habermas reminds us that this priority is ultimately dependent upon the assumption (which philosophy cannot anchor) that human beings share a common understanding of what it is to be human – an assumption that genetic engineering has begun to bring into question. 'But this "priority of the just over the good" must not blind us to the fact that the abstract morality of reason proper to subjects of human rights is itself sustained by a prior *ethical self-understanding of the species*, which is shared by all *moral persons*' (2003a: 40).

2. '...all modern societies would collapse without voluntary activities for others... Eighty million Americans, roughly 45 per cent of those above the age of 18, are involved for five or more hours a week in voluntary service for charitable purposes. In monetary terms this amounts to some 150 billion dollars' (Beck 1998: 5). 'The astonishing thing is this: for more than 75 per cent of the American population, solidarity, willingness to help others and concern for the public interest have a prominence equal to such motivations as self-realization, occupational success and the expansion of personal freedom. The real surprise is that self-assertion, enjoying oneself *and* caring for others are not mutually exclusive; they are mutually inclusive and strengthen and enrich one another' (Beck 1998: 6).

3. Benhabib notes that the similarities between Gilligan and Habermas are striking. Gilligan writes of 'equality and attachment', of the need ' not to act unfairly toward others' and not 'to turn away from someone in need'. Habermas writes of 'solidarity', of the interest each has in protecting 'intersubjective relations of mutual recognition'. '...[I]n both formulations, the ideals of moral autonomy and justice are traced back to their foundations in fragile human relations and thus "reduced to size." The generalized other of the justice perspective is always also a concrete other, and we can acknowledge this concreteness of the other by recalling those human relations of dependence, care, sharing, and neutrality within which each human child is socialized' (Benhabib 1995: 192–3).

4. Rose is understandably concerned that the therapeutic culture ignores this dialectic between welfare and the community by ignoring the latter. 'But my disquiet with the contemporary injunction to autonomous selfhood, to self-mastery and self-realization, also has an ethical dimension ... There is the pervasive sense that, whatever might be gained by stressing the autonomy and rights to self-actualization of each and everyone of us, something is lost: the ways of relating to ourselves and others that were encompassed in such terms as dependency, mutuality, fraternity, self-sacrifice, commitment to others. There is a sense of the ethical paucity of the contemporary obligation to fulfil ourselves through the mundane achievements of our everyday lives, and to evaluate all aspects of our lives in terms of the extent to which they do or do not contribute to such an inexorable trajectory of self-improvement and personal happiness through career enhancement and lifestyle maximization. And there is the sense of the poverty of the therapeutic ethic that seems the inevitable counterpart of these valorizations and obligations' (Rose 1999: xxiv–xxv). Much as I agree with this critical observation, this failure is not an *essential* feature of psychotherapeutic work but a result of its present social organization, funding, and poor moral and ethical self-understanding. By not considering the idea that the proposed link between counselling and communicative rationality requires an understanding of the distinction between moral and ethics, and an acceptance that both must be integral to counselling, Rose has an unduly pessimistic outlook. Whilst the transformation of counselling and psychotherapy into voices and movements that provide and enable a radical critique of our social world will involve a lot more than this work could dream of, it is unlikely to begin until we have a much clearer understanding of the moral, ethical and social purposes of counselling.

5. 'Conventions are norms of interaction that define reciprocal behavioural expectations in such a way that their content does not need to be justified. "Mere" conventions bind, so to speak, in a groundless fashion by custom alone; we do not associate a moral claim with them. Duties, by contrast, derive their binding force from the validity of norms of interaction that claim to rest on good reasons. We feel obligated only by norms of which we believe that, if called upon to do so, we could explain why they both deserve and admit of recognition on the part of their addressees (and of those affected)' (Habermas 1995c: 41).

6. Images and texts can create very powerful moral identifications. Although Taylor is not a devotee of discourse ethics, his understanding of moral imagery is helpful. 'Moral sources empower. To come closer to them, to have a clearer view of them, to come to grasp what they involve, is for those who recognize them to be moved to love or respect them, and through this love/respect to be better enabled to live up to them. And articulation can bring them closer. That is why words can empower; why words can at times have tremendous moral force' (1996: 96). Hillman, in

much of his work, particularly *The Myth of Analysis* (1972), also emphasizes the vital connection between image, character and social action. The sympathetic feelings of solidarity and fairness towards those experiencing violation and oppression created by aesthetic images enable us to 'feel' our moral consciousness more effectively than arguments ever could.

7. 'The ethical life...demands that I *gather* myself and detach myself from the dependencies of an overwhelming environment, jolting myself to the awareness of my individuality and freedom. Once I am emancipated from a self-induced objectification, I also again distance from myself as an individual. I pull myself out from the anonymous, scattered life that is breathlessly disintegrating into fragments and give my life continuity and transparency. In the social dimension, such a person can assume responsibility for his or her own actions and can enter into binding commitments with others' (Habermas 2003a: 6). 'Such an individual regrets the reproachable aspect of his past life and resolves to continue only in those ways of acting in which he can recognize himself without shame. In this way, he articulates the self-understanding of the person he would like others to know and acknowledge. Through a scrupulous evaluation and critically probing appropriation of his actually given life history, he constitutes himself as the person he both is and would like to be...' (Habermas 2003a: 7).

8. This sense of maintaining a recognisable identity over a life history has become accentuated in modernity. In our age the historical processes have accelerated and the future horizon is constantly expanding. The result of this, Habermas (1998c: 187–8) suggests, is that the present situation is increasingly interpreted in the light of pasts and futures imaginatively held in the present. A consequence of this is that present action will be assessed in the light of remembered pasts and anticipated futures. Thus, from the ethical perspective, there is now a social expectation that the individual will *self-reflectively* act in a *conscious* relation to the authenticity of his past and anticipated actions.

9. By using communicative reason as a foundation we are able to avoid the errors displayed by those of a Foucauldian outlook. Rose has some interesting insights into the world of psychotherapy and counselling which he calls the 'psy' industry. He correctly observes the overwhelming interest of psychotherapeutics in authenticity issues, but his conceptual framework prevents him from seeing therapy as a form of communicative action which enables us to connect it with the full range of validity claims rather than simply the claim of authenticity. This makes Rose overly negative about the social role of counselling and psychotherapy with the result that he overlooks the inherently radical potential of what he calls psychotherapeutics. 'Psychotherapeutics is linked at a profound level to the socio-political obligations of the modern self. The self it seeks to liberate or restore is the entity able to steer its individual path through life by means of the act of personal decision and the assumption of personal responsibility. It is the self free from all moral obligations but the obligation to construct a life of its own choosing, a life in which it realizes itself. Life is to be measured by the standards of personal fulfilment rather than community welfare or moral fidelity, given purpose through the accumulation of choices and experiences, the accretion of personal pleasures, the triumphs and tragedies of love, sex, and happiness' (Rose 1999: 258).

10. The current vogue in counselling and psychotherapy of emphasising freedom of choice for the client is problematic. On the one hand, the client should have the freedom to choose between particular therapists and competing therapeutic traditions. On

the other hand, once freely choosing to enter counselling the client does surrender some freedom. The client places herself in an unequal relationship (which is correctly protected from abuse by professional codes and standards) with someone who enables her to take a critical stance towards her own life history. In this new relationship the client is not necessarily the best judge over which interventions will enable her to reconstruct her life project on an authentic basis. Given that the client is free to leave counselling at any time, fulfilling client's wishes and choices will not always be possible if incommensurate with the various validity claims. This explains why counsellors cannot 'work with' certain clients if the client is unwilling to work with the issues of authenticity, truth, comprehensibility, morality, autonomy and health. These are values inherent to communicative processes, including therapy and counselling, and whilst the methodology of counselling may well suspend them in order to facilitate psychological change, this suspension can only be temporary awaiting the client's emergence as an equal partner in the therapeutic dialogue which itself acts as a prelude to the client's re-entry into society as a competent ethical and moral actor. If not placed within this context then the 'freedom of choice' ideology reflects not only the *laissez-faire* indifference of the commodified culture from which it emerges, but also represents a failure of nerve generated by an unreflective flirtation with postmodernism.

11. Indeed, it is interesting to see how Giddens' development of this thesis leads to conclusions remarkably similar to those of Habermas concerning the need for pure relationships and confluent love to be based on the validity claims associated with authenticity. 'Both accountability and authority – where it exists – in pure relationships are deeply bound up with trust. Trust without accountability is likely to become one-sided, that is, to slide into dependence; accountability without trust is impossible because it would mean the continual scrutiny of the motives and actions of the other. Trust entails the trustworthiness of the other – according "credit" that does not require continual auditing, but which can be made open to inspection periodically if necessary. Being regarded as trustworthy by a partner is a recognition of personal integrity, but in an egalitarian setting such integrity means also revealing reasons for actions if called upon to do so – and in fact having good reasons for any actions which affect the life of the other' (Giddens 1992: 191). Giddens also correctly criticizes counselling for succumbing to the hegemony of feelings and becoming overly concerned with their 'expression': 'Seen as a life-political issue, the problem of the emotions is not one of retrieving passion, but of developing ethical guidelines for the appraisal or justification of conviction. The therapist says, "Get in touch with your feelings." Yet in this regard therapy connives with modernity. The precept which lies beyond is "Evaluate your feelings", and such a demand cannot be a matter of psychological rapport alone. Emotions are not judgements, but dispositional behaviour stimulated by emotional responses; to evaluate feelings is to ask for the criteria in terms of which such judgements are made' (1992: 201–2).

12. Ingram (1997) questions the usefulness of Habermas's idea of health as an equilibrium between the validity claims. 'On Habermas's understanding of the matter, criticism of reification involves a clinical judgement of *health*, or of the right mixture of cognitive, practical and aesthetic competences requisites for cultivating happy – well-integrated and evenly developed – moral identities. Unfortunately, he nowhere shows that health is a rationally defensible value on a par with truth, justice and sincerity, all of which find a secure niche in communicative action'

(Ingram 1997: 278–9). I believe that this ignores the fact that communicative rationality is premised on the notion of achieving an agreed understanding. In order to attain such understanding, both parties have to be available to the experience of mutual personal transformation during the communicative process. This effect is only possible if *all* the validity claims are present (although they may have different emphases) – without this the genuineness of the process would be undermined.

13. 'So if the decision to act morally is the decision to act with the ultimate purpose of conforming my action to universal law, then this amounts to the determination to act according to my true nature as a rational being. And acting according to the demands of what I truly am, of my reason, is freedom' (Taylor 1996: 363).

14. Castoriadis arrives at a similar conception of autonomy. 'Autonomy comes from *autos-nomos*: (to give to) oneself one's laws. After what has been said about heteronomy it is hardly necessary to add: to make one's own laws, knowing that one is doing so. This is a new *eidos* within the overall history of being: the type of being that reflectively gives to itself the laws of its being.

    Thus conceived, autonomy bears little relation to Kant's "autonomy" for many reasons, of which it will suffice to mention one. Autonomy does not consist in acting according to a law discovered in an immutable Reason and given once and for all. It is the unlimited self-questioning about a law and its foundations as well as the capacity, in light of this interrogation, *to make, to do* and *to institute* (therefore also, *to say*). Autonomy is the reflective activity of a reason creating itself in an endless movement, both as individual and social reason' (1991: 164).

    'Freedom and truth cannot be objects of investment if they have not already emerged as social imaginary significations. Individuals aiming at autonomy cannot appear unless the social-historical field has already altered itself in such a way that it opens a space of interrogation without bounds (without an instituted or revealed truth, for instance). For someone to be able to find in him/herself the psychical resources and, in his environment the actual possibility, to stand up and say: "Our laws are unjust, our gods are false," a self-alteration of the social institution is required, and this can only be the work of the instituting imaginary...But the concrete embodiment of the institution are those very same individuals who walk, talk, and act. It is therefore essentially with the same stroke that a new type of society and a new type of individual, each presupposing the other, must emerge, and to emerge, in Greece from the eighth century B.C. on work and in Western Europe from the twelfth to thirteenth centuries onwards' (1991: 166–7).

15. 'In Kant, autonomy was conceived as freedom under self-given laws, which involves an element of coercive subordination of subjective nature. In discourse ethics the idea of autonomy is intersubjective. It takes into account that the free actualization of the personality of one individual depends on the actualization of freedom for all' (Habermas 1995b: 207).

3   The Development of Moral Character

1. Kegan holds a similar view: 'The construction of "individuality" is thus really "interindividuality"; neither any one person nor the group as an unindividuated whole, it is a category of interpenetration' (1981: 68).

2. 'It is precisely Habermas's recognition of the fundamentally inter-subjective nature
   of subjectivity, coupled with his normative ideal of non-coercive discourse, that
   makes his work attractive, and I would argue that his position remains attractive
   even if we accept Benjamin's critique...' (Meehan 1995: 240). 'The concept of
   intersubjectivity has its origins in the social theory of Jürgen Habermas, who used
   the expression "the intersubjectivity of mutual understanding" to designate an
   individual capacity and a social domain. I have taken the concept as a theoretical
   standpoint from which to criticize the exclusively intrapsychic conception of the
   individual in psychoanalysis' (Benjamin 1988: 19–20).
3. Hillman also recognized this fundamental dependence on the recognition of others:
   'As we cannot go it alone, so we cannot know it alone. Our consciousness cannot
   be divided from the other. An other is implied, not only because the soul cannot
   exist without its "other" side, but also because consciousness itself has an erotic,
   Dionysian component that points to participation' (1972: 295–6).
4. Strategic action takes no account of the subjectivity of others except in so far as it
   furthers my interests. '...an identity that always remains mine, namely, my self-
   understanding as an autonomously acting and individuated being, can stabilize itself
   only if I find recognition as a person, and as this person. Under the conditions of
   strategic action, the self of self-determination and of self-realization slips out of
   inter-subjective relations. The strategic actor no longer draws from an intersubjectively
   shared lifeworld; having himself become worldless, as it were, he stands over and
   against the objective world and makes decisions solely according to standards of
   subjective preference. He does not rely therein upon recognition by others. Autonomy
   is then transformed into freedom of choice, and the individuation of the socialized
   subject is transformed into the isolation of a liberated subject who possesses himself'
   (Habermas 1998c: 192).
5. Foucault and postmodernists, by concentrating on how subjectivity can be distorted
   by a narrow concept of rationality, do not have the conceptual tools to conceive
   of a dialectical theory of subjectivity. 'Foucault...lack[s] a mechanism for social
   integration such as language, with its interlacing of the performative attitudes of
   speakers and hearers, which could explain the individuating effects of socialization...
   Foucault compensates for this bottleneck in his basic concepts by purifying the concept of individuation of all connotations of self-determination and self-realization,
   and reducing it to an *inner world* produced by external stimuli and fitted out with
   arbitrarily manipulable, representative contents' (Habermas 1987: 287–8). 'Between
   the declared normative foundations and the concealed ones there is a disparity that
   can be explained by the *undialectical* rejection of subjectivity. Not only the devastating
   consequences of an objectifying relation-to-self are condemned along with this
   principle of modernity, but also the *other* connotations once associated with subjectivity
   as an unredeemed promise: the prospect of a self-conscious practice, in which the
   solidary self-determination of all was to be joined with the self-realization of each.
   What is thrown out is precisely what a modernity reassuring itself once meant by the
   concepts of self-consciousness, self-determination, and self-realization' (Habermas
   1987: 337–8).
6. Marcuse recognized the wider dangers to society and the environment that ensue
   from the dialectics of control as far back as 1955. 'The ego must become free, but if
   the world has the "character of negativity", then the ego's freedom depends on
   being "recognized", "acknowledged" as master – and such recognition can only be
   tendered by another ego, another self-conscious subject. Objects are not alive; the

overcoming of their resistance cannot satisfy or "test" the power of the ego: "Self-consciousness can attain its satisfaction only in another self-consciousness." The aggressive attitude toward the object-world, the domination of nature, thus ultimately aims at the domination of man by man. It is aggressiveness toward the other subjects: satisfaction of the ego is conditioned upon its "negative relation" to another ego' (1972: 88–9).

7. 'These two orientations I take to be expressive of what I consider the two greatest yearnings in human experience. We see the expression of these longings every-where, in ourselves and in those we know, in small children and in mature adults, in cultures East and West, modern and traditional. Of the multitude of hopes and yearnings we experience, these two seem to subsume the others. One of these might be called the yearning to be included, to be a part of, close to, joined with, to be held, admitted, accompanied. The other might be called the yearning to be independent or autonomous, to experience one's distinctness, the self-chosenness of one's directions, one's individual integrity' (Kegan 1981: 107).

8. This sense of invariance in the developmental process is also found in Jungian psychology. 'The "common factor" in the individuation process is the emergence of certain definite archetypes...the shadow, the animal, the wise old man, the anima, the animus, the mother, the child, besides an indefinite number of archetypes representative of situations. But also, notwithstanding the fact that the individuation process "takes the greatest imaginable variety of forms in different individuals", it has itself an archetypal character, as Jung has abundantly shown. The hero has a thousand faces...yet, despite the diversity of the adventures which befall him, his way is invariably a way of intense suffering and courageous struggle, of departure from the agreeable and the familiar, of confrontation with terror and the unknown, of radical transformation of his personality, before the treasure or the goal can be obtained... It is never a matter of the riddance of suffering, of the elimination of guilt or of the death-wish, of the reinforcement of the familiar ego-attitudes or conditioning to contented acceptance of the prevailing cultural pattern or values. On the contrary, it means an intensification of suffering, struggle and conflict, and a learning *how* to suffer, an experiencing of guilt and of personal and even cosmic disintegration. So far from eliminating death, it knows of no life except through death – through confrontation with the death-dealing powers of the psyche and the actual accomplishment of successive "deaths of the ego". Without willing renunciation of familiar forms of conscious life, the life of the whole, of what Jung calls the Self, is not realized' (White 1960: 178–9).

9. 'The horizon of the psyche these days is shrunk to the personal, and the new psychology of humanism fosters the little self-important man at the great sea's edge, turning to himself to ask how he feels today, filling in his questionnaire, counting his personality inventory. He has abandoned intellect and interpreted his imagination in order to become one with his "gut experiences" and "emotional problems"; his soul has become equated with these. His fantasy of redemption has shrunk to "ways of coping"; his stubborn pathology, that *via regia* to the soul's depths, is cast forth in janovian screams like swine before Perls, dissolved in a closed Gestalt of group closeness, or dropped in an abyss of regression during the clamber up to maslovian peaks. Feeling is all. Discover your feelings: trust your feelings. The human heart is the way to the soul and what psychology is all about' (Hillman 1989: 139). 'To feel something thoroughly does not mean to be it thoroughly. It is a mistake, a big bad mistake, to take feelings utterly literally. Psychotherapy has got itself caught in the

worship of feelings. If we took ideas literally, we would say a person was paranoid, but we take feelings as if they were the truth of who and what we are' (Hillman 1989: 156–7).

10. By falsely identifying reason with just one of its aspects (instrumentality) postmodernism is in danger of falling into its own form of 'essential otherness'. 'The critique of the Western emphasis on logos inspired by Nietzsche proceeds in a destructive manner. It demonstrates that the embodied, speaking and acting subject is not master in its own house; it draws from this the conclusion that the subject positing itself in knowledge is in fact dependent upon something prior, anonymous, and transsubjective – be it the dispensation of Being, the accident of structure-formation, or the generative power of some discourse formation . . . Once the defences of a subject-centred reason are raised, the logos, which for so long had held together an interiority protected by power, hollow within and aggressive without, will collapse into itself. It has to be delivered over to its other, whatever that may be' (Habermas 1987: 310–11).

11. Campbell (1996: 152) usefully reminds us that in recent times the term 'character' has been reduced in significance to being a mere synonym for 'personality'. This reduction ignores the fact that the term 'character' has a specifically moral dimension. This moral dimension is illustrated by the fact that 'character references' supplied to employers usually emphasize such qualities as conscientiousness, trustworthiness, honesty, diligence, punctuality and the like. These traits are taken to be indications of a person's moral standing – in other words, their 'character'. 'Thus', Campbell continues, '"character" in this sense refers to those aspects of an individual's conduct which (a) are regarded as falling under the individual's willed control, and (b) are judged, by the standards of the day, to be morally significant. Hence the nature of an individual's character will consist of the summation of all those qualities judged to be capable of being controlled by will . . . "Personality", by contrast, is a concept which, since it refers to all the behavioural and mental characteristics of a person, obscures the important distinction between that which is willed and that which cannot be willed. Consequently personality is a term which refers to all forms of behaviour, including action; whilst character is the term which refers specifically to a system of action' (153).

12. Castoriadis reminds us that this notion of the development of moral character which is here framed within a therapeutic context bears a close resemblance to the Greek conception of *paideia* whereby the moral development of the individual was inextricably linked to their political education as a citizen. And, moreover, this process was not simply 'academic' but involved the whole person. 'Only the education (*paideia*) of the citizens as citizens can give valuable, substantive content to the "public space". This *paideia* is not primarily a matter of books and academic credits. First and foremost, it involves becoming conscious that the *polis* is also oneself and that its fate also depends upon one's mind, behaviour, and the decisions; in other words, it is participation in political life' (1991: 113). 'It also becomes apparent – this is, in fact, a tautology – that autonomy is, *ipso facto, self-limitation*. Any limitation of democracy can only be, *de facto* as well as *de jure*, self-limitation . . . The least contingent of all lies in the *paideia* of citizens, in the formation (always a *social* process) of individuals who have internalized both the necessity of laws and the possibility of putting the laws into question, of individuals capable of interrogation, reflectiveness, and deliberation, of individuals loving freedom and accepting responsibility' (1991: 173–4).

13. Rowan has the courage to claim that this kind of self is achievable. 'When I first got in touch with humanistic psychology, in the early 1970s, we were very cautious about of the word "self-actualized". We thought that self-actualization was a more or less endless and unachievable aim, and that it was therefore better to talk about self-actualising people rather than self-actualized people. But now, nearly 30 years later, it all looks different, mainly because of the careful work of Ken Wilber. We now know that the self we wanted to actualize was actually quite clear and achievable...' (2000: 78).

4   Communicative Action and Counselling

1. 'In the clinical practice we find an ever-growing number of therapists presenting themselves as eclectics, combining bits and pieces of Freudian interpretation, the analyst of transference, ego therapy, the strategic and systemic interventions, etc. Nevertheless, the theory inventors in each subfield remain undaunted by such pragmatic ecumenicity' (Maranhao 1986: 232).

2. This framework has the potential to understand and underpin many of the changes in psychological and psychotherapeutic theory over the last 20 years or so. 'The theory of communicative action provides a framework within which the structural model of ego, id, and superego can be recast. Instead of an instinct theory that represents the relation of ego to inner nature in terms of a philosophy of consciousness – on the model of relations between subject and object – we have a theory of socialization that connects Freud with Mead, gives structures of intersubjectivity their due, and replaces hypotheses about instinctual vicissitudes with assumptions about identity formation. This approach can (i) appropriate more recent developments in psychoanalytic research, particularly the theory of object relations and ego psychology, (ii) take up the theory of defence mechanisms in such a way that the interconnections between intra-psychic communication barriers and communication disturbances at the interpersonal level become comprehensible, and (iii) use the assumptions about mechanisms of conscious and unconscious mastery to establish a connection between orthogenesis and pathogenesis' (Habermas 1998a: 388–9).

3. '...[P]sychoanalysis is neither a natural science nor a purely hermeneutical science; it rather incorporates a peculiar methodological model which constitutes the very heart of a branch of humanistic social science which I would call *critical-emancipatory* social science. The point of the model is, in my opinion, the *dialectical mediation* of *communicative understanding* – especially human self-understanding – by the *quasi-naturalistic objectifying and explaining* of human behaviour and human history. It is true that the analyst has to objectify the behaviour and the life story of the analysand as a quasi-determined section of nature, and he is, so to speak, entitled to this suspending of inter-subjective communication by the fact that the patient is not able to communicate about his illness because he is undergoing a partial splitting-off or estrangement of his true motives by having, himself, objectified these contents of a virtual communication by repressing them into the reified pseudo-language of neurotic symptoms' (Apel 1972: 25). Although Apel draws particularly from the psychoanalytic tradition and uses terms like 'patient', 'illness' and 'neurosis' which now are felt less appropriate, his observation is nevertheless useful.

4. 'All that has changed is that it [psychotherapy – MB] has increasingly tended to become an ally of dominant cultural assumptions rather than one of culture's most trenchant critics. In so doing, it has puffed itself up in its pomposity and uncritical sense of its own self-importance. As a result, it seems to me that psychotherapy has encased itself within a set of restrictive interventions that doom its enterprise to a stagnant mediocrity which cannot be surpassed so long as it insists upon keeping the world out of the consulting room. Worse than this, however, in adapting this isolationist perspective, psychotherapy, however inadvertently, has blunted its socially critical edge to such a degree that, currently, its major achievements are those that celebrate its growing acceptance of, and by, the status quo. In this sense, then, the once revolutionary possibilities of psychotherapy have given way to nothing more or less than the celebration of a self-serving mediocrity' (Spinnelli 2001: 18–19).

5. 'In view of the increasing awareness of the mutuality of the therapeutic relationship and the appreciation of several thinkers . . . that therapy has a moral aim it is surprising that the myth that the practitioner is morally neutral in his actual day-to-day work remains so persistent: the moral beliefs that pervade what the therapist does and says (or avoids doing and saying) are relatively unexplored' (Lomas 1999: 48–9).

6. 'It is here that the techniques of psychotherapeutics come into accordance with new political rationales for the government of conduct. They are intrinsically bound to this injunction to selfhood and the space of choices that it operates within. They are themselves predominantly distributed to individuals through free choice in a market of expertise, rather than imposed by legal or religious obligation. They are characteristically sought when individuals feel unable to bear the obligations of selfhood, or when they are anguished by them. And the rationale of psychotherapies – and this applies equally to contemporary psychiatry – is to restore to individuals the capacity to function as autonomous beings in the contractual society of the self. Selves unable to operate the imperative of choice are to be restored through therapy to the status of a choosing individual. Selves who find choice meaningless and their identity constantly fading and the inner and outer fragmentation are to be restored, through therapy, to unity and personal purpose. Selves dissatisfied with who they are can engage in therapeutic projects to refurbish and reshape themselves in the directions they desire. The psychotherapics provide technologies of individuality for the production and regulation of the individual who is "free to choose"' (Rose 1999: 231–2).

7. Jameson provides a useful reminder that the flirtation with consumerism enables us to protect ourselves from the guilt that would otherwise be generated if we were to bring to mind the conditions surrounding many of the producers of the commodities we purchase. '. . . you don't want to have to think about Third World women every time you pull yourself to your word processor, or all the other lower-class people with their lower-class lives when you decide to use or consume your other luxury products . . .' (1992: 315).

8. Hochschild (1983) illustrates, by using airline staff as an example, how the ever-cheerful and compliant self that has to be presented to customers in a consumer society can end up feeling distanced and false in relation to the worker's own sense of self. Similarly Langman, drawing on the work of Goffman, shows how our very gestures and body-language can become colonized by the intrusion of the demands of a consumer society into our very sense of self. 'This, then, fosters those expressive features of behaviour to elicit the various intrinsic and extrinsic social, psychological

and emotional rewards . . . that accrue from interaction, love, power, supplication, admiration, etc. Goffman provides a microscopic analysis of the many nuances of self-presentation, face-work and ritual, how people feign involvement and concern or distance themselves from their roles, collude with teams to define situations, give the other deference and confidence in their presentations, and convince audiences that one's own performance is genuine, etc.' (Langman 1991: 180–1). '. . . Goffman is describing the forms of alienated interaction and selfhood *generated and required* by a commodified social order. Read differently, the expressive features of interaction can be seen as the productions of commodified spectacles at the interpersonal level. This is the essential feature of modern life. As a commodity social interaction is appropriated by the market. But what that means is that in an amusement society, self-presentations as dramaturgy are the simulacra of social life and the ultimate reality' (Langman 1991: 181). Rose continues this theme with concerns about the fact that the modern self has to construct itself to be familiar with the exercise of choice – but choice within a consumerist context. 'However constrained by external or internal factors, the modern self is institutionally required to construct a life through the exercise of choice from among alternatives. Every aspect of life, like every commodity, is imbued with a self-referential meaning; every choice we make is an emblem of our identity, a mark of our individuality, each is a message to ourselves and others as to the sort of person we are, each casts a glow back, illuminating the self of he or she who consumes' (1999: 231).

9. 'Of course you should not berate, preach and exploit clients to adopt your religious, political or psychotherapeutic beliefs. Of course, you do impose your values even when you try not to. And to the extent that you are unaware of this, it is probably most dangerous . . . You could pretend to be class-deaf or colour blind. You could deny or unduly emphasize the difference in experience, you don't comment on it. When the client asks your position on homosexuality or mothers who give artificially assisted birth past their menopause, you can speak or you can explore what these issues mean for the patient. You are complicit whatever you do in supporting or suppressing values or value-verification in yourself and your client. You may think that you're truly neutral but to the extent that they are healthy, your client knows you're not' (Clarkson 2000: 55). Clarkson also reminds us of the classic participant–observer problem involved in all forms of investigation. 'It seems that experimenter expectation apparently influences the speed at which rats learn mazes; we know that children perform better academically if their teachers (falsely) believe them to be more intelligent; we know the measurements of atoms are influenced by the person of the physicist – do we really think that in the close and intimate space of the therapeutic consulting room we can keep a value-hygienic environment which no one has been able to successfully and repeatedly accomplish anywhere else in the universe?' (2000: 53).

10. '. . . [I]f the schools of therapy ever overcome their current fragmentation, then they will have to face the underlying problem of their cultural definition; that is, they will have to undertake in earnest the project of cultural reform intrinsic to a discourse which makes moral judgments about the ways in which people should leave their lives' (Maranhao 1986: 232).

11. 'When therapists are called upon to discuss the ethical imperatives of their practice they do not talk about divorce or permanence of the family, about legitimacy and illegitimacy, about piety and impiety, about commitment and reward, about the adequacy of behaviour to the prevalent social mores, or about justice and injustice.

They talk about whether they should disclose to the patient all they know about him or not, and how far they could go in the deployment of rhetorical manoeuvres. The morally acceptable standing for a psychoanalyst is the well-poised functioning of the psyche as defined by the metapsychology, and for the family therapist, the free-flowing communicative matrix that does not inconvenience any members in that circle, to the point that he or she thinks something must be done to alter the system. However, above and beyond all this Cartesian imagination, therapists do influence people's lives in moral terms, deriving the moral judgements from common sense and ideology' (Maranhao 1986: 131).

12. This interesting theme is developed by Bellah *et al.* (1988).
13. Richard Wilson, a very senior civil servant in the Labour Government in the UK in 2000 notes: 'The voluntary sector has from time to time – often perhaps – had to play the role of the conscience of government. Consciences are not always popular or convenient, and the voluntary sector has not always been popular with governments. The tireless work of voluntary and community groups has often in the past highlighted needs in society which governments would have found it more convenient to ignore. Whether they have been right or wrong is beside the point. What matters is that the potential for challenging the government of the day is a crucial part of the role of the voluntary sector in a healthy society, one which should never be lost in the very proper research for areas where cooperation is possible and desirable' (2000: 6). '. . . [P]artnership must be based on mutual respect and understanding, and with the keeping of a certain distance on both sides. I would not want the voluntary sector to get so close that it lost its capacity to warn, disagree or challenge where it thought it right to do so. The tension which I have described is one which I think government should value and not try to dispel completely' (2000: 7).

5 Issues in Psychotherapy and Counselling

1. See also Bugental: 'Long-term therapy of some depth inevitably involves times of warm communion and times of great stress – for both participants. Living through these together has a true bonding effect which is not always recognized by those who teach or practice more objective modes. Nevertheless, therapist and patient often have what can only be called a love relationship, which is by no means simply a product of transference and countertransference' (1992: 258).
2. Both Neumann (1956) and Hillman (1972) have developed the necessary connection between eros and psyche and their mythological offspring most elegantly.
3. I disagree with House's over-cautious doubts about 'the role of transference' (2003: 157). Whilst I agree with his concerns with that kind of transference which concentrates on the negative aspects of the client and assumes an over-determined causality, the validity of the transference as an expression of the living relationship between client and counsellor should not be overlooked.
4. Bauman describes how the cult of fitness may not be what it seems. ' "Fitness" is a never-to-be-reached horizon looming forever in the future, a spur to unstoppable efforts, none of which can be seen as fully satisfactory, let alone the ultimate. Pursuit of fitness, it's little triumphs notwithstanding, is shot through with incurable anxiety and is an inexhaustible source of self-reproach and self-indignation' (1999: 23).

'…[I]n the game called fitness, the player is simultaneously the fiddle and the fiddler. It is the bodily pleasurable, exciting or thrilling sensations which a fit person seeks – but the sensations-collector *is that body* and, at the same time, that body's owner, guardian, *trainer and director*. The two roles are inherently incompatible. The first requires total immersion and self-abandonment, the second calls for a distance and sober judgment. Reconciliation of the two demands is a tall order – if attainable at all, which is doubtful. [All these troubles – MB] generate a great deal of anxiety; what is more, however, that anxiety – the specifically *postmodern* affliction – is unlikely ever to be cured and stopped' (1999: 24).

5. 'Therapeutic endeavours, nonetheless take place against the background of the sequestration of experience and the internally referential systems of modernity. It is not surprising that many – not all – therapies are oriented primarily towards control. They interpret the reflexive project of the self in terms of self-determination alone, therefore confirming, and even accentuating, the separation of the lifespan from extrinsic moral considerations' (Giddens 1991: 180).

6. 'Yet pain cannot be taken for granted, nor can we let it govern our work. Simply to reduce pain is not therapy. Pain is a natural signal that something has gone wrong with the human system and needs attention. Simply quieting pain is as unwise as pasting cardboard over a persistently flashing red light on the car's instrument panel' (Bugental 1992: 203).

7. Rowan makes a similar distinction. 'Adjustment Therapy involves horizontal translation – we move from one position to a better one at the same level' (2000: 76). 'Liberation Therapy may involve vertical transformation, where our whole idea of who we are and what we are about may change quite radically' (2000: 76). He has similar concerns about the use of brief interventions. 'All forms of therapy go into the primary level, but they explain it differently. Some only aim at improving performance at the social level, and do not recognize the realising level at all. If this is a temporary measure, aimed at strengthening the social ego until it can cope with the realising level's emergence, it may be justifiable, but otherwise it can actually hinder a person's self-development' (1992: 50). 'But of course – and we know this very well in the case of therapy – each breakthrough needs a period of time so that it can be worked through. This process of working through a sharp change in our self-concept is something that cannot be rushed – it has to be given its due time. This means that the spiritual path is a long and slow one – it involves our whole being, and not just part of ourselves' (1992: 144–5).

8. 'The tendency for insurance companies to insist that cognitive-behavioural methods are the only acceptable psychological interventions has, unhappily, now passed over to Britain, the psychotherapist who works independently is currently little affected by this. The danger of being chorused into conformity of some kind stems from the health service and the process of registration' (Lomas 1999: 137).

9. 'While there is recognition by the Government of the importance of counselling interventions in Healthcare settings, this has come into direct conflict with the need for Evidence Based Medicine found in the use of RCTs. The evidence for counselling when evaluated in a clinical setting, using RCTs is equivocal. However, as we have seen from this report, there has been a profound confusion in the research field over the difference between efficacy and effectiveness. The equivocal results, so often quoted when asserting that counselling is not effective, are produced from research that is in the large part flawed. This research has used RCTs to measure effectiveness, with all the associated problems described in this report. It has largely evaluated the

practice of mental health practitioners who have used psychological interventions as part of the work, but rarely evaluated practitioners who have completed an accreditable training in those methods. It also tends to have a narrow focus' (Hemmings 2000: 29).

10. 'Moreover, the ground rules of what psychotherapy was to become were set by Freud's own private practice. This set a patriarchal precedent in a number of ways, which included (a) an interpretive discourse about the fee, and (b) a preoccupation with personal and territorial boundaries in a bourgeois domestic setting. Private practice was more of a pragmatic necessity than a model therapeutic setting. But once therapists opt to earn their living via private practice, it makes more sense to turn this into a therapeutic virtue than dwell too long on the parallels with prostitution or the charges of exclusivity and elitism it invites' (Pilgrim 1997: 53).

11. 'We forget too easily that counselling, in so far as it is linked in its origins with the radical aspects of psychoanalysis and humanistic psychology/psychotherapy, is at odds with an uncritical acquiescence in the brutalities and stupidities of capitalism. Arguing over how much (more) we should be paid is to banish more radical questions about the social and economic origins of human distress. Unpaid counselling and co-counselling are more closely associated with grassroots 'socialism', and professional salaried or high-fee-attracting counselling with capitalism. Maybe it's OK if you accept that counselling is part of an inevitable global capitalism, and the professionalization of counselling is inevitable and necessary. But surely most of us suspect that our attraction to counselling is due to its recognition of human needs and our wish to belong to the "humanisers", not the exploiters and stress-inducers. Ambivalence about fee levels may well reflect this tension' (Feltham 2003: 18).

'Shouldn't we remember that counselling is not an end in itself but part of an intuitive response to human suffering an aspiration. It is not disloyal to fellow counsellors to put counselling in its place as a tentative, fallible bid for a "more human" world rather than try to elevate it into a position of professional competitiveness' (Feltham 2003: 18).

6 Abstract Systems and the Colonization of Self

1. 'Due to the unqualified and unstoppable spread of free trade rules, and above all the free movement of capital and finances, the "economy" is progressively exempt from political control; indeed, the prime meaning conveyed by the term "economy" is "the area of the non-political". Whatever has been left of politics is expected to be dealt with, as in the good old days, by the state – but whatever is concerned with the economic life the state is not allowed to touch: any attempt in this direction would be met with prompt and furious punitive action from the world markets. The economic impotence of the state would once more be blatantly displayed to the horror of its current governing team. According to the calculations of Rene Passat, purely speculative inter-currency financial transactions reach a total volume of $1,300 billion a day – 50 times greater than the volume of commercial exchanges and almost equal to the total of $1,500 billion to which all the reserves of all the "national banks" of the world amount. "No state", Passat concludes, "can therefore resist for more than a few days the speculative pressures of the 'markets'" ' (Bauman 2000: 66–7) See also Bourdieu (2001: 42–3).

2. See Hardt and Negri (2001).
3. 'The phenomenon of sexual abuse underscores the importance of real events in the lives of people with mental health problems. There is a danger of compounding the distress of people who have been victims of circumstance by focusing on their role and responsibility (a general custom and practice in most forms of psychotherapy). This is an example of the social context of distress being evaded by focusing only on the agency of victims. For example, sexual victimization is a function *inter alia* of the power discrepancy which exists between adults (particularly men) and children. To frame it broadly as psychopathology when talking of "diagnosing" sexual abuse and when offering "therapy" to abusers as well as victims, is really to miss the point about the everyday vulnerabilities of children in society' (Pilgrim 1997: xi). Or as Bourdieu puts it: 'The return to the individual is also what makes it possible to "blame the victim", who is entirely responsible for his or her own misfortune, and to preach the gospel of self-help, all of this being justified by the endlessly repeated need to reduce the costs for companies' (2001: 7).
4. 'This question is posed as British politics drifts around a managerial centrism. There are no great political movements or inspirational causes. Voter apathy is widespread. Our political leaders are well-intentioned, but they are at a loss as to how to revive a belief in politics and public purpose . . . the public realm is in eclipse. It is almost as though citizenship has gone into abeyance' (Hutton 2002: 2). 'What strikes me is the silence of the politicians. They are terribly short of ideals that can mobilize people. This is probably because the professionalization of politics and the conditions required of those who want to make a career in the parties increasingly exclude inspired personalities' (Bourdieu 2001: 5).
5. Berman shows how this process can be acted out on a dramatic scale. The American response to the terrorist attack on New York and Washington in 2001 has parallels with the 'end of ideology' that was espoused by the Roman Empire: 'The response of the empire is to regard the attackers as the ultimate Other . . . In the main, the Romans had no understanding of noncivilization: of different values, nomadic ways of life.

    'Similarly, America views Islamic terrorism as completely irrational; there is no understanding of the political context of this activity, a context of American military attack on, or crippling economic sanctions against, a host of Arab nations – with the unilateral support for Israel constituting the central, running sore. Instead, the enemy is characterized as "jealous of our way of life", "hateful of freedom", and so on.

    'Along with this is the belief that the *pax Romana/Americana* is the only 'reasonable' way to live. In the American case, we have a military and economic empire that views the world as one big happy market, and believes that everybody needs to come on board. We – that is, global corporate consumerism – are the future, "progress". If the "barbarians" fail to share this vision, they are "medieval"; if they resist, "evil"' (Berman 2001: 2).
6. I am cognizant of the fact that in the late twentieth century the pattern of employment was moving away from what Bauman calls 'solid' modernity with lifelong employment in highly routinized factory or administrative systems (Fordism), to more flexible patterns of short-term contracts, part-time work and home-based employment patterns of a more 'liquid' modernity. Nevertheless, this should not be overemphasized. Bureaucratic and highly routinized work still dominate the work experience of most people. 'Today we stand at a historical divide on the issue of routine. The new language of flexibility implies that routine is dying in the dynamic sectors of the economy.

However, most labour remains inscribed within the circle of Fordism. Simple statistics are hard to come by, but a good estimate of the modern jobs described in Table 1 is that at least two-thirds are repetitive in ways which Adam Smith would recognize as akin to those in his pin factory. The computer use at work portrayed in Table 7 similarly involves, for the most part, quite routine tasks like data entry' (Sennett 1998: 44). The jobs outlined in Table 1 include: manufacturing, finance, insurance, personnel, computer, and data processing and government agencies. Those outlined in Table 7 include: bookkeeping, word processing, communications, financial analysis, databases, publishing, sales and marketing. Sennett goes on to argue that the new dawn of flexibility is in many senses a false one. 'To take the curse off the phrase "capitalist system" there developed in the past many circumlocutions, such as the "free enterprise" or "private enterprise" system. Flexibility is used today as another way to lift the curse of oppression from capitalism. In attacking rigid bureaucracy and emphasising risk, it is claimed, flexibility gives people more freedom to shape their lives. In fact, the new order substitutes new controls rather than simply abolishing the rules of the past – but these new controls are also hard to understand. The new capitalism is an often illegible regime of power' (Sennett 1998: 9–10).

7. Bauman, drawing on the work of Sennett, illustrates how, in some ways, flexible work patterns can increase a sense of insecurity. 'They know that they are disposable, and so they see little point in developing attachment or commitment to their jobs or entering lasting associations with their workmates. To avoid imminent frustrations, and they tend to be wary of any loyalty to the workplace or inscribing their own life purposes into its projected future. This is a natural reaction to the "flexibility" of the labour market, which when translated into the individual life experience means that long-term security is the last thing one is likely to learn to associate with the job currently performed' (Bauman 2001: 152). Also see Bourdieu (2001).

8. Bellah *et al.* come to a similar conclusion in their survey conducted in the 1980s. 'It was not that they were unwilling to make compromises or sacrifices for their spouses, but they were troubled by the ideal of self-denial the term "sacrifice" implied. If you really wanted to do something good for the person you loved, they said, it would not be a sacrifice. Since the only measure of the good is what is good for the self, something that is really a burden to the self cannot be part of love. Rather, if one is in touch with one's true feelings, one will do something for one's beloved only if one really wants to, and then, by definition, it cannot be a sacrifice. Without a wider set of cultural traditions, then, it was hard for people to find a way to say why genuine attachment to others might require risk of hurt, loss or sacrifice. They clung to an optimistic view in which love might require hard work, but could never create real costs to the self. They tended instead to believe that therapeutic work on the self could turn what some might regard as sacrifices into freely chosen benefits. What proved most emotive to our respondents, and what remains most poignantly difficult in the wider American culture, are ways of understanding the world that could overcome the sharp distinction between self and other' (1988: 109–10). 'The contradictions we have described make us wonder if psychological sophistication has not been bought at the price of moral impoverishment. The ideal therapeutic relationship seems to be one in which everything is completely conscious and all parties know how they feel and what they want. Any intrusion of "oughts" or "shoulds" into the relationship is rejected as an intrusion of external and coercive authoritarianism. The only party that is acceptable is the purely contractual agreement of the parties: whatever they agree is right' (1988: 139).

9. 'An adequate critical theory of routinization must therefore always bear in mind its darker side, for it is only from this prospective that we can examine our complicity in a way of being which constantly threatens to capture us as inert, mindless and non-reflexive selves. From this respect, routinization, particularly when considered in its recursive form, is the essential expression of "it-ness" in everyday life. Our inability to sustain an attitude of thoughtfulness when faced by the complications of life contrasts with our facility for technical thinking, where reality is inanimate and devoid of such complication. This threatens to be the cause of our downfall. We live in a world whose technical capacities increasingly threaten to overwhelm our ability to understand the question of their social value and consequences' (Hoggett 1992: 87).

10. Back in 1955, Marcuse provided us with a concept of unnecessary repression. 'Within the total structure of the repressed personality, surplus repression is that portion which is the result of specific societal conditions sustained in the specific interest of domination. The extent of this surplus-repression provides the standard of measurement: the smaller it is, the less repressive is the stage of civilization' (1972: 73–4).

11. 'To live in poverty means losing control over one's life in a number of ways which are linked to inner vulnerability and outer distress. These include the increased probability of: struggling to provide basic necessities of food and shelter; having a poor diet; resorting to comforts, such as drugs and alcohol, which impact negatively on health and well-being; aimlessness and powerlessness; cumulative debt; living in an environment which is dirty, traffic-congested and has a high crime rate; and being homeless or living in a cramped, poorly furnished home. All of these lead to a lower sense of self-worth and constricted agency in people living in poor communities. Also the direct deleterious impact on physical health of poverty has an additional indirect impact on mental health. For example, depression is common in people with chronic or multiple disabling conditions. Indeed, when the features of an impoverished context are listed like this, an apposite question could be "Why aren't *more* poor people sad, frightened or mad?"' (Pilgrim 1997: 45–6). Or, as Habermas puts it: 'We in the West do live in peaceful and well-to-do societies, and yet they contain a *structural* violence that, to a certain degree, we have gotten used to, that is, unconscionable social inequality, degrading discrimination, pauperization, and marginalization' (2003b: 35). Bourdieu (2001: 5, 39–40) recommends that economic policy makers should include in their costings all the negative social costs (delinquency, crime, alcoholism and so on) of their policy implementations.

12. 'His normative point of reference . . . is not a complete absorption of the system into the lifeworld; in his view, every complex modern society will have to give over certain economic and administrative functions to functionally specified and media-steered domains of action' (McCarthy 1991: 127).

13. Pahl believes that certain levels of friendship exhibit the properties of a pure relationship. 'These friends of virtue or friends of hope are ultimately friends of communication. Our friends who stimulate hope and invite change are concerned with the understanding and knowing. Each grows and flourishes because of the other in a spirit of mutual awareness . . . This deep communicating friend is psychologically and socially anarchistic and is qualitatively different from the friends of utility and pleasure which are more readily analysed by social scientists. Pure friendship, the friendship of character, is an alternative to society' (2000: 79).

14. Evans offers a critique of Giddens's theory of pure relationships. Empirically, she argues, not all, or even most, relationships are pure relationships. They are still conditioned by contingencies (mainly financial) such that '...what Giddens assumes as the basis of confluent relations is a degree of prosperity and economic independence' (2003: 51). I find Evans's argument a little disingenuous. First, Giddens's assumption is not unrealistic – there has been an increase in prosperity and economic independence and the number of people who might access pure relationships seems to me to extend significantly beyond Evans's rather limited estimation: '...assumptions about the arrival of more "democratic" patterns of heterosexual sexuality may correspond to the behaviour of urban professionals, but this group of largely childless individuals does not live in the same way as others in the population' (2003: 126). Secondly, Giddens is clearly trying to articulate and analyze new themes and trends which embody something different and symptomatic of the age rather than provide a full analysis of wealth distribution in late modernity. Evans also ignores the fact that Giddens clearly comments on the inadequacy of confluent love in that its contractual nature symbolizes its failure to internalize external moral values in order to create solidarity.

15. Bellah *et al.* successfully capture the notion of the moral impoverishment of relationships in late modernity. 'The contradictions we have described make us wonder if psychological sophistication has not been bought at the price of moral impoverishment. The ideal therapeutic relationship seems to be one in which everything is completely conscious and all parties know how they feel and what they want. Any intrusion of "oughts" or "shoulds" into the relationship is rejected as an intrusion of external and coercive authoritarianism. The only party that is acceptable is the purely contractual agreement of the parties: whatever they agree is right...It is the moral content of relationships that allows marriages, families and communities to persist with some certainty that there are agreed-upon standards of right and wrong that one can count on and that are *not subject to incessant negotiation*' (1988: 139–40).

16. 'Postmodernity is the point at which modern untying (dis-embedding, dis-encumbering) of tied (embedded, situated) identities reaches its completion: *it is now all too easy to choose identity, but no longer possible to hold it*' (Bauman 1996: 50).

17. Castoriadis similarly links individual autonomy to social autonomy. 'There is a goal which a few of us have set for ourselves: the autonomy of human beings, which is inconceivable except as the autonomy of *society* as well as the autonomy of *individuals* – the two being inseparably linked...(without the autonomy of others there is no collective autonomy – and outside such a collectivity I cannot be *effectively* autonomous)' (1991: 76).

18. Castoriadis (1991: 76) also draws out the connection between psychoanalysis and politics in bringing about autonomy.

7 Critique, Resistance and Transformation

1. Castoriadis (1991) emphasizes the extent to which the achievement of democracy requires radical personal transformation. 'It will come into existence only as a radical transformation in what people consider as important and unimportant, as valid and invalid – to put it briefly, as a profound psychical and anthropological transformation,

with the parallel creation of new forms of living and new significations in all domains'
(1991: 204).

2. Giddens, with some reservation, concurs with the anticipatory nature of the concept
of the ideal speech situation. 'Much the same could be said of Habermas's attempts
to develop a framework for emancipatory politics in terms of a theory of communication. The ideal-speech situation, held to be immanent in all language use, provides
an energising vision of emancipation. The more social circumstances approximate
to an ideal-speech situation, the more a social order based on the autonomous
action of free and equal individuals will emerge. Individuals will be free to make
informed choices about their activities; so will humanity on a collective level. Yet little
or no indication is given about what those choices will actually be' (Giddens 1991:
213–14).

3. Beck is bold enough to fill this out just a little. 'I'd propose to go one crucial step
further. The antithesis to the work society is a strengthening of the political society
of individuals, of active civil society here and now, of a civil democracy in Europe
that is at once local and transnational. This society of active citizens, which is no longer
fixed within the container of the nation state and whose activities are organized
both locally and across frontiers, can find and develop answers to the challenges of
the second modernity – namely, individualization, globalization, falling employment
and ecological crisis. For in this way communal democracy and identity are given
new life in projects such as ecological initiatives ... work with homeless people, local
theatres, cultural centres and meeting-places for discussion' (2000: 5–6). 'The
antithesis to the work society is not free time or a leisure society, which remained
negatively imprisoned in the value imperialism of work. It is the new self-active, self-
aware, political civil society – the "do it yourself culture" – which is developing,
testing and implementing a dense new concept of the political' (2000: 7–8).

4. 'I wish that every patient who completes therapy with me would become a societal
change agent, and I wish he would become such not from rejection of society and
standing outside of it but from incorporation of society and participation in bringing
about changes' (Bugental 1992: 257).

5. Beck (2000) and Sennett (1998) are both concerned that the practice of portfolio
working (a flexible package of part-time wage labour, family work and maybe some
voluntary work) leaves the overarching capitalist structure intact with the result that
part-time work and temporary jobs are poorly paid, lacking in sickness and other
benefits, and insecure. They therefore increase the ability of capital to move inter-
nationally to wherever labour is cheaper and more easily exploited.

6. 'It is the job of the psychotherapists to demonstrate the existence of a world constituted
by different rules and to encourage patients to be aware of available moral traditions
that opposed the moral frame by which they presently shape their lives. Through
the interactions between therapist and patient, patients will have the opportunity to
confront the implicit moral understandings enacted through their behaviours,
expectations, and emotional responses. They will be able to stretch out a picture of
the larger cultural terrain in which they were originally thrown. Finally, they will
have the opportunity to experience how their commitment to the old terrain and its
moral code has affected them, and to contrast that with the possibilities that are
presented by the moral frame offered by the therapist and those alternative frames
available but unacknowledged in their present life. By interacting with the therapist
over time, patients may notice that new emotional and behaviour possibilities have
emerged, and they may develop their own version of the morality offered by the

therapist, combine it in various ways with other traditions in their lives, and choose to commit to a different, slightly shifted moral way of being' (Cushman 1995: 295–6).

7. Kegan aligns himself with this critical conception of therapy. 'The constructive-developmental framework ought to be the most important psychological ally of any systematically excluded group because its notion of "pathology" is the least related to adjustment or coping and the most capable of detecting an unwholesome situation even when everyone seems to be functioning in ways that do not make us uncomfortable' (1981: 212).

'But when a whole subpopulation of a culture – whether or not each member needs or seeks psychiatric attention – seems to have developmentally delayed constituents, one has a way to begin analysing the possibility that the cultural arrangements are themselves deleterious. One has a way that is not defined by the dominant culture and its possibly self-serving notion of health and illness. A good psychological theory protects the least favoured members of a culture from having their status preserved by a psychology which is unwittingly the agent of the privileged' (1981: 213).

8. One price that is paid is the high level of theoretical compromise made in order to facilitate throughput and maintain a service that is essentially socially adaptive. Butler and Joyce (1998) describe Relate's approach to the unconscious. 'All of these theoretical models have one unifying feature when they are used in Relate. They all explore the fact that there is more going on in the couple's problem than the individuals involved are aware of. These extra elements might come from clients' past experiences, from deeper conflicts within clients personally or from unacknowledged struggles in the immediate groups of which clients are members. This is Relate's sense of the unconscious – the factors which affect the clients' behaviour and situation, but of which they are not conscious. *However, these factors are not so deeply buried or repressed that they cannot quickly and comparatively easily be made conscious and brought under the client's control.* Therefore, the theoretical models Relate uses in its understanding stage are accessible to the everyday experiences of counsellors and clients alike. The *concepts of transference and counter-transference have been broadened and simplified* so that they too can apply to all the theoretical models' [my italics] (1998: 18–19). 'It will be seen, then, that in the Relate Approach we expect our clients to be able to recall, albeit with gentle encouragement, the significant details that may illuminate the history of the problems. We do not ever pressurize clients to access these details, or create situations in which deeply repressed feelings may be likely to emerge. If the clients cannot offer us, after adequate respectful inquiry into a particular area, insights which are mutually useful we move to another line of inquiry and possibly to another model of unconscious interaction altogether. Therefore, *although we are dealing with matters hidden from conscious knowledge, in this counselling we are not trying to access deeply repressed material*' [my italics] (1998: 54).

9. 'If the time of systemic revolutions has passed, it is because there are no buildings where the control desks of the system are lodged and which could be stormed and captured by the revolutionaries; and also because it is excruciatingly difficult, nay impossible, to imagine what the victors, once inside the buildings (if they found them first), can do to turn the tables and put paid to the misery that prompted them to rebel. One should be hardly taken aback or puzzled by the evident shortage of would-be revolutionaries: of the kind of people who articulate the desire to change their individual plights as a project of changing the order of society'

(Bauman 2000: 5). On the other hand Bourdieu encourages political and charitable activists to '...work together against the destructive effects of insecurity (by helping them [the victims – MB] to live, to "hold on", to save their dignity, to resist destructuring, loss of self-respect, alienation)...' (2001: 86).

10. 'The counter-model to the work society is based not upon leisure but upon political freedom; it is a multi-activity society in which housework, family work, club work and voluntary work are prized alongside paid work and returned to the centre of public and academic attention...Those who wish to escape the spell of the work society must enter political society (in a new historical meaning of the term) – a society that gives material form to the idea of civil rights and transnational civil society, and thereby democratizes and gives new life to democracy. This is the horizon and the programmatic essence of the idea of civil labour...' (Beck 2000: 125). Or, even more radically, counsellors and psychotherapists might consider that 'In the age of the self-determined life, the social perception of what constitutes "wealth" and "poverty" is changing so radically that, under certain conditions, less income and status, if they go hand-in-hand with the opportunity for more self-development and more ability to arrange things personally, may be perceived as an advance and not a setback...A freedom society, not a leisure society could perhaps allow us to say good-bye to growth-oriented labour society' (Beck 1998: 8).

11. Berman (2001) provides an alternative vision. Given the unlikely prospects of radical social transformation in the *pax Americana*, one of the few viable and authentic personal options for people seeking the kind of psychological transformation that counselling and psychotherapy offer is a kind of new monasticism. Just as the Celtic monks fostered and maintained the relics of Roman and Greek culture in their libraries and scriptoria during the 'Dark Ages', people seeking and achieving authenticity and autonomy carry, in their personhood, the germ of a democratic selfhood that remains underdeveloped in the consumer capitalism of late modernity.

Bibliography

Adorno, T. (1973) *The Jargon of Authenticity*, London: Routledge.
—— (1974) *Minima Moralia*, London: New Left Books.
—— (1976) 'Introduction' in David Frisby (ed.) *The Positivist Dispute in German Sociology*, London: Heinemann.
Almond, B. (2001) 'Professional Ethics and Diverse Values', *Counselling and Psychotherapy Journal*, October 2001, Vol. 12, No. 8, pp. 4–9.
Althusser, L. (1971) *Lenin and Philosophy*, London: New Left Books.
Apel, K. (1967) 'Analytical Philosophy of Language and the Geisteswissenschaften', *Foundations of Language*, Vol. 14, Dordrecht: D. Reidel.
—— (1972) 'Communication and the Foundation of the Humanities', *Acta Sociologica*, Vol. 15, pp. 7–26.
Arendt, H. (1998) *The Human Condition*, London: University of Chicago Press.
Armstrong, J. and McLeod, J. (2003) 'Research into the Organization, Training and Effectiveness of Counsellors Who Work for Free', *Counselling and Psychotherapy Research*, Vol. 3, No. 4, pp. 255–9.
Ashley, D. (1991) 'Playing With Pieces' in Wexler, P. (ed.) *Critical Theory Now*, London: Farmer Press.
Ayer, A. (1974) *The Problem of Knowledge*, London: Penguin.
Barden, N. (2001) 'Editorial', *Counselling and Psychotherapy Journal*, October 2001, Vol. 12, No. 8, p. 3.
Barthes, R. (1972) *Mythologies*, London: Jonathan Cape.
Baudrillard, J. (1999) *The Consumer Society*, London: Sage.
Bauman, Z. (1996) 'Morality in the Age of Contingency' in Heelas, P. *et al.* (eds) *Detraditionalization*, Oxford: Blackwell.
—— (1999) 'On Postmodern Uses of Sex', in Featherstone, M. (ed.) *Love and Eroticism*, Sage: London.
—— (2000) *Globalization: The Human Consequences*, Cambridge: Polity Press.
—— (2001) *Liquid Modernities*, Cambridge: Polity Press.
Beck, U. (1998) *Democracy Without Enemies*, Cambridge: Polity Press.
—— (2000) *The Brave New World of Work*, Cambridge: Polity Press.
Beck, U. and Beck-Gernsheim, E. (1996) 'Individualization and "Precarious Freedoms": Perspectives and Controversies of a Subject-Oriented Sociology' in Heelas, P. *et al.* (eds) *Detraditionalization*, Oxford: Blackwell.
Bellah, R., Madsen, R., Sullivan, W., Swidler, A. and Tipton, S. (1988) *Habits of the Heart*, London: Hutchinson.
—— (1992) *The Good Society*, New York: Vintage Books.
Benhabib, S. (1994) *Situating the Self*, Cambridge: Polity Press.
—— (1995) 'The Debate over Women and Moral Theory Revisited' in Meehan, J. (ed.) *Feminists Read Habermas*, London: Routledge.
Benjamin, J. (1988) *The Bonds of Love*, London: Virago.
Bennett, M. (1995) 'Why Don't Men Come to Counselling', *Counselling*, Vol. 6, No. 4, pp. 310–13.
Bennett, T. (1998) *Culture: A Reformer's Science*, London: Allen & Unwin.

238

Bibliography

—— (2000) *Pasts Beyond Memory: The Evolutionary Museum, Liberal Government and the Politics of Prehistory*, Open University, Inaugural Lecture.

Berman, M. (2001) 'Waiting for the Barbarians', *The Guardian Saturday Review*, 6 October.

Bernstein, J. (1987) 'The Politics of Fulfilment and Transfiguration', *Radical Philosophy* 47, Autumn, pp. 21–9.

—— (1989) 'Self-Knowledge as Praxis' in Nash, C. (ed.) *Narrative in Culture*, London: Routledge.

Bernstein, R. (ed.) (1985) *Habermas and Modernity*, Cambridge: Polity Press.

Bertilsson, M. (1986) 'Love's Labour Lost? The Sociology of Love', *Theory, Culture and Society*, Vol. 3, No. 2, pp. 9–35.

Bettleheim, B. (1991) *The Uses of Enchantment*, London: Penguin.

Bleicher, J. (1980) *Contemporary Hermeneutics*, London: Routledge.

Bloom, A. (1988) *The Closing of the American Mind*, New York: Simon and Schuster.

Bohart, A. and Tallman, K. (1996) 'The Active Client: Therapy as Self-Help', *Journal of Humanistic Psychology*, Vol. 36, No. 3, pp. 7–30.

Bohman, J. (1997) 'Two Versions of the Linguistic Turn' in D'Entreves, M. and Benhabib, S. (eds) *Habermas and the Unfinished Project of Modernity*, Cambridge (Mass.): MIT Press.

Bond, T. (1997) *Standards and Ethics for Counselling in Action*, London: Sage.

Bondi, L., Fewell, J. and Kirkwood, C. (2003) 'Working for Free: A Fundamental Value of Counselling', *Counselling and Psychotherapy Research*, Vol. 3, No. 4, pp. 291–9.

Borradori, G. (2003) *Philosophy in a Time of Terror: Dialogues With Jürgen Habermas and Jacques Derrida*, London: The University of Chicago Press.

Bourdieu, P. (2001) *Acts of Resistance: Against the New Myths of our Time*, London: Polity Press.

Bowlby, J. (1991) *Attachment*, London: Penguin.

Brazier, D. (1995) *Zen Therapy*, London: Constable.

Bugental, J. (1992) *The Art of the Psychotherapist*, London: W.W. Norton & Company.

Bultmann, D. (1935) *Jesus and the Word*, London: Nicholson and Watson.

—— (1955) *The Problem of Hermeneutics*, London: SCM Press.

—— (1957) *History and Eschatology*, Edinburgh: University Press.

Burgess, A. and Ruxton, S. (1996) *Men and Their Children*, London: Institute for Public Policy Research.

Butler, C. and Joyce, V. (1998) *Counselling Couples in Relationships*, Chichester: Wiley.

Campbell, C. (1996) 'Detraditionalization, Character and the Limits to Agency' in Heelas, P. *et al.* (eds) *Detraditionalization*, Oxford: Blackwell.

Campbell, J. (1973) *Myths to Live By*, New York: Bantam.

—— (1976) *Occidental Mythology: The Mask of God*, London: Penguin.

—— (1988) *The Hero With a Thousand Faces*, London: Paladin.

—— (1991) *Creative Mythology: The Masks of God*, London: Arkana.

Camus, A. (1969) *The Rebel*, London: Penguin.

Card, C. (ed.) (1991) *Feminist Ethics*, Lawrence (Kansas): University of Kansas Press.

Carroll, J. (1999) *Ego and Soul: The Modern West in Search of Meaning*, London: HarperCollins.

Cashdan, S. (1988) *Object Relations Therapy*, London: Norton.

Castoriadis, C. (1991) *Philosophy, Politics, Autonomy*, Oxford: Oxford University Press.

Clarkson, P. (2000) *Ethics: Working with Ethical and Moral Dilemmas in Psychotherapy*, London: Whurr.

Cockett, M. and Tripp, J. (1994) 'Children Living in Re-Ordered Families', *Joseph Rowntree Foundation*, No. 45.

Connell, R. (1995) *Masculinities*, Cambridge: Polity Press.

Coole, D. (1997) 'Habermas and the Question of Alterity' in D'Entreves, M. and Benhabib, S. (eds) *Habermas and the Unfinished Project of Modernity*, Cambridge (Mass.): MIT Press.

Coren, A. (1996) 'Brief Therapy: Base Metal or Pure Gold' in *Psychodynamic Counselling*, Vol. 2, No. 1, pp. 22–38.

Corney, R. (1990) 'Counselling in General Practice: Does It Work?' *Journal of the Royal Society of Medicine*, Vol. 83, pp. 253–7.

Coulter, J. (1973) 'Language and the Conceptualization of Meaning' in *Sociology*, Vol. 7, pp. 1733–89.

Curtis Jenkins, G. (2002) 'Good Money after Bad? The Justification for the Expansion of Counselling Services in Primary Health Care' in Feltham, C. (ed.) *What's the Good of Counselling and Psychotherapy*, London: Sage.

Cushman, P. (1995) *Constructing the Self, Constructing America*, Cambridge (Mass.): Perseus Publishing.

Dallmayr, F. (1972a) 'Critical Theory Criticized: Habermas's "Knowledge and Human Interests" and Its Aftermath', *Philosophy of Social Sciences*, Vol. 2, No. 3, pp. 211–29.

—— (1972b) 'Reason and Emancipation: Notes on Habermas', *Man and World*, Vol. 5, No. 1, pp. 79–119.

Davies, R. (1983) *The Deptford Diaries*, London: Penguin.

D'Entreves, M. and Benhabib, S. (eds) (1997) *Habermas and the Unfinished Project of Modernity*, Cambridge (Mass.): MIT Press.

De-Haven-Smith, L. (1990) *Philosophical Critiques of Policy Analysis*, Florida: University of Florida Press.

Deleuze, G. and Guattari, F. (1986) *Nomadology: The War Machine*, New York: Columbia University.

Derrida, J. (2002) *On Cosmopolitanism and Forgiveness*, London: Routledge.

—— (2003a) *Writing and Difference*, London: Routledge.

—— (2003b) 'Autoimmunity: Real and Symbolic Suicides; A Dialogue with Jacques Derrida' in Borradori' in Giovanna (2003) *Philosophy in a Time of Terror: Dialogues with Jürgen Habermas and Jacques Derrida*, London: The University of Chicago Press.

Dews, P. (1986) Introduction to *Autonomy and Solidarity: Interviews with Jürgen Habermas*, London: Verso.

Dominion, J., Mansfield, P., Dormor, D. and McAllister, F. (1991) *Marital Breakdown and the Health of the Nation*, London: One Plus One.

Duncombe, J. and Marsden, D. (1995) 'Love and Intimacy: The Gender Division of Emotion and "Emotion Work" ', *Sociology*, Vol. 27, No. 2, pp. 221–41.

Dupont-Joshua, A. (1996) 'Race, Culture and the Therapeutic Relationship', *Counselling*, Vol. 7, No. 3, pp. 220–3.

Earll, L. and Kincey, J. (1982) 'Clinical Psychology in General Practice', *Journal of the Royal College of General Practitioners*, January, pp. 32–7.

Ehrenreich, B. (1983) *The Hearts of Men*, New York: Anchor-Doubleday.

Elliott, A. (2001) *Concepts of the Self*, Cambridge: Polity.

Ellis, J. (1976) 'Ideology and Subjectivity', *Working Papers in Cultural Studies*, Spring, No. 9, pp. 205–9.

Erikson, E. (1974) *Childhood and Society*, London: Penguin.

Erikson, J. (1988) *Wisdom and the Senses*, New York: Norton.

Evans, M. (2003) *Love: An Unromantic Discussion*, Cambridge: Polity.

Fahy, T. (1993) 'Should Purchasers Pay for Psychotherapy?' *British Medical Journal*, Vol. 307, pp. 576–7.

Farber, L. (2000) *The Ways of the Will*, London: Basic Books.

Featherstone, M. (ed.) (1999) *Love and Eroticism*, Sage: London.

Feltham, C. (1999) 'Facing, Understanding and Learning from Critiques of Psychotherapy and Counselling', *British Journal of Guidance and Counselling*, Vol. 27, No. 3, p. 301–11.

—— (ed.) (2002) *What's the Good of Counselling and Psychotherapy?* London: Sage.

—— (2003) 'Who Decides How much Counsellors are Worth?' *Counselling and Psychotherapy Journal*, December, Vol. 14, No. 10, p. 18.

Ferri, E., Bynner, J. and Wadsworth, M. (eds) (2003) *Changing Britain, Changing Lives*, London: University of London.

Feyerabend, P. (1970) 'Against Method: Outline of an Anarchistic Theory of Knowledge', *Minnesota Studies in the Philosophy of Science*, Vol. 4, pp. 17–130.

—— (1975a) 'How to Defend Society Against Science', *Radical Philosophy*, No. 11, Summer, pp. 3–8.

—— (1975b) ' "Science": The Myth and Its Role in Society', *Inquiry*, Vol. 18, pp. 167–81.

Fletcher, J., Fahey, T. and McWilliam, J. (1995) 'Relationship between the Provision of Counselling and the Prescribing of Antidepressents, Hypnotics and Anxiollytics in General Practice', *British Journal of General Practice*, September, pp. 467–9.

Floistad, G. (1973) 'Understanding Hermeneutics', *Inquiry*, pp. 445–65.

Foucault, M. (1967) *Madness and Civilization*, London: Tavistock.

—— (1972) *The Archaeology of Knowledge*, London: Tavistock.

—— (1980) *The History of Sexuality: Volume 1*, New York: Vintage.

—— (1988a) *Technologies of the Self*, London: Tavistock.

—— (1988b) *The Political Technology of Individuals*, London: Tavistock.

—— (1988c) *Truth, Power, Self: An Interview with M. Foucault*, London: Tavistock.

Freidson, E. (2001) *Professionalism*, Cambridge: Polity.

French, R. and Vince, R. (1999) *Group Relations, Management, and Organization*, Oxford: Oxford University Press.

Freud, S. (1915) *Repression*, Standard Edition, Vol. 14, pp. 146–58.

—— (1952) *On Dreams*, London: Hogarth Press.

—— (1962) *The Future of an Illusion*, London: Hogarth Press.

—— (1971) *Beyond the Pleasure Principle*, London: Hogarth.

—— (1973) *Civilization and Its Discontents*, London: Hogarth Press.

—— (1975) *New Introductory Lectures on Psychoanalysis*, London: Pelican.

—— (1991) 'Instincts and Their Vicissitudes', *On Metapsychology*, London: Penguin.

Frisby, D. (1974) 'The Frankfurt School: Critical Theory & Positivism', in Rex, J. (ed.) *Approaches to Sociology*, London: Routledge Kegan Paul (RKP).

—— (ed.) (1976) *The Positivist Dispute in German Sociology*, London: Heinemann.

Fromm, E. (1974) *The Art of Loving*, London: Unwin.

Fuchs, E. (1971) *The Hermeneutic Problem*, London: SCM Press.

Gadamer, H. (1970a) 'The Power of Reason', *Man and World*, Vol. 3, pp. 5–15.

Gadamer, H. (1970b) 'On the Scope of Hermeneutical Reflection', *Continuum*, Vol. 8, Spring/Summer.
—— (1975) *Truth and Method*, New York: Seabury Press.
Gardiner, C., McLeod, J., Hill, I. and Wigglesworth, A. (2003) 'A Feasibility Study of the Systematic Evaluation of Client Outcomes in a Voluntary Sector Counselling Agency', *Counselling and Psychotherapy Research*, Vol. 3, No. 4, pp. 285–90.
Giddens, A. (1974) *Positivism and Sociology*, London: Heineman.
—— (1991) *Modernity and Self-Identity: Self and Society in the Late Modern Age*, Cambridge: Polity Press.
—— (1992) *The Transformation of Intimacy*, Cambridge: Polity Press.
—— (1998) *The Third Way*, Cambridge: Polity Press.
—— (1999) *The Reith Lecture*, London: BBC Radio.
Gilbert, M. and Shmukler, D. (1996) *Brief Therapy With Couples: An Integrative Approach*, Chichester: Wiley.
Gilligan, C., Ward, V. and Taylor, J. (eds) (1988) *Mapping the Moral Domain*, Harvard: Harvard University Press.
Goleman, D. (1996) *Emotional Intelligence*, London: Bloomsbury.
Guggenbühl-Craig, A. (1995) *From the Wrong Side: A Paradoxical Approach to Psychology*, Woodstock (Conn.): Spring Publications.
—— (2001) *Marriage: Dead or Alive*, Woodstock (Conn.): Spring Publications.
Habermas, J. (1966) 'Knowledge and Interest' in Emmet, D. and MacIntyre, A. (eds) (1970) *Sociological Theory and Philosophical Analysis*, London: Macmillan.
—— (1970) 'Towards a Theory of Communicative Competence' in Dreitzel, H. (ed.) *Recent Sociology No. 2*, New York: Macmillan.
——(1971a) 'Questions and Counterquestions' in Bernstein, J. (ed.) (1985) *Habermas and Modernity*, Cambridge: Polity Press.
—— (1971b) *Toward a Rational Society*, Boston: Beacon Press.
—— (1971c) 'Why More Philosophy?' *Social Research*, Vol. 18, pp. 633–54.
—— (1972) *Knowledge and Human Interests*, London: Heinemann.
—— (1973a) *Legitimation Crisis*, Toronto: Beacon Press.
—— (1973b) 'A Postscript to Knowledge and Human Interests', *Philosophy of Social Science*, Vol. 3, pp. 157–89.
—— (1974) *Theory and Practice*, London: Heinemann.
—— (1976a) 'The Analytical Theory of Science and Dialectics' in Frisby, D. (ed.) *The Positivist Dispute in German Sociology*, London: Heinemann.
—— (1976b) 'A Positivistically Bisected Rationalism' in Frisby, D. (ed.) *The Positivist Dispute in German Sociology*, London: Heinemann.
——(1980) 'The Hermeneutic Claim to Universality' in Bleicher, J. (ed.) *Contemporary Hermeneutics*, London: Routledge.
—— (1981) 'Modernity versus Postmodernity', *New German Critique*, Winter, Part 22, pp. 3–14.
—— (1982) 'A Reply to My Critics' in Thompson, J. and Held, D. (eds) *Habermas: Critical Debates*, Cambridge (Mass): MIT press.
—— (1986) *Autonomy and Solidarity: Interviews with Jürgen Habermas* with Dews, P. (ed.), London: Verso.
—— (1987) *The Philosophical Discourse of Modernity*, Cambridge (Mass.): MIT Press.
—— (1989) 'Justice and Solidarity', *The Philosophical Forum*, XXI, 1–2, pp. 32–52.
—— (1991) 'A Reply', in Honneth, A. and Joas, H. (eds) *Communicative Action*, Cambridge (Mass.): MIT Press.

—— (1994) *The Past as Future*, Cambridge: Polity Press.
—— (1995a) *Communication and the Evolution of Society*, Cambridge: Polity Press.
—— (1995b) *Moral Consciousness and Communicative Action*, Cambridge (Mass.): MIT Press.
—— (1995c) *Justification and Application*, Cambridge: Polity Press.
—— (1997a) *Modernity: An Unfinished Project*, Cambridge (Mass.): MIT Press.
—— (1997b) *The Theory of Communicative Action: Volume I*, Cambridge: Polity Press.
—— (1998a) *The Theory of Communicative Action: Volume II*, Cambridge: Polity Press.
—— (1998b) *Between Facts and Norms*, Cambridge: Polity Press.
—— (1998c) *Postmetaphysical Thinking*, Cambridge: Polity Press.
—— (1999) *The Inclusion of the Other*, Cambridge (Mass.): MIT press.
—— (2001) 'Why Europe Needs a Constitution', *New Left Review*, Vol. 11, September–October, pp. 5–26.
—— (2003a) *The Future of Human Nature*, Cambridge: Polity Press.
—— (2003b) 'Fundamentalism and Terror: A Dialogue with Jürgen Habermas' in Borradori' in Giovanna (2003) *Philosophy in a Time of Terror: Dialogues With Jürgen Habermas and Jacques Derrida*, London: The University of Chicago Press.
Hadot, P. (1997) *Philosophy as a Way of Life*, Oxford: Blackwell.
Halmos, P. (1965) *The Faith of the Counsellors*, London: Constable.
Hardt, M. and Negri, A. (2001) *Empire*, London: Harvard University Press.
Heelas, P., Lash, S. and Morris, P. (1996) *Detraditionalization*, Oxford: Blackwell.
Held, D. (1982) 'Crisis Tendencies, Legitimation and the State' in Thompson, J. and Held, D. (eds) *Habermas: Critical Debates*, Cambridge (Mass.): MIT Press.
Hemmings, A. (2000) *A Systematic Review of Brief Psychological Therapies in Primary Health Care*, Staines: The Counselling in Primary Care Trust.
Hesse, M. (1972) 'In Defence of Objectivity', *Proceedings of the British Academy*, Vol. 58, pp. 275–92.
Hill, M. (1972) 'Jürgen Habermas: A Social Science of Mind', *Philosophy of Social Science*, September, pp. 247–59.
Hillman, J. (1972) *The Myth of Analysis*, New York: Harper and Row.
—— (1989) In Moore, T. (ed.) *The Essential James Hillman: A Blue Fire*, London: Routledge.
—— (1991) *Insearch: Psychology and Religion*, Dallas: Spring Publications.
—— (1996) 'Marriage, Intimacy, Freedom', *Spring*, Vol. 60, pp. 1–11.
—— (1997) *The Soul's Code*, London: Bantam.
—— (2000) *The Force of Character*, New York: Ballantine.
Hillman, J. and Ventura, M. (1993) *We've had a Hundred Years of Psychotherapy and the World's Getting Worse*, San Francisco: Harper.
Hochschild, A. (1982) *The Managed Heart: Commercialization of Human Feeling*, London: University of California Press.
Hoggett, P. (1992) *Partisans in an Uncertain World: The Psychoanalysis of Engagement*, London: Free Association Press.
Holmes, J. and Lindley, R. (1989) *The Values of Psychotherapy*, Oxford: Oxford University Press.
Honneth, A. and Joas, H. (eds) (1991) *Communicative Action*, Cambridge (Mass.): MIT Press.
Horkheimer, M. (1947) *The Eclipse of Reason*, New York: Oxford University Press.
—— (1972) *Critical Theory*, New York: Seabury Press.

Horkheimer, M. and Adorno, T. (1972) *The Dialectics of Enlightenment*, New York: Herder & Herder.

Horney, K. (1964) *The Neurotic Personality of Our Time*, London: Norton.

House, R. (1996a) 'General Practice Counselling: A Plea for Ideological Engagement', *Counselling*, Vol. 7, No. 1, pp. 40–44.

—— (1996b) 'The Professionalization of Counselling: A Coherent "Case Against"?' *Counselling Psychology Quarterly*, Vol. 9, No. 4, pp. 343–58.

—— (1997) 'The Dynamics of Professionalism', *Counselling*, August, pp. 200–4.

—— (2003) *Therapy Beyond Modernity: Deconstructing and Transcending Profession-Centred Therapy*, London: Karnac.

Howard, A. (1996) *Challenges to Counselling and Psychotherapy*, London: Macmillan.

—— (2001) 'Fallacies and Realities of the Self', *Counselling and Psychotherapy*, Vol. 12, No. 4, pp. 19–23.

Howe, D. (1983) *On Being a Client*, London: Sage.

Huch, K. (1970) 'Interest in Emancipation', *Continuum*, Vol. 8, pp. 27–39.

Hutton, P. (1988) *Foucault, Freud and the Technologies of the Self*, London: Tavistock.

Hutton, W. (1996) *The State We're In*, London: Vintage.

—— (2002) *The World We're In*, London: Little Brown.

Ingram, D. (1997) 'The Subject of Justice in Postmodern Discourse: Aesthetic Judgement and Political Rationality' in D'Entreves, M. and Benhabib, S. (eds) *Habermas and the Unfinished Project of Modernity*, Cambridge (Mass.): MIT Press.

Jacobi, J. (1967) *The Way of Individuation*, London: Hodder & Stoughton.

Jacoby, R. (1972) 'Negative Psychoanalysis', *Telos*, No. 14, pp. 1–22.

James, N. (1989) 'Emotional Labour: Skill and Work in the Social Regulation of Feelings', *Sociological Review*, No. 37, pp. 15–42.

Jameson, F. (1972) *The Prison House of Language*, Princeton: Princeton University Press.

—— (1992) *Postmodernism or the Cultural Logic of Late Capitalism*, London: Verso.

Jamieson, L. (1998) *Intimacy: Personal Relationships in Modern Society*, Cambridge: Polity Press.

Johnson, R. (1987) *The Psychology of Romantic Love*, London: Arkana.

Jung, C. (1973) *Modern Man in Search of a Soul*, London: Routledge.

—— (1975) *The Archetypes of the Collective Unconscious*, London: Routledge and Kegan Paul.

—— (1987) *Memories, Dreams, Reflections*, London: Flamingo.

—— (1993) *Aspects of the Masculine*, London: Ark.

Kegan, R. (1981) *The Evolving Self*, Cambridge (Mass.): Harvard University Press.

Keily, J. (1984) 'Social Change and Marital Problems: Implications for Marriage Counselling', *British Journal of Guidance and Counselling*, Vol. 12, No. 1, pp. 92–9.

Kind, P. and Sorenson, J. (1993) 'The Costs of Depression', *International Clinical Psychopharmacology*, Vol. 7, Nos 3 and 4, pp. 191–5.

King, M., Broster, G., Lloyd, M. and Horder, J. (1994) 'Controlled Trials in the Evaluation of Counselling', *British Journal of General Practice*, May, pp. 229–32.

Kohlberg, L. (1981) *Essays on Moral Development*, San Francisco: Harper & Row.

Kohut, H. (1977) *The Restoration of Self*, New York: International University Press.

Kop, S. (1985) *If You Meet the Buddha on the Road, Kill Him!* London: Sheldon Press.

Labouvie-Vief, G. (1994) *Psyche and Eros: Mind and Gender in the Life Course*, Cambridge: Cambridge University Press.

Lacan, J. (1970) 'The Insistence of the Letter in the Unconscious', in Ehrmann, J. (ed.) *Structuralism*, New York: Anchor.
—— (1977) *Ecrits*, London: Tavistock.
—— (1988) *The Four Fundamental Concepts of Psycho-Analysis*, London: Vintage.
Laing, R. (1969) *The Politics of Experience and the Bird of Paradise*, London: Penguin.
—— (1971) *Knots*, London: Pelican.
—— (1972a) *The Divided Self*, London: Pelican.
—— (1972b) *Self and Others*, London: Pelican.
Laing, R. and Esterton, A. (1972) *Society, Madness and the Family*, London: Pelican.
Langman, L. (1991) 'From Pathos to Panic: American Character Meets the Future' in Wexler, P. (ed.) *Critical Theory Now*, London: Farmer Press.
Lasch, C. (1985) *The Minimal Self*, London: Picador.
Lash, S. (1996) 'Tradition and the Limits to Difference' in Heelas, P. *et al.* (eds) *Detraditionalization*, Oxford: Blackwell.
Leiss, W. (1975) 'Ideology and Science', *Social Studies of Science*, Vol. 5, No. 2, pp. 193–201.
Lenhardt, C. (1972) 'Rise and Fall of Transcendental Anthropology', *Philosophy of Social Sciences*, September, pp. 231–46.
Lewis, J., Clark, D. and Morgan, D. (1992) *Whom God Hath Joined Together*, London: Routledge.
Lloyd, K., Jenkins, R. and Mann, A. (1996) 'Long-Term Outcomes of Patients with Neurotic Illness in General Practice', *British Medical Journal*, Vol. 313, pp. 26–8.
Lobkowicz, N. (1967) *Theory and Practice*, London: University of Notre Dames Press.
—— (1972) 'Interest and Objectivity', *Philosophy of Social Sciences*, September, pp. 193–210.
Lomas, P. (1999) *Doing Good? Psychotherapy Out of its Depth*, Oxford: Oxford University Press.
Low-Beer, F. (1995) *Questions of Judgment*, New York: Prometheus.
Luhmann, N. (1982) *Love as Passion: The Codification of Intimacy*, Stanford: Stanford University Press.
—— (1996) 'Complexity, Structural Contingencies and Value Conflicts' in Heelas, P. *et al.* (eds) *Detraditionalization*, Oxford: Blackwell.
Lukacs, G. (1971) *History and Classic Consciousness*, London: Merlin Press.
MacIntyre, A. (1958) *The Unconscious: A Conceptual Analysis*, London: Routledge Kegan Paul.
—— (1971) *Against the Self-Image of the Age: Essays on Ideology and Philosophy*, London: Duckworth.
—— (1982) *After Virtue: A Study in Moral Theory*, London: Duckworth.
MacPherson, C. (1970) *The Political Theory of Possessive Individualism: Hobbes to Locke*, Oxford: Oxford University Press.
Malcolm, J. (1988) *Psychoanalysis: The Impossible Profession*, London: Karnac.
Mander, G. (1997) 'Towards the Millenium', *Counselling*, February, pp. 32–5.
—— (1998) 'Supervising Short-Term Psychodynamic Work', *Counselling*, November, pp. 301–5.
Mann, D. (1997) *Psychotherapy: An Erotic Relationship; Transference and Counter-transference Passions*, London: Routledge.
Mann, T. (1936) *Freud and the Future*, London: Secker & Warburg.
Mannoni, O. (1971) *Freud: The Theory of the Unconscious*, London: New Left Books.

Maranhao, T. (1986) *Therapeutic Discourse and Socratic Dialogue*, Wisconsin: University of Wisconsin Press.

Marcuse, H. (1972a) *An Essay on Liberation*, London: Penguin.

—— (1972b) *Eros and Civilization*, London: Abacus.

—— (1974) *One Dimensional Man*, London: Abacus.

Martin, E. (1988) 'Counsellors in Medical Practice', *British Medical Journal*, Vol. 297, pp. 637–8.

Martin, H., Gutman, H. and Hutton, P. (eds) (1988) *Technologies of the Self: A Seminar with Michel Foucault*, London: Tavistock.

Martin, J. (1991) 'Habermas and Critical Theory' in Honneth, A. and Joas, H. (eds) *Communicative Action*, Cambridge (Mass.): MIT Press.

Martins, R. (1967) 'Toward a Solution of the Liar Paradox', *Philosophical Review*, pp. 279–311.

Maslow, A. (1968) *Toward a Psychology of Being*, New York: Van Norstrand Reinhold.

Masson, J. (1989) *Against Therapy*, London: Collins.

May, R. (1993) *Man's Search for Himself*, London: Souvenir Press.

—— (1996) *The Cry for Myth*, New York: Bantam Doubleday.

May, R. and Yalom, I. (1984) 'Existential Psychotherapies' in Corsini, R. (ed.) *Current Psychotherapies*, Itasca, Illinois: Peacock.

McCarthy, P. and Thoburn, M. (1996) *Psychosexual Therapy at Relate*, Newcastle: Relate Centre for Family Studies.

McCarthy, P. Walker, J. and Kain, J. (1998) *Telling it as it is: The Client Experience of Relate Counselling*, Newcastle Centre for Family Studies.

McCarthy, T. (1973) 'A Theory of Communicative Competence', *Philosophy of Social Science*, Vol. 3, pp. 135–56.

—— (1982) 'Rationality and Relativism', in Thompson, J. and Held, D. (eds) *Habermas: Critical Debates*, Cambridge (Mass.): MIT Press.

—— (1991) 'Complexity and Democracy: Or the Seducements of Systems Theory' in Honneth, A. and Joas, H. (eds) *Communicative Action*, Cambridge (Mass.): MIT Press.

McEwan, I. (1998a) *Black Dogs*, London: Vintage.

—— (1998b) *Enduring Love*, London: Vintage.

Mead, G. (1962) *Mind, Self and Society*, Chicago: University of Chicago Press.

Meehan, J. (ed.) (1995) *Feminists Read Habermas*, London: Routledge.

Merleau-Ponty, M. (1964) *Sense and Non-Sense*, Evanston: Northwestern University Press.

Meth, R. and Pasick, R. (1990) *Men in Therapy*, New York: Guildford Press.

Miller, T. (1993) *The Well-Tempered Self*, London: John Hopkins.

Moore, T. (1990) *Dark Eros*, Dallas: Spring Publications.

—— (1992) *Care of the Soul*, London: Piatkus.

—— (1994) *Soul Mates*, Shaftesbury: Element.

Morris, P. (1996) 'Community Beyond Tradition' in Heelas, P. *et al.* (eds) *Detraditionalization*, Oxford: Blackwell.

Mueller, C. (1973) *The Politics of Communication*, New York: Oxford University Press.

Neumann, E. (1956) *Amor and Psyche*, London: Routledge and Kegan Paul.

Nichols, C. (1972) 'Science or Reflection: Habermas on Freud', *Philosophy of Social Science*, September, pp. 261–70.

Nock, S. (2000) 'The Divorce of Marriage and Parenting', *Journal of Family Therapy*, Vol. 22, No. 3, pp. 245–63.

Norris, C. (1997) 'Deconstruction, Postmodernism And Philosophy: Habermas on Derrida' in D'Entreves, M. and Benhabib, S. (eds) *Habermas and the Unfinished Project of Modernity*, Cambridge (Mass.): MIT Press.

Nygren, A. (1953) *Agape and Eros*, Philadelphia: Westminster Press.

O'Carroll, L. (2002) 'Do We make a Difference?' *Counselling and Psychotherapy Journal*, Vol. 13, No. 6, pp. 10–12.

O'Connor, P. (1980) *A Review of Training*, Rugby: National Marriage Guidance Council.

Orbach, S. (1996) *Running on Empty*, London: The Guardian Weekend, 24 August, p. 6.

Pahl, R. (2000) *On Friendship*, Cambridge: Polity Press.

Palmer, R. (1969) *Hermeneutics: Interpretation Theory in Schleiermacher, Dilthey, Hedegger and Gadamer*, Evanston: Northwestern University Press.

Pattison, S. (1999) 'Are Professional Codes Ethical?' *Counselling*, December, pp. 374–80.

Phillips, A. (1998) *The Beast in the Nursery*, London: Faber & Faber.

Piaget, J. (1970) *Genetic Epistemology*, New York: Columbia University Press.

—— (1971) *Structuralism*, London: Routledge Kegan Paul.

Pierce, C. (1991) 'Postmodernism and other Scepticism' in Card, C. (ed.) *Feminist Ethics*, Lawrence (Kansas): University of Kansas Press.

Pilger, J. (2002) *The New Rulers of the World*, London: Verso.

Pilgrim, D. (1997) *Psychotherapy and Society*, London: Sage Publications.

Pirani, A. (1989) *The Absent Father*, London: Arkana.

Plato (1951) *The Symposium*, London: Penguin.

Radding, C. (1985) *A World Made by Men*, London: University of North Carolian Press.

Radnitsky, G. (1970) *Contemporary Schools of Metascience*, Goteborg: Acadmiforlaget.

Rasmussen, D. (1990) *Reading Habermas*, Oxford: Blackwell.

Rawls, J. (1999) *A Theory of Justice*, Oxford: Oxford University Press.

Reiff, D. (1998) 'Therapy or Democracy', *World Policy Journal*, Vol. 15, No. 2, pp. 66–76.

Reiff, P. (1966) *The Triumph of the Therapeutic*, Harmondsworth: Penguin.

Roazen, P. (1970) *Freud: Political and Social Thought*, New York: Vintage.

Rogers, C. (1993) *On Becoming a Person*, London: Constable.

Rorty, R. (1999) *Contingency, Irony and Solidarity*, Cambridge: University Press.

Rose, N. (1999) *Governing the Soul*, Free Association Books.

Ross, L. (1991) *Cupid and Psyche*, Illinois: Chiron.

Rowan, J. (1992) *Breakthroughs and Integration in Psychotherapy*, London: Whurr.

—— (2000) 'Back to Basics: Two Kinds of Therapy', *Counselling*, Vol. 12, No. 2, pp. 76–8.

—— (2001) 'Counselling and Psychotherapy: Different and the Same', *Counselling & Psychotherapy Journal*, Vol. 12, No. 7, pp. 22–5.

Samuels, A. (1989) *The Plural Psyche*, London: Routledge.

—— (1993) *The Political Psyche*, London: Routledge.

Sandford, S. (1998) 'Writing as a Man: Levinas and the Phenomenology of Eros', *Radical Philosophy*, Vol. 87, pp. 6–17.

Saxonhouse, A. (1984) 'Eros and the Female in Greek Political Thought', *Political Theory*, Vol. 12, No. 1, pp. 5–27

Schott, R. (1993) *Cognition and Eros*, Penn: Pennsylvania University Press.

Schroyer, T. (1973) *The Critique of Domination: The Origins and Development of Critical Theory*, New York: George Braziller.

Seidler, V. (1994) *Unreasonable Men: Masculinity and Social Theory*, London: Routledge.

Seligman, M. (1995) 'The Effectiveness of Psychotherapy', *American Psychologist,* Vol. 50, pp. 965–74.

Sennett, R. (1996) 'The Foreigner' in Heelas, P. *et al.* (eds) *Detraditionalization*, Oxford: Blackwell.

—— (1998) *The Corrosion of Character*, London: W.W. Norton & Company.

Shapiro, J. (1970) 'From Marcuse to Habermas', *Continuum*, Spring/Summer, pp. 65–76.

Sharpe, R. (1974) 'Ideology and Ontology', *Philosophy of Social Science*, March, pp. 55–66.

Sibbald, B., Addington-Hall, J., Brenneman, D. and Freeling, P. (1993) 'Counsellors in English and Welsh General Practices: Their Nature and Distribution', *British Medical Journal*, Vol. 306, pp. 29–33.

Silverman, D. (1975) *Reading Castenada*, London: Routledge Kegan Paul.

Simpson, B., McCarthy, P. and Walker, J. (1995) *Being There: Fathers after Divorce*, Newcastle: Relate Centre for Family Studies.

Slater, P. (1975) *The Pursuit of Loneliness*, London: Pelican.

—— (1977) *The Origins and Significance of the Frankfurt School*, London: Routledge Kegan Paul.

Smail, D. (1998) *Taking Care: An Alternative to Therapy*, London: Constable.

Spinnelli, E. (2001) *The Mirror and the Hammer*, London: Continuum.

Stein, M. (1983) *In Midlife: A Jungian Perspective*, Dallas: Spring Publications.

Stein, M. and Corbett, L. (eds) (1991) *Psyche's Stories*, Illinois: Chiron.

Stettbacher, J. (1991) *Making Sense of Suffering*, London: Dutton.

Stevens, A. (1990) *On Jung*, London: Penguin.

Storr, A. (1979) *The Art of Psychotherapy*, London: Secker & Warburg.

Street, E. and Downey, J. (1996) *Brief Therapeutic Consultations*, London: Wiley.

Taylor, C. (1996) *Sources of the Self: The Making of Modern Identity*, Cambridge: Cambridge University Press.

—— (2002) *The Ethics of Authenticity*, Cambridge (Mass.): Harvard University Press.

Taylor, G. (1985) Pride, *Shame and Guilt. Emotions of Self-Assessment*, Oxford: Clarendon.

Thompson, J. (1982) 'Universal Pragmatics' in Thompson, J. and Held, D. (eds) *Habermas: Critical Debates*, Cambridge (Mass.): MIT Press.

Thompson, J. and Held, D. (eds) (1982) *Habermas: Critical Debates*, Cambridge (Mass.): MIT Press.

Thorne, B. (1999) 'The Move Towards Brief Therapy', *Counselling*, Vol. 10, No. 1, pp. 7–11.

Totton, N. (2003a) 'Psychotherapy and Politics', *Counselling and Psychotherapy Journal*, Vol. 14, No. 2, pp. 4–6.

—— (2003b) 'The Ecological Self: Introducing Ecopsychology', *Counselling and Psychotherapy Journal*, Vol. 14, No. 9, pp. 14–18.

Toynbee, P. (2003) *Hard Work: Life in Low Pay Britain*, London: Bloomsbury Publishing.

Trigg, R. (1974) *Reason and Commitment*, London: Cambridge University Press.

Trilling, L. (1972) *Sincerity and Authority*, London: Harvard University Press.

Walker, J. (1994a) *Children of Divided Worlds*, Newcastle: Relate Centre for Family Studies.

—— (1994b) *Parenting After Divorce*, Newcastle: Relate Centre for Family Studies.

248 Bibliography

—— (1994c) *Children After Divorce*, Newcastle: Relate Centre for Family Studies.
—— (1995a) *Divorce in England & Wales: Counting the Cost*, Newcastle: Relate Centre for Family Studies.
—— (1995b) *The Cost of Communication Breakdown*, Newcastle: Relate Centre for Family Studies.
Warnock, M. (1998) *Altruism and Philanthropy*, London: NCVO, Hinton Lecture.
Wasdell, D. (1990) 'In the Shadow of Accreditation', *Self and Society*, Vol. 20, No. 1, pp. 3–14.
Watt, A. (1975) 'Transcendental Arguments and Moral Principles', *Philosophical Quarterly*, Vol. 25.
Weber, M. (1949) *The Methodology of the Social Sciences*, New York: Free Press.
—— (1958) *The Protestant Ethic and the Spirit of Capitalism*, New York: Scribner.
—— (1964) *The Theory of Social and Economic Organization*, New York: The Free Press.
Weir, A. (1995) 'Toward a Model of Self-identity: Habermas and Kristeva' in Meehan, J. (ed.) *Feminists Read Habermas*, London: Routledge.
Wellmer, A. (1971) *Critique of Instrumental Reason and Critical Social Theory*, New York: Herder and Herder.
Wexler, P. (ed.) (1991) *Critical Theory Now*, London: Farmer Press.
Wheeler, S. (1999) 'Can Counselling be a Profession?' *Counselling*, December, pp. 381–86.
White, S. (1988) *The Recent Work of Jurgen Habermas*, Cambridge: Cambridge University Press.
White, V. (1960) *Soul and Psyche*, London: Collins & Harvill.
Whitebook, J. (1985) 'Habermas and Modernity' in Bernstein, R. (ed.) *Habermas and Modernity*, Cambridge: Polity Press.
—— (1997) 'Intersubjectivity and the Monadic Core' in D'Entreves, M. and Benhabib, S. (eds) *Habermas and the Unfinished Project of Modernity*, Cambridge (Mass.): MIT Press.
Wilber, K. (1990) *Eye to Eye: The Quest for a New Paradigm*, Shaftesbury: Shambhala.
Wilkins, P. (1997) 'Congruence and Countertransference', *Counselling*, Vol. 8, No. 1, pp. 36–41.
Williams, B. (1993) *Ethics and the Limits of Philosophy*, London: Fontana.
Williams, B. and Montefiore, A. (1966) *British Analytical Philosophy*, London: Routledge, Kegan Paul.
Wilson, B. (ed.) (1970) *Rationality*, Oxford: Blackwell.
Wilson, R. (2000) *Modernising Government*, Hinton Lecture: NCVO.
Winch, P. (1958) *The Idea of a Social Science*, London: Routledge.
—— (1972) *Ethics and Action*, London: RKP.
Winter, D., Archer, R., Spearman, P., Costello, M., Quaite, A. and Metcalfe, C. (2003) 'Explorations of the Effectiveness of a Voluntary Sector Psychodynamic Counselling Service', *Counselling and Psychotherapy Research*, Vol. 3, No. 4, pp. 261–9.
Wittgenstein, L. (1953) *Philosophical Investigations*, Oxford: Blackwell.
—— (1969) *On Certainty*, Oxford: Blackwell.
—— (1974) *Tractatus Logico-Philosophicus*, London: RKP.
Wolf, J. (1975) 'Hermeneutics and the Critique of Ideology', *Sociological Review*, pp. 811–28.
Wollheim, R. (1999) *On the Emotions*, Yale: Yale University Press.
Zelvin, E. (2003) 'Differentiating Chat from Online Treatment', *Counselling and Psychotherapy Journal*, Vol. 14, No. 6, pp. 26–8.
Zizek, S. (2002) *On Belief*, London: Routledge.

Index

abstract systems, 9–10, 165,
    167–72, 174–86, 192, 199,
    201, 205, 209
actualization, *see* self
addictive, *see* self
adjustment therapy, *see* counselling (and
    psychotherapy)
advertising, *see* counselling
    (and psychotherapy)
aesthetic, 27, 28, 30,
    39, 54, 139, 175,
    181, 218, 220
alienation, 117, 171, 172,
    178, 236
Almond, Brenda, 118–19, 127
Althusser, Louis, 91
anomie, 26, 27, 135, 172
Apel, Karl-Otto, 105, 224
Aphrodite, 139
Apollo, 134
application, *see* moral
Arendt, Hannah, 59
argumentation, 4, 16–17,
    30–5, 39, 44, 50, 122,
    135, 196, 215
Aristotle, 41
art, 27, 54, 168, 201
    criticism, 26, 27
Augustine, Saint, 211
Austin, John, 18, 19
authenticity (including truthfulness),
    4, 8, 16, 20, 22, 23, 27, 33,
    37, 41, 42–3, 46, 53, 55, 57,
    60–1, 65–6, 73, 74, 75, 78,
    84–5, 87–8, 93, 96, 98, 99,
    101, 113, 115, 119, 121,
    126–7, 136, 138, 145, 149,
    150, 159, 164, 167, 171,
    175, 181–2, 187–90, 192–3,
    202, 218–19, 236
    congruence, 25, 54
    consistency, 55
    narrative, 94, 218
    sincerity, 25, 27
    transparency, 33, 55,
        59–60, 65, 90, 110,
        198, 206–8
authenticity and Hillman, 59

autonomy, 1, 4–10, 22, 35,
    37, 46, 51, 53, 63–8, 71,
    72, 75, 90, 99, 101, 107, 111,
    113–15, 127, 138, 143, 145,
    146, 149–50, 159, 181, 187,
    196–9, 200, 207–8, 217,
    219–20, 223
    democracy, 65, 197
    demotivation, 66
    independence, 5, 80
    interdependence, 5, 64, 127, 162,
        167, 189, 195–6, 200, 205, 220,
        223, 233
    libertarian, 5, 64, 221
    life project, 64–5, 90, 197
    personal choice, 7, 63, 66–7, 221
    reflexivity, 64–5, 197, 220
    will, 5, 66–7
    see also Giddens, Anthony;
        Habermas, Jürgen

Bauman, Zygmunt, 97, 162, 165,
    166, 174, 176–7, 180–1, 183, 190,
    199, 203, 205, 209, 227, 229, 230,
    231, 233, 236
Beard, George, 112
beauty, 138–9
Beck, Ulrich, 166, 203, 210,
    216, 234, 236
behavioural, 85, 106, 119, 139,
    141–2, 144, 147, 149–51, 154,
    162, 172, 205, 217, 223, 228
Bellah, Robert, 119, 156, 227,
    231, 233
Benhabib, Seyla, 33, 35–6, 97, 217
Benjamin, Jessica, 72–3, 74, 75–7,
    79–80, 82, 83, 135, 221
Bennett, Tony, 203–4
Berman, Morris, 230, 236
Bernstein, J., 168
Bodhissattva, 53
body language, *see* language
Bond, Timothy, 121–2
Borradori, Giovanna, 213
    Philosophy In a Time of Terror, 213
Bourdieu, Pierre, 178, 216, 229, 230,
    231, 232, 236
Bowlby, John, 64

branding, *see* counselling
(and psychotherapy)
Brazier, David, 113, 145
brief counselling, *see* counselling
(and psychotherapy)
British Association of Counselling and
Psychotherapy, 158–9
Buddhist, 39, 53
Bugental, James, 227, 228, 234
bureaucracies, 9, 168, 170–1, 175, 200,
230–1
business cycle, 162, 163
Butler, Chris, 235

Campbell, Colin, 223
capital, 8–9, 117, 161–3, 168, 170, 173,
185, 190, 230, 234
capitalism, 8, 164–5, 168, 191, 193, 194,
196, 209, 229, 231, 236
capitalist, 52, 94, 114, 161–3, 166, 170,
175–6, 180, 183, 196, 208, 231,
234
care, *see* moral
carnival, 176–7
Castoriadis, Cornelius, 165, 212, 214,
220, 223, 233
categorical imperative, 41, 43, 66,
67, 174
see also Habermas, Jürgen
character, 5, 41, 43, 55, 59, 70, 85–6,
95, 99, 101, 117, 155, 157, 179,
181, 192–3, 205, 218, 223, 232
see also moral
Christianity, 209, 211
citizen, 4, 8–9, 47, 51, 53, 55, 59, 157,
158, 162–7, 175, 176,
179, 185, 196–200, 202, 223, 230,
234
civic privatism, 166
civil society, 8, 126, 147, 234, 236
Clarkson, Petruska, 158, 200, 226
codes, *see* ethics
cognitive potential, 206–7
colonization, 9, 121, 157, 168–9, 171–2,
174–5, 182–4, 186,
192, 201, 210
commitment, 61, 67, 118, 180, 187,
217, 218, 226
commodification, 117, 173–4, 201
see also Giddens, Anthony
communication
distorted, 4, 20, 23, 25, 28–31,
42, 52–3, 102–6, 109, 149, 188,
213, 224

private, 103–5, 107, 111
public, 14, 102–5, 106–7, 108–9
reflexive, 25, 29
therapeutic, 31, 213
see also Habermas, Jürgen
communicative action, 16, 21–3,
29–31, 35, 52, 55, 57–8, 63,
71–2, 74, 78, 80–1, 83, 87, 92,
101–2, 105–7, 109–11, 115, 141,
147, 166, 168, 170–2, 175–6,
181, 183, 185, 194, 201, 205,
215, 218–19, 224
see also Habermas, Jürgen
communicative ethics, 35–6, 48
communicative rationality, 3–6, 11–39,
55, 62–5, 75–8, 81, 91, 97, 110,
113, 118–19, 122–4, 130, 135–6,
152, 158, 164, 166, 168, 187,
196, 198–9, 202, 204, 206, 210,
214–15, 217–18, 220
see also Habermas, Jürgen
comprehensibility, 3, 15, 16, 20, 23, 37,
62, 65, 74, 113, 114, 115, 127,
136, 145, 219, 224
conditional imperative, 40–1, 43
confidentiality, 1, 8, 121, 126, 154
confluent love, *see* Giddens, Anthony;
love
congruence, 21, 25, 54, 99, 110, 124
consistency, 25, 34, 55, 56, 87,
193, 194
consumer, 4, 8, 121, 128, 182, 208
choice, 4, 45, 50, 114–17, 161
consumerism, 7, 85, 146, 175, 180,
182, 225–6, 230, 236
Coole, Diana, 26, 106
Copernicus, 6, 91
Coren, Alex, 141, 145–6
counselling (and psychotherapy)
adjustment therapy, 228
advertising, 117, 173
branding, 117
brief, 7–8, 70, 83, 85, 128,
139–46, 149, 159, 166,
173, 205, 228
consumer, *see* consumer
contract, 4, 117, 157, 199, 200, 225
critique, 6, 57–8, 78, 107–9, 126–8,
201, 206, 217
countertransference, 7, 123, 127,
131–9, 187–8, 227
Critical Theory, 112, 172, 201, 213,
232
critique, *see* moral

culture, 2, 10, 85, 111, 114, 117, 119,
    124, 139, 142, 161, 186, 188, 196,
    201, 204–5, 217
  democracy, 198
  equality, 126
  erotic, 7, 55, 60, 132–8, 140,
    157, 202
  ethics, 1, 7–8, 116, 121, 153–4,
    157–60
  evolutionary development,
    7, 207, 209
  existential, 66
  humanistic, 66, 78, 82, 122, 150, 224,
    229
  Jungian, *see* Jung, Carl
  justice, 43, 135–6
  liberation therapy, 228
  management, 121
  medical model, 7, 50, 102,
    150–3, 205
  morals: moral development,
    see moral; moral emotions,
    see moral
  nonjudgmental, 6–7, 31, 113,
    125–6, 131–2, 137
  organizations, 1, 46, 51, 101,
    106, 117–18, 120, 125–6,
    139, 145–7, 153, 154–5,
    196, 201, 206–8
  outcomes, 8, 69, 142, 147, 150–2
  philosophical basis, 1–2, 11, 101,
    120–2, 158
  privatized, 49, 116, 146, 154–5, 200,
    205, 229
  see also counselling
    (and psychotherapy)
Curtis Jenkins, Graham, 152
Cushman, Philip, 79, 112, 141,
    172, 235

Davies, Robertson, 46
de facto, 176–7, 190, 199–200, 223
de jure, 176–7, 190, 199–200, 223
decentred self, *see* self
democracy, 8, 66, 122, 157, 165, 169,
    189, 196–8, 224, 233, 234, 236
  relationships, 61, 188, 197–8, 197
  self, *see* self
  see also counselling
    (and psychotherapy); Giddens,
    Anthony
demotivation, 4, 51, 66, 157
deontological, 4, 31, 34, 38, 50,
    122, 167, 211

depth, *see* hermeneutic
Derrida, Jacques, 14, 181, 213
Descartes, Rene, 92
desire, 25, 54–5, 60, 61, 65, 67, 69, 73,
    75, 79, 83, 90, 119, 130, 131–9,
    173, 180, 181, 188
development, *see* moral
Dews, Peter, 27
*Dialogues With Jürgen Habermas Jacques
    Derrida*, 213
difference between ethics and morals, *see*
    moral
Dionysian, 221
discourse, 16, 24–5, 27, 29, 31–4, 37,
    82, 86, 120, 122, 158, 188, 221,
    223, 226, 229
  ethics, 3–4, 31, 33–5, 39, 50–1,
    69, 71, 189, 217, 220
  practical, 25, 33, 109
  theoretical, 24, 33
  therapeutic, 33, 35
  see also Habermas, Jürgen
distorted communication, *see*
    communication
distorted language, *see* language
domestic violence, 30, 43, 164
domination, 6, 12, 13, 20, 21,
    22, 29, 30, 32, 38, 42, 43,
    76, 79, 83, 96, 99, 108–12,
    114, 184, 197–8, 203,
    214, 222, 232
Dryden, Windy, 139
duty, *see* moral

economic growth, 62, 162, 163,
    169, 175, 202
effectiveness, 150, 152, 228
efficacy, 151–2, 228
egalitarian reciprocity, 33
ego psychology (and self psychology) 73,
    75, 77, 195, 224
Elliott, Anthony, 185
emancipation, 26, 27, 47, 105, 107, 109,
    205, 215, 234
  see also Habermas, Jürgen
embodied self, *see* self
emotions, *see* moral
Empire, see Hardt, Michael
end of ideology, *see* ideology
enlightenment, 17, 91, 213
epistemology, 24, 52, 150
equality, *see* counselling (and
    psychotherapy); moral
Erikson, Erik, 80

Eros, 59, 131, 134, 137, 191, 211
eros, 7, 54, 60–1, 131–9, 191, 227
erotic, 7, 54–5, 60, 61, 73, 76–7,
    131–9, 140, 152, 156, 157,
    181, 202, 221
ethics, 2, 4–7, 11, 18, 21, 23,
    25–6, 29, 31, 33, 35–7,
    39–49, 51–67, 69–79, 81,
    83, 85, 88, 91, 97–9, 110,
    114–15, 122–8, 138, 153–4,
    157, 166–7, 189, 194, 202–3,
    211, 214, 216–20, 226
    authenticity, *see* authenticity
        (including truthfulness)
    codes, 1, 7–8, 116, 121, 153–4,
        157–60
    discourse, *see* discourse, ethics
    see also Habermas, Jürgen
ethnocentrism, 12, 56, 213, 216
European Union, 163
Evans, Mary, 233
evolutionary development, *see*
    counselling (and psychotherapy)
evolutionary stages, 5, 70, 80
existential, 26, 40, 42, 46, 59, 66,
    85, 95, 118, 143, 173, 174,
    181–2, 187
    see also counselling
        (and psychotherapy)
experts, 9, 171, 178
    expert systems, 178–9
expressive, 25–7, 55, 104, 175, 225–6

failed, *see* self
Feltham, Colin, 229
Foucault, Michel, 14, 82, 83,
    184, 218, 221
fragmentation, 6, 9, 96–100, 166,
    172–3, 177, 178, 185, 193–4,
    218, 225
    of self, *see* self
Frankfurt School, 201
freedom, 32, 43, 44, 45, 59,
    67, 73, 83, 114–16, 191,
    195, 197, 214, 216, 218,
    219, 220, 221, 223, 230,
    231, 236
Freud, Sigmund, 73, 80, 90,
    91, 95, 106, 108, 109,
    112, 132–4, 141, 152, 153,
    204, 224, 229
fundamentalism, 62, 122, 179, 210, 211,
    216
    see also Habermas, Jürgen

Giddens, Anthony, 2, 57, 74,
    91–2, 98, 143, 192–3, 203,
    219, 228, 234
    autonomy, 64–5
    commodification, 173
    confluent love, 61, 219, 233
    democracy, 10, 197–8; democratic
        relationships, 61, 197–8
    loss of meaning, 174–5
    pure relationships, 10, 61,
        186–9, 233
    Reith Lecture, 188
    risk, 94
    sequestration, 181–5
    shame, 89–90
    therapy as control, 121
    transformation of intimacy, 10, 204
Gilligan, Carol, 47–8, 217
globalization, 8, 10, 161–2, 186,
    209, 234
Goffman, Erving, 225–6
Guggenbühl-Craig, Adolf, 46
guilt, 5, 38, 43–4, 52–4,
    70, 86–90, 96, 97, 107,
    119, 127, 132, 143, 182,
    222, 225

Habermas, Jürgen, 2–3, 11,
    13, 14, 27–30, 33, 36, 48,
    51–2, 58–60, 64, 70, 80,
    82–3, 98, 107–12, 127,
    141, 148–9, 166, 175–6,
    179, 188, 190, 196–7, 199,
    201, 205–7, 213–15,
    218–19, 221, 223–4, 232
    autonomy, 65–7, 220–1
    communication; distorted,
        30, 102–5, 107
    communicative action, 16, 71, 106
    communicative rationality, 6, 15,
        18, 62, 81, 91, 135, 166,
        196–7, 234
    discourse ethics, 3, 33, 39, 50, 69
    emancipation, 26, 47, 105
    ethics, 4, 41, 44, 57, 216;
        categorical imperative, 43
    fundamentalism, 122
    hermeneutic, 58–9, 105
    intersubjectivity, 72, 190, 221
    justice, 38, 49
    language, 28, 106
    legitimation, 162–3, 165
    lifeworld, 63; colonization,
        168, 171, 175, 183, 210

morals, 4, 31, 38–9, 44, 47, 52, 217;
    application, 50; categorical
    imperative, 43, 67; human rights,
    45–6; Kantian, 47
motivation, 69
paleo-symbols, 103
Philosophy In a Time of Terror, 213
postmodernism, 17
*The Philosophical Discourse of
    Modernity*, 14
Halmos, Paul, 125, 156, 209
happiness, 4, 38, 46–7, 143, 189, 217
Hardt, Michael, 211, 230
    Empire, 211
health
    validity claim, 4, 7, 37, 58, 62–3,
        65, 66, 113, 114, 115, 127, 136,
        145, 219
    see also validity claims
hedonism, 175, 181
Hegel, George Wilhelm Friedrich, 91
Held, D., 166, 172
Hemmings, Adrian, 152, 229
Hera, 191
hermeneutic, 23, 53, 58–9, 105,
    109, 113, 224
    depth, 105
    see also Habermas, Jürgen
heteronomy, 22, 64, 220
Hillman, James, 59, 95, 123–4, 127,
    133–4, 137, 146, 152, 161, 191,
    217, 221, 222–3, 227
    The Myth of Analysis, 218
    transparency, 59, 139
Hobbes, Thomas, 213
Hochschild, Arlie, 60, 176, 225
Hoggett, Paul, 117, 171, 232
Holmes, Jeremy, 64–6, 114, 146, 154
House, Richard, 147, 150, 213,
    214, 227
    Therapy Beyond Modernity, 213
human rights, 4, 25, 45–6, 62, 159, 174,
    210, 216
    see also Habermas, Jürgen; moral
humanistic, *see* counselling
    (and psychotherapy)
Hutton, Will, 230
hypothetical attitude, 31, 82

ideal speech situation, 33, 107, 109, 188,
    197, 215, 234
ideology, 13, 29, 62, 95, 123, 147, 219,
    227
    end of, 8, 112, 165, 167, 230

illocutionary, 19–22, 27, 32, 99,
    213–14
IMF, 178, 216
independence, 5, 80
individuation, 5–6, 47, 49, 61, 77, 115,
    123, 135–6, 142, 166,
    175–7, 189–91, 199–200,
    215, 220–2
    managed self, 8, 142–3, 146,
        155–7, 176
    narrative structure, 10, 88, 90, 92–4,
        97, 192–3
    realization, 40, 41, 44, 46–7,
        56–8, 64, 115, 182, 190,
        193, 197, 199, 210,
        216–17, 221
    reflection, 107–9, 136, 139, 149
Industrial Revolution, 153, 209
Ingram, David, 26, 219–20
instrumental, 9, 30, 33, 40–1, 81, 116,
    182, 206, 213–14
    action, 6, 16, 22, 33, 35, 168,
        170–1, 175, 177
    knowledge, 24, 27
    mastery, 22
    rationality, 62, 76–7, 110–11, 175,
        181, 187, 189
instrumentality, 175–6, 201,
    203–4, 223
Internet, 9, 140, 164, 184, 209
intersubjectivity, 3, 5, 16–18,
    21, 24, 39, 70–3, 77–80,
    84, 90, 106–7, 115, 131–2,
    148, 164, 190, 196, 198,
    213, 215, 217, 220–1, 224
    unforced, 71
    see also Habermas, Jürgen
intimacy, 10, 56, 61, 75, 77, 81, 123,
    143, 176, 186–8, 200, 204
intrapsychic, 73, 78, 103, 172, 177, 183,
    196, 204, 221

Jacques Derrida, 213
    radical sceptic, 216
    solidarity, 49, 86, 215, 217
    strategic action, 115
    truth, 24
    universal pragmatics, 19, 26, 92
    validity claims, 3, 20, 26, 33,
        62, 219
Jameson, Frederic, 225
Jung, Carl, 95, 108, 191, 222
    Jungian, 47, 55, 59, 95, 133, 222
jurisprudence, 26, 27

justice, 1, 4, 12, 16, 35, 37–9, 43–4,
47–51, 61, 82, 86, 101, 113, 127,
135–6, 145–6, 158–9, 167, 200,
216–17, 219, 226
see also counselling (and
psychotherapy); Habermas,
Jürgen; moral

Kant, Immanuel, 43, 92, 220
Kantian, 47, 66
see also moral
Kantian, 47, 66
Kegan, Robert, 80–4, 97, 122–3,
127–9, 135, 145, 177–8, 213, 220,
222, 235
Kohlberg, Lawrence, 80
Kohut, Heinz, 77, 89
Kop, Sheldon, 60

Labouvie-Vief, Gisela, 92
Lacan, Jacques, 98, 133–4
Langman, Lauren, 225–6
language, 3, 5, 7, 13, 14, 16–20,
26, 28, 92, 95, 102, 105–6,
114, 146, 157, 170, 190,
212–14, 221, 234
body, 102, 225
distorted, 108–9, 127, 224
language games, 18, 27
private, 103–5, 107, 111
public, 14, 103–5, 107
see also Habermas, Jürgen
Lasch, Christopher, 94
law, 4, 15, 16, 35, 45, 67, 82, 164, 191,
216, 220, 223
legitimation, 70, 162–5, 167
see also Habermas, Jürgen
Leviathan, 178
Lewis, J., 126, 207
liberation therapy, *see* counselling (and
psychotherapy)
life project, 26, 40, 42, 58–9, 62, 65, 67,
88, 142, 219
lifeworld, 9, 26–7, 63, 82, 115, 168–9,
171–2, 174, 177, 183, 186–7, 201,
204–5, 210, 221, 232
colonization, *see* Habermas, Jürgen
see also Habermas, Jürgen
Lobkowicz, N. 105
Locke, John, 92
Lomas, Peter, 225, 228
loss of meaning, 9, 26–7, 146,
172, 174–5
see also Giddens, Anthony

love, 5, 7, 27–8, 39, 47, 54, 59–61,
73, 76, 86, 90–1, 123, 133–9,
143, 152, 187–9, 191, 217–18,
226–7, 231
confluent, 61–2, 73–4, 187, 198, 203,
219, 233
romantic, 61, 138, 187–8, 192
Luhmann, Niklas, 27, 54, 177
Lyotard, François, 28

McCarthy, Thomas, 32, 232
McEwan, Ian, 212
McIntyre, Alisdair, 92, 94
managed self, *see* self
management, *see* counselling (and
psychotherapy)
managerialization, 165
Mander, Gertrude, 141, 144
Mann, David, 133–4, 136–8
Maranhao, Tullio, 97, 119, 215,
224, 226–7
Marcuse, Herbert, 202, 221, 232
marriage, 60, 95, 118, 126, 164, 177,
191, 233
Martin, J., 183
Marx, Karl, 91
Maslow, Abraham, 80, 143
Masson, Jeffrey, 119
Mead, George, 224
meaning-making, 80, 84, 128–9, 149
medical model, 7
see also counselling (and
psychotherapy)
Meehan, J., 221
Mill, John Stuart, 64
modernity, 2, 8–10, 12, 26, 57, 93, 112,
114, 142, 161–3, 168, 170–1, 173,
176, 179, 183–7, 189–94, 196, 197,
199, 203, 208–9, 213, 218–19, 221,
228, 230, 233–4, 236
money, 9, 117, 168, 170–1, 178
Moore, Thomas, 144
moral, 2–7, 11–13, 16–18, 20–1,
24–5, 29, 31–5, 37–100, 108,
111, 114–15, 119, 121–30, 135–8,
140, 143, 152–3, 157–60, 164,
166–70, 174–5, 177, 179, 181–2,
189–91, 194, 196–8, 200–2, 207–8,
212–13, 216–20, 223, 225–8, 231,
233–5
application, 25, 47–8, 50–1
care, 47–50, 53, 86, 126–7
character, 5, 69–101, 157, 179, 223
critique, 13

development, 4, 53, 69–100, 115
difference between ethics and
    morals, 4, 31, 40, 42–4
duty, 6, 39, 43–7, 47, 66–7, 126–7,
    143, 165–6, 198
emotions, 53–4, 70, 85–91; guilt,
    see guilt; shame, *see* shame
equality, 4, 34, 61, 126, 162, 164,
    186, 203, 217, 232
human rights, *see* human rights
justice, 1, 4, 12, 16, 35, 37–55,
    82, 86, 101, 113, 127, 135–6,
    146, 158–9, 167, 200, 216–17,
    219, 226
Kantian, *see* Kantian
obligation, 5, 11, 24, 38–9, 42, 45, 54,
    62, 66, 189
postconventional, 4, 51–4, 70, 81
universal, 11, 12–13, 31, 33, 36, 50–1,
    69, 88, 114–15, 121
see also counselling (and
    psychotherapy); Habermas,
    Jürgen
Mormon, 36
motivation, 4, 11, 47, 51–4, 63, 66, 67,
    69, 75, 116, 130, 132, 138, 139,
    172, 208, 216
see also Habermas, Jürgen

narrative, 10, 57, 76, 86, 88, 90, 92–4,
    97, 107, 124, 127, 152, 180, 182,
    192–3, 211, 214
self, *see* self
Neumann, Erich, 211, 227
Nietzschean, 212, 223
Nirvana, 39, 53
non-judgemental, *see* counselling
    (and psychotherapy)
Norris, Christopher, 28

object relations, 73, 77–8, 224
objectification, 30, 54, 76–7, 106, 218
objectivating, 26–7, 109
obligations, 4–5, 11, 16, 24, 34–5,
    38–9, 40, 44–5, 47, 52, 54, 57–8,
    62, 66, 98–9, 115, 119, 143, 156,
    162, 175, 186, 189, 194–5,
    197–8, 217–18, 225
see also moral
Orbach, Susie, 97, 205
organizations, *see* counselling (and
    psychotherapy)
outcomes, *see* counselling (and
    psychotherapy)

Pahl, Ray, 232
paideia, 223
paleo-symbols, 103–5
    see also Habermas, Jürgen
Passat, Rene, 229
pathology, 26, 27, 112, 141, 156,
    162–3, 166, 169, 172, 176,
    196, 199, 201, 214, 222, 235
Pattison, Stephen, 158–9
pax Americana, 161, 230, 236
performative self-contradiction, 13–14
perlocutionary, 20–2, 30, 99, 213
Perls, Fritz, 222
personal choice, 7, 63, 66–7, 221
philosophical basis, *see* counselling
    (and psychotherapy)
Philosophy In a Time of Terror, 213
Piaget, Jean, 80
Pierce, C., 12, 34
Pilgrim, David, 229–30, 232
pilgrimage, 211
Plato, 133, 138
    Symposium, 133
postconventional, 4, 31, 34, 39, 51–4,
    70, 72, 75, 81–3, 90, 96, 99, 194
    universalism, 31, 36
    see also moral
postmodernism, 3, 5–6, 12–14, 17, 27,
    31, 34, 52, 64, 91–2, 95, 97, 109,
    112, 128, 172, 185, 192, 194,
    200–1, 203, 209, 213, 219, 221,
    223, 228, 233
    see also Habermas, Jürgen
poststructuralism, 91, 95, 112,
    172, 201
practical discourse, *see* discourse
practical reason, 16, 44–5, 62, 66–7
private communication,
    see communication
privatized, *see* counselling
    (and psychotherapy)
professionalization, 7–8, 49–50, 124,
    146, 153–8, 178, 195, 200,
    205–8, 210, 213, 229–30
    radical, 2, 8, 23, 29, 35, 53, 78, 95,
    117, 156, 201, 203–5, 208,
    217–18, 229, 236
    see also counselling
    (and psychotherapy)
psyche, 6, 19, 26, 53, 60, 74, 75, 96,
    102, 104, 124, 132–40, 144, 149,
    157, 161, 167–9, 172, 174, 176,
    188, 204, 212, 222, 227
Psyche, 7, 139, 211

psychopathology, 23, 26, 27, 29, 97, 102, 183, 207, 214, 230
psychotherapy, *see* counselling (and psychotherapy)
public communication, *see* communication
pure relationships, 10, 59–61, 66, 186–9, 197, 199, 203, 209, 211, 219, 232–3
  see also Giddens, Anthony

radical sceptic, 215
  see also Habermas, Jürgen
radical, *see* counselling (and psychotherapy)
Rasmussen, David, 214
rationality, 6, 19, 37, 64, 109–11, 118–20, 122, 128, 130–1, 135–6, 152, 158, 198, 202, 204, 225
  RCT, 150, 152, 154
  reconstruction of subjectivity, 58, 93, 141–2, 167, 169, 219
  revolutionary class, 204, 208
  schools, 2, 64, 73, 107, 134, 139, 201, 226
  skills, 7, 43, 121, 140, 142, 144–5, 149, 152, 155–7, 195, 208
  social context, 8, 111–12, 118, 230
  social science model, 105–6, 109, 148, 224
  socialization, 4, 6, 44, 53–4, 72, 99, 101, 135, 164, 183
  symptom relief, 4, 51, 85, 128, 146–7, 152
  technique, 7, 23, 117, 121, 123, 125, 141, 143–5, 148–9, 151, 184, 209, 225
  transpersonal, 66
  see also counselling (and psychotherapy)
rationalization, 26, 168, 201
Rawls, John, 122
RCT, *see* counselling (and psychotherapy)
reconstruction of subjectivity, *see* counselling (and psychotherapy)
reflexive, 10, 35, 57, 61, 64, 72, 82–3, 89–90, 92–9, 121, 143, 164, 185–8, 191–3, 196–7, 228, 232
reflexive communication, *see* communication
self, *see* self
Reiff, David, 154, 203, 208
Reith Lecture, *see* Giddens, Anthony

Relate, 126, 147, 207–8, 235
relativism, 3, 12–13, 17, 31, 52, 57, 91, 101, 109, 123, 212–13
religion, 3–6, 11, 38, 51, 69, 122, 129, 168, 170, 183, 187, 199, 201, 210
Renaissance, 209
resacralization, 210
revolutionary class, *see* counselling (and psychotherapy)
risk, *see* Giddens, Anthony
Rogers, Carl, 71–2, 80, 113
Roman Empire, 211, 230
romantic love, *see* love
Rose, Nikolas, 83, 142–3, 166, 217–18, 225–6
Rowan, John, 224, 228
Rushdie, Salman, 122

Saint Augustine, 211
salvation, 39, 46–7, 51
Samaritans, 139
Samuels, Andrew, 2, 78–9, 95–7, 120, 133, 161, 203, 210
  object relations, 78
  resacralization, 210
schools, *see* counselling (and psychotherapy)
self
  actualization, 71–2, 173–5, 177, 188, 217, 220, 224
  addictive, 193–4
  decentred, 5–6, 8, 10, 70–1, 91–100, 115, 122, 136, 143, 156, 175–6, 185, 194–7, 203, 209, 211
  democratic, 10, 62, 65, 96, 186, 188, 196–7, 236
  embodied, 35, 192, 223
  failed, 98, 193–4
  fragmented, 6, 96–9, 185, 193–4
Seligman, Martin, 150–2
Sennett, Richard, 179–80, 192, 231, 234
sequestration, 143, 181–5, 228
  see also Giddens, Anthony
sexual abuse, 230
shame, 5, 53–4, 56, 86–90, 97, 132, 156, 178, 218
  see also Giddens, Anthony
Silverman, David, 14, 16
sincerity, *see* authenticity (including truthfulness)
situated reason, 14, 18

skills, *see* counselling
   (and psychotherapy)
Smail, David, 161, 213
Smith, Adam, 231
social context, *see* counselling
   (and psychotherapy)
social integration, 9, 26, 168–9,
   171, 184, 221
social science model, *see* counselling (and
   psychotherapy)
socialization, *see* counselling
   (and psychotherapy)
Socrates, 138
solidarity, 4, 26, 27, 38–9, 47,
   49, 53, 61, 79, 86, 135,
   157, 166, 189, 195, 196,
   199, 215–18, 233
   see also Habermas, Jürgen
speech acts, 18–21, 27, 28, 32
Spinelli, Ernesto, 225
spiritual, 41, 210, 228
steering media, 169–71
strategic action, 15–16, 22–3,
   30, 35, 101, 102, 106, 110,
   115–16, 140–2, 147, 168–71,
   176, 177, 179, 201–2, 214–15,
   221, 224
   see also Habermas, Jürgen
strategic rationality, 6, 76–7, 202,
   203, 205
Symposium, 133
symptom relief, *see* counselling
   (and psychotherapy)
system integration, 9, 168–9,
   171–2, 181

Taylor, Charles, 43, 87–90,
   92–3, 97, 212, 216,
   217, 220
technicizing, 140, 165, 174
technique, *see* counselling
   (and psychotherapy)
telos, 22, 94, 96, 127, 211
terrorism, 14, 25, 179, 230
The Myth of Analysis,
   see Hillman, James
theoretical discourse, *see* discourse
therapeutic communication,
   see communication
therapeutic critique, 30, 33
therapeutic discourse, *see* discourse
therapy as control, *see* Giddens,
   Anthony
Therapy Beyond Modernity, 213

tolerance, 12–13, 35–6, 122,
   128, 180–1
transference, 7, 123, 127, 131–8, 141,
   145–6, 148, 156–7, 187–8, 202,
   224, 227, 235
   countertransference, *see*
      countertransference
transformation, 84–5, 145, 206, 228
transformation of intimacy,
   see Giddens, Anthony
translation, 84–5, 145, 206, 228
transparency, *see* authenticity
   and Hillman
Trigg, Roger, 212
trust, 10, 16, 21, 42–3, 59–61,
   65, 74, 89–90, 108, 118, 131,
   182, 186–9, 195, 198–9, 219,
   222, 223
truth, 1, 11–16, 20, 23–6,
   31–3, 37, 44, 55, 59,
   65–6, 69, 74, 84, 113–15,
   119, 122–3, 125, 127,
   129, 136, 145, 152,
   158–9, 166–7, 171, 202,
   212–14, 219–20, 223
   see also Habermas, Jürgen
truthfulness, *see* authenticity (including
   truthfulness)

unconscious, 2, 4, 7, 21, 25, 55,
   58, 70, 73, 83, 85, 98–100,
   102, 105–8, 112, 116–18,
   124–7, 134, 136, 163, 204,
   212, 224, 235
unforced intersubjectivity, 71
unitary, 97, 99, 193–4
unitary self, *see* self
United Nations, 46
   *United Nations Declaration of Human
      Rights*, 25
universal pragmatics, 18–19, 26–7,
   92, 102, 110
   see also Habermas, Jürgen
universal, *see* moral
universalization, 34, 36, 38–9, 46, 50

validity claims, 3–5, 7, 15–17,
   20–8, 30–4, 37, 41, 55–8,
   62–6, 69, 71, 73–4, 87,
   101–2, 109, 111, 113, 115,
   117, 119–22, 127, 135–6,
   145, 164, 166–70, 175, 194,
   213, 218–20
   see also Habermas, Jürgen

values, 1–3, 7–8, 11, 35, 37, 41,
   63–4, 101, 106, 113–14,
   117–26, 147, 152, 158–9,
   200, 202, 206–7, 226
   value-free, 6, 76, 91,
      112–18, 120, 123,
      125–7, 200, 209
   vocation, 8, 50, 155, 209
   voluntary action, 157, 207
values, *see* counselling
      (and psychotherapy)
value-free, *see* counselling
      (and psychotherapy)
Ventura, Michael, 161
Venus, 138–9
vocation, 8, 50, 155
   see also counselling
      (and psychotherapy)
voluntary action, *see* counselling
      (and psychotherapy)
voluntary organizations, 1, 8, 116,
   125–6, 205–7, 227

Wasdell, David, 99, 156
Watt, A., 215
Weber, Max, 214
Weir, A., 72, 83
well-being, 4, 46–7, 122, 166, 232
Wheeler, Sue, 153
White, Stephen, 28, 48, 82–3, 210
White, V., 123, 220
Whitebook, Joel, 106
Wilber, Ken, 80, 84, 206, 224
will, 5, 66–7
   will formation, 34, 197
Williams, Bernard, 13, 70, 129–30
Wilson, Richard, 227
Wittgenstein, Ludwig, 14, 18, 91,
   92, 215
Wollheim, Richard, 86–7, 89
World Bank, 178, 216
World relations, 26

Zeus, 95, 191
Zizek, Slavoj, 14